Music from the Tang Court · 7

Some ancient connections explored

Laurence E. R. Picken and Noël J. Nickson

with Nicholas Gray, Okamoto Miyoko 岡 本 美 代 子, Robert Walker

CAMBRIDGE
UNIVERSITY PRESS

PUBLISHED BY THE PRESS SYNDICATE OF THE UNIVERSITY OF CAMBRIDGE
The Pitt Building, Trumpington Street, Cambridge, United Kingdom

CAMBRIDGE UNIVERSITY PRESS
The Edinburgh Building, Cambridge CB2 2RU, UK   www.cup.cam.ac.uk
40 West 20th Street, New York, NY 10011–4211, USA   www.cup.org
10 Stamford Road, Oakleigh, Melbourne 3166, Australia
Ruiz de Alarcón 13, 28014 Madrid, Spain

First published 2000

Typeface   *Times 14, Apple LiSung Light 13, Osaka 13*

Printed in the United Kingdom at the University Press, Cambridge

A catalogue record for this book is available from the British Library

ISBN 0 521 780845 hardback

S.D.B.

Music from the Tang Court 7

The series of volumes of Music from the Tang Court considers a repertory of music at least 1400 years old. During the two centuries before 841 the Japanese Court borrowed a large amount of secular entertainment music from China. This 'Tang Music' (*Tōgaku*) survives in Japan in a substantial body of manuscripts, but is transformed in character in contemporary performance. This edition transcribes and comments on the music as it survives in its earliest sources. The process has revealed surprising evidence for ancient interconnections in Eurasian musics, and the essays in this seventh volume present aspects of this research to date. They provide evidence, for example, of music in a scale of four notes only from Bali and from Ancient China, as well as, most significantly, for the transportation from the Tang capital of Japan of 'several tens of scrolls of music in tablature'.

to the memory of my parents

Rosa Louisa Bevan
Ernest Frederick Picken

Contents

Preface

The present volume concerns itself with a range of historical issues
arising from studies that have now extended over a quarter of a century and
beyond.

When we began in the 1970s, it seemed necessary to set out, in as detailed a
fashion as possible for us – as foreigners, working outside the culture – the
provenance of those relatively few, precious sources that have made possible the
renewed life, as music, of a unique repertory: a vast secular repertory of Court
Entertainment Music. We felt it necessary to do this, since historical processes
and public attitudes in the home-culture have led to a complete transformation, in
contemporary performance, of the original, musical character of this repertory.

Much of this music is at least 1,400 years old. It is available to us in a
substantial body of manuscripts in tablature – in relative or absolute pitch-
notation – for five melodic instruments:

    (a) three winds –   transverse flute,
                           double-reed cylindrical pipe,
                           free-reed mouth-organ;
    (b) two plucked strings – zither and lute
    and percussion – two very different drums and a gong.

In many instances, we know from other sources the social or other occasion for
which a work was composed. In performance with the dances – inalienably
associated with this music – many of the surviving items are dance-suites, at
times approaching symphonic proportions. In some instances scores in dance-
notation survive from the thirteenth century.

Again, it has seemed to us imperative to determine what terms such as 'old'
or 'new' meant, for those immediately concerned with this 'bought' or
'borrowed' repertory in Japan, as the centuries passed in its use by the Court; as
(in due course) all items became almost unimaginably old, to the performing
musician, or to a wardrobe-master to the dancers, at the time of the Meiji
Restoration in 1876, let us say.

Finally, and still in Japan, we felt a need to consider what had probably been
the state of indigenous Japanese music when items from the Tang Court, and

from the various states of what would in due course become Korea, began to reach Japan, first having been brought by visiting musicians, Chinese or (in the broad sense) 'Korean', from elsewhere in Asia.

Inevitably, the connections between Tang-Chinese music and dance, led to enquiry into the contemporary condition of music and dance elsewhere in Asia. A consequence of that was recognition of the extraordinarily early date at which Ancient Iran and Ancient India probably discriminated notes that perform specific functions in musical discourse. When we began this enquiry, the history of music in Europe had seemed almost indifferent to these matters until the time of Rameau – according to the views of many. Our own reading – of medieval Latin and later vernacular sources – revealed that there existed, for Europe also, a history of functional terminology. This European history seems to have developed independent of knowledge of Asian traditions, and perhaps its most surprising feature is the presence of a precise definition of a chant-final, already in the 10th century and again in the 11th, in terms that reveal the pitch-relationship of the final with every other note of the chant. In today's term, the medieval 'final' is revealed as 'a tonic'.

That we should wish to demonstrate the relationship between what survives of the 28 modes of the Tang-Chinese system of classification of musical items, and that part of the early Tang repertory which survives in the manuscripts of *Tōgaku*, was not perhaps surprising. What is surprising is the extent of our Table (see Chapter 6) that summarises relationships between mode-keys of the survivals. Our Table also reveals the marked instability of the mode-key *Taishiki-chō / Dashi-diao* 大 石 調. The fact that the mode-key system seems to be related to the two modal note-sets of the Indic jāti has been noted elsewhere in the text.

It is perhaps in relationships between Indonesia, Ancient India and China, that the most surprising evidence for ancient interconnections in music, as well as in note-systems, has come to light. As yet our suggestions are necessarily provisional; but they encourage us to add the sub-title: 'Some Ancient Connections Explored' to the title of this volume.

Volume 7 includes a first quotation from a 9th- or 10th-century Balinese chant, surely deriving from an ancient Sanskrit tradition, transcribed by Mr Nicholas Gray. This now takes its place in the series along with the restored chant, published in our treatment of 'Bodhisattvas' in Fascicle 4. It is hoped it may be joined, in due course, by a summary of studies by Dr Markham on Buddhist chant, in the Sino-Japanese tradition[1].

---

[1] See also Elizabeth Markham (1983): *Saibara* – Japanese Court Songs of the Heian Period, Volume 1: *Text*, Volume 2: *Music*, Cambridge University Press, Cambridge.

The transcription into staff-notation, and publication, of the remaining 72 titles of this repertory, known in particular from manuscript-sources of Fujiwara no Moronaga and Minamoto no Hiromasa, will henceforward be greatly facilitated by Professor Wolpert's development of computer-software[2]. This will enable any score in tablature to be reproduced in a printed version of its tablature-signs, following the same layout in column-breaks as the original. (It can also produce another layout, such as column-breaks determined by the ends of ostinato-units.) The computer program will also generate an automated transcription in staff-notation of any score in tablature provided. In addition, a basic score for any of the five melodic instruments can be generated from any one of the five.

For the future, Volume 8 will offer (for many items) a first full-score, headed by a flute-score of the tenth century, first transcribed by Professor Allan Marett (University of Sydney, Australia) in his Cambridge Doctoral Dissertation of April, 1976. As one of the original 'Tang Music Group', and as a contributor in one way or another to all Fascicles and Volumes of *Music from the Tang Court*, as well as to our other series, *Musica Asiatica* (1977–91), Professor Marett's participation in the project is greatly valued.

Continuing assistance in research on the musical and theatrical life of the Tang Court – such as has so often illuminated our project over the years – has been promised by the Tang Studies Society, the president of which, Elling Oliver Eide (for many years now a greatly valued friend), was uniquely helpful in bringing to our attention a collection of Japanese musical manuscripts that, as the nucleus of our collection of source-materials, revealed so much before ever a library in Japan had been visited. (See *Music from the Tang Court* (1981), Fascicle 1, *Introduction*, p. 7.)

With description and analysis of items in the *Ichikotsu* and *Sada* modes now complete, we look forward to exploring, in subsequent volumes, other musical works of the Golden Age of the early Tang Dynasty, in particular the extended dance-suites, and with these the surviving song-texts (so far unexamined), in the hope of re-creating the vocal aspect of this music, thus far neglected. Initial studies of dance-scores of the early thirteenth century lead us to hope it may be possible to restore the dances also. These were an essential aspect of the Court Entertainment Music – 'The Banquet Music' of the Tang. Indeed, in this context *we* must always think in terms of 'Music-with-Dance' rather than 'Music'.

---

[2] See also R. F. Wolpert (1977): A ninth-century Sino-Japanese lute-tutor, *Musica Asiatica*, 1, 111–165, Oxford University Press, Music Department, London (1981): A ninth-century score for five-stringed lute, *Musica Asiatica*, 3, 107–35 (1995): Toward a grammar of *tōgaku*, *Oideion* 2, Leiden.

Thanks to the generous sponsorship of the Library of Congress, a set of Compact Discs to accompany earlier fascicles, Volumes 6 and 7, and future volumes, is now in preparation. Soon it will be possible to hear this music in performance for the first time after a lapse of 1,400 years. Performing materials for Western instruments, as well as for original instruments, are in preparation, so that musicians worldwide may participate.

From the beginning it has been our wish that the repertory be brought to life as living music. Its quality as music has been beyond doubt for us, since the very first transcriptions were made. We both transcribed and performed the works ourselves, playing from original notations, on Chinese and Japanese, or equivalent European, instruments.

'Music for a Thousand Autumns' – a birthday wish for the Taizong Emperor, first played on the 5th day of the 8th month in the year 728 – was performed in the Great Hall of Yale University under the baton of Professor Sotirios Chianis on 4 April, 1973. Sadly, the piece was again to be performed in 1976, in the Dwight Memorial Chapel of Yale University, at a Memorial Service on 19 October for Professor Arthur Wright, prematurely deceased, a valiant supporter of the work of our group.

Earlier in that year, on 19 June, in the grounds of Lucy Cavendish College (Cambridge), a concert took place of which the programme appears in the 13th-century *Kokonchomonshū*, consisting of items of *Saibara*, *Tōgaku* and *Komagaku*, as originally performed before a retiring Japanese Emperor. That same year, the suite in six movements: 'The Singing of Spring Warblers' (*Music from the Tang Court*, Fascicle 2), edited by and under the direction of Professor Wolpert, was performed in that same College.

In 1990, thanks to the initiative of Professor Chen Yingshi, the suite 'The Emperor Destroys the Formations' was performed (on Chinese musical instruments, including exquisite replicas of Tang instruments, made by the *Suzhou Minzu Yueqi Yichang* 蘇州民族樂器一廠), by professors and students of the Shanghai Conservatory of Music, under the direction of Professor Noël Nickson (University of Queensland, Australia), who had prepared a first, justified score from unedited transcriptions of the oldest manuscripts.

Most recently, this suite (the score further revised by Professor Nickson, and with percussion added) was performed on Western instruments by the Philharmonia Orchestra of Yekaterinburg, under the direction of Sarah Caldwell, Artistic Director of Opera Boston.

Acknowledgements

For help of many different kinds we are indebted to Dr C.J. Adkins, Charles Aylmer, Dr Clare Y. Barlow, Anthony Bowen (Public Orator in the University of Cambridge), Dr Karel Brušák, Professor Chen Yingshi, Ms Cheng Yu, Professor Mary N. Craighill and Professor Lloyd Craighill, Dr Ian Cross, Professor Christopher Darwin, Dr Robin Donkin, Dr Shailaja Fennell and Dr Stephen Fennell, Professor Fukushima Kazuo, Tessa Gardner, Dr Ilya Gershevitch, Phyllis Giles, Michael Good, Nicholas Gray, David Hindley, Dr Nobuko Ishii, Professor K.L. Johnson, Professor Kárpáti János, Professor John Killen, Professor Kishibe Shigeo, Dr P. Kornicki, Dr Vivienne Law, Dr Graeme Lawson, Michiko Matthews, Professor D.L. McMullen, Dr C.P. Melville, Dr Douglas Mills, John Moffett (Librarian, The Needham Research Institute), Dr M. Morris, Professor Peter Nolan, Ms Inok Paek, Dr Carole Pegg, Richard Ranft, Dr Susan Rankin, Professor Nicholas Sims-Williams, Dr Richard Skaer, Professor Denis Twitchett, Robert Walker, Dr Marnix StJohn Wells, Margaret Widdess and Dr Richard Widdess, Dr J. Woodhouse.

A list of Japanese helpers who contributed so much to Chapter 2 will be found at the end of that Chapter.

To all these must be added, with particular emphasis, the names of distingushed former pupils, without whose devoted collaboration over more than twenty years, this series would never have come into existence:

Dr Jonathan Condit,

Dr Elizabeth Markham,

Professor Allan Marett,

Professor Rembrandt Wolpert,

to which list I would add my 'spiritual pupil', Dr Stephen Jones, and the name of my wonderful colleague, tireless collaborator, indispensable and most tactful critic, and devoted friend, Professor Noël J. Nickson. Readers of the series will know that any outrageous views encountered are those of Laurence Picken rather than Noël Nickson.

Chapter 1

How the *Tōgaku* Repertory was acquired; and the processes of 'Acculturation' that followed that acquisition. (L.E.R.P. – with invaluable help from Allan Marett.)

The *source* of the various sources of the 'Tang Music' repertory in Japan, and the manner of importation of those sources, both require consideration. The term 'borrowed' has been used by us, since the Banquet-Music of Tang was certainly not imposed on the Japanese; its acquisition was willed by the recipients. Some part was presumably 'acquired' from visiting musicians from Korea (the ancient states of Paekche, Silla, Koma) and from Tang and Wu (see Chapter 3, p. 80); but what has appeared to us since 1972 as a last and massively substantial acquisition, by Fujiwara no Sadatoshi, and from Liu Erlang (Fascicle 5, p. 124), was (in part at least) paid for in gold. A gift of 200 'ounces' (*ryō* 兩) is reported to have been made when *biwa/piba*-lessons were solicited in the Tang capital, Chang'an. The gift of instruments, and scrolls in tablature, reportedly made when Sadatoshi's stay there ended, was surely a *quid pro quo*: an equivalent response to an earlier gift received. Before this sojourn in Chang'an – if indeed it occurred – Sadatoshi had unquestionably stayed in Yangzhou in 838, and received a gift of scores in *biwa*-tablature from his teacher, Lian Chengwu, the substance of that *MS.* conveniently referred to by us as *FBBF*.

There is no evidence in Japanese musical sources that such materials ever formed part of the transmission of *Tōgaku* to Japan. The standard version (*KKS* 8, p. 157) of the succession from *biwa*-Master to *biwa*-Master runs from Lian Chengwu through Sadatoshi to Prince Sadayasu 貞 保 親 王, without mention of Liu Erlang; and careful inspection of prefaces to all items of the repertory in *JCYR*, *SGYR* and *HFF*, has failed to disclose reference to the collection supposedly acquired by Sadatoshi from Liu Erlang in Chang'an.

The primary constitution and integrity of *FBBF*

Our early acceptance of the importance of Fujiwara no Sadatoshi was primarily due to having been privileged to see, in 1972, the lute-manuscript (*FBBF*) of the Fushimi no Miya 伏 見 宮 family[1] in its integral condition; as assembled (on

---

[1] In 1972, L.E.R.P. was permitted to see this manuscript-scroll. He declined the honour of unrolling it; this was done by a member of Staff of the Imperial Palace Library. The impact made was that of an incontrovertibly single manuscript. The quality and type of paper, the manner of ruling of the sheets, the placing of major headings, and the identity in writing-hand

scholarly advice) by the Staff of The Library of the Imperial Palace in Tokyo *Kunaichō shoryōbu* 宮 內 聽 書 陵 部.

A superb facsimile was published in 1962 and, as stated in the pamphlet that accompanied that facsimile, paper and calligraphic style both establish the original as a mid-Heian document of tenth-century date. Again (as stated at the outset in the anonymous pamphlet), before the bequest was made by the Fushimi no Miya family, the document existed as three separate manuscripts, separately titled in the library-catalogue of that family.

Two of these titles were actual, present sub-titles of sections of the *MS.* as now constituted: 'Things for all modes for lute' *Biwa sho chōshi hon* 琵 琶 諸 調 子 品 and 'modal things' 調 子 品. (For this use of 'things' see later.) In the present condition of the manuscript, these sections amount to 9 and 2 sheets respectively, with their titles appearing top-right, on initial cream-paper sheets of the scroll: nos. 16 to 24 for the former; 14 and 15 for the latter.

The third section of the manuscript appeared in the family-catalogue under the title: 'Musical scores [of preludes] in five modes' *Go chōshi-fu* 五 調 子 譜. These form the bulk of the first section of the document as now assembled. The original heading of the entire manuscript: 'Preface to scores for lute' *Biwa-fu jo* 琵 琶 譜 序 precedes a preface (top-right, in first column), again on an initial, cream-paper sheet of the scroll. The 'five' in the original catalogue's title represented the number of different modes (and, of course, mode-keys, in the sense of modal octaves of identical structure transposed to various keys) for which modal preludes were supposedly provided in this section of 12 sheets. In reality, the list of contents names six mode-keys of which only four are represented by extended modal preludes; a fifth mode is illustrated by a tuning-piece. This first section comprises Preface, summary list of contents, and modal preludes.

Doubts regarding the integrity of the *MS.* as now constituted are due, presumably, to the fact that the three component sections were first examined separately. The view, that they were and are indeed three separate *MSS.*, was endorsed by the stance of Hayashi Kenzō 林 謙 三, who first undertook serious musicological examination of the components.

It seems to us, however, that those who now wish to re-dissociate these components, to 'deconstruct' the *MS.*, have never allowed themselves time to

from end to end, left no room for doubt as to the original integrity of this National Treasure. At that time the Library Staff were mystified by Hayashi Kenzō's insistence that only the *Biwa sho chōshi-hon* constituted the gift to Sadatoshi from Lian Chengwu, his Teacher. At all events, the date 920/921, towards the end of the Preface, fits paper-type and quality, and the calligraphic style of the hand. There is no room for doubt that this is the copy of Sadatoshi's *MS.* as received from Lian Chengwu; a copy probably made (with some insertions) by Prince Sadayasu.

read it through in its entirety, or to consider, step by step, the implications of its contents.

Before deploying our arguments in favour of respecting the conclusion to which the staff of the Library of the Imperial Palace came, something must be said in regard to technical terminology, since the precise meaning of the terms used is of such importance in the interpretation of *FBBF*. A reading of Professor Wolpert's sequential examination of the entire scroll (Wolpert, 1977) is an essential preliminary to understanding the present discussion, which is merely an extension of his pioneering analysis and transcription.

The language of Chinese modality

As already indicated (Volume 6, p. x) the Chinese term *diao* 調 is used (among other ways) as a verb: 'to tune' (Karlgren 1957, p. 280, **1083 x**). This usage occurred already in the 'Record of Rites' *Liji* 禮 記 ('a ritualist's anthology of ancient usages, prescriptions, definitions and anecdotes'. See Riegel, 1993, p. 293). '*diao xian*' 調 絃 is still used with the meaning 'to tune strings'. The word may also be used as an adjective: 'in tune', as in the phrase: '[the zithers] *qin* and *se* are in tune' 琴 瑟 調 合, used as a metaphor for domestic harmony. Certainly well on into the Sui 隋 dynasty (581–618), *diao* was also used by musicians to refer to a mode as we understand the term (p. 205). It seems likely that the addition of an unemphatic particle *zi* 子 (an 'enclitic') arose first in Tang usage, making the modal meaning explicit. The binome: *diaozi/chōshi* 調 子 thus becomes recognisable as the name of a *thing* (even if in part an abstract conceptual 'thing') as opposed to any meaning of *diao* as action.

The bulk of *FBBF* is a document in the Chinese of the Tang dynasty. It appears to include later interpolations in Chinese (strictly speaking in Sino-Japanese) not merely in the Preface, but also in the body of the *MS.* (see later), but for the most part the style is purely Chinese. That it is a Japanese manuscript-copy of a Chinese original is evident from the handwriting and from the many anomalously formed lexigraphs in the text. Modified from its original condition though it be, this document still retains instances of the Sui (and earlier) use of *diao* (without the particle *zi*) as 'mode'. This only occurs, however, where qualification of the lexigraph 調 by the *name* of a mode removes ambiguity, as in mode-titles such as 'Wind-Fragrance Mode' *Fengxiang diao* 風 香 調.

Although the enclitic *zi* establishes *diaozi* as a noun with the meaning of 'mode' – not (be it noted) 'tune' (another potential meaning of this lexigraph, Volume 6, p. x) – definition of 'mode' required a further, descriptive step, in making the concept 'concrete', in 're-ifying' it, before a stringed instrument could be prepared for playing in a particular *diaozi*.

For a zither, played on open strings, no more was necessary, however, than to specify the pitch of a note in the modal note-set to which each string was to be tuned.

For a lute, with four strings and four frets, however, more information was necessary, if the pitches available at all fret-positions on all four strings were to be specified. That information was in first place the pitch to which each string was tuned. In addition, however, it was necessary for the player to know where tuned open-strings were in unison with stopped strings, so that the accuracy of tuning could be tested. This information was also necessary to the composing, improvising musician, since alternation between the different timbres of stopped and open-string sounds, at the same pitch, adds greatly to the musical interest of a lute's discourse.

All this information is categorised as the *pin/hon* 品 of a mode – *diaozi pin/chōshi hon* 調 子 品. The lexigraph 品 (as Karlgren (1957, p. 178, **669, a-d**; and p. 51, **122, a, b**) recognised), represents a generalised group of objects. In lexigraph **122, a-b**, these are shown stored in a receptacle, as in the graph that forms the left-hand side of this lexigraph: 歐. Already in the 'Book of Documents' *Shangshu* 尚 書 (or *Shujing* 書 經), *pin/hon* has the meaning 'kind, class', and parts of this text may date from the end of the first millennium BC (Shaughnessy, 1993, p. 379).

Pin/hon may function both as verb: 'to classify', 'to order'; or as a general noun for a 'thing'. It is used in both these senses in *FBBF*. The more important use (from our standpoint) is that of 'thing', as in (for example) an expression such as 'food stuffs' *shipin* 食 品. This is homologous with the expression in *FBBF*: *diaozi pin* 調 子 品 = 'modal things' or 'matters', where the 'things' are locations of pitches at frets over which the four strings run, together with the pitches of the open strings themselves.

Pin (in a verbal sense) occurs in 'rules for ordering (in the sense of tuning) the strings' *pin xian fa* 品 絃 法, or merely *pin xian* – 'to tune strings'.

Wolpert (1977) very suitably translated *diaozi pin* as 'frets in a mode', since this is patently what the expression means, as the text (displayed on sheet 14 of the *MS.*-facsimile) shows.

On the Tang *piba*, however, the proper name for 'frets' seems to have been 'posts' *zhu* 柱, qualified as 'string-posts' 絃 柱, as in the *Suishu* reference to tuning (p. 210). On the modern *piba*, frets on the table are referred to as *pin* 品; those on the neck (four in number) as *xiang* 相. When these terms came into use is not known; but since frets glued to the table seem not to have existed, or at least to have been rare, before the Song dynasty, it may be that the new names appeared then. The term *xiang* may relate to the morphological *similarity* of the four neck-frets seen today; they are, in fact, survivals from the Tang lute. *Pin* is

4

surely no more than 'thingumajig', and in no way a specific word for a 'fret' in general. The later use of *pin* for frets on the table of a lute seems never to have reached Japan.

As a last topic in 'meanings', *FBBF* uses *diaozi* itself in two senses. The most common meaning is that of 'mode'/'mode-key' in general. As already seen, if qualified by a modal name, the *zi* becomes superflous. For *FBBF* it is of supreme importance, however, that *diaozi/chōshi* also means a highly organised, musical composition, intended to display the melodic possibilities of a given modal note-set, including all aspects of that mode; perhaps even including characteristic formulae in use in that mode.

(Wolpert's translation of the term '*diaozi*' as 'modal prelude(s)' makes use of a term invented by him in the light of the thing itself. Even the most extensive, and the most modern, of Chinese-Chinese dictionaries affords no help in determining the precise meaning of technical, musical terms such as this; and no Chinese-Chinese Dictionary has as yet been constructed in the manner of *The Oxford English Dictionary*, so that it is possible to determine the meanings of words/lexigraphs at a particular point in time.)

The outline structure of Chinese modal preludes

Inspection of the modal preludes transcribed from *FBBF* by R.F.W. shows that such a musical piece is an organised, articulated (but *senza-misura*) linear discourse, largely in notes of equal duration, segmented as melodic fragments of unitary, binary, ternary and even larger units, separated by marked breaks (丁 *tei* / *ding*), some marked as 'small'. These latter were perhaps to be treated as pauses of a single beat's duration, as opposed to longer pauses of two beats or more. Such pauses frequently occur following pitches from the note-set of a given mode that are musically fitted to act as cadences. Such preludes almost invariably end in an arpeggiated, skeletal version of the note-set: triadic, or reduced to modal octave and fifth, in a final cadential formula (Picken, 1998).

To call such *diaozi* 'Preludes' (as R.F.W. and we have done) is not legitimised in the *MS.* by the use of any such term as *Xu* 序, which identifies the opening movements of Tang 'Large Pieces'. Use of the term 'Prelude' is validated, however, by the structural parallels between *diaozi* as they occur in *FBBF* and named *Xu / Jo* in the tablatures of surviving *Daqu / Taikyoku* 大 曲.

Structural features of *FBBF* that confirm its integral character

In our view, the firm basis for regarding *FBBF* as having originally been constituted as it now is, lies first in the colophon (Wolpert, 1997, pp. 146, 147). It is the statement of what Sadatoshi received from his venerable teacher, Lian Chengwu 廉 承 武. First, that he (Lian Chengwu) *'chuan xi'nong diaozi'* 傳 習 弄 調 子. Second, that *'boshi Chengwu song pu reng ji er'* 博 師 承 武 送 譜 仍 記 耳.

The first of these might be translated *either* as: 'taught playing of exercises' (or 'practice in playing') [and] 'modes/mode-keys/modal preludes'; *or* as a single phrase: 'practice in playing modes/mode-keys/modal preludes'; the second, that 'Master Chengwu sent a gift of examples in tablature as a lasting record' (with acknowledgement to R.F.W.) – since *song* carries overtones of a gift, and there is a similar extra-meaning of something 'exemplary' about a *pu*.

As already stated, no distinction in Tang terminology appears to have been made between 'mode', a 'transposed mode' (a 'mode-key'), and a 'modal prelude'. (The dot in the *FBBF* manuscript between the lexigraphs 弄 and 調 is no more than an involuntary blot, an accident, not a comma. In printing the text of the colophon, the descriptive pamphlet shows no such element. The manuscript-text, like Tang texts in general, is unpunctuated save by spacing.)

Of the alternative translations just suggested, it is perhaps preferable to read: 'practice in playing modes/mode-keys/modal preludes', since Sadatoshi must already have had some skill as a lute-player on his arrival. One does not acquire proficiency on a hitherto unknown instrument in 22 days. (The colophon states that the teacher arrived in Yangzhou on the seventh day of the eighth month of the year 838 and instruction was completed on the 29th of the same month.) The character of the instruction given must have been highly specialised, and the contents of the entire scroll suggest that instruction was exclusively directed to initiating Sadatoshi into the art of playing – almost certainly also composing, and perhaps even improvising – modal preludes in all the modes and mode-keys.

He was certainly not sent to China to acquire the basic technique of *biwa*-playing, but rather to develop skill in the special style used for modal preludes; to acquire knowledge of all the modes and mode-keys used in the Tang repertory; and surely to acquire understanding of the principles on which modal preludes were devised. What Sadatoshi gained for the future was, in first place (as the manuscript shows) an extended body of formal modal preludes for lute, exemplifying the older plectrum-technique, as well as (for the Tang) the more recent finger-plucking technique.

For Sadatoshi the scroll represented a harvest of extended, *model* modal preludes in what by 838 (see later) had become the principal modal types of the *Tōgaku* repertory: Mixo-Lydian and Dorian – as is still the case in the surviving *Tangyue/Tōgaku* repertory today (see Chapter 7, p. 253). The first great musical prize of the Mission of 838 was this collection, of which the surviving *MS.* is a copy. Very properly it occupies first place in the sequence of items in the *MS.*

How remarkable it was, that its acquisition should have been the goal of Sadatoshi's instruction, has not hitherto been recognised. The music of the scores in *FBBF* is Chinese music of the Tang period; what is more, it represents the music of the only period in Chinese history when the Chinese reveal any interest in 'pure music' – in music without a non-musical reference. Apart from the surviving *qin*-pieces known as *diaoyi* 調 意 – 'the meaning of the mode' – of which specimens survive in the popular Yuan-dynasty encyclopaedia: *Shilin guangji* 事 林 廣 記, this is the only surviving Chinese music intended to display the properties of particular octave note-sets. The main thrust of Lian Chengwu's teaching, as we can now see, was an induction into the abstract musical art of playing preludes in a limited number of different modal octaves in different keys. The tunings in the final section of *FBBF*, however, would (in theory) have enabled Sadatoshi to tune the lute for improvisation in any of the 28 mode-keys (minus one – as Hayashi first pointed out).

The discrimination of standard (minor) and contrary (major) forms of modes on the same final
The actual, specimen-modal-preludes of the first section of *FBBF* (as the transcriptions of R.F.W., 1977, pp. 152–64, showed) exemplify two different modal octaves only: Dorian and Mixo-Lydian in Western (Glarean) terms. These are each demonstrated in two keys with finals a fourth apart.

    The inter-relationships between the demonstration-preludes may be summarised as follows:

1. *Fengxiang diao* 風 香 調   = *Yu* 羽 mode
   (*Fukō chō*)   (Dorian) on *A*

2. *Fan Fengxiang diao* 返 風 香 調   = *Shang* 商 mode
   (*Hen fukō chō*)   (Mixo-Lydian) on *A*

3. *Huangzhong diao* 黃 鍾 調   = *Yu* mode on *E*
   (*Ōshiki chō*)

4. [*Fan Huangzhong diao* 返 黃 鍾 調   = *Shang* mode on *E*]
   (*Hen Ōshiki chō*)

(Only one of these names, 3, survives in use today. It is indeed a *Yu*-mode, but the final is *A*, not *E*.)

The use of *fan/hen* 返 in relation to (2) is of great interest, since a similar term: *fàn* 犯 was used (some three centuries later) by *Song Bai Shi Daoren*, Jiang Kui 宋 白 石 道 人，姜 夔 in the context of his collected songs and pieces (Picken, 1966, p. 161), as set out, in particular, in relation to his Song (16). The primary meaning of *fan* 返 (an alternative form is 反) is of reversal, contrariness, even rebellion; in a modal context perhaps simply 'contrary'. In 1966 *fàn* 犯 was translated as 'clashing'.The juxtaposition of modal preludes in these forms in *FBBF* shows plainly that it is the condition of the third degree of the note-set that is in question; this is the point of contrariety, of 'clash' between 1 and 2. Their note-sets are otherwise identical:

$$A\ B\ \underline{C}^{\sharp}\ D\ E\ F^{\sharp}\ G\ a$$

$$A\ B\ \underline{C}\ D\ E\ F^{\sharp}\ G\ a$$

Jiang Kui's example perhaps shows that clashes between modes on the same final could occur in respect of two degrees – as in *Gong* 'clashing' with *Shang* on the same final. Song (16) invites experimental use of $f^{\sharp}$ and f, c and $c^{\sharp}$, at appropriate points.

In the listing of *diaozi* that follows the end of the Preface on sheet 2 of *FBBF*, three are listed as existing in the *Fan* condition, namely *Fengxiang diao* (already considered), *Huangzhong diao* and *Qingdiao*.

Regarding the *Huangzhong diao* pair, it is surely the case that Wolpert's III 3 among the modal preludes (1977, p. 163) represents *Fan Huangzhong diao*.

In its designation of this last-named piece in the body of the text, and in relation to a particular modal prelude, *FBBF* discloses another way of distinguishing those modes that differ only in the character of the mediant, whether a minor or major third above the final. III 3 is labelled (see sheet 11 of manuscript) as *tong diao lü yin* 同 調 呂 音: 'Same mode, *lü*3-note', whereas the two previous *Huangzhong diao* preludes are labelled 律 *lü*4 *yin*. The label surely implies that an all-important note that distinguishes one note-set from the other belongs either to the *lü*3 (= 呂) series of pitch-pipes (where '3' indicates the third segmental tone), or to the *lü*4 (= 律) series ('4' = fourth tone). Although this way of discriminating normal from *Fan* forms of a mode is not used in the summary index (see sheet 2 of manuscript), we may safely identify the *lü* (律) *yin* preludes of *Huangzhong diao* as the normal form of the mode, and the *lü* (呂) *yin* form as *Fan Huangzhong diao*.

It is beyond question that this ancient Chinese nomenclature is also the source of Japanese discrimination and designation of *ritsu* (律) and *ryo* (呂) scales (see later). This nomenclature first appears in *Hanshu* 漢 書 in the recognition of two categories of Chinese pitch-pipes: 律 and 呂(see *Hanshu, Lüli zhi di yi shang* 律 曆 志 第 一 上). The discrimination goes back to their respective methods of generation, distinguished as 'Superior Generation' (上 生) and 'Inferior Generation' (下 生). The date at which this distinction was established in this form cannot be later than the work of Liu Xin 劉 歆 (46 BC – AD 23) in his 'Treatise on the Pitch-Pipes and on the Calendar' (Hulsewé, 1993).

This technical nomenclature arises from the fact that the Superior Generation are pitch-pipes derived from a pipe a fourth higher in pitch, by lengthening that same pipe by one third of its length.The Inferior Generation are obtained from a pitch-pipe a fifth below in pitch, by shortening the length of that pipe by a third.

The six members of the Superior Generation are known as the 'six *lü*4' (六 律). In the *Hanshu* their initial notes are displayed as: *Huangzhong* (黃 鍾) *Taicu* (太 簇) *Guxian* (姑 洗) *Ruibin* (蕤 賓) *Yize* (夷 則) *Wuyi* (無 射). They may be represented as: $C\ D\ E\ F^{\sharp}\ G^{\sharp}\ A^{\sharp}$. These are the 'Male *Lü*4' (*Yanglü*4 陽 律).

The six members of the Inferior Generation are known as the 'six lü3' (六 呂): *Dalü* (大 呂) *Jiazhong* (夾 鍾) *Zhonglü* (中 呂) *Linzhong* (林 鍾) *Nanlü* (南 呂) *Yingzhong* (應 鍾), to be represented as: $C^{\sharp}\ D^{\sharp}\ E^{\sharp}\ G\ A\ B$. These are the 'Female *Lü*3' (Yinlü3 陰 呂).

In theory, *Huangzhong* might be regarded as belonging to either or both series, since it may be generated as the fourth below *Zhonglü*, thus belonging to the Superior generation, or as the fifth above *Zhonglü*, and therefore of the Inferior Generation. Its status as the fundamental of the entire system of pitches demanded (presumably) that it be assigned to the Superior Generation.

What decides whether a modal note-set is regarded as 'male' (= minor) or 'female' (= major) is: whether the *Gong*-note in the octaval note-set of that mode belongs to the Superior or Inferior Generation of the pitch-pipes. In *Fengxiang diao* (a *Yü*-mode – since the note-set is *Yü, Biangong, Gong, Shang, Jiao, Bianzhi, Zhi* (let us say $A\ B\ C\ D\ E\ F^{\sharp}\ G$)), *Gong* – that is, the third degree ascending, (C) – belongs to the Superior generation (if *Huangzhong* is defined as the pitch C). That is to say, the *Gong*-pitch is male. Therefore this note-set is 律 音, the masculine mode-key on the final A.

In *Fan Fengxiang diao* (a *Shang* 商 mode) – of which the modal prelude in the body of the text is described as being 呂 音 – a different note-sequence is displayed, though the set starts on the same pitch, A: *Shang, Jiao, Bianzhi, Zhi, Yü, Biangong, Gong*, to be represented as: $A\ B\ C^{\sharp}\ D\ E\ F^{\sharp}\ G$. If *Shang* is A, *Gong* (in this Mixo-Lydian note-set) must be G, and G belongs to the set of six lü3 (六 呂). For this reason, the corresponding modal prelude is described as 呂 音.

The fourth mode-key, *Qing diao* 清 調 (though listed along with the other three (sheet 14), and given formal expression in a *diaozi pin/chōshi hon* 調 子 品

(but without flute-pitches) is not embodied in a modal prelude, even though it (and for that matter the other three principal mode-keys) are shown as tuning-testing pieces: *xian he/ito-awase* 弦 合, in the appropriate section of the manuscript that precedes the colophon.

What function the *Qing diao* tuning (with its strings II and III in unison) served, is unknown. That they were indeed so tuned is strongly suggested by the tuning-testing piece (Wolpert, 1977 (18), p. 128), with its multiple repetitions of pairs that correspond in pitch to the tuning of these strings. It is noteworthy that *Qing diao* too is stated (in the summary index of modes, mode-keys and modal preludes) to exist in a *Fan* (= 'contrary') form. This is not illustrated by a *xian he/ito-awase*: by analogy with the *Huangzhong lü3 yin*, *Fan Qingdiao* should have been a Mixo-Lydian octave on *B*, matching *Qingdiao*'s Dorian note-set on *B*.

Turning now to the final section of the manuscript: musical materials that precede the colophon, the claim [still made by some Japanese, that all Sadatoshi received from Lian Chengwu was the collection of 'string-harmonisings' *ito-awase / xian he* 絃 合 (sheets 16–23)] is incompatible with the statement of what he was taught. As has been demonstrated, *diaozi* are not merely modes/mode-keys, they are also (in our sense) modal preludes. The tuning-testing pieces of Sheets 16 to 23 are in no sense 'modal preludes'.

Only someone sadly persuaded (as was Hayashi Kenzō) that all that Sadatoshi received in score from his teacher was that portion of the *MS.* entitled *Biwa sho chōshi hon*, could have thought that *ito-awase* were to be equated with *chōshi* in the sense of 'modal preludes'. It is evident that, as late as a publication from 1969 (*Biwa-fu shinko*), Hayashi held that the only document received from Sadatoshi's teacher, Lian Chengwu, was the *Biwa sho chōshi hon*.

In seven instances, the transcriptions of R.F.W. mark all open-string notes in the tuning-testing pieces, and it is plain that the *ito-awase* are constructed (in general) from chains of open and stopped strings sounded in sequence; pairs of strings, tuned either to unison, or to a consonant interval of octave, fourth or fifth. Diatonic sequences of notes only appear (if at all) *after* the four strings have each been correctly tuned. A further reason for denying these tiny pieces the status of 'modal preludes' is that, with a single exception, the *ito-awase* never disclose the complete note-set of the mode/mode-key. The exception is the *Sada-chō/Shatuo diao* tuning-testing piece.

That the nature of these short pieces has been completely misunderstood is evident from the immensely solemn performance of the *ito-awase* for *Fengxiang diao* on the first side (item 5) of the disk: *Tempyō. Heian jidai no ongaku* 天 平。 平 安 時 代 の 音 樂, edited by Hayashi. The performance defeats the primary purpose of *xian he/ito-awase* 絃 合, which surely was to hear whether unison or

10

consonance had been established between pairs of strings. To achieve this, it is essential that the sounds of the pair be heard in quick succession, and certainly without the addition of confusing lower open strings.

No less troubling is the suggested performance of the beginning of the score in staff-notation, prepared by Shiba Tsukehiro, printed at the end of the *FBBF*-pamphlet. It represents the beginning of the *Fengxiang diao* prelude. The pace – as suggested by the abundance of white notes – is funereal; durations are (without exception) arbitrary; and a pause is made on an interpolated cadence (unmarked either in *FBBF* or in the version of *FBBF* in *SGYR* – also examined by R.F.W.). There seems to be no understanding here of the musical value of a modal prelude as an anticipatory exposition; of its function: to remind those about to take part in a collective performance of some piece, both of the tuning in which they are expected to play or sing, and of the melodic properties and potentialities of a particular mode.

Unlike this fragment, R.F.W.'s transcription of the first *Fengxiang diao* Prelude reveals rational cadence-points, on the final and on the fifth above the final, at the ends of phrases. The piece is an exposition of a Church Dorian series: *A B C D E F♯ G*, with one anomalous cadence on the super-final, *B*, and one conspicuous descending leap of a tritone, between *c* and *F♯*.

Of great importance, in relation to the constitution of the *MS.* as a whole, is the fact that only in the section headed *Biwa sho chōshi hon* did Lian Chengwu provide *essential information on the pitches of specific modal flutes to which specified strings were to be tuned.*

The extended preludes of the first sheets of the scroll cannot (and could not) be played without information from the *Biwa sho chōshi hon.* The Table of tunings for the four groups of preludes, headed *Chōshi hon* on sheet 14, includes no pitch-data. Only if the player already knew the pitches of one or two strings, in a particular modal set, would it have been possible (using the *Chōshi hon* instructions) to tune, so as to play the corresponding preludes not merely in the correct mode, but in the correct key.

As stated (in his paper of 1977, p. 116, paragraph 1), in transcribing the extended preludes that follow the Preface and the brief list of contents, Wolpert made use of flute-pitch information furnished *either* in the *Biwa sho chōshi hon* section of *FBBF*, *or* in the version of the *Biwa-fu* in *SGYR*. It is evident from his translation that the data on pitch-equations between open-string and stopped sounds for the principal modes in *SGYR*, also include the necessary flute-pitches (unlike the display in *FBBF*, under the heading *Chōshi hon/diaozi pin* 調 子 品, sheet 14). This again re-inforces the need for the *MS.* (as received from Lian Chengwu) to have been constituted as it is today. The notations of the preludes could not have been realised by Sadatoshi (or any later Japanese player) without

11

the information in the section that precedes his colophon, that is: *Biwa sho chōshi hon*.

Examination of the collection of *Chōshi* of various kinds transcribed and published by Shiba Tsukehiro 芝 祐 秦 (1972, volume 4) has not revealed any obvious survivals from the modal preludes of *FBBF*. Nevertheless, in the section: *gaku biwa sho chōshi hon* 樂 琵 琶 諸 調 子 品 (Shiba 4, p. 53) it is evident that the structure of *ito-awase* in *FBBF* has influenced their design.

It is also to be noted that the term *ito-awase* itself (the Japanese reading of *xian he*) seems not to have been accepted into the *Tōgaku* vocabulary. Its place seems to have been taken in part by *hongen* 品 絃, presumably a vestige of *pin xian fa/hongenhō* 品 絃 法.

Observations linking *FBBF* with present tunings and modal categories in today's *Tōgaku* practice

As shown in Wolpert's Table of Mode-Keys (1977, pp. 131–2) the pitches of lowest strings (in the various tunings) all lie between *E* and *A*, as they do today. It is apparent that some identical tunings served for different modes, and that the tunings prescribed for named mode-keys are not those prescribed for pieces in *SGYR*. For example: *Shatuo-diao* and *Yiyue-diao* (that is: *Sada-chō* and *Ichikotsu-chō*) in *FBBF* share the same $F^{\#} B e a$-tuning, whereas today's tuning is *A d e a*. What determines the sequence of mode-keys in this same Table (pp. 131–2) is not apparent; even the sequence of lowest-pitched strings is not continuous.

Of the names of mode-keys in the Table of 28 Modes as reconstructed from data in *Yuefu zalu* (*YFZL*) (Picken, 1969, p. 98; for corrections see this Volume, p. 105), about half appear in the Table in *FBBF*; but their sequence is not reconcilable with that in the *YFZL*-Table, and in no instance is a mode in *FBBF* qualified by one of the 'pentatonic' modal names '*Gong*', '*Shang*', etc. In the Table of 1969, *Gong* and *Jiao* modes are so specified; but this type of qualification never occurs in *FBBF*.

Chromatic alteration occurs in certain sections of the modal preludes in the second tuning, the *Fan Fengxiang diao*, where the leading-note is not infrequently sharpened, changing the mode from Mixo-Lydian to Ionian.

In the case of the third group of preludes, the name: *Huangzhong diao* survives to the present; but its tuning: *E B e a*, is not that specified for items in *Ōshiki-chō/Huangzhong diao* today, but rather the tuning of today's *Hyōjō/Pingdiao*. The table reconstructed from *YFZL* (Picken, 1969) includes, however, a *Yü*-mode named *Huangzhong diao*, but with final *G*. As argued later (p. 257), this entire table requires raising in pitch by a tone throughout so that this

12

Yü-mode ends on *A*, in order for there to be correspondence with the real pitches of *Tōgaku* mode-keys. Accordingly, as practised today, *Huangzhong diao/Ōshiki-chō* corresponds to the same named mode in the *YFZL*-Table. In the *Gong*-set of the *YFZL*-Table there also existed, however, a *Huangzhong Gongdiao*黃 鍾 宮 調 mode on *C*. *Huangzhong diao* on A would then be the *Yü*-mode of that *Huangzhong Gongdiao* octave (see also p. 258).

Turning now to mode-key names of other modal preludes, *Fengxiang diao* (a *Yü*-mode on A) appears (in the light of this discussion) to be equivalent to today's *Ōshiki-chō/Huangzhong diao* as well as to the same named mode-key in *YFZL*. The *Fan Fengxiang diao*, a *Shang*-mode (Mixo-Lydian) on A, would then correspond to the *Xiaoshi diao* 小 石 調 of *YFZL*, as well as to the same-named mode-key in *FBBF*, but to be played there in the *Hyōjō*-tuning. Unfortunately there is no 'string-harmonising' (*ito-awase*) piece for *Xiaoshi diao* in *FBBF* [Wolpert, p. 124, (8)].

A beginning has been made in examining the music of the extended preludes in *FBBF* (in terms of musical structure and stylistic idiom) in a study of a single prelude (Picken, 1998). Preliminary comments on (1) *modal variability* in all three groups of preludes as they survive in *FBBF*, and (2) *structural variance* between their versions in *FBBF* and *SGYR*, were made in Fascicle 5, pp. 109, 110. While these items are certainly 'Tang music' (*Tangyue/Tōgaku*), they are not part of the entertainment-music repertory today and are only known from these two sources: *FBBF* and *SGYR*.

The effect of the open-string, undamped notes in low register, so frequent in these specimen-preludes from Lian Chengwu, is: to furnish a quasi-harmonic bass-line to the activities of melody-notes in tenor-register. Indeed (as R.F.W. frequently demonstrated in performance in the 1980s), the ear is reminded of what Ernst Kurt termed 'linear counterpoint', with lower notes at times sketching a descending 'bass-line', for example: E - D - B - G - E'- E', against which a tenor-line descends: $c^{\#\prime}$ - d' - $c^{\#\prime}$ - b - d' - g - $f^{\#}$ - e, as in Prelude III. 5 (Wolpert, p. 164).

Among the modal specimens [and reminiscent of the great Prelude in *Ōdai-hajinraku/Huang-di pozhenyue* (Fascicle 1, 1981)] are the frequent repetitions of quaver/eighth-note pairs, with a descent of a tone or minor third between members of a pair.

Sadatoshi's tablatures (received from Lian Chengwu in 838) might be expected to represent a somewhat earlier Chinese summary of the mode-key system than that summarised in the *YFZL*, itself dating from the end of the ninth century (Gimm, 1966, p. 58). Furthermore, in view of the fact that his teacher in Yangzhou was 85 years old, his gift to Sadatoshi may have been more representative of an earlier phase of the modal system, as perceived by a lutenist.

The use of pitch-pipe names, in the titles of mode-keys in the *YFZL*-Table, gives an impression of greater formal organisation of the mode-key system than does the serial list of titles of tunings in *FBBF*, where names of mode-keys reveal no musical characteristics.

Possible grounds for an intentional dissociation of this manuscript

It now seems to us possible that the *MS.* known as *FBBF* may have been dissociated deliberately, for the sake of convenience. The most useful section for a performer – and this will have remained true long after the passing into oblivion of the introductory preludial use of *chōshi* – was surely the collection of tuning-testing pieces for 27 of the mode-keys of Tang. Facilitating neat dismemberment, the *Biwa sho chōshi hon* begins precisely at the top of sheet 17; there was no need even to cut a sheet!

A break at the beginning of the sheet headed *Chōshi hon* is again a useful and rational place to break the sequence of sheets, since this short section includes not merely the tunings for four principal mode-keys (even though lacking pitch-information), but also a continuation of the précis of tablature-signs from the last modal prelude on sheet 13. *That* précis had begun with symbols for finger-plucking. By 838 these would have been of primary importance for a Chinese *piba*-player, since by the middle of the eighth century the use of fingers had largely replaced use of the plectrum in Tang China (Gimm, 1966). For Japanese performers, retaining (to this day) the older technique of the plectrum (*bachi/bo* 撥), the rest of the tablature-signs (on sheet 15) will have been of more general importance.

The practical needs just stated may well have dictated separation of first and last sections of the *MS.* The remaining sheets, 14 and 15, had value (for the performer) as a glossary of tablature-signs (excluding those for 'finger-plucking').

Lian Chengwu speaks of his pupil

These same two sheets are of great importance in other respects, however.

First, they include a comment on Sadatoshi's performance that can only have come from his teacher, Lian Chengwu. In this statement, Sadatoshi is significantly referred to by his Japanese title: 'Sadatoshi Ason'. In China, Lian Chengwu may well have called him: 'Zhenmin *Chaochen*', as one might say: 'Mr "Spiritual Diligence", Minister of the Court'.

'Zhenmin *Chaochen* finally played all.'

A stop (unique in this *MS.*): ◦ , is inserted, following 'all' *zhu/sho* 諸, and the lexigraph *diao* 調 is written small, to the right, in the space between two columns of lexigraphs, so that the sentence is to be completed as: 'all modes/mode-keys' 貞 敏 朝 臣 究 彈 諸 ◦ 調.

R.F.W.'s translation continues (p. 120): 'There was nothing we did not work through; but some of his notes were neither good nor bad, and some were not in tune with the flute.'

Such frank assessment of Sadatoshi's achievement can only have come from his teacher. Under no circumstances would such an opinion have been expressed by Sadayasu, for example, who certainly followed him in the *biwa*-tradition in Japan, and possibly was taught by Sadatoshi.

On the other hand, in the passage that follows the tablature-signs and their use and meaning (sheet 15), while Wolpert held that Sadayasu is writing of Sadatoshi in describing 'the Master' as 'adding many strings' and 'many ornamental notes' in performance, as compared with Tang practice, Wells (1993) suggests it is Sadatoshi writing of his Master, Lian Chengwu. Which view is correct would seem to turn on which of the two, Sadayasu or Sadatoshi, would be more likely to make comparison with Tang practice. Surely it would have been Sadatoshi who had observed that practice.

The final sentence (on sheet 15) ties together, indissolubly, the modal preludes of the first section (sheets 1–13) and the tuning-pieces of the *Biwa sho chōshi hon* (sheets 16–23): 'In addition, in respect of every score for all the modal preludes there is a tuning for the strings.' 加 以 諸 調 子 譜 中 皆 有 品 絃. That comment can only have come either from Lian Chengwu, describing the completeness of what he is sending, or from someone who has only experienced the manuscript as an integral whole, as it now exists thanks to the intelligence of the Library Staff of the Imperial Palace.

One more passage must be considered. It is the parenthesis (presumably from Sadayasu), added to a statement from (we infer) Lian Chengwu: 'The four modes/mode-keys prepare for refined music' 四 調 備 雅 樂. Here once more we see *diao* functioning, as in the earlier usage, for 'mode/mode-key'. The parenthesis that follows may mislead. R.F.W. properly translated *chōshi* 調 子 in this parenthesis as 'modal preludes'. In the following statement, however, the phrase: 'That is, these four *diaozi*', cannot refer to 'modal preludes', since the number of preludes notated amounts to 13 (one is incomplete, and the missing sheet presumably carried one more, completing the total of 14 as stated on sheet 3). The statement must mean: 'That is, these four mode-keys'.

What is stated by Lian Chengwu about the four modes *preparing* for *refined music* is not to be understood in the sense of preparing for *Yayue/Gagaku* in the

15

sense of Confucian Ritual, or Court Ritual, or Ceremonial Music, either Chinese or Japanese. It means only 'refined music' as opposed to 'popular music' 俗 樂. It is a statement of wide significance.

As Professor Mabuchi (1989, 1990) has demonstrated (see our p. 90) the term *Gagaku/Yayue* did not come into use in Japan until relatively late (16th – 17th century). Even in Chinese sources the term is rare. Here in this scroll it means the music of cultured Chinese; it does not mean (in this particular context) the music of Confucian or Ancestral worship. It signifies only that it was proper to introduce any music (other than popular music) as it would be introduced at an Islamic or Indian Court, by a modal prelude that displays the musical and affective properties of the music that will follow.

In Japan, it was undoubtedly early Heian practice to play a modal statement of some kind before performance of items from the Banquet Music. In respect of a majority of items in *RMS* (1133), it is expressly stated that the entrance of dancers and musicians to perform a piece is to be accompanied by the appropriate *chōshi* (frequently dancers and musicians also retire to the same accompaniment). It is evident that modal preludes, rather than the various types of *Ranjo/Ranjō*, were still in use for this purpose in the time of Ōga no Motomasa.

The parenthesis goes on to attribute the tradition (of using these four modes/mode-keys in this introductory manner) to 'the old Vice-Governor of Mutsu Province, Yoshiharu'. This statement in no way implies that Yoshiharu had anything to do with the origin of the modal preludes of sheets 1–13. Whoever wrote the parenthesis was merely using the Tang term: *diaozi* for mode/mode-key.

We conclude that *FBBF* is still, substantially, as it was when Lian Chengwu wrote it for Sadatoshi, at the end of a period of intensive training in the composition of modal preludes. Gamō Mitsuko (1989), too, accepts as original, the condition of *FBBF* as re-united by the Library of the Imperial Palace in 1962, and confers on Sadatoshi the distinction of having systematised the modal system of *Tōgaku* as it survives in Japan. That is to do Sadatoshi too much honour. It was his teacher, Lian Chengwu, who imparted the systematics, and the technique of composition also, we may suppose.

As a final comment on these modal matters, so importantly defined in *FBBF*, it is evident that by 838 (when Sadatoshi wrote the colophon), a considerable restriction of the 28 mode-keys had occurred in China. The major needs of *piba/biwa* players could be satisfied by two heptatonic modal note-sets, each in two keys only. As we shall see, this remains largely true of the *Tōgaku* repertory as a whole as it survives in manuscript form today.

Inspection and consideration establishes indeed that with knowledge only of the mode-keys illustrated by modal preludes in *FBBF*, there would be no need of

16

knowledge of any other tunings. All the modes in use in the Tang Chinese musical world could be played using those tunings alone. All such modes began with a first upward step in pitch of a tone – matching the standard fret-layout – and the only difference between the principal modes lay in the character of the mediant: whether minor or major. Differences between quasi-Dorian and Aeolian-type scales, should these be required, could readily be accommodated where frets were a semitone apart.

Wholly unexpected, and surely of enormous historical significance, is the fact that these two modal note-sets that survive are precisely the two octave-sets from whence the modes of the ancient Indian system were derived in the days of the jāti (p. 202): the *Sā-grāma* (Dorian on *C*) and *Mā-grāma* (Mixo-Lydian on *F*).

Fujiwara no Ason Sadatoshi 藤 原 朝 臣 貞 敏

The role of Sadatoshi in the history of Chinese and Japanese music merits particular emphasis since, as we argue, it was he who furnished the most extensive, synchronous collection of musical materials, representing and illustrating the significance for *piba/biwa* performance, in China and Japan, of what are known as 'the 28 Modes of the Tang' (Wolpert, 1977, pp. 152–64).

It is now certain that Sadatoshi did not return to Japan as soon as his studies with Lian Chengwu were completed (see pp. 39–48). What he did before his return later in 838 (or – if the biographical notice in *Sandai jitsuroku* is authoritative – in 839) is disputed in some quarters.

His journey

The colophon to *FBBF* (Wolpert, 1977) makes plain that Sadatoshi had been briefed (as a member of the Mission to Tang in which he participated) to seek instruction on *biwa* from a Chinese Lute-Master. The length of his stay in Tang is unclear; and his biography in *Sandai jitsuroku* (Fascicle 5, pp. 124, 125) is not entirely compatible with statements in *FBBF* of which the authority may not be questioned. The Japanese Mission of 838 included a Buddhist Monk, Ennin 圓 仁 ('Complete Benevolence') (793–864), posthumously known as *Jikaku Daishi* 慈 覺 大 師 ('Great Teacher Aware of Compassion'). Ennin's Diary of the Mission (very much seen from his personal standpoint) survives and was translated by Reischauer (1955, i), who examined its contents in a further publication of the same year, in which he related these to Tang history and geography.

The reference (in the colophon to *FBBF* – Wolpert, 1977) to an occasion when a petition to the Chinese authorities for a *piba/biwa* master was made (*via* Wang Youzhen) on the 7th day of the 8th month, is only reflected in the Diary (perhaps) by reference to a visit (by Wang) to the official inn on the 9th day of that month.

Sadatoshi's period of instruction from his 85-year-old teacher lasted (as already stated) no more than 22 days; and (as indicated by Wolpert) the story (in *Bunkidan* 文 機 談, repeated by Kikkawa) of his being taught *piba* in 835, is impossible, since he did not reach Yangzhou until 838. From Ennin's Diary (Reischauer, 1955, i, p. 22), the Mission did not arrive in Yangzhou until the 25th of the 7th month of 838. The explanation of this discrepancy between *Bunkidan* and the Diary may well be the considerable delay in the departure of the flotilla from Japan, as shown in the table of Japanese Missions to China assembled by Tōno, Haruyuki 東 野 治 之 (1995).

Although Sadatoshi undoubtedly participated in the Mission, it is evident (from entries in the Diary) that his capacity as a musician was either unknown to Ennin or too unimportant to be mentioned. The size of the Mission (651 members, according to Fujiie Reinosuke, 1988, p. 95) perhaps makes understandable Ennin's limited knowledge of the full range of competences even of someone who interested him as a co-religionist. Sadatoshi is mentioned on four occasions only, and these show him to have been a man of considerable gifts – as was already plain from the very unusual objective of his Mission: to receive training in a theoretical aspect of Chinese musical studies.

On the 24th of the 7th month he is named by Ennin as Acting Administrative Officer and is said to be suffering from what appears to be a dysentery. On the 29th of the 11th month he 'has for some time being lying ill and suffering' and 'has resolved to make pictures of the Boddhisattva Miyōken 妙 見 and of the Four Heavenly Kings 四 天 王' (Reischauer, i, p. 60), and this resolution was implemented on the 30th day of the 11th month of 838. On the 9th day of the 12th month he also offered a 'maigre feast' in the *Kaiyuansi* 開 元 寺 temple (where the Mission stayed in Yangzhou); made offerings to the new pictures and to more than 60 monks, and had copies of older paintings made (Reischauer, i, p. 64). This is the last occasion on which Sadatoshi is mentioned in the Diary. He is described on the 9th day (as also in the colophon to *FBBF*) as an Administrative Officer of the first ship of the Mission.

The manner in which Sadatoshi reached Chang'an – if indeed he did so as stated in the brief biographical notice in *Sandai jitsuroku* (Fascicle 5, pp. 124–5) – remains obscure. On the 5th day of the 10th month of 838, the ambassador and the bulk of the Mission boarded five ships for the first part of the journey to the capital, Chang'an; but the Diary tells us that Sadatoshi was still with Ennin's group on the 9th day of the 12th month of 838. We are further informed that the ambassadorial party reached Chang'an on the 3rd day of the 12th month of 838 (Reischauer, i, p. 64). [When at last the party embarks to continue its voyage, *via* the Grand Canal, Reischauer's interpretation of the abbreviated name and title of a member of the Fujiwara clan: 'Commander of the Fourth Ship', as a reference to Sadatoshi, cannot be sound, since the Diary shows he did not leave for Chang'an when the bulk of the Mission left.]

Reischauer (1955, ii, p. 308) suggests that the diary 'indicates that Sadatoshi never went to Ch'ang-an but remained in Yang-chou with Ennin'. This goes somewhat beyond the text of the diary, which merely reveals that he was still with Ennin after the departure of the ambassadorial group. We are told, however, that it was then the intention of Wang Youzhen (the Chinese Official responsible for the Mission and for the activities of its 651 members) to proceed shortly to the capital. Conceivably Sadatoshi went with him – the former's status of 'nobleman' must always have stood him in good stead in China. It seems highly unlikely that he could have made his way alone to Chang'an. Nor does it seem reasonable to suppose that he remained (by permission of the Chinese authorities) alone in Yangzhou – for further instruction on *biwa*/*piba* for example – in view of the almost daily difficulties (*vis-à-vis* the Chinese authorities) experienced by the group of four religious, when they sought permission for Ennin to stay on in China and visit holy places, after the embassy (with its ambassador) had departed for Chang'an.

In the eyes of the Chinese authorities, Ennin's group, consisting of himself, two disciples and a servant, appeared to have been 'abandoned' in China. According to a letter from the subprefecture (Reischauer, i, p. 138) the Chinese authorities described the group as thus treated 'by the Japanese ships' that left for Japan on the 15th day of the 7th month in 839; and this is confirmed by a statement in a later letter – from the Government General of Dengzhou, addressed (presumably) to the Regional Commander of Qingzhou, on the 9th day of the 3rd month of 840 – repeating that the party had been 'abandoned' by the returning ships of the Japanese Mission that left for Japan on the 15th day of the 7th month of 839 (*Kaicheng* 開 成 4) (Reischauer, i, p. 187). The four travellers left behind in China overwintered from 839 to 840 in Qingningxiang, and then proceeded (*via* Wutaishan and Taiyuan) to Chang'an. Ennin himself remained in China for nine years. What happened to Sadatoshi is not reported.

It is abundantly clear that Sadatoshi's period of training with Lian Chengwu was of a theoretical as well as practical character, and it is questionable whether, participating as he plainly did in Buddhist religious exercises of one kind or another, he would also have contact with Entertainment Music from the Tang Court while in Yangzhou. Nevertheless he is said – by *RMS, JCYR* and *SGYR* –

to have brought back to Japan, as a *biwa*-piece, a single item of the Banquet-Music. The piece in question is the Quick of 'The Palace of Congratulations' (*Music from the Tang Court*, 3, 1985; see pp. 20–9).The oldest source testifying to this is the *RMS* of 1133. The entry occurs on p. 31 of the edition of that work in *Gunsho ruiju* 群 書 類 從 卷 第 342: '貞 敏' '(being a person called Sadatoshi) copying it on *biwa* came with it from Tang'. 貞 敏 。 さ だ と し と い ＾ る 人 な り 。 唐 よ り 琵 琶 に な ら ひ て 。 き た る な り 。 At some time, therefore, Sadatoshi must have had opportunity to hear at least one item of Entertainment Music of the Court; and the Court resided at Chang'an.

Valuable as are the entire contents of *FBBF*, it was Sadatoshi's sojourn with his second teacher – did it indeed occur – that may have furnished in bulk most of the *Tōgaku* items that survive, to this day, in manuscript tablatures in Japan. It was in Chang'an, and from Liu Erlang 劉 二 郎, that he is reported (in the brief biographical note in *Sandai jitsuroku*) to have later received 'some tens' of scores (*sujū/shu shi* 數 十) of scrolls: 'Liu Erlang made a gift of musical scores in several tens of scrolls' 劉 二 郎 贈 譜 數 十 卷 。(See Fascicle 5, p. 124.) These scores in this quantity would surely have constituted a very substantial transmission of virtually all that the Japanese ever received from China as 'Tang music'.

In an attempt to get over the difficulty of two persons named as instructors in *biwa*, Gamō Mitsuko 蒲 生 美 津 子 (1989, p. 732c) permitted herself to offer an alternative opinion as to who taught *biwa* at the Kaiyuansi 開 元 寺 in Yangzhou. In a parenthesis she states: 'In a different version, Liu Erlang' 異 説 で は 劉 二 郎. That one may be free to doubt Sadatoshi's signed witness to what happened at the Kaiyuan Temple in 838 would not occur to a foreigner.

The other musician
Notwithstanding the evident quality of his musicianship, Sadatoshi was not, according to the sources, in charge of musical activities on the Mission of 838. That function is stated to have been performed by Ōto no Kiyogami (Seijō) 大 戶 清 上 (see Marett, 1976, pp. 11, 12 for his place in the Tang flute-tradition in Japan, and pp. 16–18 for limited biographical details; see also our pp. 21–22). Kiyogami was named as 'Head of Music' in the Mission to Tang: 遺 唐 の 音 樂 長. Gamō Mitsuko (1989, p. 732c) has more recently confirmed his presence and role in 838. This appointment had been made in 837 or 835 (see Marett; see also Haruyuki), and the Mission undoubtedly finally left Japan for Tang in 838. One of the returning ships is reported to have been wrecked on a small island near Taiwan, and Kiyogami (who did not return) is said to have been killed by

the inhabitants. (A.J.M. suggests that his loss may also have occasioned loss of scores, collected by him in person.)

A number of smaller items in the *Tōgaku* repertory are indeed associated with his name, as now here summarised:

RMS (1130) mentions Kiyogami's name in relation to three items: *Ōtenraku* 應 天 樂, *Kaiseiraku* 海 青 樂, *Seijōraku* 清 上 樂.

JCYR, *SGYR*, (post 1170) mention Kiyogami twice only in relation to *Ōtenraku* and *Seijōraku*.

KKS (1233) states that Kiyogami 'made': *Jusuiraku* 拾 翠 樂, *Ōtenraku* (Hamanushi made dance), *Shōwaraku* 承 合 樂, *Ittokyō* 壹 團 嬌, and *Seijōraku*, but is uncertain whether Kiyogami or Hamanushi 'made' *Kaiseiraku*. (*JCYR/SGYR* say – according to Nangū – that the last was 'played' by Kiyogami.) *Seijōraku* is the piece most certainly composed, in our sense, by Kiyogami before his departure.

JCYR and *SGYR* give relatively lengthy accounts of this, and these are more accurate by one lexigraph than the account in *KKS*, though the latter text was evidently modelled on theirs. The formulation in *RMS* is quite different.

What seems of importance is that nowhere is any item attributed to Kiyogami as *collector*. Even if every one of the handful of pieces listed were indeed 'made' by Kiyogami, this tells us nothing regarding the source of the enormous, surviving manuscript-repertory, of which in fifteen years we have so far transcribed, and published in transcription, perhaps less than one third. A small fraction only of that repertory is performed today in Japan as single movements, sometimes the last surviving memory of a *taikyoku* or 'Large Piece'.

A single reference in *HFF* (Marett, 1976) links Kiyogami with the flute-score of a *taikyoku* piece that was evidently known to Hakuga. The piece is *Moto-uta* or *Genka / Yuan ge* 元 哥 – for 歌; presumably 'First Song'. (See Marett's *Dissertation*, p. 260.)

Ōto no Kiyogami's high standing seems to have been due to the fact that he was a fine flute-player, and to the no less important fact that he was very well-born and enjoyed imperial favour. Had he indeed collected on the Mission of 838, the loss of his person need not, of course, have meant loss of the materials collected.

If, however, the silence of Ennin on the subject of Sadatoshi's musical abilities and duties is regrettable, the absence of any reference whatsoever to Ōto no Kiyogami is surely extraordinary. Reischauer's index to the Diary includes no instance of the family name 'Ōto'; nor does any component of his name, read either in the Japanese or in the Chinese manner, appear there. Conceivably, the considerable size of the Mission precluded knowledge on Ennin's part even of important members, if their duties were purely secular. The Table of Missions to

Tang, from 632 onwards, drawn up by Fujiie (p. 95), shows that Kiyogami, if appointed to a Mission in 837, must indeed have participated in the Mission that left in 838 and returned in 839 and 840. (839 is the year of the reported shipwreck. See also Tōno Haruyuki, 1995.)

What happened to Ennin

For the record, we owe to Ennin himself an important observation on Tang Chinese performance of a single musical item that survives to this day in the *Tōgaku* repertory. While staying in the Long'xingsi temple 龍 行 寺 in Qing'zhoufu he may have witnessed (on the 24th of the 3rd month of 840) a performance of 'The Prince of Qin Destroys the Formation' *Qin-wang pozhenyue/Shinnō hajinraku* 秦 王 破 陣 樂. The diary-text has: 'Spring Festival Formation-Destroying' 春 節 破 陣 樂; but Reischauer and others suggest that 'Spring Festival' 春 節 is a mis-copying of '*Qin-wang*' 秦 王 (Reischauer, i, p. 195).

Ennin himself returned to Japan on the 9th day of the 9th month of 847. It seems possible that this date is responsible for the confusion between Chinese and Japanese dates, as recorded in the biographical notice of Sadatoshi in *Sandai jitsuroku* (Fascicle 5, p. 125). The Chinese date (*Dazhong* 大 中 1) 847 is the year of Ennin's return to Japan, and it may have been known to the biographer that Sadatoshi travelled with the Mission that included Ennin. The Japanese date that is mistakenly equated with that same Tang-Chinese date (847) in the biography, is in fact *Jōwa* 承 合 6, namely 839.

It is not impossible that Sadatoshi in fact returned to Japan in that year, if he was able to participate in the ambassadorial Mission that set out for Japan from 'the east inlet of Mt. Chi in Chingning-hsiang' in 839 (Reischauer, i, p. 187). The return of Sadatoshi to Japan would then match the chronology of *Sandai jitsuroku*, according to which he arrived in Chang'an already in 838 (travelling perhaps with Wang Youzhen, after the main body of the Mission had left Yangzhou on the 5th day of the 10th month in 838). Subsequently, having stayed for two to three months with Liu Erlang, he could have left Chang'an (with the ambassadorial party) to meet ships departing for Japan in 839. It is suggested that the biographer muddled the dates of Ennin's and Sadatoshi's respective returns to Japan.

And if Sadatoshi did not reach Chang'an and Liu Erlang, what then?

The implications of Ennin's account of his contacts with Sadatoshi, as well as what the colophon and contents of *FBBF* suggest about Sadatoshi, is that he was a person of much more intellectual substance than the description 'skilled in playing *biwa*' implies. His contribution to modal understanding of the *Tōgaku* repertory by the Japanese was, and remains, of immense importance, even if he did not reach Chang'an and bring back a gift of scores; and this, notwithstanding his description, in the colophon to *FBBF*, merely as *hankan* or *hōgan/pan'guan* 判 官 'Administrative Officer'. His interest in religious paintings suggests that he was, perhaps, also himself a painter. The remark in his biography (Fascicle 5, p. 125) that he 'had no other artistic ability' 無 他 才 藝 reads rather oddly – unnecessarily, perhaps – as if some competence were being denied. Such an attitude would be in keeping with the slightly dismissive tone of that biography.

It has been suggested – but this may be no more than gossip – that the outline bibliography in *Sandai jitsuroku* is not to be trusted since it was not written until perhaps 60 years after the death of Sadatoshi; furthermore, that it is an invention intended to explain the otherwise unexplained acquisition of the bulk of the *Tōgaku* repertory.

In regard to the first criticism, delay in documentation is no novelty in the historical process. The dated account of the consecration of the Great Buddha of the Tōdaiji, which occurred in 752, post-dates the occasion itself by almost a century, since the records of the temple did not begin until the ninth century. Regarding the second suggestion, surely if the story were an invention with a purpose, some attempt would have been made to improve Sadatoshi's image. He emerges, however, as no more than an able *biwa*-player, of modest standing in rank and appointments.

If Sadatoshi did not bring back 'musical scores in several tens of scrolls', we have no notion how the repertory reached Japan in the bulk represented by the surviving source-manuscripts, the volume of which today is utterly unsuspected by a majority of Japanese musicologists. As to when and how the repertory came to be organised as we see it in the principal manuscripts, classified by mode-key and by size, we would then have no inkling. Had the repertory been received from Sadatoshi in the form of copies of Chinese musical manuscripts, however, items would surely already have been ordered, in modal, and perhaps also in size, categories.

What happened to the repertory from Tang?
Certain critics – and conspicuously Reese (1986, p. 81) and Lam (1989, p. 345) – have charged us with paying insufficient attention to the possibility that the Banquet-Music Repertory from the Tang Court was transformed, and in particular that the *scores* of the music, and not merely their performance-practice,

were transformed in the Japanese environment, as a result of a process of acculturation.

A major element that had impelled the Japanese to secure *scores in notation* – rather than (say) merely to hire visiting musicians, competent to perform the Tang Entertainment Repertory – was, surely, the interest in that repertory shown by a literate and musically educated nobility, able to read Chinese, and therefore able to read and perform from tablatures or pitch-notations written in Chinese. Theirs was, of course, not just an interest in *music* (as we understand the term), but an interest in the complex of Music-with-Dance, in *Yue* 樂, as the term was understood by the Chinese from the earliest times, down to, and including, the Tang (see Fascicle 2, p. 102).

Of the climate of noble, musical performance at the Heian court, 'The Tale of Genji' (in Waley's translation, 1935) gives a vivid picture; as (for example) in the 'The Flower Feast' (Chapter viii, p. 147):

'About the twentieth day of the second month the Emperor gave a Chinese banquet under the great cherry-tree of the Southern Court. Towards dusk the delightful dance known as the Warbling of Spring Nightingales (*Shunnō-den/Chunying zhuan*, Fascicle 2, p. 45) was performed... When it was over the Heir Apparent placed a wreath on Genji's head and pressed him so urgently that it was impossible for him to refuse. Rising to his feet he danced very quietly a fragment of the sleeve-turning passage in the Wave Dance (*Seigaiha/Qinghai bo*, Wolpert *et al.*, 1973). In a few moments he was seated again, but even into this brief extract from a long dance he managed to import an unrivalled charm and grace. Even his father-in-law who was not best pleased with him was deeply moved and found himself wiping away a tear.'

In regard to the second item from the Flower Feast: 'Waves of Kokonor', Lady Murasaki's novel itself dates from about the year 1000; the transcription of the piece [from the *Shinsen gaku-fu* (*HFF*) of Minamoto no Hiromasa (Hakuga), completed in 966] by Marett, 1976 (see also Marett, 1977, p. 55) may therefore be taken to represent its condition, in a flute-version, in the time of Prince Genji. It is a heptatonic melody in a mode (*Banshiki-chō/Banshe-diao* 阪 蛇 調) known to Chinese court-musicians at least since the sixth century AD (p. 213). Its style resembles that of no known Japanese music, either ancient or modern.

Beyond question, the Banquet-Music from Tang has been transformed in performance out of recognition, by processes of acculturation, over the 1200-year (or more) span of its survival in Japan. We accept that the word 'acculturation' covers all that happens, over time, in the adaptation of any aspect of imported cultural materials or behaviour, in a new cultural environment.

Processes of acculturation

Much indeed happened over time:

(a)   the enormous retardation in performance deduced by us;

(b)   *shō*-technique was changed;

(c)   *gaku-sō* technique was changed;

(d)   *gaku-biwa* technique was changed;

(e)   the status of these three instruments was reduced from melody-bearing to accompanying;

(f)   *ryūteki* and *hichiriki* became free of the melodic restraints of the original modality;

(g)   the last two instruments came to perform increasingly florid variations on the basic melodic line of the Tang original.

All these are aspects of acculturation; but they are evidently not what Lam and Reese have in mind. Both critics imply significant Japanese modification, already in the first century or so after importation, of the essential qualities of the basic musical materials received from Tang. Both postulate a modification such that even the hitherto unrecognised melodies of *shō*, *gaku-sō* and *gaku-biwa* scores (unrecognised until revealed by L.E.R.P., 1957, 1967, 1969) underwent transformation – 'japanicisation' – so that (in Reese's words) our title should have been 'Music from the Heian Court'.

Of any *profound* revision of the tunes that survive *in unambiguous, fixed-pitch tablature, in the scores for mouth-organ* (which do not of course display the cluster-chords of today's performance-practice) there is no trace. The tunes as transcribed from the mouth-organ scores today remain unmistakeably Chinese in character. From their judgements, it is evident that neither critic has ever heard of 'circumstantial evidence': 'Evidence of facts not in issue from which can be inferred a fact in issue' (C. B. Curzon: *A Dictionary of Law*, many editions). As will become clear at the end of this Chapter, there is now direct evidence of transmission of instruments to Japan when Sadatoshi returned, as well as the link of an item of the *Tōgaku* repertory with such a transmission.

The nature of adaptive change in the new cultural environment

Nevertheless, changes occurred that served to adapt the repertory to Japanese taste. The period from mid- to late-Heian was precisely a period during which many aspects of borrowed Chinese culture were adapted to Japanese circumstances. In this period, it is already apparent that adaptation was taking place; but the nature of the adaptive process in relation to music was not – as it later became – fundamental.

25

Tablatures in chronological sequence – from *Gogen kinfu* 五 弦 琴 譜 to *Hakuga*, to Moronaga's *Sango-yōroku*; from *Ko Sō-fu* to *Ruisō-chiyō* and Moronaga's *Jinchi-yōroku*; from *Kofu* to *Shinsen-shōteki-fu*; and from *Hakuga* to later flute-*MSS* of all kinds – show us that what happened first (during the Heian period) was a reduction in *bulk* of the primary musical material embodied in tablatures: a shortening of items, from perhaps five or six movements in the flute-score *HFF*, to a single movement in the string-scores of Moronaga and the *shō* scores of the thirteenth and early fourteenth centuries.

In addition, there was an enormous reduction in the number of *titles* of items present in the performing-repertory of the Tang Court-musicians, as compared with the number of items that survive in the great manuscript collections of Fujiwara no Moronaga and Minamoto no Hiromasa. The repertory in *SGYR* amounts approximately to 110 titles, of which a high proportion are suites in two, three, or more movements. These too have undergone further subsequent shortening, by the omission of movements.

The collection of items, in scores for the three winds: mouth-organ, flute and reed-pipe, available today for amateur use, and comprising items both from the *Tōgaku* and *Komagaku* repertories, amounts to no more than some sixty titles of single movements (with one exception, where two movements of one title are still performed).

In addition to these quantitative changes, the scores (for each of the five melodic instruments used in *Tōgaku* performance today), when examined in chronological sequence, show an increase (over the centuries) in the degree of decorative embellishment applied to the primary melodic lines of the earliest manuscript tablatures.

For example: in the zither-tradition, the versions of items in the *Ko sō-fu* (*KSF*) 古 箏 譜 *MS.* (Tenri Library perhaps of the tenth century; see facsimile, with commentary by Hayashi Kenzō 林 謙 三, Tōkyō, 1974) are in general less embellished than are Moronaga's versions of the same items in *JCYR* (see transcriptions by Dr Jonathan Condit in Picken, 1974). In the case of *Etenraku*, for example, minims/half-notes in *KSF* are replaced by repeated crotchets/quarter-notes in *JCYR*; quavers/eighth-notes are interpolated between pairs of quarter-notes; *glissandi* are extended in compass in *JCYR*.

In general, the kinds of additions to be observed in the decoration of zither (and lute) versions are of the familiar categories of appoggiatura, passing-note, anticipation, auxiliary notes (in mordents and *Pralltriller*), and échappées. [Interestingly, however, Moronaga has preserved, in second place, a 'same-tune' version (*dō-kyoku* 同 曲) of *Etenraku* in *Banshiki-chō* that is even less decorated than is the Tenri *KSF* version.]

In the same mode-key, Wolpert (1981, pp. 81ff.) set out in parallel (1) the version from *HFF* of *Chūmeiraku/Chongming yue* 崇 明 樂 'Respect for Wisdom' (this piece is now known as *Sōmei-raku/Zongming yue* 宗 明 樂 'Ancestral Wisdom'; see also Marett, 1977, p. 49); (2) the version of this piece in *GGKF* (now judged to be, like *HFF*, of the eleventh century in its writing); and (3) the lute-version from *SGYR*. (1) includes rather more quaver-movement than does (2), but infinitely less than does (3). This last abounds with finger-plucked mordents, as compared with only two *Pralltriller* in *GGKF*. (A.J.M.'s version of the piece in *HFF* shows mordents – on the beat, or delayed – in almost every measure; on flute these amount to minimal, effortless decoration, playable at speed.) The parallel assemblage of transcribed scores in staff-notation of the piece 'Waves of Kokonor' *Seigaiha/Qinghai-bo* 青 海 波 (Wolpert *et al.*, 1973, pp. 8, 9) may serve to display the total range of decoration from the version of *HFF* to those of later, zither-, lute- and reed-pipe-scores.

This increase over time in the density of embellishment may well be correlated (as we would argue) with slowing down in performance-speed and this again with the revision downwards, over the centuries, in the number of repeats of a piece, or of a suite-movement, as specified by Moronaga. The latter's authorities for larger numbers of repeats in earlier times are his predecessors: Prince Sadayasu, and Minamoto no Hiromasa (Hakuga). As a single instance, regarding the complex performance of 'Bodhisattvas' (*Bosatsu/Pusa* 菩 薩), *JCYR* and *SGYR* state that the Prelude is to be played once; they note, however, that Prince Sadayasu's 'Southern Palace Score' states that 'the Prelude should be blown four times' 序 可 吹 四 反 (see Fascicle 4, p. 66). The time-interval between Prince Sadayasu and Fujiwara no Moronaga would have been rather more than two centuries; so perhaps this downwards revision of the number of repeats of the Prelude may be interpreted as a maximal reduction in performance-speed to a quarter of that adopted in the time of Prince Southern Palace.

In the score of the 'Large Prelude' of *Bosatsu* (Fascicle 4, pp. 76–80), attention should be drawn to the important flute-glosses in *JCYR*, and their agreement (in large measure) with the text of the older mouth-organ score: *KF/HSF/RK*. It is reasonable to suggest that these two sources approach the condition of the piece as received from Tang; and that the minimal decoration of the flute-version is in itself an indication of an original, relatively *short* duration of the quarter-note, in this and other music from Tang.

Marett (1991, p. 132) has commented: '…if a Chinese musician from the Tang period… could have been transported to twelfth-century Japan and had listened to how the Japanese were performing one of the Tang tunes he had known in China three centuries earlier, he would no doubt have been surprised at how the tune had been treated in Japan, but would probably nevertheless have been able to recognise the tune'.

Subsequent to that time, however, as already demonstrated (Marett, 1985, pp. 409–31), it is plain that: '...the ancient Chinese melodies of *Tōgaku*, which persisted in Japan up until the twelfth century can no longer be heard; the melodies carried today by *ryūteki* (flute) and *hichiriki* (reed-pipe) – now regarded as the main melodies – have emerged at some time after the twelfth century'.

Indeed, it is the view of Japanese scholars, as well as of the Court musicians themselves, that 'it is the *hichiriki* and *ryūteki* that carry the main melody and that other melodic instruments have a subsidiary role' (Marett, p. 409). Furthermore, this melody is held to be 'decorated harmonically by the *shō* (mouth-organ) and strings' (Gamō Mitsuko, 1970, cited in translation by Marett, p. 409). This implies that Gamō wrote unaware that mouth-organ, zither and lute, all three, still carry (as we have shown over the past 18 years) the original Tang melody in a form appropriate to the physical properties of the respective instruments.

The emergence of formulaic melodic embellishment
In this same paper (1985) Marett demonstrated how formulaic melody-lines began to evolve in flute-practice, as revealed by flute-versions of the same piece in a family of manuscripts known as: *Chū Ōga ryūteki yōroku-fu* (*CORYF*). One copy of this survives from the end of the thirteenth or the beginning of the fourteenth century (the original has not survived). Parallel display of the item *Seigaiha/Qinghai bo* 青 海 波 (in *Banshiki-chō/Banshe diao* 般 蛇 調) (Marett, 1985, pp. 424–5), transcribed from *CORYF* and from *HFF*, reveals that whereas the only ornaments applied to the *HFF* recension, in versions available in *SSSTF* and *SGYR* ('Heian-style ornamentation') are appoggiaturas, ligatures and mordents; in *CORYF* the bulk of figures may not (in the light of Heian practice) be regarded as merely 'ornamental'.

Two figures only may be regarded as 'extended appoggiaturas', in which an appoggiatura is applied to an already existent appoggiatura; this operation is then repeated, forming a conjunct chain of notes. The new type of decorative figure is further distinguished from the earlier, Heian type, in that it may be used where no return of the same melodic unit of the original melody occurs. That is to say, there is already a tendency for the amplificatory figures to behave as independent formulae.

Example 1. *Seigaiha*, transcribed from *Chū Ōga ryūteki yōroku-fu*, and *Hakuga no fue-fu*

An extended sequence of such figures (from *CORYF*) is shown by Marett (Example 1) in parallel with developments therefrom in modern flute-performance (Example 2). From the present-day version for flute (lowest of the three staves) it becomes evident that the modality of the piece in *HFF* is transformed in the modern version by the disappearance of $g^{\sharp}$. Yet as shown in another of Marett's examples (Marett, p. 423, example 5), the musical line of *HFF* is to be traced even today, in a melodic line modally transformed but metrically defined by the original structure, as we see it in *HFF*.

Example 2. *Seigaiha* (part only), transcribed from *Chū Ōga ryūteki yōroku-fu*, and according to modern practice

The fact that the modern melodies of *ryūteki* and *hichiriki* are, in both instances, constructed of 'small units of fixed melody (*koteiteki-na senritsu no shō-tan* 固定的な旅律の小單)' had already been recognised by Gamō Mitsuko (1970, p. 145); but the relationship between these elements and any primary melody was not recognised by her (Marett, 1985). That these same elements recur *throughout* the *Tōgaku* repertory would seem at first sight to exclude any possibility that the florid, modern melodies of these two wind-instruments are still today related to *different*, original melodies from the Tang. Nevertheless they are so related.

Modality: mouth-organ resistance to hemitonic pentatonicism

The scores for *shō* remain to this day (for the most part) *in their modal condition as specified for pieces of same title in Chinese historical sources.* No trace of Japanese hemitonic, pentatonic modality is to be heard *in the shō-melodies,* as they appear in the mouth-organ tablatures – in striking contrast to what happened

30

in the elaborate variant-versions for *ryūteki* and *hichiriki* as currently and traditionally performed.

No trace of modal change of this kind is detectable in the *shō*-scores of 'small' and 'middle-sized' pieces; in the case of the 'large pieces', not only is there no such modal change, but their extended complex heptatonic melodies have no parallel in any kind of Japanese melody known to us in history, or in present performance-practice, in any genre of traditional Japanese music (see Chapter 2, pp. 59–62, 74–75.). It is probably significant that it is the Large Pieces (*Taikyoku/Daqu*) that have almost disappeared from the repertory of *Tōgaku* as performed today. Where two movements of one such *Taikyoku: Shunnō-den/Chunying zhuan*, survive in the repertory, it is the rhythmically regular movements – rather than the rhythmically irregular movements – that are still performed.

The modal system from Tang in the Japanese environment of the Kamakura period

A glimpse of Kamakura-thinking about the modal system of Tang as acquired along with *Tōgaku*, is afforded by a comparative table in *Zoku kyōkunshō* (*ZKKS*) 9, p. 360. This sets out *shō* pipe-names in parallel with corresponding flute-pitches at named flute-fingerholes. The nine columns bear the names of six of the mode-keys under which the bulk of the repertory is classified. Three columns, however, bear titles of mode-keys not mentioned either in *FBBF* or in the Chinese data from *YFZL* (see p. 32). In each instance a column is headed by the final of the mode-key and is followed by a vertically descending sequence of pitch-names, as for a heptatonic, modal note-set, but with added alternative pitches.

The first column, with *e* as initial pitch, suffices both for *Hyōjō* and for *Taishiki-chō*; and this is made possible by the fact that the note-set of the *shō*-pipes includes both *g* and *g$^{\sharp}$*, *c* and *c$^{\sharp}$*. The parallel display of flute-hole names is unfortunately incomplete: *g* is omitted; *c$^{\sharp}$* is present; but *d* also is absent.

This precedent is followed for all the modes in turn, in each instance both natural and sharp forms of each pitch are shown, pitches that in the original mode would be either one or the other, but never both.

The entire table appears to be part of that set out in the sixteenth-century *Taigenshō* 體源鈔 (*TGS*), pp. 1440ff. *ZKKS* shows note-sets on nine notes only, rather than on the 12 notes of the *Taigenshō*-Table, where *Shinsen*, *Kamimu* and *Shimomu* – non-Tang note-sets – are exhibited along with others, likewise unknown to Tang. This latter Table also includes a note-set on *g$^{\sharp}$*, named as 'Bird-Bell Mode' *Chōshō-chō* 鳥鍾調.

Of interest is the fact that unlike the Table in *ZKKS*, the *TGS* Table sets out the series of finals in ascending order from *D* to *E'*, where *ZKKS* runs the series of finals from *E* to *D'*, although in neither instance is tessitura explicit. Furthermore, it is evident in *TGS* that it is the *Shō/Shang* 商 pentatonic set of the *Ichikotsu* mode-key that determines the structure of the *TGS* Table and the sequence of mode-keys in *ZKKS*. In the latter, *Hyōjō* and *Taishiki-chō* occur at the same locus, since each can be regarded, skeletally, as utilising the same pentatonic framework: *e*, *f♯*, *a*, *b*, *c♯*. The Table of seven *Shang/Shō* modes in the Tang-set of *YFZL* (Picken, 1969, p. 98) only furnishes Chinese names for five of the twelve Japanese, pentatonic, *Shō* mode-keys of *TGS*, and five of the nine such of *ZKKS*.

It was, presumably, because of the importance of, and lowest-pitched final of, *Ichikotsu* that the 23.56.1-skeleton was adopted as pattern for the entire Tang mode-key system, as viewed by the Japanese in Kamakura and Muromachi times. The prime position of that mode (along with the modes with the 6.123.5-skeleton) is linked, we suggest, with the influence that stemmed from the exposition of Chinese modes in *FBBF*, after Sadatoshi's return from Tang.

Unfortunately, however, even the *ZKKS* Table that shows all possible pitches, both for flute and for mouth-organ, does not show what modal-practice was, in thirteenth-century performance. The flute fingerhole-set for *Sōjō* does indeed show *f♯* and no *f♮*, but it includes both *c* and *c♯*. The *Shuangdiao* 雙調 of the Tang was in fact a Mixo-Lydian set: *g a b c d e f*. Nevertheless, the note-set as shown by *ZKKS* would have embraced the resultant practice of winds and strings in today's performance of items in this mode, with *biwa* sounding both *c♯* and *c*, and flute sounding *c♯* and *c*, as well as *f* and *f♯*. The *g♯*, present in the mouth-organ pipe-set shown in *ZKKS*, is used today in the six-note cluster-chord on *f♯*, but the *c♯* (shown in *ZKKS*) is not.

The absence of defined, differentiated, modal note-sets in these nominally 'modal' displays, surely implies a weakening of regard for such differentiation. The progressive loss of perception of original modality, as performance-speeds were continuously reduced, made possible the re-shaping of the most conspicuous instrumental lines in formulae that are frequently 'hemitonic'. The plurality of alternative pitch-values, for degrees that were once decisive in determining modal character, tended to reduce all 'modes' to the condition of chromatic 'keys'.

Attention may be drawn again to elements of modal, and mode-key variability of much earlier date, previously discussed (Fascicle 5, p. 109), including evidence that comparable variation between modal variants of the same piece was present in the Chinese environment before transmission to Japan.

The 'national' scales, and the historic role of Yatsuhashi *Kengyō*

Readers with knowledge of the distinctive hemitonic pentatonic scales characteristic of one part of Japanese folk-music, and so very characteristic of the popular *koto* (*zoku-koto* 俗 箏) and *Kumi-uta* 組み 歌 traditions, and of the music of *Naga-uta* 長 歌 and *Kabuki* 歌 舞 伎, may have supposed that any revision of Chinese tunes by Japanese musicians (in an attempt to render them more acceptable) would long since have manifested itself, had it occurred, by a change from the Chinese-type anhemitonic pentatonic scaling of Tang tunes, to the Japanese hemitonic type.

It is the case, however, that the characteristic *in/yin* 陰 scale (as opposed to the *yō/yang* 陽 scale) does not appear in notation in Japan until the seventeenth century. (Of interest is the fact that a gender-distinction is made between the two types: the former as female, the latter as male. They differ in the size of the interval between the first two notes of the two scales; in the *in*-scale this is a semitone; in the *yō*-scale, a tone.)

The *in*-scale first appears in the scores of compositions for voice with zither-accompaniment, namely, the song-suites for voice and *koto* known as *kumi-uta* (Adriaansz, 1973). Strictly speaking, hemitonicism in these scores is not implicit in the *notation* as such – which is for the most part as for *gaku-sō* scores: a numbering of the strings in sequence from the lowest pitch upwards. Hemitonicism was determined by the specified scalar-tuning of the string-set.

This introduction of a type of scaling that had previously belonged (we infer), exclusively, to the oral tradition of Japanese folk-music, was made by a musician born in 1614, blind from birth, who made his living as player of the *shamisen/sanxian* 三 味 線 / 三 弦, a three-stringed, long-necked, unfretted lute with a snake-skin table. The instrument appears to have been introduced from China to the *Ryūkyū* islands, and to Okinawa in particular, early in the seventeenth century. Later in life the musician took the personal name of 'Yatsuhashi' ('Eight Bridges' 八 橋). He died in 1685.

He had been taught *koto* 箏 by a monk from Kyoto who was on a visit to Edo (today's Tokyo). The monk, Hōsui (法 水 'Water of the Law'), was a pupil of Priest Genjo (玄 恕 'Mysterious Reciprocity'), who in turn had been pupil to Kenjun (賢 順 'Virtuous Obedience'). The last was both founder of a school of *koto* -performance and priest at the Zendōji (善 導 寺 'Temple of Virtuous Guidance') at Kurume 久 留 米 in Tsukushi 筑 紫, a region of Kyūshū. The instrument of Kenjun and his pupils is known as the *Tsukushi-goto* 筑 紫 箏 'the zither of Tsukushi'. Their style of performance was certainly influenced by the *gaku-sō* tradition of the great religious houses, which in turn reflected (at least in technique) that of the Court.

In view of his training-background in *koto*, it is at first sight surprising that Yatsuhashi made use of the *in*-scale. It would seem probable that this was determined by the modal tradition of music of his childhood in Iwashiro 岩 代 – specifically in what was once Mutsu on the 'Eastern Mountain Circuit' (*Tōsandō* 東 山 道).

The great tradition of the *zoku-koto* ('the popular zither'), embodied in items such as *Rokudan no shirabe* 六 段 の 調 'Melody in Six Sections', of *Hachidan no shirabe* 八 段 の 調 'Melody in Eight Sections', of *Midare* 亂 'Disorder' and others, embraces solo-instrumental items attributed – but with no great certainty of attribution – to Yatsuhashi *Kengyō* ('Master'); nevertheless, it may surely be accepted that these seminal compositions issued from the *ryū* 流 (the school) founded by Yatsuhashi.

It must be remembered, however, that Hirano Kenji 平 野 健 次 and Mabuchi Usaburō 馬 淵 卯 三 郎 convincingly demonstrated the metamorphosis of an originally anhemitonic pentatonic piece of *Minshin-gaku* 明 清 樂 – the 'Chinese' musical tradition of the Ming and early Qing dynasties – into Yatsuhashi's *Rokudan* (see Cumulative bibliography). There can be no doubting the tremendous consequences of the introduction (from China) of the Okinawan long-necked lute, *shamisen*, for the evolution of Japanese music.

How profoundly different this style of *koto*-composition is from the *gaku-sō* scores in tablature of Moronaga's *JCYR*, leaps to the eye when transcriptions of the two are compared. Nor is the major difference one of modality; texture, and finger-technique also, are profoundly different. Furthermore, the process of melodic development does not resemble that manifest in such immense movements from Tang *Taikyoku/Daqu* as (for example) the Prelude of *Ōdai hajinraku*. In this context see again Chapter 2.

The authenticity of Tang survivals in the *Tōgaku* manuscript-repertory

Perhaps the most important witness to the uncontaminated genuineness of the earliest Sino-Japanese *Tōgaku MSS.* is the history, character and content of the documents themselves. A.J.M. had shown this already (Marett, 1976) by his analysis of the sources utilised by Minamoto no Hiromasa (Hakuga) 源 博 雅 in assembling his 'Newly Edited Music Scores' (*Shinsen gaku-fu* 新 撰 樂 譜). These sources are listed in the Postface to *HFF*.

Hakuga's immediate source was a set of three scrolls coming from Prince Sadayasu (873–924). Inspection revealed that at least six different systems of notation are to be distinguished in *HFF*. Representing these by Roman numerals from I to VI, it was possible to show that systems III–VI are probably older than systems I and II, in which the greater part of Hakuga's score is written. At the end of the Postface, Hakuga states explicitly: 'but this score adopts the tablature-style(s) of the time' 但 此 譜 以 用 當 譜 之 體. It is probable, that pieces in *HFF* that share the same system of notation derive from a single manuscript. One system (III) is to be identified with the score (in date *c.*830) of Ōto no Kiyogami (Seijō) (Marett, Dissertation 1976, p. 33). Kiyogami himself taught flute to at least two members of the Minamoto (源) clan; but who was responsible for Hakuga's personal training in flute is unknown.

Of great importance for the history of the flute-tradition in Japan is the sequence of teacher-pupil relationships to be deduced from Hakuga's Postface (Marett, Dissertation 1976; Table, p. 32):

Itaburi no Kamataba 板 時 鎌 束 – Kiyose no Miyatsune 清 賴 宮 經 – Ōto no Kiyogami 大 戶 清 上 – Wanibe no Ōtamarō 和 邇 部 大 麻 呂.

Assuming that, in order to be a teacher, each of these must have reached a minimum age of 20 before taking pupils, a rough estimate of the number of years represented by this sequence can be made. In fact, Wanibe no Ōtamarō was 24 when himself appointed teacher of Korean flute in the Bureau of Music. If Ōtamarō (born in 798) was taught in his late teens by Kiyogami (say, in 818), the sequence may carry us back to the first half of the eighth century. That is to say, we are perhaps brought within 50–100 years of the moment of 'composition' of many of the items from the early Tang period, so abundant in the *Tōgaku* repertory.

It can be asserted with confidence that the only stylistic changes between the scores preserved by Hakuga and the zither-scores of Moronaga (the latter assembled in the twelfth century) lie in the degree of embellishment of the latter, the use of broken (or simultaneous) octaves, and frequent pedal-notes on the final (or other notes below the melody-note) to reinforce the decaying sounds of plucked strings.

Japanese performance-practice on *gaku-biwa* today adds lower open-strings, struck along with all primary tablature-signs, but these additions are not indicated in Moronaga's *SGYR*. They reflect a style of Chinese lute-playing current in the Sui and the first half of the eighth century of the Tang; indeed this practice is still in varying degrees common to lute-performance across Asia from East to West, and on into Turkey and the Balkans.

There exist, however, certain modal aspects that require comment when considering the extent to which *Tōgaku MSS.* may be regarded as representative of the Tang tradition. Many of the tunes classed as *Ichikotsu-chō* items are now hexatonic only. They are no longer strictly speaking representative of the *Shang* mode. They may lack the fourth: *g*; and the seventh (if present) may be sharpened: $c^{\sharp}$.

Again, *HFF* retains the unsharpened *f* of the *Sōjō/Shuangdiao* mode-key of Tang in the only two such items that survive in *HFF*. In later Japanese *MSS.*, the *f* is sharpened. Again, notwithstanding Moronaga's careful statement of the character of the *Sada-chō* mode-key, a number of mouth-organ scores of such items are not Lydian in their modality. There are grounds, however, for accepting that, in some instances, the mode of certain items had already been changed in China, before they reached Japan.

Such criticisms as those of Reese (1986, p. 81) and Lam (1989, p. 345) reveal the presence in their minds of a crypto-hypothesis, namely: that in the early Nara period, in the earliest phase of importation of Tang-Music, performed at the Japanese Court by Korean or Chinese musicians (at a time prior to a putative importation of scores in tablature from China in 838 or 839), there existed in Japan a musical culture such that the primary melodic material of imported music of Tang China could have undergone significant re-shaping at the hands of Japanese musicians.

Nothing of what is known of Japanese musical culture at that time suggests, however, that it was capable of exerting such influence on an incoming music of so different an order of complexity. The musical culture of Tang exemplified a 'sound-ideal' and structural concepts very different in character from those of any Japanese music previously known to us. (See Chapter 2.)

Most genres of today's 'Japanese Music' originated subsequent to the importation of musics from Paekche, Silla, Koma, Tang and Wu

Almost all the genres of music that come to mind when today we think of 'Japanese music' – in the sense of music represented by surviving *scores* – are in date much later than the Nara and Heian periods. *Kabuki* and *Naga-uta*, the *Zoku-koto* ('popular' *koto*) and *Kumi-uta* (song-suite) repertories, and *Minshin-gaku* (originally Chinese music of the Ming and Qing dynasties) are all of the seventeenth and eighteenth centuries. Earlier, *Bunraku* (puppet-plays of the sixteenth and seventeenth centuries); *Nō* (fourteenth century, but beginning with the *Sarugaku-nō* – perhaps two centuries earlier); *Jōruri*, and the *shakuhachi* solo-repertory, beginning in the thirteenth century; the various narrative-traditions, with *biwa* used dramatically and percussively rather than melodically; *Imayō* ('modern-style' songs – beginning in the eleventh century); the dramatic monologues with scraper (*sassara*) such as *Sekkyōbushi*, probably beginning in the Heian period (Ishii, 1989, pp. 297, 298). *Rōei* ('Clear Voice') itself – tenth to eleventh centuries – may have arisen already in the Heian period in imitation of a type of Chinese literary pursuit, combining the singing of improvised verse with drinking, as described in connection with the piece: 'The Eddying Bowl' (Fascicle 3, p. 46).

Shōmyō – Buddhist cantillation – began to be imported from China conspicuously in the ninth century (and possibly earlier). There is an earliest surviving manuscript from the twelfth century, and there are manuscripts (in a floridly melismatic melodic style) in neumatic notation from the thirteenth and fourteenth centuries onwards.

Other texts with neumes survive from the Heian (and even from the Nara) period: *Fūzoku*, *Mikagura*, *Azuma-asobi;* but the attempts to transcribe these have rested on graphic parallels with neumatic notations of much later, thirteenth-century, or even later date.

The dates suggested in the preceding paragraphs are based mostly on dates of earliest known texts, and they may well be late by a century. Even so, they reinforce the probability of what has been asserted: that virtually all the genres we think of as representative of Japanese music are post-Heian in origin. That summary statement is confirmed in some detail by the first Table: 'The stream of Japanese music' (*Nihon ongaku no nagare* 日 本 音 樂 の 流) in the useful *Nihon ongaku daijiten* (Hirano *et al.*, 1989).

The Reader may well be wondering what has happened, in this summary, to the *Saibara* repertory. Is that not to be considered as source for an early and distinctively Japanese style of vocal melody? The existence of song-texts of this genre, and of its practice by the nobility, are attested from 900 onwards; but the studies of Dr Elizabeth Markham (1983) showed decisively that we may scarcely regard any *Saibara*-melody, even in the condition in which these were first recorded in notation (towards the end of the twelfth century by Fujiwara no Moronaga, in his *JCYR* and *SGYR*), as representative of a primary *Japanese* melodic condition. Markham summarised the position definitively – and devastatingly – as follows:

'Inspection reveals that all of the ten melody types [into which the 55 *Saibara*-melodies may be grouped] except number 3 (*Koromogae*) include at least one *Saibara* linked with a *Tōgaku*- or *Komagaku*-piece.The four *ryo*-melody-types (7–10) are of particular importance in that all these types include *Saibara* linked with both *Tōgaku* and *Komagaku* repertories, and the final three melody-types (8, 9 and 10) also include songs stated to be folk-songs.

'The implications of this apparent confusion (to be pursued at a later date) are manifold and far-reaching:

'The three repertories, *Saibara*, *Tōgaku* and *Komagaku*, are not, as has been generally held, mutually exclusive. Each includes melodies found in one, or both, of the other two.

'The *Saibara* repertory consists of Japanese poems sung *either* to melodies that are largely borrowed from other genres (*Tōgaku*, *Komagaku*, and possibly *Fūzoku-uta*); *or* to melodies that (no matter what their ultimate origin may have been) were later arranged as new *Tōgaku-* or *Komagaku*-pieces; *or* to melodies that were themselves composite in origin: in part "borrowed" and in part "original".' (Markham, 1979, volume 1, p. 247; 1983, volume 1, p. 250).

A notable feature of the vocal lines of *Saibara* – restored (by Markham) in the light of the 'pointed' song-texts of the [*Tenji-bon*] *Saibara-gakushō* [天 治 本] 催 馬 樂 抄 (1125), and of the undated *MS.* (esteemed as earlier), the *Nabeshima-fu* 鍋 島 譜 – is the prevalence of anacrusis in the musical treatment of text-lines. A song may begin (as does: 'Cherry-Man' *Sakurabito* 櫻 人) on the first beat of the first measure; but subsequent text-lines are sung to phrases that begin either *before* or *after* the first beat of a measure in the *go-byōshi* 五 拍 子 ('five-beat') percussion-pattern. This use of anacrusis – such that the vocal line is always in rhythmic counterpoint with the fixed pattern of the percussion – is a common feature both of Japanese and Korean song. For that reason it may not, necessarily, be regarded as evidence of the Japanese origin of any item in the *Saibara* repertory.

Dr Yi Yonhi 李 寧 熙 has shown that passages in *Manyōshū* 萬 葉 集, written phonetically in Chinese characters, but making no sense as ancient Japanese, make sense as ancient Korean (see Yi Yonhi, 1989). This suggests that the involvement of Korean culture in that of Japan may be far deeper than has hitherto been acknowledged; and indeed this is the emphatic message of J.C. and A. Covell (1984), in their study of the Korean impact on that culture. None of this, however, affords any clue to the condition of Japanese music at the time when music from Tang and Wu began to reach the courts of the nobility in Japan. We would merely caution against the notion that the *Saibara* repertory offers us a purely Japanese, melodic tradition.

There would seem to be only one remaining, potential source of ancient Japanese melody: the music of surviving local religious festivals throughout the length and breadth of Japan, the music of local *matsuri* 祭. This Chinese lexigraph consists of 'hand' with 'flesh', and 'to show' and 'to inform', as determinative. In Chinese it has always meant 'sacrifice', both in the sense of the making of funerary offerings, and in the sense of a sacrifice for spirits, good and bad. In both meanings, the action involved is the making of offerings, rather than the sacrifice of a victim. In Japanese, the verb *matsuru* means to offer prayers, to celebrate, to worship; but *matsuri* itself has come to mean a festival or feast. Though such an occasion still demands the making of offerings to spirits, it will hardly be thought of today in Japan, in quite the same way as the Chinese character suggests.

Chapter 2 offers a preliminary investigation of such music, and suggests that its study reveals a style of Japanese music that has hitherto escaped attention; a style that is profoundly different, in scalings and in structures, from anything presented to Japanese musicians by the arrival of *Komagaku* and *Tōgaku*; a style in which the evolution of melody proceeds in a manner unlike that of *Tōgaku* melody; a subtle style, the subtleties of which are at odds with the bold sweeps of melodies from Tang, Wu, Paekche, Silla and Koma.

The style disclosed by this analysis, moreover, is a style that could not have made a significant impact on incoming styles from Korea or from Tang, so profoundly different in character and complexity is it from them. The style itself might be described – if a general term is felt to be necessary – as the style of *Shintō* 神道 'The Way of the Spirits'; with the qualification that this is the music of folk ritual, not the music of State ritual, today associated with the word 'Shinto' in Western use.

The reality of Sadatoshi's visit to Chang'an

Evidence has recently come to light that Sadatoshi's visit to Chang'an is unlikely to have been a figment of an inventive historiographer's imagination, as now disclosed. Readers who have followed our series may recall that, as reported in Fascicle 5, p. 125: 'On the brink of his [Sadatoshi's] making his farewells, Liu Erlang prepared a farewell banquet and presented *biwa* of purple Sandalwood and purple *Wisteria*-wood, one of each.' Evidence of knowledge of the existence of these *biwa* in Japan in later times has recently been presented by Li Youbai 李 尤 白 (1995) in his collected studies of 'The Pear Garden' *Liyuan* 梨 園 and its role in the creation and development of all arts associated with theatrical performance in China (*Liyuan kaolun* 黎 園 考 論, 1995, Shaanxi renmin chubanshi, Xi'an).

In pursuit of a Chinese report of a Japanese having visited Chang'an during the Tang dynasty, Mr Li wrote to Japan, and in due course received a reply from Mr Tanabe Shirō 田 邊 史 郎 (Department of Musicology, University of the Arts *Geijutsu daigaku* 藝 術 大 學, 樂 理 科), now deceased. This reply was first published in the journal of the Xi'an Conservatory in 1986. In his letter, Mr Tanabe cited two extracts from the *Gakkaroku* 樂 家 錄 of Abe no Suenao 安 李 尚 (1690). These and other extracts from texts mentioned by Mr Tanabe are assembled on pp. 45, and are translated and discussed from here onwards. With passages of text closer together, it may be easier for the eye to pick out tacit quotes or mis-quotes of each by other.

The extracts leave no doubt that two *biwa* (received as gifts from his second teacher, Liu Erlang) returned with Sadatoshi to Japan. The instruments were individually named, and were known and treasured already in the time of Emperor Nimmyō (833–50) and for some centuries thereafter. Of greater interest and importance (as it seems to us) is the fact that an historical romance from the late twelfth century (referred to by Mr Tanabe) also includes important material concerning the two lutes from Tang China. The work in question is 'The record of the rise and fall of the Minamoto and Heike clans' *Gen-Pei seisuiki* 源 平 盛 衰 記 (*GPSSK*).

According to Editor Ishikawa Kaku 石 川 核 [responsible for the text of the *Yūhōdō-bunko* edition 有 朋 堂 文 庫, Meiji 44 (1911)], this latter work is concerned with historical events that occurred during the reign-periods Ōhō 應 保 (1161, 1162) and Jūhei 壽 永 (1182–4). The compilation of *GPSSK* came later. The two lutes from Liu Erlang are described in the chapter numbered 希 卷 第 三 十 一 (Chapter 31, pp. 185–90 in this edition). The first sentence of this chapter summarises (in effect) a number of phrases in the account in *Sandai jitsuroku* (Fascicle 5, p. 125). On the other hand, much of the text of this same chapter is an expansion of information common to the later *Gakkaroku* account of 1690; that is to say, it is (in respect of the later text and in the Chinese sense) a *yanyi* 演 義: a formal text expanded in a more popular version.

The preceding Chapter 30 (p. 183), headed: *Tsunemasa mairo Ninnaji no miya koto* 經 正 參 仁 和 寺 宮 事 'The matter of Tsunemasa's Visit to the Palace of the Temple of Benevolent Harmony', ends with a reference to one of the two lutes: that in which Chapter 31 displays the greater interest, known by the name of 'Green Mountain' *Seizan* 青 山, on which four items from the *Tōgaku* tradition were played by Tsunemasa: *Rindai, Seigaiha, Sokō* (presumably *Sogōkō*) and *Manjūraku*.

The succeeding chapter (p. 185) is headed: *Seizan biwa riyugin takaboku koto* 青 山 琵 琶 流 泉 啄 木 事 'The matter of "Green-Mountain" lute [& the lute-pieces:] "Flowing Spring" [&] "Woodpecker" '. It begins:

'In the beginning, and regarding this *biwa*, in the second year of Jōwa (835–47), the Head of the Housekeeping Bureau, Sadatoshi, subject to an imperial edict, travelled to the Great Tang Country; and, having called on Lian Chengwu, received by way of [Lian's] instruction certain secret pieces and obtained [from him] two *biwa*: Genzō ["Black Elephant"] [*or* Genshō "Mysterious Symbol"] and Seizan ["Green Mountain"]. While the Master constantly played [one of] these *biwa* in teaching pieces to Sadatoshi, amidst the green treetops of "Green Mountain", a Deva, descending from Heaven, (end of text on p.45) fluttered its sleeves like whirling snow. The Master, surprised by this good omen, gave the *biwa* the name of "Seizan". Furthermore, [in regard to]

40

this *biwa*'s manner of construction: from a trough[2] of purple *Wisteria*-wood the body was extracted; from a branch-end of Chinese quince-wood likewise [was made] a Heavenly Head; the plectrum was likewise [fashioned from] a cloven branch-end of boxwood, while after being applied to [a sheet of] Chinese juniper, tiger-skin formed the lower segment of the plectrum-face. As to the picture on the plectrum-surface: in the azure sky above a summer-mountain there was painted the likeness of a bright moon rising. It also had the name "Seizan" attached to it.'

'This is just like the *biwa* that has a Grazing Horse painted on the plectrum-surface being called "Grazing Horse".'

[As will be shown, the substance of the two preceding paragraphs is also present in *Gakkaroku*, but in Chinese (*kambun* 漢文) rather than Japanese.]

Continuing the account of 'Seizan':

'In olden times, in the reign of Emperor Murakami (946–67), when the moon shone brightly, unobscured by clouds, and the wind was soughing and it was most chill, near midnight one Autumn night, His Majesty, enjoying a quiet moment of leisure, put himself in a tranquil state of mind and deigned to take out this *Seizan*. He himself honoured us by playing the secret piece "A myriad Autumns", and as the plectrum by turns produced sound and silence, at the tip of the eaves, lit by moonlight, the Deva deigned to descend during 5 or 6 Sections of the secret piece, fluttering its sleeves like whirling snow, and then ascended to the vault of the Heavens.

Never since have men experienced such an auspicious sign in connection with a biwa.'

The association of Emperor Murakami with a *biwa* having a same-sounding name as the other *biwa* from Tang: *Genzō/Genshō*, also occurs in *Gakkaroku*. The preceding extracts are close translations of passages from *GPSSK* – a text that presents considerable difficulties for the translator.

The style of that text is to be compared with the following passages from *Gakkaroku*. These all occur in a chapter entitled 'Precious Instruments of Music' *Ongaku chinki* 音 樂 珍 器 (*Gakkaroku* pp. 1308–16).

---

[2] In a recent publication: 古 代 樂 器 の 復 元, 1995, the ancient technical term for the body of a *biwa*: 槽, meaning 'trough', is translated as 'shell'. In terms of joinery, the body of lutes of the *gakubiwa*-type (the type in use in the *Gagaku* ensemble) is a coarsely grooved, shaped, block of wood, of thickness such that the term 'shell' is not obviously appropriate. The thickness of the body of the *gakubiwa* has much to do with the acoustic properties of the instrument. The many bodies of *biwa* visible in 1988 on the premises of the late Mr Satake, sometime maker of instruments to the Imperial Court of Japan, plainly revealed the procedure that led to the *grooving* of their internal surface by the use of an adze-like tool.

The first 'precious *biwa*' to be described (p. 1309) is *Genshō*, written 玄 上, rather than 玄 象, the second of Sadatoshi's *biwa*.

'An honoured object of the Emperor Murakami. Trough of purple *Wisteria*-[wood], plectrum of water-buffalo [horn]; the plectrum-face painted with persons on horseback playing polo, playing with a ball on the belly, like a dance, and so on.'

A second 'precious *biwa*' (also p. 1309, text not supplied) is named 'Grazing Horse':

'An honoured object of the Engi Emperor [901–22; during the reign of Emperor Daigo]. A grazing horse was painted on the plectrum-face.'

This *biwa* again was at times confused with *biwa* from Sadatoshi.

As to the *Genzō/Genshō* of Sadatoshi (*Gakkaroku*, p. 1309), under the heading 玄 象, this name can be read in two ways: as *Genzō* 'Black Elephant' or as *Genshō* 'Mysterious Symbol'. The former recalls a famous surviving *biwa* of Tang date in the *Shōsō-in*, with the lower area of the table painted to show an elephant, carrying musicians and dancers.

The text reads:

'An honoured object of Emperor Nimmyō: of purple sandal-wood, a trough, one item, with a black elephant [or mysterious symbol] painted on the plectrum-face, this was a *biwa* of Great Tang.' More detail is given under *Seizan* (p. 1310). Some records state that 玄 象 is the same instrument as 玄 上 [This name too is read as *Genshō* with the meaning 'Mysterious Superior'.]

The *Gakkaroku*-account (p. 1310) now turns to the *biwa* that so plainly took first place in *GPSSK*.

' "*Seizan*": this was Emperor Nimmyō's honoured object with its trough of purple *Wisteria*-wood. Ancient records state that in the second year of Jōwa (835), the Head of the Housekeeping Bureau, Fujiwara no Sadatoshi, received an imperial decree to go to Tang. He visited Lian Chengwu (簾 承 武), studied secret pieces for *biwa*, and obtained, of *biwa*, two. *Genzō* and *Seizan* were these. While Lian Chengwu was transmitting pieces to Sadatoshi, from amidst the green treetops of "Green Mountain" a Deva descended from Heaven, fluttering its sleeves like whirling snow. 'The name "Green Mountain" (*Seizan*) was from this.' One version states that the plectrum-face was painted with a scene where a bright moon emerged from the blue void over a mountain in Summer. From this it was called 'Green Mountain', just as, 'n the case where a grazing horse was painted on the plectrum-surface, the *biwa* was called *Bokuba* 'Grazing Horse'.

[It is of course the case that Sadatoshi received *biwa* not from his first lute-teacher, Lian Chengwu in Yangzhou, but from the second, Liu Erlang in Chang'an.]

Although from a work compiled rather more than 500 years later than the *Gen-Pei seisuiki* (for that text see our pp. 45–46), the *Gakkaroku* passages now translated here are in Chinese rather than Japanese, and are punctuated with signs (*kunten* 訓 點) that indicate the order in which Chinese words are to be read in their Japanese equivalents. This system of markings – literally 'instructive dots' in Sino-Japanese – has existed (in some form or other) in Japanese use at least since the Heian period (Crawcour, p. xiv, 1965). By contrast, the earlier *Gen-Pei seisuiki* is for the most part in Japanese. All features of Japanese word-order and Japanese syntax are explicit in the earlier text of the *GPSSK*, which makes use of no *kunten*-symbols, and the Japanese reading of virtually every Chinese lexigraph is given in *hiragana* syllables.

Notwithstanding its later date, *Gakkaroku* (our p. 45) seems to reflect parts of original sources written in Chinese – in *Kambun* 漢 文. A few short sequences of Chinese lexigraphs are reminiscent of sequences in the *Sandai jitsuroku*'s account from the *Rikkokushi* (Fascicle 5, p. 124). Sadatoshi himself is described as *Ason* 朝 臣 – courtier – in the latter: 掃 部 頭 藤 原 朝 臣 貞 敏; but in relation to *Seizan* (*Gakkaroku*, p. 1310) this courtesy-title is omitted from that sequence. In *Gen-Pei seisuiki* (p. 45) his patronymic: 藤 原, too, is missing.

In *Sandai jitsuroku* the gift of the two *biwa* had been described as 贈 紫 檀 紫 藤 琵 琶 各 一 面: 'presented with purple sandalwood and purple *Wisteria*-wood *biwa*, of each one item' [面, as well as meaning 'face', is a numerary adjunct for flat objects].

The account of Emperor Nimmyō's *biwa* 玄 象 *Genzō* in *Gakkaroku*, p. 1309, begins: 紫 檀 槽 一 枚 ' purple sandalwood trough, one item' [where 枚 is again a numerary adjunct]; and in the same work, the 青 山 *biwa* of that emperor is defined as 紫 藤 之 檀: 'trough of purple *Wisteria*-wood' where 之 is an attributive particle.

In *Gen-Pei seisuiki*, though the gift is said to have come from Lian (廉) Chengwu (in Yangzhou) rather than from Liu Erlang (in Chang'an), the substance of the gift is still stated as two *biwa*: 二 の 琵 琶 を 得 た り き 玄 象，青 山 是 也。 'Two *biwa* were obtained. *Genzō* and *Seizan* were these.'

Thus the form and constitution of a number of phrases in the accounts in *Gakkaroku* in some instances resemble, or indeed are identical with, parallel phrases in the *Sandai jitsuroku* that relate to Sadatoshi's visit to Tang and

Chang'an, and (in particular) to the gift there of *biwa* of sandalwood and *Wisteria*-wood.

It is also clear that, notwithstanding the joint testimony to a single teacher in *FBBF* and *Sandai jitsuroku*, these various documents make evident that Sadatoshi did indeed enjoy instruction by *two* teachers, even though in later accounts the two persons are confounded, in the matter both of instruction and of the gift of lutes. Furthermore, assonance has probably re-inforced confusion between two instruments, or else has led to dissociation of one into two, as two instruments of similar-sounding name, associated with two emperors: Nimmyō (833–50) and Murakami (946–67), namely 玄 象 and 玄 上 respectively, both to be read as similar sounding names: Genzō/Genjō/Genshō.

A last literary and historical association links the *Seizan-biwa* with the fortunes of the Heike 平 家 – the Taira clan. Tradition relates that, having been housed in the Imperial Palace for several centuries, *Seizan* was transferred to the Palace of the Temple of Benevolent Harmony *Ninnaji no miya* 仁 和 寺 宮, where it was presented to Taira no Tsunemasa 平 經 正. This was the personage already associated with the playing of items from the *Tōgaku* repertory in the 31st Chapter of the *Gen-Pei seisuiki* (p. 183). Following Tsunemasa's death in battle, however, it was for a time lost, and only later returned to the *Ninnaji no miya*.

To us, it seems that these fragments of information, even in garbled form, strongly suggest that Liu Erlang's gift of two lutes, one of purple sandalwood, one of purple *Wisteria*-wood, did indeed return with Sadatoshi to Japan. If these gifts returned with him to Japan, the reality of the alleged visit to Chang'an is established (notwithstanding confusion of the two teachers), as is (associated therewith) the probable truth of the gift of several tens of scrolls of musical tablatures: 'Liu Erlang presented, of musical scores, several tens of scrolls' 劉 二 郎 贈 譜 數 十 卷 (Fascicle 5, p. 124).

Taira no Tsunemasa figures also in the *Heike monogatari* (*HM*) 平 家 語 物 in association with the two named *biwa* and with the *Ninnaji no miya*. The edition consulted (again in the series *Yūhōdō bunko*) (Taishō 11=1922) was revised by Nagai Ichikō 永 井 一 孝. In his preface he indicates that the *Heike monogatari* was compiled between the time of Go Saga Tennō (Kangen 1=1243) and that of Go Fukakusa Tennō (Kenchō 1 & 2=1249–50). The Gen-Pei War occurred in the 1130s, with Taira being defeated in 1185. The historical events narrated in *HM* and *GPSSK* are roughly contemporary; but *HM* is later in compilation. It is perhaps not surprising, therefore, that memory of Sadatoshi appears to be fading in the somewhat later romance, as compared with the earlier.

In the later compilation, the story is changing; events and names are no longer those of the historical record of the *Sandai jitsuroku*. In the passage

44

headed 'The affair of "Green Mountain" ' (p. 340) the story is taken back to the time of Emperor Nimmyō and the third year of Kashō 嘉 祥 (850):

'In the time of the journey to Tang of The Chief of the Household Supplies Department, Fujiwara no Sadatoshi, meeting with the *Biwa*-Master of Great Tang, Ren Sōfu 廉 妾 夫 (or Shōbu if *kun* readings are adopted), three pieces being transmitted, he returned to Japan. At that time, three *biwa* were conferred: *Genzō/Genshō*, *Shishimaru* 獅 子 丸 "The Lion's Ball", and *Seizan*.'

This 'Ren Shōbu' is the Japanese reading (given in *hiragana* syllables) of a name clearly modelled (in phonetic terms) on that of Ren Shōbu – the Japanese reading of 'Lian Chengwu' – Sadatoshi's *Biwa*-Master in Yangzhou: 廉 承 武. Evidently the sounds of the personal name are remembered (albeit imperfectly); the original Chinese, and the original meaning of the personal name, have been forgotten. Somewhat surprisingly, a Chinese-style sentence is preserved unmodified in this thirteenth-century romance as a component of a longer sentence that is completely Japanese in grammatical construction. It is suggested that the embedded Chinese construction survives from a document in Chinese, in *kambun*, a document of the same period as the *Sandai jitsuroku* account. The sentence: 掃 部 頭 貞 敏 渡 唐 is augmented by the addition of の..., 'in the time of' or merely 'when', leading to the reading: 'When the Head of Housekeeping, Sadatoshi, crossed to Tang,'– continuing in Japanese: 大 唐 の 琵 琶 博 士 廉 妾 夫 に 逢 ひ 'meeting with the *Biwa*-Master of Great Tang, Ren Shōbu...'(for text see our p. 46).

In these various documents, we see progressive failure of memory. Sadatoshi is stripped first of his rank (junior Fifth Grade, upper rank), then of his courtesy title *'ason'*, lastly of his distinguished clan-name: 'Fujiwara'. His second lute-teacher, Liu Erlang, is forgotten and the gift of lutes is attributed to Lian Chengwu, his first teacher (as a teacher certainly the more important in the transmission of modal knowledge); the gift of scrolls in musical tablature is forgotten. The number 'three' that appears in the phrase 'three pieces were transmitted' may be a partial memory of Liu Erlang's offer of 'instruction in two or three modal systems' 即 授 兩 三 調。 Of Lian Chengwu, only the patronymic is correctly remembered; the two-component personal name is corrupted to a same-sounding, but surely derisory, personal name: 'concubine's husband' 妾 夫, rather than 'inheritor of martial qualities' 承 武. For ease of comparison, various fragments of texts are set out in sequence below.

Passages from *Sandai jitsuroku* 三 代 實 錄

掃 部 頭 藤 原 朝 臣 貞 敏

承 和 二 年 (835) 為 美 作 椽 兼 遣 唐 使 准 判 官 ， 五 年 (838) 到 大 唐 ， 達 上 部 ， 逢 能 彈 琵 琶 者 劉 二 郎 .

臨 行 劉 二 郎 設 祖 筵 ，贈 紫 檀 紫 藤 琵 琶 各 一 面面控

Passages from *Gakkaroku* 樂 家 錄 卷 之 四 十 一 ，音 樂 珍 器
p. 1309 玄 上 added two lines (p. 42)
p. 1309 玄象 仁 明 天 皇 御 物 也 。 紫 檀 槽 一 枚 ，撥 面 畫 黑 象 ， 是 大 唐 琵 琶 也 (p. 42)
p. 1310 青山 仁 明 天 皇 御 物 也紫 藤 之 檀 也 舊 記 日 承 和 二 年 掃 部 頭 藤 原 真 敏 蒙 敕 宣 唐 度 ， 謁 于 簾 承 武 習 琵 琶 之 秘 曲 ， 而 得 琵 琶 二 玄象 青 山 是 也 。 簾 承 武 傳 曲 于 真 敏 之 時 ， 自 青 山 綠 梢 天 人 降 ， 翻 迴 雪 之 袖 。自 是 名 之 青 山 也 (p. 43)

(It is to be noted that *Gakkaroku* does not use the correct form of Lian Chengwu's patronymic: 廉.)

Passage from *Gen-Pei seisuiki* 源 平 盛 衰 記:
p. 185 青 山 琵 琶 流 泉 啄 木 事 抑 此 琵 琶 は ， 承 合 二 年 に 掃 部 頭 真 敏 が 敕 宣 を 蒙 ， 大 唐 國 に 度 っ 蒐 ， 廉 承 武 に 謁 して 祕 曲 を 傳 へ 習 しに ， 二 の 琵 琶 を 得 たりき 。 玄象 ， 青 山 是 也 。 博 士 此 琵 琶 を 彈 じっ、曲 を 真 敏 に を し へ し に ， 青 山 の 綠 の 梢 に ， 天 人 天 降 っっ...

Passage from *Heike monogatari* 平 家 物 語:
p. 340 青 山 沙 汰 ， 大 唐 の 琵 琶 博 士 ， 廉 姜 夫
Ren Shō-bu

[L.E.R.P. is deeply indebted to Dr P. A. Herbert, an independent scholar of Perth, Western Australia, for critical reading of the translations of texts, *GPSSK*, *HM* and *GKR*. In regard to the apparent preservation (in the texts in Japanese) of phrases present in the *kambun* biographical note on Sadatoshi in *Sandai-jitsuroku*, Dr Herbert authorises quotation of her opinion: 'I am sure all the texts come from one (probably lost) source close to Sadatoshi's time.'

Returning for a moment to our hero, Sadatoshi, in this story of transmission of Tang Music to Japan, Reischauer (1955, ii, p. 52) indicates that Liu Erlang's offer of his daughter was accepted by Sadatoshi. L.E.R.P. (Fascicle 5, p. 125) now agrees. In translating 琴 箏 as '*kin* and *biwa*' when stating that Miss Liu '["played"] these instruments "outstandingly well" ', he evidently suffered a grievous mental lapse. 'Biwa' was a figment of the imagination, and the compound *kin no koto* surely stands for the Chinese seven-stringed zither: *kin/qin*. Use of the binome was probably intended to help a Japanese reader understand what sort of thing a Chinese instrument – not widely known in Japan – was: 'the *kin*-sort of *koto*', just as *shō-teki* 笙 笛 at one time identified the mouth-organ: *shō/sheng* 笙: 'the *shō*-sort of flute'.

A further lapse was that of translating the biographical notice's: 以 能 彈 琵 琶，歷 仕 三 代 as: 'By virtue of his being able to play *biwa* excellently, he remained in office throughout three reigns.' It should have read no more than: 'Because he was skilled in playing *biwa*, he…'. Looking back, 'excellently' was an unjustifiable attempt to add a word of praise to so grudging an account of his services to Japanese – and indeed to Chinese – music.]

In the light of our more recent reading of *Sandai jitsuroku*, of Reischauer on the travels of Sadatoshi and Ennin, as well as a recent account of Japanese embassies to Japan and their ships, by Tōno Haruyuki 東 野 治 之 (1995), the dates of Sadatoshi's departure on his field-trip to Tang China (*Music from the Tang Court*, Fascicle 5, p. 124) should be given as '7th month, Jōwa 承 和 3 (836); redeparted 7th month, Jōwa 4 [837]; redeparted 6th month, Jōwa 5 [838]'; and arrived, '12th month, K'ai-ch'eng, 開 成 3 (838)'.

These data from Tōno Haruyuki show that the statement (in *Shoku-Nihon-koki* 日 本 古 記; see Marett, 1976, p. 17) that Ōto no Kiyogami / Seijō 大 戸 清 上 was invited to the Tang Court in the early years of the Jōwa era – 837, fifth month, eighth day – and left Japan in 838, is entirely compatible with the facts regarding departure recorded by Tōno Haruyuki's Table 1 (1995, p. 49).

The 'redepartures' (Dr Herbert suggests) were due not merely to the hasardous effect of the onset of storms, associated with the start of the monsoon-period towards the end of Summer, but also to the fact that Japanese Missions were tributary, and (as Tōno Haruyuki argues: pp. 58, 59) it was imperative that an embassy reach Chang'an before the New Year, since it was required to attend the New Year audience in the capital. If weather conditions suggested that timely arrival were doubtful, departure would be postponed. The journey, from landing to the capital, usually took three to four months. Only in very exceptional circumstances were members of an embassy permitted to make use of post-horses.

The content of pp. 37–46 are surely most important in relation to the question whether Sadatoshi reached Chang'an or not. It makes certain that he did: he was a member of a Mission, where the Mission went he had to go; unless (as with Ennin) there were a special reason for him not to do so. He would not have been permitted to detach himself from the body of the Mission (even when sick) without an escort.

In concluding this first chapter, gratitude must be expressed for the 'moral support', as well as for the invaluable photocopies of passages from recent publications, given to us by Mrs Satomi Toyonaga 豐 永 聰 美, in advancing the view that Fujiwara Ason Sadatoshi did indeed return to Japan, bringing with him two lutes, received as gifts from Liu Erlang in Chang'an, thus increasing the probability that 'the several tens of musical scores', also presented by Liu Erlang, also returned safely with him.

Chapter 2

In Search of the Music of Pre-Nara Japan (N.J.N.; L.E.R.P.;
with field-assistance from Mrs Okamoto Miyoko 岡 本 美 代 子)

A survey of the *titles* of items in the *Tōgaku* repertory, shows that many are of
items current in Tang during the 7th and 8th centuries AD (unpublished
observations by Dr Stephen Jones). If one asks where in Japan today – if indeed
anywhere today – might one expect to find traces of early styles of Japanese
music – styles (dating from, or before, the 7th century) that might reasonably be
compared in age with the style of these earliest items from Tang – it would seem
reasonable to begin the search by examining musics of folk-religious rituals such
as are celebrated at the present time in innumerable localities all over Japan.

The music of state-ritual in Japan has evidently been subject to interruption
over the centuries; and the process of reconstruction and restitution has depended
on hazardous interpretation of written sources in the light of later, traditional
practice. In the case of Japanese folk rituals, we have immediate, aural access to
musics that have either never, or only recently, been entrusted to, or confined by,
any kind of notation whatsoever: music that formerly existed and survived only
in the memories of those who performed it.

Two areas of surviving folk practice have been considered. The first,
arguably of immense antiquity, is that of bird-dances. The second, from a
tradition extending backwards at least to the end of the ninth century, is that of
the instrumental music performed by musicians on the principal floats that
participate in the great annual, July-festival in Kyoto, the *Gionmatsuri* 祇 園 祭;
the Gion Festival.

The primary meaning of the Chinese *ji* 祭 is 'sacrifice'; but the character of
the occasion nowadays is more adequately reflected by the word 'festival'. '*Gion*'
itself, 'The Garden of *Gi/Qi*' 祇 園, refers to the Jetavana, the Sanskrit name for
the garden given by Prince Jeta to Sakyamuni, as a place for tranquil meditation
and spiritual refreshment. This sense of the name of the festival seems not to be
generally known in Japan nowadays; but the name bears witness to a primary
religious and Buddhist association. Use of the lexigraph *gi/qi* 祇 today permits
interpretation as 'national god' or 'local god' in Japanese. In Chinese the
meaning is 'earth spirit'; but in the original Sino-Sanskrit the lexigraph was
presumably borrowed because of the resemblance between its sound and that of
the first syllable of the name of Prince Jeta [cf. Karlgren (1957) **867 i** **g'ieg /
g'jie* / k'i, p. 229].

The music (with which this Chapter is concerned), the performers, and the ensemble of instruments and instrumentalists, are all named by the Japanese phrase *hayashi* 囃 子, written as は や し in the *hiragana*-syllabary. The Chinese lexigraph only occurs in the largest Chinese/Chinese dictionaries; and it never carries the range of meanings of Japanese *hayashi*. In Chinese use it is described as 'a tune/music that assists dancing': 助 舞 聲, or as 'noise' 嘈 雜, to be compared with 'clamour' as defined by 口 喧. It is to be noted that the lexigraph is compounded from 'mouth' 口, and 'mixed' or 'confused' 雜 = 囃. Its old-style Chinese 'spelling' is given thus: 七 合 音. This supplied an aspirated initial (in today's orthography '*c -*') and a final '*a* '= *ca*. (*zhā* and *za* are alternative pronunciations with different meaning-extensions.) The presence of the 'mouth' determinative (口), not merely in 囃 but in 嘈 and 喧 as well, suggests that 囃 was originally applied to a vocal rather than instrumental sound; so that 'dance' was perhaps anciently 'assisted' by song. In Japanese the word *hayasu* 囃 means 'play an instrument; accompany; beat time; banter, jeer; applaud' (Nelson, 1975, p. 30). The *on* pronunciation of the character – that is the Japanese form of the ancient Japanese pronunciation of the Chinese – is given as *satsu*; this is evidently related to the range of Chinese sounds previously shown. A further Japanese phrase is suggestive: *hayashi kotoba* 囃 子 詞 signifying 'meaningless words in a song (for rhythm)' (Nelson, 1975). This again suggests a primary significance of this lexigraph as vocal sound.

Be that as it may, it is certain that the lexigraph for *hayashi* is not a Japanese creation, but a nowadays-forgotten Chinese character, acquired by the Japanese in the earliest period of lexical borrowing, the Han dynasty. These two facts: the age of the lexigraph and its probable primary meaning of vocal sound associated with dance, reinforce the view (see pp. 66, 72) that the original function of the instrumentalists was to provide an accompaniment for dancing. As we have seen, in the light of the Chinese etymology of the lexigraph used for the Japanese word *haya-* (as in *hayashi*), it seems possible that, in the remote past, this accompaniment was vocal. It is the case that certain items in the repertory are still danced on the floats themselves, the dancers being largely invisible, save to senior persons and musicians on the float.

Music of Bird-Dances
Turning to the matter of bird-dances, cave-paintings give graphic evidence of the existence of bird-cults in the Palaeolithic Period (Armstrong, 1958, p. 11); and we are told by Plutarch that 'The Crane' was danced by Theseus and his companions when he and Ariadne landed at Delos (Armstrong, 1943, p. 71). Plutarch's source was Dicaearchus of *c*.300 BC. In China, Crane Dances

certainly existed as early as the fifth century BC. The costume of the two male dancers – first seen (by L.E.R.P.) at the Yasaka Shrine in Kyoto in July 1972 – suggested that the birds represented (male and female) must be Cranes of the genus *Grus* (Chinese *he* 鶴); but the birds are always referred to by the Japanese as *Sagi* 鷺, and these are Herons (Chinese *lù* 鷺). Herons and Egrets, however, do not exhibit the striking mating-dances of Cranes. It is perhaps the case, that with the lowering of the water-table in Japan, and a consequent reduction in the extent of areas where Cranes are still visitors, the ancient Crane Dance has come to be attributed to a more familiar bird.

Sagimai 鷺 舞 – or, more popularly, *Sagi no mai* 鷺 の 舞 – are known from several localities: they occur in Kyōto itself at the Yasaka Jinja 八 ±反 神 社; and at Tsuwano 津 和 野 in Shimane Prefecture 島 根 縣 (confusingly, the railway-station for Tsuwano is on the Yamaguchi 山 口 line). In Tsuwano the dance belongs to the Hachiman Jinja 八 幡 神 社 – the Shrine of the War God – and to the *Gionmatsuri* of that shrine. At intervals over the centuries the dance, being lost in one locality, Kyoto or Tsuwano, has been revived with help from the other.

Such dances also occur at several localities in Kanagawa Prefecture 神 奈 川 縣, most notably at the War God's Shrine in Nakai-machi 中 井 町.

As a map of Japan shows, these several localities are quite widely separated in space, with Kanagawa in the Northern half, and Kyoto and Tsuwano in the Southern half of the island of Honshu. This wide geographical separation may be linked with distinctive differences in costume, properties and character of the dance and its associated music, in Tsuwano and Nakai-machi.

The music from Tsuwano seems to have been first recorded on July 20, 1955, by the Japan Broadcasting Corporation (NHK: Nihon Hōsō Kyōkai 日 本 放 送 協 會). Victor SJL-2188-M (from which the Tsuwano music has been transcribed by us) is one of 38 LP discs (2166–2204): *Nihon no Minzoku Ongaku* 日 本 民 俗 音 樂. This series was compiled by Dr Honda Yasuji 本 田 安 of Waseda University (information kindly supplied by Professor Kishibe Shigeo).

Our examination of these items has been made possible by the availability of such recordings, and by published accounts of the ceremonies, in particular those edited over the years by Takahashi Hideo 高 橋 秀 雄 and Yamaji Kōzō 山 路 興 造, including the printing (in 1978) of an account (by Miyata Kagaya 宮 田 輝) of the *Sagimai* at Tsuwano, and an article by Higuchi Akira 木 通 口 昭 (1988) that reprints a transcription of the music from Tsuwano, first published by him in 1968.

A brief account of *Sagimai* in Kanagawa-ken (where Dragons – and Lions too – participate in dancing along with *Sagi*) is to be found in *A History of Kanagawa Prefecture* (folk-customs section): *Kanagawa-ken kakuronhen 5 minzoku, dai 7 hen, Minkan geinō, dai 1 shō geinō*, p. 878. A more detailed account of a performance is available in reports from Nagata Hirayoshi 永田衡吉 (1968) in *Kanagawa-ken minzoku geinōshi* (pp. 296–8). (A calendar, *Kanagawa-ken hyakka jiten*, gives the date of such a performance in 1983 as 29 April.) For *kanji* of these publications see Cumulative Bibliography.

In a future publication, it is hoped to publish *in extenso* our transcriptions in score of the music of Heron dances from both areas, as well as items from the music of the *Gionmatsuri*, as transcribed by us from recordings, along with descriptions of the rituals to which these musics are integral. The present account offers no more than an abridged summary of observations, transcriptions and analyses.

A single, striking feature, that links performance of music associated with the Heron Dance with that of the Festival Bands (*Matsuribayashi* 祭はやし), is the use of contrived dissonance in the stately Introit (*TS1*) to the song that accompanies the dance at Tsuwano (*TS2*): paired flutes play at a distance approximating to a minor ninth, as they do throughout the repertory of the Long Halberd Float (*Naginataboko* 長刀鉾) that leads the procession in Kyōto, and indeed throughout the repertory of other floats as well. (Regarding this form of the lexigraph 鉾 *hoko/feng*, see p. 63.) The immediate purpose and function of such dissonance may originally have been to increase carrying-power in open-air performance; but it may also have the function of dispelling malign influences – an apotropaeic function. In any case, it is a practice to be compared with the contrived out-of-tune-ness of paired 'unison'-pipes, to be observed in widely separated environments: twinned duct-flutes in the Balkans, double-chanter droneless bagpipes in North-Eastern Turkey and the Caucasus, and on the Great Highland Bagpipe itself (Picken, 1975, *passim*).

The Tsuwano instrumental Introit (*TS1*), the Tsuwano dance-with-song (*TS2*), and the Kanagawa music for the *Sagimai* (*KS*) now follow. The in-stave figures are the numbers of quarter-note beats of the *hayashi*-interludes.

Example 1. *Tsuwano* (*TS1*): Introit, Transcription

The melody is written in half-note values. A quarter-note unit is valid, but not always strictly adhered to by the flute-players – although the percussionists are insistent in maintaining the same heavy pulse throughout.

Table 1. TS1: *Weighted-Scale Data*

	b	*d*	*e*	*f#*	*g*	*a*	*b'*		
(1) Durations (numbers of beats)	4	30	36	4	41	22	5	=	142
(2) Occurrences	2	14	17	2	17	10	3	=	65
(3) Initials & Finals	2	5	6	2	9	2	0	=	26
TOTALS	8	49	59	8	67	34	8	=	233
Percentages	3	21	25	3	29	15	3	=	99

Example 2. *Tsuwano* dance-with-song (*TS2*), Transcription

Table 2. TS2: *Weighted-Scale Data*

	$c^{\sharp}$	e	$f^{\sharp}$	$g^{\sharp}$	a	b		
Durations	4	28.5	73.5	2	1.5	39.5	=	149
Occurrences	4	36	82	4	3	43	=	172
Initials & Finals	4	6	17	0	0	11	=	38
TOTALS	12	70.5	172.5	6	4.5	93.5	=	359
Percentages	3	20	48	2	1	26	=	100

Example 3. *Kanagawu Sagimai (KS)*: Heron Dance, Transcription

Table 3. KS: *Weighted-Scale Data*

	b	c	e^b	f	g	a^b		
Durations	1	20.25	16.5	21.5	8.25	2.5	=	70
Occurrences	1	19.00	22.0	23.0	13.00	2.0	=	80
Initials & Finals	1	8.00	2.0	4.0	6.00	1.0	=	22
TOTALS	3	47.25	40.5	48.5	27.25	5.5	=	172
Percentages	2	27.00	24.0	28.0	16.00	3.0	=	100

Ignoring complexities of intonation introduced by the flutes, note-sets of the three pieces, with final cadences marked with a pause, are seen to have some notes in common.

Example 4. Note-sets of *TS1*, *TS2* and *KS*, drawn from Examples 1, 2 and 3

To assist comparison, note-sets of *TS1* and *KS* (Example 4) are transposed down by 10 and 11 semitones respectively (Example 5); like pitches now appear in vertical alignment.

Example 5. Note-sets positioned to show common notes in alignment

A: transposed down ten semitones (*TS1*)
B: transposed up one octave (*TS2*)
C: transposed down eleven semitones (*KS*)

Note-sets now demonstrate a common sequence of five notes: *c* # - *e* - *f* # - *g* # - *a*.

Returning to *TS1* at its original pitch (Example 1), it can be seen that, notwithstanding the final cadence on *g*:

(a) all notes of a 123.56, five-note scale on *g* are present, plus one added note, *f* #;

(b) phrases are short and cadences are frequent – on *a* (2), *e* (2), *d* (3) and on *g* (6); and

(c) *g*, *e* and *d*, are notes most often sounded throughout the piece; yet despite all this, and the fact that there is no direct half-tone step in the linear context, an over-all feeling of Chinese, anhemitonic *Gongdiao* 宮 調 modality is not strong. What are striking in *TS1*, though, are the rising and falling fourths, and the leaps of superimposed fourths in the first and sixth phrases; and the fact that the fourth is stretched even further in phrases 11 and 13, to become a fifth, and then sixths, three times.

Further evidence of the importance of the fourth in Japanese, pre-*Tōgaku* musical style is exposed in *TS2*, where falling conjunct tetrachords: *b*-*f* # and *f* #-*c* #, define the principal pitch areas of the two contrasting sections of the Song.

In typical Chinese 123.56-modality, 6 (= *e*, if 1 = *g*) would be the least important note (according to ancient perceptions of a note-hierarchy) (Picken, 1966, p. 157). It must be remembered, however, that according to the *Qinding Da Qing huidian* 欽 定 大 清 會 典, the sixth above *Gong* was the modal dominant (*zhu diao* 主 調) (Picken, 1956, 1957, p. 162). In Zhu Xi's six melodies in a heptatonic *Gong*-mode, however (Picken, 1956, 1957, pp. 152–6), movement is always from, or to, the sixth by step, so that its role in those compositions is very different from that of the sixth note of the scale (*e*) in *TS1* where movement to and from *e* to *g* occurs by leap many times – that is, only if one regards the gap between 6 and 1 in a rising or falling prime modal scale as a leap.

Turning to the note-set of *TS2*, transcribed as $c^\sharp$ - e - $f^\sharp$ - $g^\sharp$ - a - b (Example 4), the scale might be regarded as a *Yudiao* 羽 調 (6.123.5) inversion of a *Gongdiao*-set on e, with a added; but the final note is $f^\sharp$, and the principal notes of the Song are $f^\sharp$, b and e, though e has no cadence, not even in conclusion. There are, in fact, 19 cadences in all: on $f^\sharp$ (13), $c^\sharp$ (4) and b (2), discounting the final cry on b as beyond cadential purpose and weight; but e's capability in this role is entirely rejected.

Notwithstanding the superficial appearance of a 6.123.5 formation on e, the choice of cadence notes shows that further reference to that modality would be mistaken. Nevertheless, it is interesting to observe that the item operates in two, distinct, structurally-interlocking segments. There are two principal phrases, one to each segment, each falling the distance of a fourth, the first, b-$f^\sharp$, and the second, $f^\sharp$-$c^\sharp$. The overlapping note-sets of the two phrases accommodate corresponding formulae: b - a - $f^\sharp$, and $f^\sharp$ - e - $c^\sharp$, out of which comes a third, subsidiary phrase on two repeating notes, the two notes common to the principal phrases, e and $f^\sharp$, which reiterates dactylic rhythm each time the text repeats the line *Sagi ga hashi o watashita*.

As a striking example of how rapidly folk-tradition may change, a recording entitled: *Kagura*: Japanese *Shinto* Ritual Music 1990 (Hungaroton SLPX 18193) – being materials collected, with commentary, by Professor Kárpáti János – includes a version of TS2, sung by a six-membered, unison male-chorus, in which the compass of the melody has been extended from a seventh to an octave. In terms of our chosen pitch, the lowest note becomes $c^\sharp$ rather than b. This version of the *Sagimai*-song was recorded by Professor Kárpáti on 26 November, 1988, at *The National Festival of Performing Arts* in the 'Hall of Japanese Adulthood', *Nihon seinenkan* 日 本 成 年 館 Tokyo. In his notes accompanying this recording, Professor Kárpáti notes that the *sagimai* – the complex of ceremonies that support the dance – is not properly speaking a *kagura* – a revelation of the dwelling of a god, but a *furyū*; that is, a ritual that averts evil influences. To us it seems likely that the *sagi*'s function is to conduct a divinity or divinities into, and in due course from and out of, the world of men.

Coming now to KS, the transposed note-set: c - $c^\sharp$ - e - $f^\sharp$ - $g^\sharp$ - a (Example 5), again includes the five notes, $c^\sharp$ to a, of the preceding pieces; but the presence in this scale of two semitone steps and a three-semitone leap rules out any tentative consideration of a 123.56 *Gong*-scale in a primary or inverted position (for example). The same, of course, applies to the original note-set in Example 4. No single note finds notes a major third and perfect fifth above itself with which to attempt to argue a modal pentatonic structure. a - $c^\sharp$ - e are present, but do not function in *Gong* manner. It has only 3 major thirds (transposed, $g^\sharp$ - e), but 18 minor thirds ($c^\sharp$ - e - $c^\sharp$).

Could this note-set as first transcribed (not as Example 5) be a modified, Japanese-style *ritsu*-scale on b - c - $e^\flat$ - f - g - $a^\flat$? Not with both f and b; and the absence of d from the lower trichord would be unusual in a *ritsu*-scale. Both $a^\flat$ and b are non-conforming elements, from the standpoint of either *Tōgaku* modes, or Japanese *ryo*- and *ritsu*-scales, or indeed of any *in* 陰 and *yo* 陽 forms. Though $a^\flat$ and b are seeming intruders in this scale-series, it is noted that $a^\flat$ occurs only twice, and only in the first three notes of the composition, and that b sounds once only and at great distance from the opening $a^\flat$.

In each of the three melodies, *TS1*, *TS2* and *KS*, as shown by the weighted-scales (Tables 1, 2 and 3), four of the shared notes of the transposed scales (Example 5): $c^\sharp$ - e - $f^\sharp$ - $g^\sharp$, account for more than 74 percent of the tunes. In *TS1*, the original sequence of b - d - e - $f^\sharp$ contributes 55 percent to the value of the 13 phrases. *TS2* places yet greater importance on the equivalent sequence: $c^\sharp$ - e - $f^\sharp$ - $g^\sharp$, to the extent that it provides 73 percent of the total value. *KS*, however, virtually lives on its equivalent set: c - $e^\flat$ - f - g, which accounts for 95 percent of the total, 11 phrases.

None of the data presented so far can be reconciled with *Tōgaku* models. In the latter, however, the study of 31 items (including three Large Pieces: *Daqu* 大曲) has revealed: (1) the importance of standard formulae relating to the opening and closing of movements; (2) respect for pentatonic sub-structure in melodic style and tonal relationships; and (3) prevalence of the binary principle in form, structure, metre and rhythm.

The next step in analysis of the Heron-Dance tunes was to look for shared formulaic material. Only one common formula is observed, one that holds together as a melodic idea shared by *TS2* and *KS* (Example 6). This is measures 16–19 of *TS2* (heard four times), and measures 6–9 heard once in *KS* (with a hint of itself in measures 29–31).

Example 6. A formula shared by *TS2* and *KS* (transposed)

In items so far analysed in 'Music from the Tang Court', modal obligations evidently require final cadences to be standard, formulaic statements. Example 7

shows the three approaches to the final in the three melodies: by descent in *TS* movements (*TS2* transposed up a semitone), by ascent in *KS*. *TS1* concludes with a cadence-pattern previously heard, in full, as the completion of phrase 11; it is formal in pattern and in note-durations: *d - b - a - g* (phrase 11) and *d - b - g*, the latter compressed and dogmatic, each note taken by leap.

Example 7. Final Cadences of *TS1*, *TS2* (transposed) and *KS*, compared

The foundation of each of these cadence-formulae is the same.

The six crotchet-beats of *TS2*-transposed (Example 7) are even more emphatic than the ten beats of *TS1*; but abrupt as the transposed *TS2*-cadence looks in isolation, the phrase it terminates, extending over six measures – six binary beats (measures 97–102) – insists throughout that, in transposition, *c* leaps down to *g* to finish the song. These two notes occupy five unit-beats at first occurrence (measures 97–9) and seven beats the second time (measures 99–102). This kind of modality is inescapable throughout *TS2*. Every phrase repeats the notes *b* and *f♯*, with *f♯* always preceded by *b* (see Example 2). The weighted-scale of *TS2* confirms the role of *b* as near two-thirds of the value (and importance) of *f♯*.

In a harmonic sense, the final formulae in *TS1* and *TS2* are not comparable; but in the modal and melodic sense they are. The *TS1*-cadence moves from *d* (49 in weighted-scale *TS1*) to *g* (67); while the *TS2*-cadence moves from *b* to *f♯* – sub-dominant to final – in weighted-scale, 94 to 173. The difference of approach in *KS* at first seems of major significance; but in fact the final cadence is approached, in both melodies – *TS1* and *KS* – in precisely the same way, *via* a chain of thirds, minor third followed by major third: *TS1* descending *d - b - g*; *KS* ascending *c - e♭ -g*.

Example 8. Intermediate Cadences of *TS1*, *TS2* (transposed) and *KS*, compared.

Looking at other cadence-formulae (Example 8), *TS1* displays six cadence-forms, of which the first four are somewhat related, as variant formulae adapted to context and function. The remaining two are positive, dominant and final-note cadence-forms.

TS2 – a very repetitive tune of nineteen phrases – has only four phrase-endings. The first and third are distinctive formulae, the third particularly so, since it closes a catchy little phrase that momentarily escapes the hegemony of *b* and *f*$^{\sharp}$, the powerful sub-dominant and final.

KS makes use of a variety of cadence-notes, with two out of the six formulae closing on the same note. The nature of the scale removes it from detailed comparison with the previous item, thus permitting – even providing for – greater variety in cadence-forms than the *TS*-movements required. The four non-final *KS* cadence-notes, approached (as they are) from above, have about them a different tonal ambience, whereas *TS1* and *TS2* cadence-forms sound somewhat alike. Two *KS*-cadences employ the same notes: *e*$^{\flat}$ - *f* - *g* and *g* - *f* - *e*$^{\flat}$. They cover the same segment of scale which in isolation brings *ryo*-tonality to the ear.

Comparing the non-final cadences in the three compositions (Example 8), six patterns stand out which, despite varying numbers of beats, notes and rhythms, are distinguished by the same underlying features. They are all drawn from oral traditions, in which diversity of detail disguises a primary core-agreement. Three of the cadences (in Example 9) fall from the final of a note-set to a dominant note one fourth below, while the remaining three cadences imitate

61

the falling interval, and so establish and achieve a corresponding, complementary effect.

Example 9. Selected cadence patterns for *TS1*, *TS2* (transposed) and *KS*, compared.

Rhythm, intervallic structure, and position in the scale, all tend to endorse differences rather than likenesses. The two phrases that stand comparison have been pointed out already (Example 6); and even these structures: *TS2*, measures 16–19; *KS*, measures 6–9, have separate identities.

Two structural observations remain to be made:

First, all three items consist of odd-numbers of phrases. The length of these phrases differs in the course of a single piece; furthermore, both duple- and triple-time units occur in all three structures. Such variability in phrase-length and in metrical structure, and the existence of non-binary structure in terms of numbers of phrases, are of course phenomena not commonly encountered in measured items of *Tōgaku*.

Secondly, both Introit and Song from Tsuwano are integrated, structurally speaking, by the insertion between (in the case of the Introit), and between and over, melodic phrases (in the Song), of a passage for percussion alone, which extends from seven to 13 beats. A striking feature of this passage is that all beats are of equal weight, so that there is no defined sense of a measured pulse – of a metre – associated with particular beats.

In its shortest version, the first *TS1* interlude, the passage consists of a sequence of (a) three beats on a larger drum (described as 'braced *taiko*'); (b) three beats on a pair of gongs, pitched a fifth apart on $c^\sharp$ and $g^\sharp$; (c) two beats on a small drum or a pair of such. This percussion-phrase, or a variant thereof, separates each melodic phrase of the Introit.

In the Song, although the percussion-phrase enters after the singing of the first line of the Song, subsequently (and lengthened from seven to eight beats by a quarter-note rest) it is repeated approximately ten times in succession, in parallel with the remaining phrase-lines of the Song. Only on the final note of the Song do the flutes of the Introit enter again in a brief *Coda*, supported by larger drum and gongs.

Music of the *Gionmatsuri*

The second area of folk-ritual music to be examined is that of music played (with two exceptions only) *on* the floats that process through the streets of Kyoto during the Gion Festival. The term 'float' is here used as an analogous term for one of the two types of wheeled vehicle, respectively known as *hoko/feng* (originally – and in Chinese – 'the point of a sword') and *yama/shan* 'mountain'. The character most commonly used, by the floats and by the authorities in Kyoto, for 'float' is a variant of a more usual lexigraph: 鉾. The variant is composed from the same determinative: *jin* 金, with *mou* 牟 on the right: 金牟. This variant is not available to us in our founts of Chinese characters.

A first and all important step towards examination of this repertory was a visit to The National Ethnological Museum in Ōsaka by L.E.R.P. in the company of Professor Mary Nute Craighill of the Kansai University of Foreign Studies. Professor Craighill acted as interpreter in conversations with the Staff of the Museum and in particular with Professor Tanushi Makoto 田 主 誠, then Director of the Museum. It was our singular good fortune that Professor Tanushi had for ten years acted as principal director of the *Gionmatsuri*.

Examination of items from this repertory was made possible (for details see p. 76–77): (1) by information from Professor Tanushi and Mr Ōsugi Ryūichi 大 杉 隆 一; (2) by published recordings of items from the repertory of the Long-Halberd Float (*Naginataboko* 長 刀 鉾) [(P) 1086 King Record Co. Ltd]; (3) by gifts of cassette-recordings from Japanese friends.

Thanks to the first we were able to purchase the privately printed volume of transcriptions in staff-notation of the repertories of ten of the principal floats (published in 1988 under the title *Gionbayashi* 祇 園 ば や し). These are transcriptions prepared from tapes of the performance of the float-bands, made in 1968 and 1979. Above all, we have been privileged to receive a private recording of the entire repertory of the Chrysanthemum-Water Float (*Kikusuiboko* 菊 水 鋒).

The home of this 'Chrysanthemum-Water' Float is now the district of Muromachi 室 町in Kyoto. The district was once known as *Ebisu-chō* 惠 比 須 町, because of the presence there of the Shrine of the God of Wealth: Ebisu. In the Muromachi period, and from 1338 onwards, the float had a different form from that of today, being a '*yama*', rather than (as now) a '*hoko*'. The society and its float was known, accordingly, as *Ebisuyama*. By the fifteenth century, the form had changed again, and the structure was referred to as *Shisuiboko* 止 水 鋒 'Still-Water *hoko*'. Finally, about 1500, it became *Kikusuiboko*. This *hoko* and its furnishings were destroyed by fire in 1864. Restoration did not occur until 1953, so that the society did not participate in the annual *Gionmatsuri* for almost a century.

The transcriptions in the volume: *Gionbayashi*, are (to some extent) schematic in that, while providing a rhythmic framework that illustrates the activities of gongs and drums, and a pitch-framework for the flute-melody, they do not attempt precise notation of what the ear perceives. The justification for such an approach is: that this is music known only from performance, largely preserved in the memories of the musicians – the *hayashi*; only to a limited extent does it depend on written documents – 'practice books': *keikobon* 稽 古 文 that prescribe (to some extent) the actions of the percussion-instruments, both gongs and drums. (We were privileged to receive a bound photocopy of the manuscript *Keikobon* of the *Kikusuiboko*, dated 1863, as a gift from Mr Ōsugi.) The bulk of such a score sets out prescribed patterns for gong-strokes, together with the all-important, guiding calls: the *kakegoe* 卦 聲, made either by the lead-drummer alone, or in chorus by the drummers. Only occasionally, where drums alone perform, does the score show a continuous, sequential, symbolic notation of drum-stroke patterns. This happens, for example in the *Jibayashi* 地 囃 子 ('local music'?) piece with which the *Naginataboko*-musicians begin their repertory.

The published transcriptions show that three differentiated tone-colours are available from the gongs (鉦 *shō*), according to whether the drum-stick (or beater) strikes *either* the centre of the internal circular face, *or* the angle between plate and rim, below or above, *or* centrally, but 'with restraint'. The drum – named *taiko* (太 鼓) but in reality a cord-braced, squat drum, resembling the same-named drum of the typical *Nō* 能 ensemble, and not resembling the *taiko* of the *Gagaku* ensemble – is beaten on one head as it rests on a stand, with that head sloping down towards the player.

64

Eight types of simple stroke are distinguished by *hand* (right or left), by *position*, or by *weight*; and there are three further differentiated strokes, including a roll. At least some of this stroke-differentiation on gongs and drums is reflected in the percussion scores, and is indicated *either* by different symbols, *or* by annotations in a mixture of syllables, both *katakana* and *hiragana*.

An invaluable feature of the *Gionbayashi* volume is that the surviving scores of nine (out of the ten repertories transcribed) are reproduced following the transcriptions in staff-notation. The missing score is that of the *Kikusuiboko* of which we are privileged to have a photocopy. Inspection shows that the scores use a shared repertory of symbols. In lay-out they are usually written in vertical columns, but in one instance in horizontal rows.

The flutes learn their tunes nowadays from entirely separate scores, written in a style known as *shōga* 唱 歌 (literally 'singing-song'), similar to that used by learners [of flute (*ryūteki*) and other instruments] in *Gagaku* performance.

Other than the implications of their linear geometry, the percussion-scores offer no guide to metre and rhythm; and they evidently serve principally as reminders to performers who already have some memory of previous performances. We believe it to be historically important that the drums lead the ensemble, even though the bulk of the score is concerned with the different types of stroke on the gongs. These latter are dish-shaped, flange-rimmed, cord-loop suspended, hand-held gongs that scarcely existed, even in China, before the fifth century AD. They cannot have been in use in Japan until the establishment of Buddhism among the nobility in the sixth century, say.

How odd the first gongs must have appeared to Japanese musicians when they first arrived in Japan is suggested by the name adopted for the entirely similar (but not hand-held) gong in the *gagaku*-ensemble, known as *shōko* 鉦 鼓. This Chinese binome, *zhenggu*, originally had the sense: 'the gong to sound the retreat; the drum to sound the advance'. Its apparent meaning in Japanese would merely be: 'gong-drum'; and in the mouth of a non-Chinese musician, *shōko* would merely be a disyllabic name for a foreign instrument.

It is evident that items in the 'practice-books' of the musicians are conceived as complete pieces in their own right. They do not consist of repeating, colotomic patterns, based on measure-like units. Without flutes, the performance by drums and gongs alone would still be valid as music, just as purely percussive items flourish in the practice of the provincial Chinese Music Associations investigated by Jones and Xue (1991) (see in addition Stephen Jones, 1995).

Each float-band performs up to 60 differently named items. The sequence of these in performance is continuous, and seemingly standard for a given float and its society (*Yama* or *Hoko*). A number of differently titled items follow one after the other in performance, without a break between, although the entire repertory may be interrupted at two or three points. In some float-traditions, the musicians distinguish between a sequence of items played on the outward journey from the site of the building in which the float is housed, and a sequence played during the return. In such case, the two halves of the repertory are distinguished as *watari* 渡 and *modori* 戻, literally 'crossing' and 'returning', respectively.

The sequence of titled items is linked together by standard pieces, shorter and longer, and standard for a particular float, referred to as *Nagashi* 流し and *Age* 上 げ .The former movement often appears to act as a multi-purpose interlude; the latter, either as a general *Coda* or as a short, linking episode. The reason for these terms being used with these significances in this context, is not understood.

The transcription of the music of the floats into staff-notation is rendered difficult, and in some degree inadequate as a representation of what is heard, for two reasons: First, the sustained use of contrived dissonance on the part of the flutes. Each float carries a minimum of six flute-players, some of which mimic the melody at a distance approaching a semitone or ninth from the others, while one or more performers play in the upper octave – in so far as the compass of the now standard flute, 能 管 (the *nōkan*, as used in the performance of *Nō*) permits this. Secondly, the scaling of such flutes (as with *nōkan* in general) is neither standard, nor rational (in a technical sense); and their use in the hands of the performers results in great variability of the perceived pitch, even of notes that might be regarded as 'the same'.

Two performing groups today make use of *Shinobue* 篠 笛 rather than *nōkan*; that is, flutes (*fue* 笛) made from 'a small kind of bamboo'= *shino* 篠. This is the type of flute still in use by the *Sagimai* flute-players. Mr Ōsugi expressed the view that players on a majority of the floats adopted the *nōkan* under the influence of the once popular genre of *Sarugaku* 猿 樂 ('monkey-music').This latter, having both Buddhist and Shintō associations since the eighth century, probably derived from the Chinese genre of *sangaku* 散 樂, literally 'free music', known to have featured as part of the music played during celebrations at the Tōdaiji in the year of its consecration.

The two groups in question have only recently been revived: *Ayagasaboko* 綾 傘 鉾 and *Shijōkasaboko* 四 條 傘 鉾. (In Japanese use, the lexigraph *jō* 條 in the latter title is reduced to the right-hand component only. The meaning remains the same: 'a stretch or length', in this instance, of road or street.) Members of these two societies each assemble as a small group of participants (including both musicians and dancers), promenading together with a large, short-cylindrical umbrella: the *Kasaboko* 傘 鉾 'umbrella-halberd'. Both societies make use of a simple bamboo-flute. That it is indeed made from a particular species of bamboo, the one commonly designated when the term *shino* is used, has not as yet been determined.

A Shintō-Priest kindly informed Mrs Okamoto Miyoko that at one time a *hoko* existed known as the *Kasasagi-boko* 'The Magpie-Halberd' 鵲 鋒 and that the *Sagimai* was danced by members of that society. One is tempted to suppose that both the dance and the characteristic umbrella, arose from popular word-play on the name of the bird: 'magpie' = *kasasagi*. The components: *kasa* and *sagi* sound like 'umbrella' and 'heron', respectively. The other components of the names of the two societies are street-references.

Whatever the explanation, these two societies offer a possible image of the structure of the procession before the development of wheeled floats: a sequence of promenading groups of musicians and dancers, together with those carrying – by turns – the essential protection from July elements of sun and rain – a vast umbrella, in shape a transverse segment of a cylinder. In this instance, the instrumental ensemble takes what may be a pre-Buddhist form, consisting as it does of flute and drum only – as for *Sagimai* at Tsuwano or Nakai-machi.

Our transcriptions of *Matsuribayashi* pieces offer, so far as staff-notation allows, a rationalised version of the melodic material presented to the ear by the recordings. Even so, this body of melody is something new in our experience of Japanese music. It is a body of music that seems never to have been subjected to detailed scrutiny before. This may well be due to the absence of historical documents, and because it is a music that survives only (or largely) in the memory of the performers, assisted by a type of score that only serves as a memory-jogger. In structure and in 'modality' it is a music unique of its kind, a music indeed *sui generis*.

Two items have been transcribed and subjected to detailed analysis. These are *Karako* 唐 子 and *Shishi* 獅 子. The former title might be translated as 'Tang Child' or 'Korean Child', or more generally: 'Foreign Child'. The latter is 'Lion' and immediately leads one to think of the 'Lion Dances' common in China, Korea and Japan.

A piece entitled *Karako* occurs in the repertory of five floats (out of the ten of which the repertories have been transcribed and published), and the percussion-scores of all five, same-titled items, are very similar, as are their versions in transcription. *Shishi* too is a title that appears in the repertories of other floats. Indeed, a number of titles are shared between repertories of the ten principal floats; and this suggests perhaps that there was once a common repertory, with pieces of the same title sharing the same percussion-score. Where percussion-scores are shared, the melodic lines also seem to be versions of each other.

Karako

A piece in three Sections, played with continuous acceleration.

Example 10. *Karako*: melody transcribed from *Gionbayashi* cassette, *Kyōto Naginataboko hayashi-kata renjū* 京 都 長 刀 鋒 は や し 方 連 中 (K23H-5257).

The scale may be represented simply as: d^b, f, g, b^b

68

Example 11. *Karako*: the note-set in simple scalar form

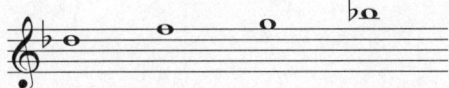

The three Sections, primarily repetitions, are played with increasing speeds. The complete melody consists of four notes only; and from these, two- and three-note patterns are drawn: falling patterns, g - f and g - f - d^b; and rising patterns, d^b - f and d^b - f - b^b. These may vary slightly in repeats, as tempo increases. As transcribed, the melody reduces in time, since the duration of beats diminishes as tempo increases. (In determining note-durations and frequencies of occurrence from which to determine a weighted-scale, only the second half of the third section of the piece has been used, since only there is the value of the beat a single crotchet/quarter-note.)

Table 4. Karako: *Weighted-scale data (of the final repeat)*

	d^b	f	g	b^b		
Durations	8.5	13.5	18	6	=	46
Occurrences	7.0	10.0	15	3	=	35
Initials & Finals	3.0	7.0	7	1	=	18
TOTALS	18.5	30.5	40	10	=	99
Percentages	19.0	31.0	40	10	=	100

The three Sections of the whole melody are constructed from phrases derived from the falling and rising note-patterns: A, AB and BC, where the letter-symbols denote the growth of second (AB) and third (BC) phrases from a predecessor. In Sections 1, 2 and 3, A is 13 notes long; AB, 11–13 notes long (depending on durations and repetitions); and BC is 8–12 notes long (according to durations and repetitions). The form of each Section is shown in the following table.

Table 5. Karako: *structural formulae of three sections*

Section 1: A, A, AB, BC

Section 2: A, AB, BC

Section 3: A, AB, BC; A, AB, BC

The structure is maintained by the forward impulse of successive note-patterns, from the first descending g - g - g - f onwards, to the ultimate leap to the final note. Every phrase reaches out to its cadence: g, f, b^b. The central core-pattern: - g - f - d^b - f - occurs just once in each repetition.

As transcribed, and in approximate terms, Section 1 accelerates from 66 to 104 quarter-note beats per minute, with note-values reducing along the way. Acceleration in Section 2 is slight, from 92 to 100 quarter-note beats per minute, with note-values diminishing. Section 3, moving more rapidly, plays the tune twice, with note-values decreasing each time: first time through, from 108 to 152 unit-beats per minute; second time through, 112 to 152 unit-beats per minute. Metronome-markings are, of course, what a tape-recording of a single performance reveals.

The acceleration recorded in *Karako* is a phenomenon not uncommonly to be observed in performance of Japanese traditional music. In the performance of *Karako* it is evident from the outset; and the transcription reflects this in its notation, with whole-notes (the 'beats' of the Japanese structure) becoming dotted half-notes, later half-notes, and finally quarter-notes, with tempo steadily increasing. Reduction of note-values assists both eye, and mind's ear, to appreciate the energy that underlies form, style and performance of the genre.

70

Table 6. Three Sections of Karako: *comparison of numbers of notes in the three discrete phrases*

		$g\text{-}f\text{-}g$		$g\text{-}f\text{-}d^{\flat}\text{-}f$		$d^{\flat}\text{-}f\text{-}b^{\flat}$		
Section 1		13 + 13	+	13	+	12	=	51 notes
Section 2		13	+	13	+	10	=	36 notes
Section 3	(1)	13	+	11	+	9	=	33 notes
	(2)	13	+	11	+	11	=	35 notes
TOTALS		65		48		42	=	155 notes

Every phrase contains, or stands for, 13 beats, or notes. Phrases of less than 13 notes are variant forms of 13-note phrases.

The numbers of notes in each phrase, sometimes reducing as tempo gathers, are sustained by patterns of 13 drum-beats per phrase, and by complementary patterns of 11 gong-beats per phrase: that is, the gong does not mask the fourth and eighth drum-beats. The rhythmic-block pattern as a whole is eleven gong-beats to the same metrical duration and tempo as thirteen drum-beats, and thirteen primary melodic notes.

In the transcription, one prime melody-note is represented as a whole-note in Section 1, a dotted half-note in Section 2, a half-note in the first time of Section 3, and a quarter-note in the second time. Each of these values equates with one beat of the music in Japanese terms. It is evident that drums, gongs and melody are wholly interdependent: for example, the drum alone sounds with the note f, when the melodic line descends from g. (Early in the performance of the piece, the drum-strokes are preceded by a short up-beat; but this is omitted as the pace increases.)

At intervals during this – and, indeed, during all pieces in the *Matsuribayashi* repertories of the ten principal floats – metrically defined di- or tri-syllabic ejaculations (*kakegoe*; see p. 64) are chanted from time to time by one (or more, in unison) of the drummers. Each syllable is precisely timed and supported by a 'restrained beat' on a drum. Typically, the calls and drum-strokes occur at the ends of the thirteen-beat phrases. It is noteworthy that the drums add no beats *between* the primary beats that underlie notes, nor between a cadence-note and the impending phrase-initial.

The gong-players evidently follow drums and flutes (drums anticipating flutes) until the second, thirteen-beat phrase of *Karako* 3, at which point all play *with the beat* until the last note.

The percussion-score clearly prescribes (by implication) all notes and all beats of each entire phrase. Be there 8, 10, 11, 12, or the standard 13 notes in the melody (as played by the flutes), the regular thirteen drum-beats dictate the structure, the duration and the cadence position, of all thirteen phrases of *Karako*.

It is worth emphasising the difference between what is revealed by the *performers* concerning the nature of 'a beat' in this music, and what the Western ear seeks to impose. 'Japanese beats' are evidently counted by drum-beats. The first phrase of Section 1, for example, consists of the thirteen notes and thirteen drum-beats; but the same phrase requires a count of 54 slow, regular Western beats – crotchets or quarter-notes. Not until the second time of Section 3 do Japanese beats equate with Western beats in value. Even then, however, cadence-notes are subsumed under a single drum-beat, regardless of their duration. No aspect of the remarkable details of this music appears to be determined by a conscious conceptual, theoretical framework.

Shishi

A second item (from the repertory of the *Naginataboko* is 'Lion' 獅 子. It is in three Sections played in numerical sequence without breaks.

Example 12. *Shishi*: flute melody (transcribed from cassette: K23H-5257).

Since Lion-headed dancers join with Heron-dancers in Kanagawa Prefecture, it seems not unlikely that *Shishi* was at one time a danced item throughout the

Gionmatsuri. Closely musically related pieces of the same title occur in the repertories of several of the floats that participate in the Gion Festival.

Example 13. *Shishi*: Hexatonic Scale.

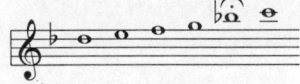

The note-set of the flute-melody of *Shishi* is hexatonic, but *e* is only to be heard in Section 2, and there only three times, as auxiliary to *f*. With b^b as final, one recognises a structure of modal interest. The significant scale is: b^b - *c* - d^b - *f* - *g* (where b^b and *c* are lowered by an octave). *f* functions as tonal centre, and *g* is next in precedence. In the preparation of the weighted-scale, only the third Section of the piece has been used.

Table 7. Shishi: *weighted-scale data from three sections*

	d^b	*e*	*f*	*g*	b^b	*c*		
Durations	20	4	90	44	20	16	=	194
Occurrences	19	3	47	22	6	8	=	105
Initials & Finals	1	0	13	6	2	2	=	24
Totals	40	7	150	72	28	26	=	323
Percentages	12	2	46	22	9	8	=	99

f is the convergence of tensions from opposite directions: d^b to *f* and *f* to b^b, with *g* supporting *f* as focus of the repeating pattern: *g* - *f* - d^b - *f*. This latter accounts for 84 percent of occurrences of the three notes *g* - *f* - d^b and 80 percent of the time-durations of the tune.

   g - *f* - d^b - *f* is the single prominent formula of *Shishi*, and the pattern is heard sixteen times in the course of the whole; the same notes occupy 78 binary beats of the entire composition. It is the same pattern that forms the central phrase of the three Sections of *Karako*.

   The tune itself is very short; and Sections 2 and 3 are varied repeats of Section 1. Indeed, it is evident that the piece could be prolonged indefinitely – were there lions still participating – by extended repetition. A major difference between Sections is the unaccountable ending of Section 2. Detailed discussion of this is postponed for a future publication. What immediately strikes the ear is the appearance of *e*, unrelated to anything preceding or succeeding.

A minor difference between Sections is that in 2 and 3 the flutes begin their tune one binary beat later than in Section 1. In both sections this is compensated for by reducing the duration of the fourth note – from its condition in Section 1 – to one binary beat instead of two. This phenomenon, leading (as it does) to a momentary shift in the relationship of a down-up-down sequence on the gongs to the line of the flutes, is shown in notation in the published transcription in score (*Gionbayashi*, 1988, p. 18), as well as being audible in the published cassette tape-recording of a selection of festival-music from the Long-Halberd Float. It is evidently a feature of today's performance. Tradition falters, and Time exonerates.

In regard to scales, it is plain that the same formation is present in both *Karako* and *Shishi*: *g - f - d^b- f* to which *Karako* adds *b^b*. *Shishi* too adds not only *b^b*, but also *e* and *c*. Both pieces consist of three Sections; and in each case these are slightly varied repetitions of a single tune. That single tune is of the same duration as the extended *MS.*-score for drums and gongs.

While the scale-formations of both pieces are dissimilar from those of the *Tōgaku* modal-tradition, *Karako* and *Shishi* share similar note-series – series that are distinctive of a *Gionbayashi* style, as is evident from the total repertories of the ten principal floats. Neither the scale-formations of *Karako* and *Shishi*, nor the interrelations and functions of notes in the series, are to be compared with the practice and theory of the *Tōgaku* modes.

The lengths of the two pieces are comparable with those of single-movement items of the Tang Music; but the basic musical materials, and the methods of formal construction, are radically opposed to *Tōgaku* practice. The *Gionbayashi* items imply fewer phrases, and fewer notes; and a single phrase may be heard in extended, consecutive repetitions, before moving to a new phrase. These items are each constituted from a lesser amount of musical material than are *Tōgaku* items; and repetition is literal – extended without variation. *Karako* shows how each of its three phrases emerges from the preceding phrase by adding (and/or discarding) notes. *Shishi*, on the other hand, consists largely of a single formula of four notes, repeated many times with very little variation.

Karako differs from *Shishi* in the marked escalation of tempi displayed; *Shishi* moves steadily and regularly, with little change in tempo. Formulae in both items are few, where whole phrases are constructed from a single note-pattern. Both share one phrase: the third phrase of *Karako* (Section 1), and the basic formula-phrase of *Shishi* heard at the same pitch *g - f - d^b - f*. Both realise the potential of the augmented interval for textural colour and individuality; but *Karako* makes use of it in each Section, while *Shishi* builds almost all of its three

Sections from it. In addition, *Shishi* also makes use of the other augmented interval: d^b - *e*.

Profoundly different from the colotomic structure of a majority of *Tōgaku* items is the 'through-composed' character of the percussion-scores, specific to each item. It is important to recognise that each score is unique to a particular named item. Furthermore, each score, in performance *without* a melody-instrument, would be as complete a structured piece of music as it is *with* a melodic instrument.

The interpretation of the percussion-scores in terms of durations – in the sense of 'colotomic or block-structural durations' – is not specified in the scores in terms of numbers of beats to a measure (as it is for a majority of Tang-Music scores); but examination of the rhythmic structure of a series of scores reveals the presence of unexpressed duration-values in their interpretation and execution, values of which the percussionists may not themselves be consciously aware.

The evidence for fundamental stylistic differences between the music of the *Matsuribayashi* (including the archaic bird-dances) and the repertory of *Tōgaku* – as preserved in Sino-Japanese *MSS*. ranging in date from the eighth to the thirteenth centuries – surely justifies recognition of the persistence in Japan of a body of Japanese music virtually uninfluenced by importations, in the Sui and Tang periods, from the mainland of Asia.

It is to be noted, that the irregular phrasing – shown by arching phrase-lines in the transcription of *Shishi* – is not a phenomenon unknown to the folk music of China today. The *baban* 八 板 tune-family, of such importance in the Southern 'Silk and Bamboo' tradition (Jones, 1995, pp. 144–6, 276 and elsewhere) exhibits both symmetrical division of the group of eight binary beats into two groups of four, and asymmetrical division as three+two+ three. This latter segmentation is comparable with what is shown by phrasing in the transcription of *Shishi*.

In a private communication (letter of 21 October, 1995), Stephen Jones stresses, however, that 'four-square' as well as 'long and short phrases' co-exist. Chinese observers of this phenomenon are inclined to link it with the occurrence of long and short verse-lines in the texts of *ci* 詞 and *qu* 曲. (This view on the part of Chinese observers is perhaps mistaken. The musical length of long and short song-text lines should more probably be the same. By this means differences in pace between lines may come to add greatly to their emotional effect.)

In the performance of *Shishi*, the phrasing shown is underlined by fast upward *glissandi* on the flutes on quitting the end-note of each phrase. Our concern is merely to demonstrate that the type of rhythmic irregularity observed in *Shishi*, though not a feature of the Tang-Music repertory thus far transcribed, is not unknown to the folk-music tradition of China as it survives today.

75

For that matter, it should perhaps be remembered that 'the six great net-ropes' 六 大 綱 that transect Korean scores in tablature from the time of King Sejo (1455–68) (Condit, 1984, p. 4), subdivide columns of eight squares into three groups of 3 - 2 - 3. Although Condit sought to demonstrate that the group of two was read – in the case of ternary pieces – as a unit of three, one recalls the existence today of Chinese-Buddhist percussion-patterns of 3+2+3 beats. The possible occurrence of non-regular subdivision of a unit of eight, once widely distributed as a folk practice in East Asia, perhaps common to China, Korea and Japan, has to be born in mind.

As suggested in Chapter 3 in regard to the concepts of 'Old' and 'New' Musics in Japan, far from the Japanese having embarked on a profound modification, at the time of their importation, of musics that reached them from Tang, Wu, and Koma, it seems probable that their own 'elite' music was transformed, almost beyond recognition, in the course of time, by the styles of what was imported.

The effectively unwritten music of *matsuri*, surviving today in every district of Japan, suggests to us some of the characteristics of an ancient music, the most distinctively Japanese of all the musics of Japan; music in a style that may have existed in Japan, long before importations from elsewhere on the mainland of Asia reached The Land of Ama-terasu Omikami.

This somewhat speculative Chapter on the music of pre-Nara Japan could not have been written without the help of Japanese friends who responded warmly and generously to enquiries instituted on our behalf by Mrs Okamoto Miyoko 岡 本 美 代 子 and others, over the years from 1991 to 1995. Their names are set out here in the sequence in which their help came:

Professor Tanushi Makoto 田 主 誠 (formerly Director of The National Ethnological Museum *Kokuritsu Minzokugaku Hakubutsukan* 國 立 民 族 學 博 物 館, Ōsaka) and Mrs Tanaka Yukiko 田 中 雪 子 (formerly of the same museum) drew our attention to the publication: *Gionbayashi*, and directed us to Mr Ōsugi Ryūichi 大 杉 隆 一 (at one time Secretary to the *Gionmatsuri Yamaboko Rengokai* 祇 園 祭 山 鉾 連 合 會); and his successor, Mrs Teraura Keiko 寺 浦 桂 子 .

From Mr Ōsugi we received a bound photocopy of the *Keikobon* 稽 古 本 of the *Kikusuiboko* (p. 64).

Mr Kawatsuka Kinzō 川 塚 錦 造 (Head of Music of the *Kikusuiboko*), kindly prepared for us cassette-copies of the private recording of the repertory of this *hoko*, as performed today.

Mr Yoshida Satoru 吉 田 舜, formerly a member of Staff of *Nihon Gakushi-in* 日 本 學 士 院 (Tokyo), generously sent a photocopy of an article on *Sagimai* from *The History of Kanagawa Prefecture* together with a video-tape of the Festival at Nakai-machi, in Kanagawa-ken.

Dr Itō-(Tanese) Yōko 伊 藤 (種 瀬) 陽 子 (a distinguished former doctoral pupil of L.E.R.P.) responded with unparalleled kindness to our request for help in the search for source-materials for this study – materials of some rarity even in Japan.

To her we owe introduction to Mr Fukuda Minoru 福 田 稔, Chief Producer, International Department, The King Record Company Limited, Tokyo, who with great generosity furnished us with copies (no longer otherwise obtainable) of cassette-recordings of music from various *matsuri* of the Edo region.

To her we also owe introduction to Mrs Takahashi Mito 高 橋 美 都, a folklorist familiar with Kanagawa-ken, who most kindly sent us a large map of the Prefecture, photocopies of articles by Nagata Hirayoshi, an article by Higuchi Akira, cassette-recordings of music associated with Heron-dances (both in Kanagawa and at Tsuwano), and a video of ceremonies (including *sagimai*) at Nakai-machi, in Kanagawa-ken.

A final note must be added, again remembering with gratitude the occasion when Professor Mary Nute Craighill and L.E.R.P. first visited *The National Ethnological Museum* in Ōsaka in 1991, and all that flowed from that visit, thanks to our meeting with Professor Tanushi Makoto.

Chapter 3

'Old music','New Music', and other classificatory terms in the musical vocabularies of late Nara, and Heian, Japan (L.E.R.P.)

The significance of the terms 'old' and 'new', as applied to music, and in particular to the Tang Music (*Tōgaku/Tangyue* 唐 樂) of the *Gagaku* 雅 樂 repertory, is a matter on which a variety of opinions have been expressed in different sources, at different times, and by different persons. The late Professor Eta Harich-Schneider (1973, p. 110) offered the following definition: '*Kogaku* (old music) or *Shingaku* (new music) – that is, early or late Heian music.' The statement is made without citing any authority; and in our view, having examined both the sources and Japanese discussions of the topic, it is exact; even though we would extend its validity – at least as regards 'old music' – to the Nara period.

Our investigation of this matter has been enormously facilitated by the generosity of Professor Kishibe Shigeo 岸 邊 成 雄, in providing photocopies of articles by himself and by Mr Hayashi Hirokazu 林 廣 一, and a Table by Mr Tōgi Shintarō 東 儀 新 太 朗 – the two latter being former Court Musicians. All three of these photocopied-articles formed part of Programme-Notes for a Public Performance of *Gagaku* (the fourteenth in succession), given in the Small Theatre of the National Theatre, on 3 March, 1973 [*Shōwa 48 nen* (1973) *sangetsu, go jitsu, Kokuritsu Gekijō, Shōgekijō, daijushi kai Gagaku Kōen, Kangen, Ikko-gaki* 昭 和 四 十 八 年 (1973) 三 月，五 日，國 立 劇 場，小 劇 場，第 十 四 回 雅 樂 公 演，管 弦，一 鼓 搔]. The most recent observations and views of these scholars will be considered subsequent to a prior discussion of the implications of 'old' in Nara times (pp. 91, 95).

I

The classification of items, in Matsushima Yorimasa's invaluable articles on ancient inscribed remnants of clothing, etc. in the *Shōsō-in* (1952, 1953; 1978), is of great importance in relation to the meaning of the term 'old music', as applied to musical items from the Tang repertory, performed as *Tōgaku* in Japan. In the first, and (historically speaking) for us the most important division of his review: 'Items relating to the Eye-Opening Ceremony of the Great Buddha of the Tōdaiji' (in 752), Matsushima sets these out under a number of heads.

At the outset, it is to be observed that the language in which these brush-written inscriptions on garments etc. are written, is a species of minimal Chinese

/ *Kambun* / *Hanwen* / 漢 文. The name of the temple itself: *Tōdaiji* 唐 大 寺, is frequently abbreviated, most commonly to *Tōji* and occasionally to *Tōdai*; while in discussing items from Tang, the phrase: 'Tang old music' [= 'Old music from Tang'] *Tō ko gaku/Tang gu yue* 唐 古 樂 may be reduced to *Tō ko* or even to *ko*. Once, it appears as *ko Tōgaku*; and once *ko/gu* 古 is replaced by *chū/zhong* 中, in a context where this can only be an error. It is of importance that *Tō/Tang* is used exclusively in the sense of a state or administrative area in contrast to other states; it has no chronological implications.

An important matter of idiom and style is the total absence, the non-occurrence, of the word for a musical 'piece' (*kyoku/qu* 曲) throughout the inscriptions that relate to items performed at the Tōdaiji in 752. In every instance, if any term apart from the remainder of the title is added, the term 'music' *gaku/yue* (樂) rather than 'piece' is used. 'Emptying the Cup' is given thus: 傾 杯, without adding either *bu/wu* 舞 (dance), or *gaku/yue* (music), or *kyoku/qu* (piece). It is also to be noted that the term *Gagaku* nowhere occurs.

The same classificatory terms here used by Matsushima are also in use in the 'Essential Records of the Tōdaiji'. [*Tōdaiji yōroku* 唐 大 寺 要 錄 records of the temple from the ninth century to the the beginning of the Kamakura period in the early-twelfth century.] The information concerning *titles* of pieces performed – available to us as recorded in ink-inscriptions on costume-remnants and dance-properties now in the *Shōsō-in* – is not, unfortunately, given in the Tōdaiji's record of the eye-opening ceremony.

Harich-Schneider (1973, p. 72) seems to have been mistaken in stating that 'the complete sequence of dances' is contained in the second scroll of the record. What is given there is the list of categories of music-with-dance, as defined by Matsushima. Only one item is mentioned by title in the second scroll, namely, *Batō* 拔 斗, one of the so-called Rin'yū 林 邑 items (p. 72): '*Batō* and other dances 拔 斗 等 舞'; but this statement does not relate to the eye-opening ceremony performed on the Ninth Day of the Fourth Month of the Year *Tempyō-shōhō* 天 平 胜 寶 四 月 九 日 (*TDJYR*, p. 47). The *number* of dances from each of categories (1), (2) and (3) (see later) is given, and (on occasion) the number of dancers as well. Unfortunately, the lexigraphs 舞, and 舞 with the ninth determinative: 人, are used interchangeably in Japanese, and while it seems probable that the latter originally meant 'dancer' as opposed to 'dance' 舞, Moronaga (for example) uses either graph in either of these senses. The passages in *TDJYR* (p. 49) show that this was also probably so when the document describing the ceremony was drafted.

Classification based on that of Matsushima Yorimasa of items performed at consecration of Tōdaiji, 752

(1) 'Great Song' *Ō-uta* 大 歌
(2) Tō/Tang
(3) Koma/Korea (not considered here)
(4) Tora/Dvāravati (Waterhouse, 1991, pp. 73–101) (not considered here)
(5) Go/Wu

(1) 'Great Song'
A first group of items covers Japanese music. The qualification 'Great' is perhaps derived by association with titles of great ceremonial occasions, such as imperial coronations *Daijōe* 大 嘗 會 or *Daijōsai* 大 嘗 祭. The original *Chinese* meaning of these terms was: 'Buddhist Ceremony *or* Festival of the Autumnal Offering of First Fruits to the Ancestors'. The items in this first category, both danced and sung, are now *Shintō* 神 道, rather than Buddhist in character, however.

[The remaining groups are geographical or regional, defined by names of states or administrations: Tang (= China); Koma (anciently a region of what is now modern Korea); Dora (perhaps the South-East Asian kingdom of Dvāravati); Wu (anciently a Chinese province of the Eastern seaboard). (Though not distinguished as a category in listing these remnants, it is known from *TDJYR* that Rin'yū (Çampa) also was represented.)]

(2) Tang
Inspection shows that the names of categories discriminated by Matsushima have been taken by him from the inscriptions themselves. Under 'Tang' he distinguishes three sub-categories: (2, a) Old music from Tang 唐 古 樂; (2, b) Middle music from Tang 唐 中 樂; (2, c) Free/Popular music from Tang 唐 散 樂.

(2, a) Old music from Tang 唐 古 樂. It is not immediately clear whether 'old' meant musical items that were indeed 'old' in the Tang tradition at the time of acquisition by the Japanese; or musical items that were acquired by the Japanese at an early date. At the outset, it must be emphasised (in the light of all that is now known) that the terms 'old' and 'new' were not used in Chinese in any specific sense in relation to current music. There was no use of 'old music' other than, perhaps, in the sense of music of ancient and idealised times, when music was perfect. The term 'new' (新) was indeed applied to the Banquet Music in the

Tang Dynasty in the phrase: 'New Banquet Music' *Shin yanyue* 新 燕 樂, with reference to new items devised in 649 by Zhang Wenshou 張 文 收.

The category (2, a) includes costume-remnants and dance-properties from four pieces:

(2 a, i) 'Destroying the Formations' 破 陣 樂;

(2 a, ii) 'Gentleman An' 安 君 子;

(2 a, iii) 'The Prince of Lanling' 蘭 陵 王 (Fascicle 5, p. 2); and

(2 a, iv) *Sohōhi* 蘇 芳 菲 (see later).

(2 a, i) cannot refer to 'The Emperor Destroys the Formations' (Fascicle 1), since that title is separately listed in category (2, c) (see later, p. 90). It seems possible that entry (2 a, i) refers to a piece known nowadays by a more ancient title: 'The Prince of Qin Destroys the Formations'. The future Taizong Emperor, born (in 599, perhaps) as second son to the Emperor Gaozu, was made 'Prince of Qin' 秦 王 in 618 when his father, Li Yuan, was enthroned as Emperor; and according to tradition it was in 620 that he, as Prince of Qin, defeated the rebel soldiery of the pretender, Liu Wuzhou. Among the prince's forces the victory was celebrated (again according to tradition) by the creation of a ballad: 'The Prince of Qin Destroys the Formations'. This is recorded in *JTS*, *TD*, *THY*, *XTS* and elsewhere (see later, however).

As to the dating of these last named four sources, on a previous occasion it was argued that Chapter 28 of *JTS* relates to events before, or not much later than, 755 (Picken l965, p. 82). Twitchett (1992) concluded that the first section of this chapter, down to the Kaiyuan period of Xuanzong's reign (713–41) derived directly from the *National History* and from sources probably written in the early part of that period. *TD* (*Tong Dian*) (801, 803) and *THY* (*Tang huiyao*) – supposing that such a politically neutral piece of information existed already in the *HY* recension of 801 – both attest the same provenance of a first piece relating to the Prince of Qin. *TD* (p. 761) states that, at the time of the victory, 'among the people there was a popular ballad, the piece of 'The Prince of Qin Destroys the Formations' 人 間 歌 謠 有 秦 王 破 陣 樂 之 曲.

THY describes Taizong's own account, given to a banquet of officials in 627, of how the piece arose: 'in consequence, among the people there was this song' 世 間 遂 有 此 歌. The Emperor went on to admonish those present against the performance as *Yayue* of such a warlike piece. What was performed in 627, however, was not presumably the popular ballad of 620 – if indeed such a ballad had ever existed.

The account of origin in *JTS* is fuller than that in *THY*, but not as full as that in *TD*; and the fullest account of all is to be found in *XTS* (2, p. 467): 'When Taizong was Prince of Qin he destroyed Liu Wuzhou, and [those] in the army

81

together made the music-piece: 'The Prince of Qin Destroys the Formations' 太
宗 為 秦 王，破 劉 武 周，軍 中 相 於 作 秦 王 破 陣 樂 曲. (In passing,
the parallel with the circumstances under which the first version of the piece 'The
Prince of Lanling Penetrates the Formation' arose is to be noted; Fascicle 5, p. 2.)

Nevertheless, the story appears to be untrue. The Prince of Qin certainly did
not destroy Liu Wuzhou in the sense of killing him at any time. He was killed in
622 by the Eastern Turks. Up to that year, Liu caused constant trouble in
Northern Shanxi, but seems never to have been the object of an attack by the
Prince of Qin (Li Shimin). (See Wechsler, 1979, pp. 162–86.) Li Shimin
(together with the Heir-Apparent) was indeed involved, however, in the repulsion
of the forces of Xieli Qaghan, when the latter invaded Taiyuan in 622 (Wechsler,
p. 181). The occasions may have been confused.

*The documents, taken together, surely attest the creation of a piece entitled
'The Prince of Qin Destroys the Formations'; but we cannot be certain of the
existence of a piece of that title until Li Shimin was enthroned in 626.*

It is the case, that a piece of this title, in *Taishiki-chō/Dashidiao* survives in
GGKF (now regarded by some as of eleventh-century date, calligraphically akin
to Buddhist documents of the 12th or 13th centuries, but surely incorporating
much earlier materials). A piece of this title also survives in *KF/HSF/RK*, *SSSTF*,
JCYR and *SGYR*. These versions are related to that of *GGKF*, as shown by N.J.N.
(Volume 6, 1997, pp. 233–78). Performances of pieces entitled 'Destroying the
Formations' are recorded in *JTS*, *XTS* and *TD*, on at least a dozen occasions
between 627 and 829. These, however, were all court instrumental performances
with dancers, unlike the first (possibly fictitious) spontaneous ballad of the
soldiers (perhaps with a martial dance) in 620. In one only of these performances
is the ballad-title referred to, namely, that of 633 (*TD*, p. 761; *XTS*, p. 467), where
the original title of a piece, known as 'Seven Virtues Dance', is said to have been
'The Prince of Qin Destroys the Formations'.

The limited information available in the sources does not permit firm
identification of a particular version of a 'Destroying the Formations' piece as the
one performed at the Tōdaiji in 752. The presence of two swords, their scabbards,
and a fragment of scabbard (Matsushima 1978, p. 51), seems to indicate,
however, that this was a version of a dance performed with weapons – unlike the
weaponless version listed in category (2, c) (see later). Nor does such information
as exists regarding modality, afford clues to the identity of a particular version. In
THY (pp. 615-l8), a survey of titles (submitted to the Throne for approval in 754)
lists five 'Destroying the Formations' items; all are in the Mixo-Lydian mode, but
in five different keys. The listing of so many versions, at a date only two years
later than the consecration ceremony at the Tōdaiji, reinforces the suggestion

(made earlier) that 'old' cannot refer to age in the Tang repertory, but must refer to 'age' in some other respect.

The order of presentation of the modes and keys in *THY* may be significant. The pitch *Taicu* 太 簇 (a tone above *D*, namely *E*) is named first, and the sequence of modes (on the *Taicu* degree) that follows is: *Gong, Shang, Jiao* – that is: Lydian, Mixo-Lydian and Aeolian, all on *E*. Is it only coincidence that our earliest version of 'Destroying the Formations' (from *GGKF*) is in the *Taicu Shang* mode-key, equated (in *THY*, p. 616) with the Tadjik Mode on *E* (*Dashidiao* 大 食 調)? (The finals of the versions in other keys in the survey of 754 are set out in the sequence *A, D, G, B*. The entire sequence of finals is then *E, A, D, G, B*. That is to say, the 2nd, 3rd, and 4th keys follow a cycle of fifths (or their inversions to fourths): *E-A-D-G* – fourth up, fifth down, fourth up.

The sequence suggests that the original key may indeed have been *E*, the key of the earliest version known to us. It is to be noted that yet another 'Destroying the Formations' item exists in the same mode-key: *Sanju hajinraku/Sanshou pozhenyue* 散 手 破 陣 樂. This item, in two movements (see *SSSTF*) is not, however, obviously musically related to the other *Hajinraku/Pozhenyue* items.

From this summary, it is evident that any one of a number of Chinese versions of 'Destroying the Formations' was available for transmission to Japan, in the early Nara period, between 627 and (say) 678; but it seems improbable that items associated with persons of imperial rank would have been disposed of by the Chinese Music Bureau to 'despised' foreigners until a decent interval (two generations, or three?) had elapsed since they were last played at the Chinese court.

In 752, how long would any such version have to have been present in the court repertory of Japan, for it to be regarded as 'old'?

(2 a, ii) 'Gentleman An' is attributed (*YFZL*, p. 58) to the end of the Sui dynasty, and indeed to the end (in 616) of the reign of the Yang-*di* Emperor. If 安 弓 字 (or 子) (*Ankyūji* in Sino-Japanese reading) may be identified with *Anjunzi* 安 君 子 (read as *Ankunshi* in Sino-Japanese), this latter piece survives (in *JCYR* for example); and it, too, is in the Tadjik mode. In the dialect of Chang'an (*c.*AD 600) the triplet-titles would have been similar, reading *an/kiung/tsi* (Karlgren 1957 **146 a - c**; **90 a - d**; **964 a - j**) or *an/kiun/tsi* (K. **459 a - c**). A further graphic variant of the title: 安 公 子 would also have sounded approximately the same in the dialect of Chang'an, namely: *an/kung/tsi* (K. **1173 a - f**). There is no reason, therefore, to regard 安 弓 子 or 安 弓 字 as a title different from 安 君 子 or 安 公 子 – the piece from the reign of Yang-*di* of Sui.

(2 a, iii) 'The Prince of Lanling' (Fascicle 5, and Volume 6, N.J.N., Appendix 1, p. 88; Appendix 5, p. 233) is, as we have seen, a title that originated

in the Northern Qi dynasty (550–77); certainly a piece of closely related title appeared then, in celebration of the victory of Prince Wu of Lanling at Mangshan in 564 (Fascicle 5, p. 2). Observations and arguments from analyses (N.J.N., Volume 6, Appendix 5) support the view that the surviving Entering Broaching is indeed of pre-Tang date.

(2 a, iv) The last title in the 'old music' group is a plant-reference. It appears to mean 'The Fragrance of *Pirella*' (*Sohōhi/Sufangfei*) 蘇 芳 菲. The plant, *Sufangfei*, is identified as *Pirella frutescens var. crispa* (Labiatae). This item is said by *RMS* (p. 41) to be both 'new' and 'old' music, but by *KF/HSF/RK* to be 'old'. The title is not known to the Tang lists, but the piece was clearly important in Japan, where it was played on imperial journeys and – in particular – on journeys by boat. It occurs as a single movement of nine bars in *SGYR* and *CORTYF*, but is described in the former as 'new music' and as a 'middle-sized piece' (中 曲). Since, however, the prefatory comment to the lute-tablature also states that the number of times the piece is to be played depends on the dancers, it may have been for that reason that in spite of being a single movement the piece was regarded (by *SGYR*) as 'middle-sized'. Very remarkably, the dancer's costume for this piece included a dog's head, though the shape is described as 'lion-like' (*KKS*, p. 86).

From the classification, it is evident that *Sohōhi* was undoubtedly 'old' for those who inscribed costume-remnants worn at the Eye-Opening Ceremony in 752; furthermore, from Chinese sources, the other titles in this group are to be attributed (as argued) to the last years of the sixth and the early years of the seventh centuries. Since Sui and early Tang overlapped by one year, 'old' (if used for 'Gentleman An') would apply quite as well to 'Destroying the Formations'. If, however, 564 was the year of creation of a first version of 'The piece: "The Prince of Lanling Penetrates the Formation" ', that date pre-dates both Sui and Tang dynasties.

It would seem then, that whatever meaning was ascribed to 'old' in 752, it could not mean for all four items '*antedating* the Sui and Tang dynasties'. At that time (in 752), the Japanese capital was still at Nara; and if we reckon the beginning of dateable Japanese history from 593, only one of the 'old' items perhaps originated before that date.

It is suggested then, that 'old' related rather to music as practised at the Japanese Court; that it meant items of Tang music that were 'old' in 752 from the standpoint of their date of acceptance into the repertory of the court-music. Plainly, 752 antedates by almost a century the reported return of Sadatoshi in 839 with his 'several tens of scrolls' (Fascicle 5, p. 124). It does not appear that the repertory was substantially augmented before that date.

The use of the descriptive term 'old', in relation to part of the Tang-music repertory as it existed in 752, implies the existence of other items that were not 'old' in that particular sense. Moreover, it was evidently unnecessary at that time to distinguish them as 'new' in relation to others, since the term 'new' is not used in any of the inscriptions on garments or properties. Their distinctive attributes are perhaps indicated by the class-titles of groups (2, b) and (2, c), yet to be considered. The apparent use of this particular item, *Sohōhi*, as 'background-music' on journeys by the imperial family, might be reconcilable with the other specification that the number of repeats of this item in performance is indefinitely extensible.

Finally, regarding this set of titles (Category (2, a): 'old music from Tang'), it may be significant that 'The Prince of Qin Destroys the Formations', 'Gentleman An', 'The Prince of Lanling' and 'The Fragrance of *Pirella*', all exist as *single* movements in the surviving manuscripts. The importance of this observation will emerge later.

An alternative interpretation that has to be considered is that 'old' (*ko/gu* 古) was used as a convenient, same-sounding abbreviation of the lexigraph 胡 *ko/hu*. Originally this was a Chinese name for Northern foreigners – Turkic peoples – at one time China's chief enemies. In the Tang, however, 'Hu' usually meant peoples on the Western borders, and the term was more commonly applied to Sogdians than to Turks; Hu were still foreigners, however. From a Japanese standpoint, all pieces from Tang and the other regions (categories 2–5) were 'foreign', even though not necessarily 'barbarous' – a meaning often attached to 'Hu'.

We prefer to think, however, that to the Japanese of 752, *ko/gu* 古 meant in some sense 'old'; and it is important to note that it is being so used in the Nara period. That is to say, it is so used before 797, in which year the capital moved from Nara to Heian-*kyō* 平 安 京, the new capital.

(2 b) 'Middle music from Tang' 唐 中 樂
The heading of the second category of items from Tang presents (at first sight) even greater uncertainty of interpretation than the first. By the twelfth century, and possibly earlier, the Japanese distinguished three sizes of piece in the Tang-music repertory: small, *middle-sized* and large. In China, however, only the third of these categories was used as a technical term. There, from Han times onwards, the Large Pieces (*Daqu* 大 曲) were suites. In the repertory of the seven-stringed zither (*qixianqin* 七 弦 琴) extended items are still so-called today; smaller items are referred to as 'small pieces' (*xiaoqu* 小 曲); but neither term has a well-defined structural significance. Commonly, the *xiaoqu* are pieces first learned by

a beginner; and there is no category of *qin*-pieces referred to as 'middle-sized pieces'.

This 'middle-music' category of items performed at the Tōdaiji includes three dance-pieces:

(2 b, i) 'Three Towers' (*Sandai/Santai* 三 臺);

(2 b, ii) 'Emptying the Cup' (*Keibairaku/Qingbei-yue* 傾 杯 樂); and

(2 b, iii) 'Bird(s) of the Qin River' (*Shingachō/Qinhe niao* 沁 河 鳥).

(2 b, i) A number of 'Three Towers' scores exist. The earliest notated example is the single movement in *Hyō-jō* in *GGKF* – perhaps a movement in 16 bars of 4/2, but unmeasured as written. *HFF* includes a single movement of 16 bars (in *Ōshiki-chō*), entitled 'Emperor's Three Towers' (*Ōdai sandai/Huang-di santai* 黃 帝 三 臺) described as 'new music'. *RMS* records a 'Commoner's "Three Towers" ' *Shonin sandai/Shuren santai* 庶 人 三 臺, in 16 bars (in *Taishiki-chō*) (not qualified as either 'new' or 'old'), as well as an 'Introit to the "Three Towers" ' *Sandai-en/Santai-yan* 三 臺 豔 in *Hyō-jō*). This consisted of Broaching and Quick, each in 16 bars, described as 'new music'. By the time Ōga no Motomasa wrote *RMS* (1133) the Prelude to this duplet was extinct.

(2 b, ii) The most famous 'Emptying the Cup' piece first appears either newly composed or refurbished in the reign of the Xuanzong Emperor 玄 宗 (712–55) and is linked with the performance of the Dancing Horses; but the 'making' (*zhi* 製) of a first 'Emptying the Cup Piece' in the reign of the Taizong Emperor (627–49) is only recorded in *XTS* (21, p. 471). This creation is attributed to Zhangsun Wuji 長 孫 勿 己 – as *JTS* (p. 2446) puts it: 'a good friend of Taizong from early years' 少 於 太 宗 友 善. Indeed they were probably born on the same day and their friendship continued throughout life, with Wuji becoming Chief Minister on Taizong's accession (Wechsler 1979, p. 194).

The piece was one of four ordered by Taizong to be made 'in conformity with Inner Banquet [usage]' 因 內 燕 (*XTS*, p. 471). All four items are said to have been in the *Gong* 宮 mode (Lydian) (see later, however). Unfortunately (as pointed out to us by Professor David McMullen) the *XTS* text is extremely terse. The four items are listed in sequence; but the fourth, celebrating Taizong's favourite 'Yellow piebald charger' (the horse that died under him in 650), cannot have been composed until late in the reign.

Professor McMullen suggests the translation: '[Earlier] when the Emperor [then Prince of Qin] had defeated Dou Jiande, the horse he had [then] been riding had been called *Huangzongpiao*. [Later] when he campaigned in Gaoli, this horse died on the road, and he was much aggrieved by it. He then ordered the musicians to compose the *Huangcong die qu* 黃 驄 疊 曲.' (This form of the title: 'The piece: Variants of "Yellow piebald-charger" ' is of musical interest, in that it clearly establishes a meaningful difference between *die* 疊 and *qu* 曲.) As an obviously appropriate title for banquet-usage, however, we may perhaps assume that Zhangsun Wuji's 'Emptying the Cup Piece' 傾 杯 曲 was composed not much later than 627, in the first years of Taizong's reign.

No mention of an 'Emptying the Cup' associated with Taizong occurs in *JTS*, however. The only reference to such a title in that source is linked with Xuanzong and relates to a first appearance of thirty pairs of Dancing Horses (*JTS* 28, p. 1051) and their 'doing the "Emptying the Cup" piece' (為 傾 杯 曲). No reference to *composition* of the piece is made. Conceivably this latter tune was a reworking of the earlier piece; but if so the mode was changed from Lydian (*Gong*) to Mixo-Lydian (*Shang* 商) as is the piece that survives today in *Taishiki-chō*.

Several versions in notation, made (apparently) during the Tang, have survived to this day. Two widely differing, single-movement pieces of this title are preserved in the *Dunhuang pibapu* 敦 黃 琵 琶 譜 (see Chen Yingshi 陳 應 時, 1990, pp. 3 and 10). One of these (p. 3) is in a hexatonic *Re*-mode (Chinese *Yudiao* 羽 調 on *E*), the other (p. 10) is heptatonic and ends in a Lydian *Do*-mode (Chinese *Gongdiao* on *C*). (See also Rockwell & Picken, 1998.) The entire *MS*. is probably of the tenth century. On modal grounds this piece could not be the original tune for Taizong's Dancing Horses.

The existence, however, of an item in the *Dashidiao* list (*THY*), entitled 'Yellow piebald light-foot' (see later), recalls the title of the fourth item made at Taizong's command (by a musician – *yuegong* 樂 工) in memory of the horse that died under him: 'Yellow piebald charger'. The title is given in *XTS* (21, p. 471) as *Huangcongdie qu* 黃 驄 疊 曲. In *THY*, the similar title is given as 'Yellow piebald light-foot' 黃 驄 喋.

The third and last *zi*, however, needs 馬 on the left as determinative, not 口 as shown here in 喋. Under Karlgren's **633** (p. 169), lexigraphs that shared the same phonetic as *ye* 葉 ('leaf') had sounds such as *iap* or *d'iep*, in the dialect of Chang'an. The sound of 疊 (K. **1255 a-b**) was *d'iep*.

It begins to look as if a suitable, horse-related homophone ('Light-Foot' 馬 + 葉), has been substituted for the original 'repetitions' or 'variations' (疊) on 'Yellow Piebald'. Such a substitution would have been encouraged if *piao* ('charger' 驃) were written indistinctly and read, for the sake of its sound, as if the phonetic were as in *ye* 葉. Conceivably the mode of the *Huangcongdie*-piece may have been *changed* from original Lydian to Mixo-Lydian, as the popularity of the latter mode grew during the later Tang (see Picken 1956, pp. 170ff).

A further reference to what is indubitably Taizong's 'Emptying the Cup' occurs in *THY* (33, pp. 609, 610). 'At the end of the Zhen'guan [reign-period – that is *c.*648] there was a certain Pei Shenfu whose lute-interpretations were

87

marvellous. He did three pieces: "The Slave from the Conquered Barbarians"; "Fire Phoenix"; "Emptying the Cup". The single notes were clear and beautiful. Taizong greatly loved these.' 貞 觀 末 有 裴 神 符 者 妙 解 琵 琶 作 胜 蠻 奴 火 鳳 傾 杯 三 曲 聲 度 清 美 太 宗 甚 愛 之。.

In addition to the report of Xuanzong's 'doing' 'Emptying the Cup' with 30 pairs of horses, *XTS* (22, p. 477) gives an account of a yet more elaborate presentation, with 100 pairs of horses, adding that the musicians were 'young and comely, some tens of men' 樂 工 少 年 姿 秀 者 十 數, and that 'some tens of pieces of Emptying the Cup were danced' 舞 傾 杯 數 十 曲. This is the first indication that the music of Xuanzong's item of this title consisted of a number of subdivisions (= 'pieces').

The information is important since what survives of *Qingbeiyue*, in *MSS*. later than the *Dunhuang pibapu*, is a middle-sized suite, known to Moronaga as having consisted of Prelude, Broaching and Quick, of which the first movement had already disappeared when *JCYR* and *SGYR* were compiled. Nevertheless, the Prelude was known to have consisted of 16 drum-beat periods. The surviving Broaching and Quick each consist to this day of 16 measures.

Regarding the modality of Xuanzong's version of the 'Emptying the Cup' piece, no information is given in *JTS* or *XTS*, for example. The mode-key and title-lists in *THY* (pp. 615–18), however, establish the existence (at the end of the eighth century) of two versions of this piece in the *Shang* mode in two different keys: one in the *Yuediao* (Mixo-Lydian on *D*) and one in the *Shuangdiao* (Mixo-Lydian on *G*). The surviving Broaching and Quick in *KF/HSF/RK*, however, are in *Taishiki-chō* (Mixo-Lydian on *E*).

(2 b, iii) Regarding the item: 'Bird(s) of the Qin River' (Volume 6, pp. 63, 156), the piece is described as 'old' in the prefaces to the sources in tablature. *RMS* knows only a single movement in 10 bars, to be treated as either 'new' or 'old'. *ZKKS* (see p. 65) indicates that the piece once consisted of Prelude and Broaching, and that the dances for both had disappeared by the time *ZKKS* was written. This piece – if we accept that it did indeed come into existence at the time of the canal-developments undertaken by Yang-*di* of the Sui dynasty – cannot be later than about 616. Its treatment as 'old' or 'new' in Japan (it has been suggested) was indicated by the use of the *ikko*, rather than the *kakko*, in religious as opposed to secular contexts, the *kakko* being used in the latter.

Summarising, then, information available regarding items in Category (2, b) ('Middle music from Tang'): what is common to them is that while only single-movement forms survive, all three titles are known to have existed also in forms in two or three movements. The *length* of individual movements differed: 16 bars in 'Three Towers' and 'Emptying the Cup'; 10 bars in 'Bird(s) of the Qin River'. Furthermore, versions of each item in a variety of mode-keys are reported: 'Three

Towers' in *Hyō-jō*, *Ōshiki-chō* and *Taishiki-chō*; 'Emptying the Cup' pieces in a variety of mode-keys and measure-dimensions, with a surviving two-movement version in *Taishiki-chō*.

Items in Category 2, b: i, ii and iii, did not, therefore, share a common modality or movement-length; what they shared was the attribute of being classed *together* (by *KKS*, for example, but also in the prefaces to these items in certain *MSS*.).

Items (i), (ii) and (iii) of Category (2, b) are all, however, 'middle-sized'. By age of *title*, (iii) is older than both (i) and (ii). (i) is traditionally linked (in *KKS*, for example) with the Empress Wu Zetian, Gaozong's widow, born in 623 or 624, who seized the throne in 685 and died in 705 or 706. (ii) may derive from Xuanzong's Mixo-Lydian version of the piece in *Taishiki-chō*.

What (i), (ii) and (iii) have in common is neither age nor modality, but their 'middle-sized' character, attested by their position (in *KKS* 3, pp. 49ff) in a list of items headed 'Narrative of dance-pieces inherited by legitimate family descent; middle-sized pieces' 嫡 家 相 傳 舞 曲 物 語; 中 曲 等 (the reference is surely to descent within the Koma clan). It is therefore suggested that in 752 the heading: 'Middle music from Tang' meant 'Middle-sized Pieces'.

Finally, it is to be noted that the stylistic practice of the inscriptions is *never* to use the term 'piece' as it was later used in Heian and Kamakura times in size-categories: 'small piece' (*shōkyoku* 小 曲), 'medium-piece' (that is: 'middle-sized piece') (*chū-kyoku* 中 曲) and 'large piece' (*taikyoku* 大 曲) . We are probably justified therefore in interpreting the term *chūgaku/zhongyue* 中 樂 as meaning 'middle-sized pieces from Tang'. In structure 中 樂 and 中 曲 are homologous constructions in the particular style of minimal Chinese used by those who inscribed garments, etc. after the Consecration.

There would seem to be no reason for regarding this group of items as in any sense intermediate in age, whether in the Japanese environment or in China.

(2 c) 'Popular Music from Tang'. The term for the third category of music from Tang is here translated as 'popular music' (*Tōsangaku/Tang sanyue* 唐 散 樂). The original meaning of the lexigraph *san* 散 (K.**156**) appears to have been 'to disperse'; but by Late Zhou times (say, 500 BC) meaning-extensions of 'undisciplined' and 'useless' were known (Karlgren 1957, p. 62, **156**). According to *THY*, the term had existed for generations (as *sanyue*), and such music 'was not in the Palace-Entertainment class' 非 部 伍 之 聲, but was a variety-performance of comic turns, songs and dances. 'It was called "The Hundred Turns" ' 謂 之 百 戲. *THY* lists the titles of many of these; but the list includes neither of the two items named in this third category.

One of these is a *kodatsu/huntuo* 渾 脱. [Only in Japan is 褌 (read *kun* or *gun*) substituted for 渾.] The Sino-Japanese homophone used in the inscribed dance-piece title, *hun* 渾, originally meant the sound of running water, hence 'confused' or 'turbid'. Three dance-music pieces with titles that include this binome exist in the *Tōgaku* repertory, two in *HFF*: 'Sword-Vapours *kuntou*', and 'Miss Cao's *kuntou*' (see Marett 1977, pp. 24, 25, 52, 59). (After more than twenty-years' acquaintance with the repertory, Professor Wolpert suggests this title is perhaps better translated as '*Kuntou* of the Girls from Cao'.) The first of the two *HFF* items is in *Banshiki-chō*; the second, in *Kaku-chō* (Marett, p. 9). From the specimens in *HFF*, it is evident that the *kodatsu/huntou* was a specific type of dance, musically characterised by metrical irregularity. A third *kodatsu* survives as 'Rotating-Drum *kodatsu*' (*Rinko-kodatsu/Lun'gu-kuntou* 輪 鼓 渾 脱) in *Taishiki-chō*. In the eyes of the Japanese, and on grounds of propriety rather than musical characteristics, any *kodatsu* will have been seen as of a category different from that of other items.

The placing of *Ōdai-hajinraku* in the 'popular music' category is bewildering, since the position of this item in late Heian and Kamakura scores and handbooks suggests that the piece was greatly esteemed. In its original Chang'an environment, however, the music-with-dance piece: 'Destroying the Formations', was in the fullest sense 'popular' as a Banquet-Music item. Indeed this title may be said to have become almost a National Anthem in Tang China, from its prototype ('The Prince of Qin Destroys the Formations') onwards. The energy and political stature of Taizong insured persistence of the title into later reigns, even though both music and dance evidently underwent successive transformations in time.

It is to be noted that while a category of what has here been called 'popular' music was distinguished, there is no occurrence of the term 'refined' – *ga/ya* 雅. Professor Mabuchi Usaburō (1989, 1990) has shown that early Japanese sources, such as *Shoku Nihongi* 續 日 本 記 (797) and the *Ryō* 令 (718) and its commentaries (880), referred to the imported Banquet Music as 'Tang Music': *Tōgaku*, never as *Gagaku*. The erroneous equation of 'Tang Music' with *Gagaku/Yayue* may well have arisen in the seventeenth century, among Confucianist circles of the Edo period.

As Mabuchi also shows, the term *Yayue* 雅 樂 in the ritual music and music-monographs of Chinese histories – from *Shiji* 史 記 to *Suishu* 隋 書 – has scarcely any concrete content. The term is used rather in a quasi-poetic manner, its content ideal rather than real. Even in the historical sources (as Mabuchi reveals) the term itself is used once only in relation to a concrete musical repertory: in the *Songshu* 宋 書 of Shen Yue 沈 約 (441–513), and then in regard to the restoration of ancient music, and the authorised new-composition of four *Yayue* songs.

(5) Go/Wu 吳. Finally, in regard to this Nara-period classification of musical items from China, it is important to note how many items are consigned to the category *Go/Wu*. This was an ancient province-name dating from the period of the Three Kingdoms (*Sanguo* 三 國 – AD 229–80) of Wei 魏, Shu 蜀 and Wu 吳; geographically, Wu is modern Jiangsu Province. In the Tang (763) this area consisted of portions of Huainan, Zhexi and Zhedong (Peterson 1979, p. 488). [Japanese use of the term *Go* does not, of course, refer to the late Tang and post-Tang period, when Wu became one of the Ten Kingdoms of the Lower-Yangzi delta and South-Eastern coastal area (Somers 1979, p. 789).]

In the Sui and Tang periods, Wu was a pronouncedly different linguistic region from that of North China (as indeed that region still is). The dialect of Wu differed from that of Chang'an (the Tang capital) as reflected in the *Qieyun*, 切 韻 – a pronouncing-dictionary of the Chang'an dialect from *c.*AD 600. The oldest Sino-Japanese pronunciation of Chinese lexigraphs reflects the dialect of Wu; these indeed are referred to as *Go-on* 吳 音 'sounds of Wu', and such sounds were accepted by the Japanese in pronouncing Chinese characters before use of the later *Kan-on* 漢 音 'sounds of Han' – representing the Northern dialect-area – became common.

Conspicuous among the articles classed under 'Music from Wu' are masks, many costumes or garments for Lion-Dancers, and (surprisingly) 'Emptying the Cup' again ('emptying' 傾 being written without the determinative 人), as well as many items for a piece entitled 'Drunken Barbarians' (= Sogdians?), etc.

In summary then, it is suggested that in 752 'old music' meant an item accepted into the Japanese court-repertory early in the Nara period. In Heian use, 'new' appears to have been applied to pieces acquired at a later date. In late Heian and Kamakura times, the same piece could be performed on occasion either as 'new' or 'old' music.

For 'old music' performance, the small drum in the ensemble was the *ikko* or *ichi-no-tsuzumi* 壹 鼓 (in the Nara period, a waisted, two-headed, cord-braced drum, hung round the neck, the body thereof made of glazed earthenware).

In performance as 'new music', the small drum was the *kakko* 羯 鼓, cylindrical wooden body, with two heads, cord-braced, beaten with characteristically rightangle-bent sticks on both heads. According to Harich-Schneider (1973, p. 108) alternative use of *ikko* or *kakko* continued until the end of the Tokugawa period. In the late Heian and early Kamakura sources, it is evident that percussion-treatment as 'old music' was appropriate when pieces were being played during Buddhist ceremonies.

The inclusion of *Ōdai hajin-raku/Huang-di pozhenyue* in the class *Sangaku* is perhaps understandable if, in the Nara period, the Japanese were aware of the popular character of Banquet-Music-versions of 'Destroying the Formations'. The presence of a *Kodatsu/Huntou* in this category surely indicates the 'popular' character of pieces consigned to the class.

The separate treatment of *Tō/Tang* and *Go/Wu* items suggests, perhaps, two routes of importation of items from China: (a) more immediately from Wu on the Western seaboard; (b) from the North, and ultimately, perhaps, from Tang *via* Korea.

II

It has seemed to us advisable: first, to consider the probable significance of terms used in the classification of *Tōgaku* items at the time of the Eye-Opening Ceremony at the Tōdaiji in 752, and to do so virtually without reference to later views. To the topic of later meanings, we now turn.

The useful 'Song & Dance Handbook' (*Kabu hinmoku* 歌 舞 品 目, 1857) states (五 上 古 樂, p. 269): '*Kogaku* ("*old music*") names the period of transmission of many pieces. Because this classification is used in the following section that lists various pieces, I record that opinion here.' 古 樂 コ レ ハ ， 諸 曲 ノ 傳 來 ノ 時 世 ヲ 定 ム ル 名 目 ナ リ 。 下 ノ 樂 曲 品 目 ノ 部 ニ コ レ ヲ 分 別 ス ル ニ ヨ リ テ ， コ ， ニ 其 説 ヲ 錄 ス 。

The quotation that now follows in the same handbook [taken from *Taigenshō* (*TGS*) 題 源 抄 (1510–12)] shows at once, that already by the date of this much earlier handbook, the notion of *ko* 古 had ceased to be linked merely with a period of transmission/introduction to Japan, and had become a matter of date of origin in China, as well as of transmission to Japan. *TGS* goes on to list eleven of the Chinese dynasties, back to Xia and Yin-[Shang], as if these were potential sources of 'music from China'. 'As to "Old Music": that is called "old song" which is in the old style, in the old manner of Xia and Yin. ("song" is music.) [This gloss on *TGS* (from *KBHM*) is adopted here and later.] The small beats are played with the *ikko*, and so forth. For example [the music from] the Xia dynasty... to the Chen, dynasty by dynasty, and so forth.' 古 樂 者: 古 之 風 俗 ，夏 殷 ， 舊 俗 ， 日 之 古 歌 ， ［歌 者 樂 也］ 小 拍 子 ニ 用 一 鼓 云 云 。 譬 ハ 夏 殷 周 秦 漢 魏 晉 宋 齊 梁 陳 等 之 時 ， 已 上 十 一 代 ヲ 古 ト 云 … 。

In regard to 'New Music' (*KBHM*, p. 270), *TGS* quite as confidently asserts: 'As to "New Music", in modern style, originating at the Tang Court, this is called

"New Song". ["song" is music.] The small beats are played with the *kakko*. For example [the music of] Sui and Tang from Taizong... to Wuzong...' 新 樂 者: 今 之 風 俗 唐 祚 ノ 始 成 ル 日 之 ヲ 新 歌 。 [歌 者 樂 也 。] 小 拍 子 二 用 羯 鼓，譬 ヲ 隋 唐 太 宗... 武 宗... (Here omitting the sequence of dynasties and rulers.)

Hayashi Hirokazu (this volume, p. 78), quoting from the seventeenth- to eighteenth-century *Yoshino Yoshimizu-in gakusho* 吉 野 吉 水 院 樂 書, equates *ko* with *ko koku* 胡 國, the land of the Northern Barbarians in China, while suggesting that *shingaku* 新 樂 is an abbreviation for Silla-music: 新 樂 八 新 羅 國 樂, adding that this is not a 'considered opinion'. It was indeed a view already advanced (and from the same source) in *Kabu hinmoku*. For the present, however, sufficient (and perhaps more plausible) alternatives than these of Mr Hirokazu are suggested by the sources examined.

It is certain that the inscriptions on garments and properties used at the Eye-Opening Ceremony at the Tōdaiji in 752 were not written by historical musicologists – by people like Toyohara no Sumiaki (author of *TGS*) for example – but by servants of the temple, responsible for the care of temple-property. The inscriptions may have been written forthwith, on the morrow of the great and glorious day, long before the date of the first colophon to the *Tōdaiji-yōroku*, namely, 848; but we have no evidence of this. Certainly the account of the Eye-Opening Ceremony itself was not written when the ceremony was performed. Nevertheless, the inscribed garments and properties probably bring us nearer to the technical use of terms in the Nara period than does any other source.

In his Programme-Notes (see our p. 78), Professor Kishibe Shigeo has considered items not only from the Tōdaiji ceremony of 752 but also from a ceremony some 28 years later (in 780) at the Saidaiji 西 大 寺, also in Nara. Instead of items being labelled as under (2, a) (see p. 80), the Saidaiji items are labelled in four different ways: 'Performance Music' *Gigaku / Jiyue* 伎 樂, 'Large Music from Tang' *Dai Tōgaku /Da Tangyue* 大 唐 樂; 'Music from Tang' *Tōgaku/Tangyue* 唐 樂; and 'Music from Korea' *Koraigaku/Gaoliyue* 高 麗 樂. Kishibe suggests that the two Tang-divisions, distinguished by Tōdaiji and Saidaiji, are to be equated – as first suggested (he reveals) by the late Professor Hayashi Kenzō 林 兼 三.

Terms:

	Tōdaiji		Saidaiji	
	'Old'	'Middle-sized'	'Old'	'New'/'Large'?
	Kogaku	*Chūgaku*	*Tōgaku*	*Dai Tōgaku*

Returning to Kishibe's proposed identification of Saidaiji's *Tōgaku* 'Tang Music' as 'Old Music', and *Dai Tōgaku* 'Large Tang Music' as 'New Music', it might be argued (as it seems to L.E.R.P.), that the term 'Middle-sized Music' (*Chūgaku*) should rather be equated with 'Large Tang Music' – since both religious houses (Tōdaiji and Saidaiji) make no use of the term for 'piece' *kyoku*. For both, '*gaku*' is evidently 'a piece'. And since, as shown previously, three of Tōdaiji's 'old' items are single movements, it would be rational to contrast a group of single-movement pieces with items in several movements. To contrast 'Old' with 'Middle-sized pieces' would then be reasonable. *Dai Tōgaku* might be construed as 'Large pieces from Tang' rather than 'Music of Great Tang', and would then indeed form a parallel to 'Middle-sized Pieces', in contrast to the single-movement items of 'Old Music [= pieces] from Tang'.

The eleventh-century Lute-Score of Minamoto no Tsunenobu 源 經 信 (facsimile published in 1990) includes, however, an item: *Sohōhi* in one movement; but since other items in this manuscript, known to have consisted of several movements (for example: *Shin Raryō-ō* 新 蘭 陵 王), are also represented there by single movements, no certainty can exist regarding the status of *Sohōhi*. Both in *SGYR* and *CORYF*, however, the piece of this title is an item in a single movement, with no suggestion that it ever consisted of more, even though described as a 'middle(-sized) piece'. It was previously suggested (p. 76) that the size-category may have been conferred on this piece because of its suitability for indefinite repetition.

As we have seen, attempts to distinguish between 'older' and 'newer' items, in relation to their history in China, do not fit probable dates of origin of items included in Tōdaiji's *Kogaku* and *Chūgaku* divisions (see pp. 80–89). It remains unclear why Saidaiji's *Tōgaku* needs to be interpreted as 'Old Music from Tang'. May not the preliminary assortment leading to classification have been made by separating the repertory into smaller and larger *sizes* of piece?

Of interest is the fact that music from Korea (*Koraigaku*, *Komagaku*) seems never to have been graded in regard either to size or to date of appearance in the Court Repertory of Japan. In fact, importation of music to Japan from states that became Korea (Silla, Paekche, Koma) had begun already in the second and third centuries AD according to Reid (1946). All items from that source and of that time would therefore have been 'old' in Japanese terms of date of introduction or acquisition. Indeed, examination of the titles of items of *Komagaku* performed in 752 (to be recognised from inscribed garments and properties) shows that, making allowance for some small verbal changes, virtually all the *Komagaku* items now present in the Japanese repertory (as summarised by Hirade, 1982) were perhaps already known in Japan in 752.

The role of *Komagaku* in the evolution of Japanese music (as we know it today) has surely been underestimated. The total number of *Komagaku* items performed at the Eye-Opening Ceremony in 752 amounted to about two-thirds of the total number of *Tōgaku* items performed at that time.

A highly significant Table, prepared by Mr Tōgi Shintarō (p. 78), shows an overall transfer of items from the category 'old' to that of 'new' over time, according to data recorded in the manuscripts of tablatures, and in the *Gagaku* handbooks from *RMS* (1133) onwards: *JCYR* (*c*.1192), *KKS* (1233), *Roseishō* 蘆 聲 抄 (*RSS*) (1341), *TGS* (1511), *GKR* (1690), continuing through *Kabu hinmoku* (*KBHM* 'Listing of terms relating to song and dance' 歌 舞 品 目) to the present. From this Table it is evident that the earliest handbook (*RMS*) is much less concerned to declare the 'old' or 'new' character of a given group of items than are (for example) *JCYR* and *KKS* in regard to the same set of items.

Particularly striking is the evidence (in *RSS*) that at least 14 'old' items (out of a sample-repertory of 37 titles) were to be played with *kakko* rather than *ikko*, notwithstanding their being classed as 'old'.

This entire Table surely demonstrates that no conclusions whatsoever, regarding the real age of any Tōgaku *item, are to be drawn from its designation as 'old' or 'new' in a Japanese context (age, that is, from date of origin in China).*

The signed items of clothing and dance-properties now in the Shōsō-in and believed to date from the ceremony of 752, show that 'old' items were undoubtedly 'old' in some sense from the standpoint of Nara or early Heian wardrobe-masters. The real dates of origin in China (so far as these can be ascertained) show that 'old' cannot, however, refer to date of creation of a piece in China. Items designated 'old' are evidently no older than those allocated (by their inscriptions) to the 'Middle-Music' category.

Professor Kishibe (p. 93) equated Saidaiji's *Dai Tōgaku* with Tōdaiji's *Tō chūgaku*, and both of these with Heian *Shingaku* ('new music'); but he also sets out the instruments used in performance of two categories of 'Tang Music' discriminated by Saidaiji, both of these as recorded in the 'Register of Mobile Property of the Saidaiji' *Saidaiji shizai ryūkicho* 西 大 寺 資 財 流 記 賬. The lists of instruments are profoundly – and to us, inexplicably – different. Moreover, they bear no resemblance to any previously known Japanese ensemble employed in the performance of Court Music, whether Tang Music or any other. In hand-written notes, Professor Kishibe kindly drew our attention to the difference between these lists and those for *Dai Tōgaku* and *Tōgaku* as cited in *TGS* (11, 1476). The Saidaiji list for *Tōgaku* includes no less than nine different percussion instruments along with three kinds of flute, 18 mouth-organs and a lute. *Dai Tōgaku*, on the other hand, was played by a single drum (and no other percussion-instrument), along with *kin/qin* 琴, *sō/zheng* 箏, and *kūgō/konghou* 箜 候 (angled harp).

III

From our preceding surveys (I, p. 78) and (II, p. 92), it seems probable, then, that even when the term 'old' was written on garments and dance-properties used in the Eye-Opening Ceremony at the Tōdaiji in 752, its meaning was *not* that the items (in which those garments or properties were employed) were 'old' Chinese music-with-dance items – as a *Chinese* might have used such a description; it meant only *relatively old* as an item in the Japanese repertory.

Use of the term 'old' surely implied also that, at the same time, other items present in the then repertory were not so old; but in the Nara period it was (seemingly) unnecessary to distinguish them as 'new'. It appears to have been more important to record that they were *larger* items, in terms of the number of movements of which they were composed. More movements would probably imply greater duration in performance; and that attribute may have been of importance for those required to devise a sequence of items, to be performed in the time-space of a particular ritual sequence. The fact that the 'old' movements seem all to have been *single movements* may be significant. These 'oldest' items in the repertory had presumably been brought to the Court, and to the homes of the nobility, by visiting Korean and/or Tang-Chinese musicians, before the participation of Sadatoshi (and Ōto no Kiyogami) in Ennin's journey (see Chapter 1, pp. 17, 19). Perhaps they were single-movement pieces because single movements are easier to remember.

A question remains as to why no category of 'large' pieces seems to have been recognised at this earliest date. If 'middle music' does indeed mean 'middle-sized pieces' (as has been argued), the term itself would seem to imply knowledge of a yet larger category: the *Taikyoku/Daqu* 大 曲 – the only size-category formally distinguished in the Chinese nomenclature. An answer might be that such items from the repertory (a) were not as yet performed, even if available, because of their musical demands on the performers; or (b) had not as yet been transmitted as scores to Japan, even though (through Korean and Chinese informants) Japanese musicians may have been aware of the existence of this size-category. *Taikyoku/Daqu*-scores are available in *GGKF* and *HFF*; but there is no evidence that the substance of these manuscripts was available to musicians in the Nara period.

Although the term 'new' does not occur on clothing or properties from 752, it is understandable that return (in 838 or 839) of the Mission to Tang of 838 [bringing – as alleged – 'musical scores in several tens of scrolls' (Fascicle 5, pp.

124–5; this volume, p. 20), scrolls bestowed on Fujiwara no Sadatoshi] would have flooded Court musicians with – in the most direct sense – 'new music'.

The earliest, post-Nara, classificatory use of the terms 'old' and 'new' would seem to be that in Minamoto no Hiromasa's tenth-century *Shinsen gakufu* 新撰樂譜 (otherwise: *HFF* – see Marett, 1977, 1976). Of the 48 items transcribed by Marett (1976, pp. 233–309), 15 titles are qualified by one or other of these terms. Three are said to be 'old'; twelve, 'new'. None of these 15 items, however, was heard at the Tōdaiji in 752. Of the three 'old' pieces, the title of one may indeed have been transmitted to Japan at an early date. It is the piece *Somakusha/Sumozhe* 蘇莫者.

As first suggested by Pelliot (1934, p. 104), this Chinese spelling of the name of a festival celebrated in the oases of Kuchā and Turfan suggests Sanskrit *samača: 'a gathering'. The fertility rites practised in these localities on the occasion of the festival recalled to him those of Eastern Persian *Naurōz*. It is indeed the case that this *Tōgaku* item of music-and-dance had rain-making associations, as entertainingly summarised and set-out by Wolpert (1988, p. 504).

On this matter, Eckardt (1953) surveyed relevant Chinese references from the early eighth century onwards. Of these a memorandum to the Chinese Throne suggests that the practices associated with *Sumozhe* may have been known in Tang China for some time before the dates of various memorials submitted to the Throne.in protest. The grounds for classifying *Somakusha/Sumozhe* as 'old' (in the Nara-sense) in *HFF* may therefore have been substantial.

An item classed as 'new' in *HFF* is 'Waves of Kokonor' (*Seigaiha/Qinghaibo* 青海波). It is known that this was a favourite tune of the greatly esteemed poet Li Bai, 李白; but his pleasure in dancing to this tune when drunk can scarcely have been widely known before he reached literary eminence at the Court of Tang Minghuang (Xuanzong, 712–56). It seems likely that the tune was an eighth-century acquisition from outside the territory of the then imperium. A piece that did not reach China until the reign of Minghuang is necessarily likely to have been regarded as 'new' by the Court musicians – as indeed it was stated to be by Hakuga (Minamoto no Hiromasa).

No descriptions of items as 'old' or 'new' attach to items in *Gogen kinfu* (*GGKF*): music in tablature for the Chinese five-stringed lute *wuxian/gogen* 五弦. This manuscript is now judged to be of the eleventh century, but was ostensibly written in the ninth century; its contents, however, are probably of much earlier date. The copy of *HFF* from which the surviving late copies of that *MS*. derive was also of the eleventh century; but *GGKF* contains much less in the way of related information – variant readings, for example – than does Hakuga.

HFF as it survives is a truncated version of Hakuga's original; it lacks the repertories in *Ichikotsu-chō*, *Sada-chō* and *Taishiki-chō*. Furthermore, as shown by Fujiwara no Moronaga's frequent quotations from Minamoto no Hiromasa's flute-score, the text of *HFF* as we now have it is not as extensive as was that of the version known to Moronaga. Information regarding numbers of repeats of entire pieces, or of sections of pieces, cited by Moronaga from Hakuga, and contrasting with the practice of his day, is conspicuously lacking in the text of *HFF* as now available to us in the surviving late manuscript-copies.

Thus *HFF* occupies a position intermediate in time between the documents from the *Kaigene* 'Eye-Opening' at Tōdaiji in 752, and the testimony of *RMS*. It appears to mark the first use of the term 'new' (*shin/xin* 新) as opposed to 'old' (*ko/gu* 古); and we suggest that the need for 'new' did not arise until indeed a 'new' and important increment, changing the dimensions of the repertory, reached Japan, perhaps with Sadatoshi (Fascicle 5, pp. 124, 125; this volume, p. 20), or as material collected by Ōto no Kiyogami that may have survived the loss of his person (as privately suggested by A.J.M.).

In the light of our surveys **I** (p. 78) and **II** (p. 92), it is perhaps now possible to see how the original meanings of 'old' and 'new' came to be forgotten with the passage of time, as the entire *Tōgaku* repertory assumed the character of 'old' – 'ancient' even – as the centuries rolled by. That the two terms really meant, respectively, 'what we've had in stock for some time', and 'what has just come in', will scarcely have occurred to anyone in post-Heian times. One can well understand why Toyohara no Sumiaki 豐 原 流 秋 (compiler of *Taigenshō*) felt it necessary to undertake a survey of interpretations current in the sixteenth century (p. 93).

We may surely now lay aside any thought that 'old', as applied to items from the *Tōgaku* repertory in the Nara period, ever signified items of 'old Chinese music'. By late Heian and Kamakura times, however, it is evident that compilers of sources in tablature and of the *Gagaku* handbooks, thought the term 'old' *might* imply age since date of origin in China. This is shown, for example, by the 'history' of 'Sogdians Drinking Wine' (*Konju/Hu yin jiu* 胡 飲 酒), as recounted in *KKS*, where the origin of the piece is linked with the name of a Chinese Minister of State in the fifth century BC (see Fascicle 4, p. 1). This item, a middle-sized piece, consisting of Prelude and Broaching, is described as 'old' both by *KF/HSF/RK* and by *JCYR*, *SGYR*. This perhaps suggests that by later Heian and Kamakura times, items formerly in the 'Middle Music' category (唐 中 樂) were more conveniently relegated to the 'old-in-the-repertory' category. Eckardt (1953) suggested that by the year 900 much of the Chinese evidence regarding the history of *Tōgaku* items had been forgotten in Japan.

Nevertheless, though 'old' does not and never did mean 'ancient Chinese', the first appearance in time of certain *titles* antedates the coming to power of the Tang. This does not *necessarily* mean that the associated *music*, as known to us today from the manuscripts – including even that from the oldest Sino-Japanese sources – may be regarded as pre-Tang in date. Beyond question, the title: 'The Prince of Lanling' (Fascicle 5) – a piece that celebrates a victory against the Northern Turks at Mangshan (芒 山) in 564 – is pre-Tang; and in Volume 6, Appendix 5 (p. 278) N.J.N. offers substantial evidence that the *music* of the Entering Broaching of *Ryō-ō* may well be older than that of other items of which it may have been the parent. Again, it is probable that the piece: 'A Jade Tree's Rear-Court Blossom' 玉 樹 後 庭 花, derives from a setting of a six-line lyric itself written by the last ruler of the Chen 陳 dynasty (557–87). The sources in tablature, however, refer to the former as 'old', and to the latter as 'new'. By date of origin their titles were equally old, and the music of the former may well date from the sixth century.

Chapter 4

Locational and functional names of notes in modal note-sets across Eurasia
(L.E.R.P., N.J.N.)

Introduction

It is commonly held by those interested in ethnic musics that the locational and
functional names applied to the degrees (= the notes) of diatonic octaves for
example, names such as 'tonic', 'dominant', 'mediant', etc., are so strongly
linked with Western harmonic conceptions (as enshrined in eighteenth-century
harmonic theory) that their use in the description of any non-Western music or
any Western folk-music is inappropriate. Indeed, in a generous, detailed and
judicious review of our first three fascicles, we were chided for using 'such
inappropriately loaded terms as "dominant", "sub-dominant", etc.' (Widdess,
1987, p. 178).

In our defence, it should be stated immediately that we only permitted
ourselves such usage after analysis of the frequency of occurrence, location, and

function of each note of the mode appeared to justify this. It had become evident (in the course of that analysis) that in frequency of occurrence the 'dominant' (here the fifth above the mode final) not uncommonly 'dominated' in that regard the musical structures analysed.

Respecting the susceptibilities of those who would deny to a modal final the quality of tonic – even though that prohibition too has lost force (in our view) in the light of historical data – we have consistently used the term final, but the other names for notes in their locational significance – sub-dominant, mediant, sub-mediant, as well as super-final and sub-final – are so useful for descriptive purposes in that locational significance, that we have felt justified in retaining them in that role.

In volume 6 of *Music from the Tang Court* (1998, p. 203) an essay by N.J.N. traces the source of this taboo (on the use of the terms 'dominant' and 'tonic') to its probable origin in caution originally expressed by Abraham and Hornbostel, and sets out in detail the procedure adopted by himself in the preparation of 'weighted-scales' for analytical purposes. In essence, our analyses (Picken, 1956, 1957; Nickson, 1985, 1987–99) have been variants of Hornbostel's procedure.

The discrimination of two kinds of names for notes in a diatonic octave rests on two criteria: where a note is in relation to others in a standard sequence of names; and what a note does – its function as manifested in the course of a tune. The question 'where?' (it must be understood) relates not to position in a time-sequence, but to position in a linear sequence in musical space, the ascending pitch-sequence of notes in a particular modal note-set. The sequence may be a segment of an alphabet (in the Western world), a sequence of specific note-names (in the Middle East or in South or East Asia), a sequence of pitch-names as well as a sequence of note-names (in East Asia); and such sequences may have relative or absolute pitch-values. (No attempt will be made on this occasion to discuss the etymology of note- and pitch-names – a field somewhat oddly disregarded. A few observations will be made, however, in regard to certain Chinese names, and to meaningful relationships between note-names at one time in contemporary use in Ancient China and India, pp. 207–215).

In all instances, if pitches are expressed as frequencies of vibration of a resonant material, the numerical value increases, from the member of the series of lowest frequency, upwards. In the most familiar Western case a modal note-set will consist of seven degrees, spaced in various patterns of diatonic intervals of tone or semitone; and such a heptatonic set may be transposed up or down in musical space as in the independent singing of one-and-the-same tune by children, women or men. In any octave, the direction of the sequence of pitch-frequencies is conveniently regarded in the West as rising from the lowest note on which the series begins and on which a tune most commonly ends. The note in this position in the sequence is the final. The final ends tunes in time; but it is also located in a fixed position in the modal note-set. Elsewhere in the world, scales may be thought of as ascending or descending, at various times and in different places.

With the term 'final' we confront a difficulty in classification: the discrimination of two classes of names, 'locational' and 'functional' is imperfect in a logical sense, since the two classes overlap. The final (for example) is both a locational and a functional name. This classificatory imperfection (imperfection from the standpoint of the Logic of Classes) arises from the manner in which the descriptive vocabulary developed through time. It need not trouble us. What is important is that we should not confuse locational and functional terms. Musical cultures worldwide differ in respect of the number of functions discriminated and their allocation to particular sites. From an early date the Indian system (for example) discriminated more and rather different functions (see p. 202) than did the Western system; while until recent times the Chinese system distinguished fewer functions.

Again, the term 'dominant' is conspicuously a functional term for a degree that occurs frequently in the course of a tune, at intermediate cadences as well as elsewhere, and thus (in a statistical sense) may dominate the musical structure. In the West and nowadays the dominant (in the standard tradition) is invariably a note at the interval of a fifth above the final. It has a precisely defined intervallic relationship with the final; its whereabouts in pitch-space are fixed.

In other musical cultures, a dominant – or as an approximately equivalent functional component is now called (following Widdess) in Indian music 'a predominant' – is not necessarily a note at this particular pitch-distance from the final. This was and is conspicuously so in Indian music, and is so in Middle Eastern music today. Dominants may lie, therefore, at times at other intervals than a fifth from the final.

Looking ahead, it may be helpful at this point to expand somewhat what has just been stated, and to anticipate what it is hoped to establish in the course of this essay.

From the history of terms in the Western modal vocabulary, it is apparent that the discrimination of the melodic functions of notes in tunes occurred gradually. The mere naming of degrees, regardless of function, began in the West with the use of letter-names from an alphabetical segment. This usage was borrowed from the practice of the Roman world, and by Roman authors from the Greeks in principle, though not in detail.

A first major note-function to be discriminated in the West was that of ending a chant or song: a final note became a final.

Single-note initials of tunes were discriminated in a second major functional discrimination by the tenth century and were recognised as being in precise intervallic relationship with the final; but they were not restricted to a single pitch in the note-set, as was the final. Unlike the final, their position in the modal note-set was not, and in many cultures still is not, fixed.

A third discrimination was that of the tenor or repercussa. Although the term 'tenor' appears to have been used first for a 'held' (sustained) note (as the meaning of the Latin word implies), it is probable that by the beginning of the twelfth century this term was also applied to a reciting-note in each of the Eight Tones (p. 162). The texts also suggest that tenors were notes judged suitable for ending (or beginning) intermediate phrases in a chant. Such notes were, therefore, another kind of 'final': finals of intermediate phrases (a third discriminated function). Already in the early twelfth century, tenors were notes that lay at a fifth above the final in all 'authentic' modes other than the Third Tone. They are evidently precursors of the dominants (p. 170) discriminated by the early seventeenth century.

The locations, and the functions of final, initial, finals of intermediate phrases, and of tenor/dominant, were discriminated in that process of progressive analysis of chant-structure which led, eventually, to a procedure by which chants could be classified. Other notes (of the 7-note-set) cluster about the two functional poles of final and dominant; but their distance from either (in intervallic terms) varies with the structure of each particular mode. It is nevertheless convenient to be able to refer to the location of other notes relative to the position of final or dominant, without having to specify intervallic distances.

Locational terms such as 'super-final' and 'sub-final' are handy for notes immediately above or below the final; and knowledge of the modal octave concerned will at once decide whether 'super-' or 'sub-' denotes an intervallic separation of a semitone or tone. These terms denote locations without specifying intervals; they can be used in the description of a melodic line within the context of a stated mode without need of further qualification.

From the history of note-terminology, it is evident that terms derived from Latin *medius* – such as 'mediant' – have no other significance than that of being, in some sense, 'between'. They have never carried any significance of functional mediation, in the sense in which the term 'mediation' is most commonly used; and in the West they appear in history long before the harmonic role of the interval of a third in the constitution of triads had been recognised. Originally the term 'mediant' had no harmonic implication, even though the intervallic character of mediants (as major or minor thirds) had been defined at an early stage (using the monochord), in terms of the harmonic or arithmetic division of the interval of a fifth. The mediant was the third above the final: a mean between the pitch of the final and that of the note a fifth above.

The sub-mediant is the mean between final and the fifth below the final – the fifth identified by Rameau (1726, Chapitre 7, p. 38) and by Riemann (1897) as the 'sub-dominant'. Sub-mediants too may lie at a minor or major third below the final. All these terms that relate notes – within the musical space of a modal octave – to final and dominant do not (of themselves) define pitches; they specify relative locations.

It is precisely the absence of fixed, intervallic significance in their relationships that makes the set of locational terms: final, super-final, sub-final, dominant, sub-dominant, mediant, sub-mediant, so useful in describing melodic structure; and it is to be noted, yet again, that even dominants do not invariably stand worldwide in the same fixed intervallic relationship to the final of a given mode.

Alternative systems of nomenclature – the names of notes, or their serial numbers (counting the final as '1') – are less conveniently used to define locations in relation to the polar functions of final and dominant. Their lesser convenience arises from the fact that the serial order, both of names, and of numbers, changes of necessity, with each change in mode. Any note-name or serial number may occupy the locus of every one of the locational names in turn. The locus of 'mediant' in relation to a final in one of the seven diatonic modal note-sets may be occupied by any name or number; but its character as 'mediant' will only be evident if the entire note-set is completely defined. On the other hand, the term 'mediant' (applied to a note) at once informs us that it lies above the final at a distance of a major or minor third.

As to any charge of 'ethnocentricity' in our use of both locational and functional names as in Western harmonic music, it suffices to remind readers that there is good reason to accept, as fact, that the system of seven diatonic modes was fully developed and in use, in Old Babylonia, in the second millennium BC (see pp. 106–107).

If this sketch of a view of modal octaves, in functional and locational terms, appears already unpalatably destructive of received opinions, be assured that every statement just now made, regarding evolution of the vocabulary devised for the description of anharmonic melody (that is, of melody without Western-style harmony), will be supported by the sources in original and in translation.

A journey begins; and recalling the title of this series, it will scarcely surprise the reader if we begin a journey of historical enquiry in China.

No Chinese or Japanese text has ever revealed any modal properties of the Tang *Yue*-mode (Japanese *Ichikotsu-chō*) – or indeed of any other mode of the Tang system (Picken 1969, p. 98)[1]– other than the pitch of the final (frequently also functioning as initial), together with those intervallic relationships within the note-set that are implicit in the names of the corresponding pitch-pipes. In Tang Chinese practice, the *Yuediao* was a heptatonic, Mixo-Lydian octave-species (using the Glarean nomenclature). In Moronaga's practice for lute (and, it is to be supposed, for zither also) his tablatures (but no verbal statement) show that he chose to interpret *Ichikotsu-chō* as a Lydian note-set. (See Fascicle 1, p. 27.)

It was in the hope of discovering how a Chinese composer of the Sui or Tang set about creating a piece in this first mode-key group, that N.J.N. began the process of analysis in 1980. In the light of that continuing analysis, our use of the term 'dominant' is both functionally correct in relation to melodic structure, and frequently locationally correct as well in its application (in this mode-key) to the fifth above the modal final [see for example the first Half-Section of the Prelude of 'The Emperor Destroys the Formations' (Fascicle 1, Table 5, p. 85); in the second Half-Section, the sub-mediant narrowly exceeds the fifth above the final in frequency of occurrence as phrase-final].

As familiarity with the contents of this group of items has increased, N.J.N. and L.E.R.P. have become more and more impressed by the similarity between their twentieth-century insights into these musical structures, and the practices of anonymous 'composers' of the Tang. It is possible, however, that the tune-makers of that time were wholly unconscious of the constructional procedures discriminated and named by N.J.N.: repetition, sequence, transposition and inversion, with or without variation.

The work of Thrasher (1988) has suggested that Chinese musicians of today are themselves unconscious of such practices – in the contemporary, Hakka-Chaozhou 客家潮州 instrumental tradition (for example). Such unconsciousness has been affirmed with evident satisfaction in regard to traditional Japanese musical genres (Kikkawa 1979, p. 73; 1984, p. 64). This situation should not surprise us, however, for it is surely the case that Schenkerian analysis generally reveals far more than was ever consciously present in the mind of the composer subjected to that dissection.

If, however, we find our musical susceptibilities appreciative of the compositional procedures of musicians at work more than a thousand years ago, musicians who lacked our formulated concepts – concepts that derive from modal and musical analysis of our generation – should we not at least pause to enquire

---

[1] This Table (p. 98) includes three Printer's Errors: in *Lin-chung chiao*, delete *E*; in *Hsien-lü tiao*, delete *B*; in *Pan-shê tiao*, insert *B* in line with *B*s in lines 2 and 3 of the *Yü*-group.

whether the establishing of the Western major/minor harmonic system in the eighteenth century did indeed mark so great a change (as postulated by ethnomusicologists) in concepts relating to modality and musical structure?

That question has led us inescapably to a re-examination of the history of diatonic modal systems throughout Eurasia. A first stimulus thereto came from the late Dr Benjamin Rajeczky (Musicological Institute of the Hungarian Academy of Sciences), who drew our attention to the view of Seidel (firmly expressed in *Riemanns Musik Lexikon*, 1967, p. 237): that the concept of dominant antedates the emergence of major/minor tonal music. Seidel cites seventeenth-century use of the term, applied to the fifth degree of Church Tones in their authentic condition. In that same article, reference to the use of the term 'dominant' as alternative to Repercussa, Tenor, or Tuba, in the description of the reciting-note in psalmody, already suggests a measure of historical continuity, underlying the nomenclature both of modal functions and of degrees, from an earlier to a later period. This observation again suggested the potential value of, and indeed the need for, a re-examination of the history of modal systems and of their description and classification.

It is infinitely to be regretted that in the most recent encyclopaedic review of Mode, Powers (1980, pp. 376–450) saw fit to make no mention of the fact that, 'as early as *c*.1800 BC, the Babylonians tuned the strings of a nine-stringed lyre[2] to a quasi-diatonic set of notes covering an octave + one note, in seven different "Pythagorean" octave-species at the same pitch' (Picken, 1975, pp. 601–8). The evidence for this statement had already been published in detail, and discussed at length both by Akkadian specialists and by musicologists, before the date of the latest reference in the bibliography of Powers. That same statement rested on work, over a period of years, by at least three specialists in the Sumerian – Akkadian field, and by two musicologists at home in the history of early musics of the Middle East and Greece.[3]

Powers was not alone, however, in ignoring these developments. Winnington-Ingram[4] removed mention (present in earlier of his writings) of

---

[2] Duchesne-Guillemin (1969) advocated the giant Sumerian ZAG.SAL. This name, however, now read as ZAMI (in Akkadian as *sammû*), seems to be the name of a *harp*, rather than a *lyre*, and Gurney and Lawergren (1988) argued for the horizontal angular harp with nine strings. West (1994, p. 166), however, argued for a lyre of the Sumerian type 'with its soundbox embellished at one end with the head of a bull or cow'. Recently, however, Professor Gurney (1994) has renewed the argument that the *sammû* was the horizontal angular harp, on which (as held by the performer) the row of fastenings of strings on the soundboard would mark the shortest strings as 'in front'. The player would then run up the scale in ascending pitches by plucking the strings towards his body in sequence, from front to back of the horizontal soundboard. Gurney and West now agree on the Sumerian type.

[3] For references, see Picken (1975, p. 601) and that bibliography.

[4] R.P. Winnington-Ingram, 'Greece', *I, *Groves' Dictionary...* (1980), pp. 659–72.

Babylonian 'precursors', in his most recent account of Ancient Greek Music and the Greek modal system. In Winnington-Ingram's case, the rejection of Old Babylonian evidence from the second millennium BC may have sprung from a general reluctance of classicists of an older generation to accept evidence that 'Greek' culture owed anything of significance to the Orient.

In the case of Powers, it seems that he did not wish to examine historical interconnections. The sequence in which he examines non-European modal systems is (coincidentally) largely that of their hypothesized transmission eastwards and in time (as set out in Picken 1975, pp. 600–9); but he makes no suggestion of any such relationship between the terms of this sequence. Fortunately, a recent study of Hurrian musical texts by an eminent scholar in the field of Greek music at last makes public, in that context also, the authentic priority of the Old Babylonians as the first to utilise a set of seven diatonic octave note-sets in the composition of song-melodies (West, 1994).[5]

It is one thing to express caution, or indeed scepticism, in regard to new findings in any field; it is quite another to fail to mention evidence.

Of particular importance, as it seems to us, is the fact that the Old Babylonian tuning-techniques were applied to separate strings attached to a lyre-yoke or to the arch of a harp. These procedures resulted in the tuning of open strings as seven different diatonic modal note-sets (see West, 1994, pp. 165–7). The manner of retuning between modes has recently been set out again, in detail, by Gurney (1995), in a re-examination of text *UET* VII 74 (a fragmentary text from Ur, previously published by him in 1968). This tablet confirms not merely what cyclical tuning achieved for each mode, but how re-tuning from one diatonic mode to another was effected by operating on the tritone.

In one procedure, one member of the tritonic set is tuned up a semitone from one mode to the next; in the other, one member is tuned down by a semitone at each transition. Whatever theoreticians may have had to contribute, by way of rationalisation and standardisation, such a contribution could only have been made subsequent to the satisfaction of the requirements of singers, and subsequent to the established practice of instrumentalists accompanying their own performance or that of others.

In any re-examination of the origins and history of Eurasian modal systems, it is today essential to begin with the information that has come to us from the second millennium BC. It is also essential to remain aware of the practical needs of instrumental performance. Furthermore, it is to be stressed that the living

[5] West, M.L. (1994) 'The Babylonian Musical Notation and the Hurrian Melodic Texts', *Music & Letters*, 76, pp. 161–179.

folk-music traditions of the relevant geographical regions must of necessity be examined, when considering any account of the history of diatonic modal systems – the folk-musics of countries of the Mediterranean Basin, from East to West, as well as those of the countries of Eastern and Western Europe to the North.

Judging from lists of references, it is plain that neither Isobel Henderson (1957), Winnington-Ingram (1936, 1956, 1980), nor Chailley (1964), felt impelled to refer to any studies of surviving folk traditions in these regions.

Chailley (1964, p. 4) described as a chimera the objective of the attempt [made in the ninth-century *Alia musica* ('Other Things Musical')] to achieve a synthesis between (1) the writings of the last Latin commentators on Greek music, and (2) the body of chant peculiar to the Western Christian Church. He justly states: 'Ecclesiastical chant descended from traditions without any relationship with classical Greek music.' (*Le chant ecclésiastique était issu de traditions sans aucun rapport avec la musique grecque classique.*)

Nevertheless, as first pointed out by Baud-Bovy (1978), the continuity of language (both spoken and written) and of beliefs, in Greece, over a span of more than three thousand years, of itself encourages one to suppose that the living musical traditions of the folk, in Greece today, may yet preserve types of melodic structures of historical importance. At the other end of Eurasia, the persistence of types of musical construction over a span of twelve hundred years and more, perhaps even over two-and-a-half millennia, is now established (Picken *et al.*, 1981–99).

Chailley went on to add to his previous strictures: 'This [= classical Greek music] had died without posterity; the tetrachordal system had existed, the "tonoi" of tessitura no longer corresponded to any practical notion; of the three Greek *genera*, two had disappeared [chromatic and enharmonic], and only the diatonic remained in use.' (Celle-ci était morte sans descendance; le système tétracordal avait vécu, les 'tonoi' de hauteur ne correspondaient plus à aucune notion pratique; des trois genres grecs, deux avaient disparu, et le diatonique restait seul en usage.)

He wrote injudiciously if he intended his statement to imply that, with the passing of Ancient Greece, melodies of the compass of a tetrachord, and the use of tetrachords as building-units in musical structures, had vanished from the earth. The music that survives today in Mainland Greece, throughout Thrace and Anatolia, and in Macedonia, as 'folk tradition', is not necessarily a 'genetic' descendant of any once extant, classical Greek music; but all over this area tetrachordal structures are very much alive and in evidence at the present time.

Further to the West, and in the body of ecclesiastical chant itself, the importance of tetrachordal structures is conspicuous. This is markedly so in the most ancient elements of Ambrosian and Hispanic/Mozarabic chant.[6]

Still further West, perhaps the most archaic melodies of the Irish repertory, preserved by Bunting (1840),[7] are constructed from a pair of tetrachords, conjunct or disjunct. The late and much regretted Samuel Baud-Bovy (1967, 1978) has furnished examples of Greek folksong in which the essential notes are a trichord of fourth and major tone. It is to be deplored that his work should have been persistently overlooked or ignored.

Further afield, but still in the cultural zone of Ancient Greece, namely in Anatolia, song-melodies (to be heard today) may consist of a descending chain of fourths, conjunct or disjunct – again a demonstration: that musics of which tetrachords are the building-units are still extant (Arsunar, 1962). Numerous examples are to be found, in particular in the category of 'long song' (*uzun hava*), in the first comprehensive survey of Anatolian Turkish folksong by Sipos (1994).

The existence of chains of tetrachords does not mean, however, that melodies of octaval, or greater, compass do not exist today, side-by-side with these more 'archaic', non-octave types. Tunes of octave-compass are to be found over the entire area; in certain districts pairs of disjunct tetrachords may predominate in certain types of song. (All folksong-traditions are, of course, to be interpreted as diachronically stratified, preserving both archaic and more recent melody-types.)

In Turkish art-music also, the complex *makam* are frequently extended upwards by a tetrachord or pentachord; and in modal exposition of the so-called *basit* ('simple') *makamlar* – as in a *taksim* before a song – melodic evolution tends to proceed by tetrachords, from lower to upper tetrachord – or conversely – in accordance with the convention attaching to a particular *makam*.

Yet further afield, Jairazbhoy (1970, *passim*), in describing practices of the North Indian, Hindustani tradition, noted a division of the octave into balanced conjunct or disjunct tetrachords in rāga-exposition. And again as shown by Widdess (1980, p. 126 and Table IV) the most frequently used range of melodies,

[6] Anglés, Higini (1954) 'Latin chant before St Gregory', *New Oxford History of Music*, 2; see, for example, specimens of Ambrosian recitatives (pp. 65, 67); the antiphon-formula Dominus dixit ad me, p. 69; the Kyrie eleison from the Gallican Office, p. 76; and in particular the Hispanic/Mozarabic Paternoster, perhaps of the fourth century. See also Dom Jean Claire (1962, 1963), this volume, p. 120.

[7] Bunting, Edward (1840) *The Ancient Music of Ireland arranged for the piano forte To which is prefixed A dissertation on The Irish Harp and Harpers, including an account of the Old Melodies of Ireland*, Dublin: Hodges and Smith. Chapter VI: notices of the more remarkable pieces and melodies of the collection, pp. 83–9; music pages *post* p. 88 'Lamentation of Dieidre for the sons of Usneach' (III. *Neaill glubh a Dheirdre*) item 1; 'The battle of Argan More' (V. *Argan Mór*), item 3.

in the second chapter of the Saṅgitaratnākara of Śārngadeva (first half of the thirteenth century) is an octave extended upwards by a tetrachord. (See also Widdess, 1995.) Indeed the existing grāmarāga-melodies 'normally remain within a range of not more than an octave and a fifth…' (Widdess, 1975, p. 273).

The need for a theoretical procedure by which to generate different modal octaves within the same pitch-limits (as on lyres and harps) disappeared in the West with the development of an unaccompanied vocal tradition and repertory in the Christian Church, both East and West; but the image of the Greater Perfect System of the Greeks, in its double-octave form, with added lowest note, lived on for the post-Carolingian theoreticians. It is indeed the case, as Chailley stressed, that Western Europe and the North exhibit only the diatonic genus; but in countries of the Eastern Mediterranean, and increasingly as one travels East and South therefrom today, the incidence in folk-musics of chromatic tetrachords becomes conspicuous.

In all three statements, therefore, Chailley's résumé was in some respects incorrect.
The advent of Indo-Europeans in the territory of mainland Greece did not occur until about 2000 BC (Murray, 1989). The territory of Greece was of course populated long before that event, and there is abundant evidence of this in the language and mythology of Ancient Greece, as well as in the place-names of Greece, both today and in Antiquity.

The most probable homeland for the Proto-Indo-Europeans, however, appears today to have been the territory between the Black and Caspian Seas. Even in that territory, however, there is no evidence of their presence before, say, 4500 BC. Their presence there is made probable (in particular) by evidence of extensive linguistic contact between them and their immediate neighbours to the North of that hypothesised homeland, speakers of Finno-Ugrian languages (Murray, 1989) in the region between Volga and Dnieper.

While close affinities between Vedic Sanskrit and the Old Iranian Language of the Avesta are recognised, there is evidence that 'attests the existence of a very archaic form of the Indic language as early as 1600 BC' and again 'this indicates that a separate Indo-Aryan language had already diverged from Iranian by this time and that the putative period of proto-Indian-Iranian "unity" must predate this, perhaps by as much as a half-millennium or more.' (Murray, 1994, p. 38.) This implies a period of unity falling within the third millennium BC. Remembering that 'there are possible (though disputed) Indic traces in the names of a few gods revered by the Kassites', and that these people were 'the dynasty from the Zagros region [in Iran] that assumed control of the Babylonian empire'

110

– may not one sentence, concerning string-length ratios and pitch-relationships, have been carried further eastwards by a lyrist or harpist, a sentence that derived ultimately from observations made by musicians of Old Babylonia in the second millennium BC? Such a sentence might have been carried by one of those first to ride horses in their original homeland – between the Black and Caspian Seas – an Indo-European of Western Asia. The Chinese in fact reported that their knowledge of the ratios came from Daxia 大夏, namely Bactria.

'Diffusion', 'Transit', 'Transmission', 'Transport' of ideas and artifacts

Both anthropologists and archaeologists may well be critical today of a vague 'diffusionist' approach to the history of modal theory, and of reference to 'transmission' or 'transfer' of musical instruments. Let it be stated at the outset: our ideas assume no 'migrations'. We require as mechanism nothing more than that which can be transmitted in speech from one person to another; transmitted to one person given access to a written document, or receiving an instrumental demonstration.

A perfect example in action of the essential process as we conceive it, has been provided by Edward James (1982, p. 109)[8] in his tracing of 'the slow movement of particular customs from one monastery to another across Gaul…'. His example follows the progress of the practice of 'perennial praise' (laus perennis) by which, in any monastery, a group of the community is always at its devotions, thanks to the organisation of a shift-system.

Coming originally from Constantinople, the practice is first recorded in Gaul at St-Maurice d'Agaune in 515; then, successively, at Chalon-sur-Saône in 585, at St-Denis in the seventh century, and in the eighth century at Tours, St-Riquier and elsewhere. This amounts to a speed of radiation, from St-Maurice d'Agaune to St-Riquier, of 600 km in the space of at least two centuries (say from 515 to 715).

It was Kroeber (1940) who first distinguished clearly between 'direct diffusion' and what he was first to name as 'stimulus diffusion'. Of the former process, the history of music in East Asia affords unambiguous examples: (1) the transmission to China in the sixth century (by a Kuchean musician) of knowledge of seven diatonic modes derived from the Indian system (this volume pp. 205–213); (2) the transmission to Japan of knowledge of Chinese arithmetico-acoustic theory, and of musical scores from the Court Entertainment musics of the Sui and Tang dynasties; (3) the transmission to the Korean Court (as a political bribe) of musical scores and instruments for the performance of

[8] *The Origins of France: from Clovis to the Capetians, 500–1000* (1982), p. 109.

111

Confucian *Yayue* ('Refined Music') in the reign of the Huizong Emperor (1101–26) of the Song dynasty.

Our concern (in 1975) was (and still is) the role, in hypothesised processes of transmission, not merely of 'direct diffusion' but of 'stimulus diffusion'. Kroeber (1940, p. 20) characterised the latter phenomenon as 'new pattern growth initiated by precedent in a foreign culture'. Needham (1954, I: pp. 244ff) wrote: '…the wholesale taking over by one people from another of idea-systems or patterned structures is not a necessary supposition. A simple hint, a faint suggestion of an idea, might be sufficient to set off a train of development which would lead to roughly similar phenomena in later ages, apparently wholly independent in origin.'

Later (1965, IV:2, p. 6), when well advanced into the fifth discrete volume of his gigantic work, and in his introduction to the topic of Mechanical Engineering, Needham observed: 'Hardly anyone in the Middle Ages would have noted that technology had a history, but at the Renaissance it gradually dawned on historians that the ancient Romans did not write on paper, knew nothing of printed books, and used no collar harness, spectacles, explosive weapons or magnetic compasses.'

Among the works of the Renaissance that draw attention to inventions to which 'the whole of antiquity has nothing equal to show' (the same, p. 7) particular mention may be made of the *Nova Reperta* (New Discoveries) of Johannes Stradamus, completed in 1638 (see Needham), wherein of nine new discoveries and inventions, six 'were directly derived, at the very least by stimulus diffusion, from China'.[9] These six were: (1) the magnetic compass, (2) gun-powder weapons, (3) the printing press, (4) the mechanical clock, (5) silk, (6) the stirrup.

If it be objected that in the discussion of the history of modal systems we are dealing with ideas, with concepts, not inventions and techniques, we must insist that these ideas were not merely conceptual aspects of their tuning-procedures. The failure to recognise and explain the practical roots of these 'idea-systems' (as Needham would call them) accounts for the failure of generations of recent scholars to make plain (to any musically interested reader) the practical purpose of any particular exposition of modal theory, from post-Carolingian times to the present.

It is not proposed to set out again the stages in the apparent eastwards transit of knowledge of an arithmetical finding, a ratio, a relationship between lengths of resonating agents, such that their equivalent pitches were at the consonant

---

[9] Particular instances of stimulus diffusion are discussed in some detail on pp. 271, 476, 533, 544, of Needham, IV: 2.

interval of a perfect fifth – a ratio, whether expressed as 2 : 3 or 3 : 2, a relationship capable (without further knowledge) of generating in theory, among literate peoples from Old Babylonia to China, musical systems comprising seven different diatonic octave note-sets.

It need only be emphasised that for China, Japan and Korea, we have documents – not merely written texts, but instruments – that make plain both the occasion of a critical transfer of information, and the role of instruments as vehicles in that transmission.

It is proper now, however, to consider the relatively late transmission of modal ideas Westwards from the Greeks – via Roman authors – to the Europe of the early Middle Ages, as part of the same secular processes (processes extending over time) of both direct and stimulus diffusion.

Long before the elucidation of Old Babylonian tuning-procedures, Robinson (1962, p. 177) had suggested 'that there radiated east and west from Babylonia the germ of an acoustic discovery which was developed in one way by the Greeks and in another by the Chinese…'. In the context of the present exposition, Robinson's conclusion may be amplified: 'developed in one way by the Greeks and their neighbours to the West, and in other ways by the Arabs (direct inheritors of the Greek theorists), by the Persians, and ultimately by the Chinese, Koreans and Japanese'.

From a previous account of an apparent eastwards transmission of modal systems (Picken, 1975, p. 601) it is plain that, as the Greeks made original use of certain elements only of Old Babylonian theory, so too the Chinese used the cyclical procedure – the theoretical generation of quasi-octave-sets by a cycle-of-fifths tuning-sequence – in original, non-Greek and non-Babylonian ways. Indeed, one might extend the sequence of transformation of what was received by the Chinese to that which Heian and post-Heian Japan made of the Chinese system – and, for that matter, what the Koreans made of it. Always, the process of stimulus diffusion exhibits selection, rejection and local modification of whatever elements of a given idea-system were offered at source.

In recent years, it has become increasingly clear that, like the Old Babylonian procedure (of the second Millenniun BC) for changing from mode to mode by operating on the tritone, like the Greek theoretical procedure (of the fourth century BC) for generating seven different, diatonic note-sets within the same, fixed pitch-limits, the generation by the Chinese in the fifth century BC of a 12-note 'octave' (never so regarded by the Chinese) did not necessarily depend on knowledge of any kind of 'cycle-of-fifths' procedure. The Chinese development seems rather to have emerged from empirical observations of the acoustic properties of bronze bells of a particular configuration (our p. 199). Only at a later date is there textual evidence of Chinese knowledge of the cyclical procedure, and even then the arithmetico-acoustic knowledge that it embodied was used primarily as a theoretical development, giving intellectual satisfaction to those whom we would call, in today's terms, theoreticians, mathematicians, acousticians, rather than performing musicians.

Not until the time of Jing Fang 京房 (*fl.*45; *d.*37 BC) (see *Hou Hanshu* 候漢 書, 11, 3a–16a) is there documentary evidence of the use of a stringed instrument in tuning-operations on bronze bells. Such an instrument was used by Jing Fang in his extension of the cycle-of-fifths procedure, first documented in the third century BC (see later). (Reports in the Guoyu 國語 – containing late Zhou 周, Qin 秦, and Han 漢 materials – do not state of what material the pitch-standards were made; and that source is, in any case, too late to be regarded as evidence of the practice of the Zhou in tuning bells.)

As with Greek lyrists and kitharists, in China also, tuning was achieved by empirical methods in which the skill of the craftsman and the ear of the musician (at times the same person) were all that was necessary. The tuning-practice of instrumentalists in China still today relies on tuning to consonances judged perfect by the ear, whether the instrument be a lute, a zither, or a free-reed mouth-organ; and recent investigations into the tuning of bells have established that the Chinese had no need, in the fifth century BC, of any set of pitch-pipes to guide them in generating remarkably accurately tuned sets of bells (Ma, 1981; Picard, 1986; Falkenhausen, 1993).

The tuning of Chinese stringed instruments today rests entirely on the tuner's judgement of the perfection of fifths, fourths, octaves and unisons. On the seven-stringed zither (*qin* 琴), the perfection of unison between harmonics may be used as a final refinement of the tuning process. In the tuning of the free-reeds of mouth-organs (Chinese *sheng*; Japanese *shō* 笙), the perfection of fifths, fourths and octaves is judged by ear; but though the process takes place in Japan in a standard 'cyclical' sequence, it is not a 'cycle-of-fifths' procedure.

The tuning of ancient Chinese cast-bronze bells, intensively examined in recent years as a result of archaeological finds between 1957 and 1978, has revealed wholly unexpected use, made by the bell-founders and tuners, of the acoustic properties of bells that are not radially symmetrical in cross section about the vertical axis, but bilaterally symmetrical. The cross-section is not ellipsoidal (as is that of many cast animal-bells all over the Middle East), but has the shape (see diagram beneath) of a leaf-like segment (properly a 'lune').

In general, a lune is the figure enclosed by the intersection (on a sphere or plane) of two circles of equal radius. A bilaterally symmetrical, leaf-like lune results when their centres are equidistant from the plane that passes through the points of intersection. (For detailed studies of bells of this conformation, see Falkenhausen, 1993.) In bells that are lune-shaped in cross-section, the pointed ends of the lune act as acoustic nodes; as a consequence the bell yields two notes of different pitches at different points of striking (see diagram below).The precise pitches obtained depend on differential thinning of the wall.

Diagram 1. Geometrical construction generating the curve known as 'Lune', also showing, diagrammatically, carved-thickness of bell-wall, and striking points for contrasting pitches

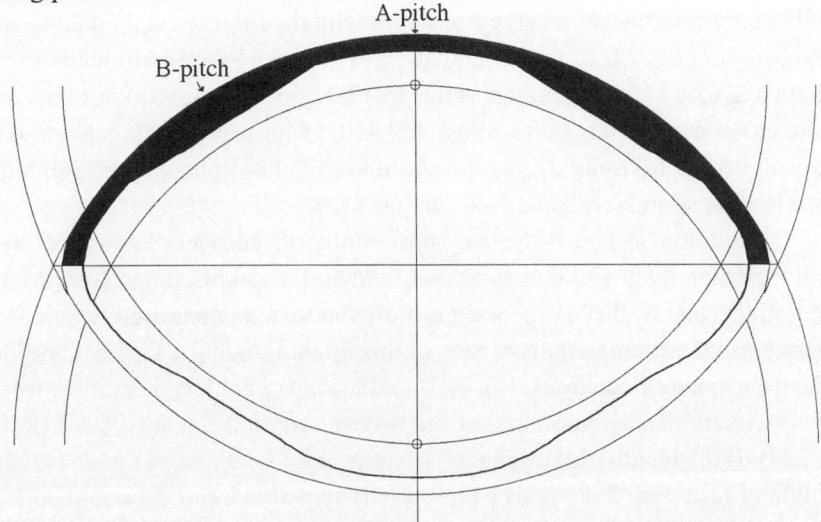

Over the centuries, the preferred practice of the founders and tuners came to be such that the pitch-difference (between the two notes yielded by one bell) was either a minor or a major third. The latter type is only about half as numerous as the former (Liang, 1985, pp. 70–5; Picard, 1986, p. 9). Falkenhausen (1993, p. 85) notes 44 bells with a minor third difference and 20 with a major third difference among the bell-chimes of Marquis Yi of Zeng. From the ancient Chinese nomenclature of the striking-points, there can be no doubt that the fabrication of two-pitched bells became a conscious goal. Furthermore, by making use of the lower pitch (the A-tone), as well as of the pitch a minor or major third higher (the B-tone), scales could be assembled. In effect quasi-chromatic scales of semitone-degrees in sequence, composed of chains of interlocking thirds, were available by the Mid- to Late-Zhou Period (say 475–221 BC).

From the evidence of these two-pitched bells, we can be certain that no knowledge of 2/3 and 4/3 ratios applied to bamboo-tubes, for example, were *necessary* to facilitate the achievements of bell-founders and tuners in China in the fifth century BC. Falkenhausen suggests, however, that pitch-pipes might have been used as a refinement in the tuning-procedure, since the tuning of some sets suggests that already, at this date, knowledge of the string-tuning-principle known as *san fen sun yi fa* 三 分 損 益 法: 'the rule of adding or subtracting a third' existed among the bell-founders and tuners (Falkenhausen, p. 301). It seems certain, however, that this was only applied at that time to the tuning of 'notes' (*yin* 音) in a scalar set, and not (as later) to the tuning of pitch-standards.

It is evident that the teasing, arithmetico-acoustic problem of the cycle-of-fifths procedure: that an octave consonant with the fundamental could never be reached (no matter how far extrapolation of the cycle were continued), excited Jing Fang (p. 114) to extend the series of 12, to 60 pitches, working with a thirteen-stringed tuner; and in about AD 450, Qian Lezhi 錢 樂 之 [Astronomer Royal of the (Liu) Song dynasty] was led to calculate values to the 360th term (see Robinson, in Needham, 1962, 4:1, p. 219).

In addition, as late as the late 16th century, Prince Zhu Zaiyu 朱 載 堉 was still experimenting with bamboo-pipes, and both recognised the existence of the end-effect (that is, that a pipe sounds more flat than its measured length warrants), and attempted to correct for this by introducing a factor related to the diameter in his calculations. His most extraordinary achievement, however, was the discovery of the importance of the twelfth root of 2 – that is: $12\sqrt{2}$ (Robinson, p. 223). If the length of the primary string is unity – let's say at pitch C – the length of the string that yields a pitch a half-step above C ($C^\sharp$) would be $1/12\sqrt{2}$. That length, say x, divided in turn by $12\sqrt{2}$, would yield D, and so on. Prince Zhu almost certainly worked this out on strings, and then turned his attention to pipes.

Again we see an entirely theoretical, mathematico-acoustical, Chinese, line of enquiry, very different from – yet in its theoretical character similar to – the intellectual activities of the Greeks themselves in 400 BC at the latest. It seems to us that the very uselessness, in practical terms, of knowledge of the properties of strings of different lengths, to a people already capable of remarkably accurate tuning of chromatic octave sets of bells, using empirically developed procedures of the fifth century BC, speaks for the impact of some prestigious piece of information suddenly coming into the system from outside.

And why, one may ask, if this knowledge was not imported, was the process of generating the pitch-pipes specifically linked with geographical regions that lie to the West of China, whither travelled (according to Lü Buwei 呂 不 韋, writing in the third century BC) Ling Lun 伶 倫 (a late addition to the pseudo-historical list of 'Discoverers'), even to Daxia 大 夏, commonly equated with Bactria?

'As Pythagoras to the East, so Ling Lun to the West' (Robinson, 1962, p. 176). In the European environment, the same type of observation is to be made. The

Greeks did not adopt the method by which the Old Babylonians modulated from one octave-species to another by operating on the tritone. The post-Carolingian, Latin-writing theorists in their turn took (and we must suppose gratefully) from writers such as Martianus Capella (for example) the nomenclature and structure of tetrachords and pentachords, but rejected – or at least in due course lost interest in – the Boethian exposition of seven different *tonoi* generated by modulation within the space of an octave.

The Western theorists preferred a double-octave system of toni (= Tones) in which top-tail inversion, rather than retuning, generated different octave-species. And always it must be remembered that, while the Greeks may have had no need of Pythagoras in order to generate 'Pythagorean' scales (as Winnington-Ingram observed), so too the Gregorian melodies of the Roman Church originally owed no debt to any precedent theoretical system. As Anglés (1956, p. 111) remarked, the idea of classifying Gregorian melodies 'according to the *Oktoechos* [the Byzantine family of eight modes] is no older than the eighth or ninth century', though the Byzantine *Oktoechos* itself goes back to Severus, who was the Monophysite Patriarch of Antioch from 512 to 519. [Regarding the Theory of Music in Byzantium see most recently (and worthily), Richter (1998).]

The system of modal classification was constructed in order to codify and classify melodies that had been written, and collected together, centuries earlier. The *Oktoechos* itself became a feature of Byzantine practice: '…the systematic use of modes through the liturgical year… the eight-week cycle of hymns… a week of hymns in the first mode… followed by a week of hymns in the second mode…' (see Abraham, 1979, p. 64). The Western practice had originated in the Syrian Church; but let us not forget the comparable Chinese practice of changing key and mode each month in performance of the hymns of Confucian ritual, from the Han dynasty onwards. The texts of these latter hymns go back at least to the fifth century BC, and elements of their music may well be of the same date (Picken, 1969, 1977).

What makes the Western European history of modal theory of such interest is, in part, that we can plainly see 'stimulus diffusion' in operation in this context, since we have available not merely the original documents that furnished a major stimulus – Martianus Capella and Boëthius, for example (to name but two) – but also the treatises of the later, Western European, Latin-writing authors from the ninth, tenth and eleventh centuries onwards. These two types of document show both what was offered and what was accepted, according to the needs of the recipients.

As an East Asian parallel, we know the year – probably AD 589 – in which a first demonstration of seven heptatonic octave-species was made to Chinese musicians by a lutenist from Central-Asian Kuchā (p. 205), and we may plausibly suppose (in view of the known cultural bonds between Kuchā and South Asia) that at least some elements of early Indian musical theory and practice[11] were at that moment available and accessible to Chinese musicians had they wished to accept them. Evidently, in the light of later Chinese musical history, they did not so wish.

Again, we can see, from Tang sources, what was available to Japanese musicians; yet the Sino-Japanese modal system, as exemplified in the surviving *Tōgaku* repertory, has its own distinctive features (see Chapter 7), notwithstanding its evident derivation from the system of 28 modes of the Tang (four diatonic octave-species, each in seven keys), as set out in *Yuefu zalu YFZL*.[11]

The diffusion analogy and the role of need

In the literal sense the Latin verb *diffundo – fudi – fusum* means no more than 'to pour out on all sides'. What causes such an overflow and spread of an idea-system? Molecules of a substance in solution wander from a region of higher to one of lower concentration, and at constant temperature the rate of movement is directly proportional to the difference in concentration between the two regions. If complete ignorance of any cultural trait be equated with zero-concentration, one might imagine a uniformly advancing, circular wave – the advancing front of an idea-system – steadily spreading from its point of origin, throughout human societies the world over.

Observation shows, however, that this did not happen to the arithmetico-acoustic idea that related string-length ratios to musical intervals. In fact, the echoes of Old-Babylonian and Ancient-Greek modal conceptions appear to have excited far more extensive developments in Europe and the Middle East, than in East Asia; the non-Islamic musical cultures of Africa south of the Sahara appear to have remained largely untouched by those conceptions. Surely, stimulus diffusion is facilitated where there is, culturally speaking, not zero-concentration,

[10] The relevant passage from the Sui History (Suishu 隋書, 14) had previously been translated in part by Picken (1955, p. 4); Gimm (1966, p. 209); and by Wolpert (1975, pp. 106–11). The relevance of this passage to the Indian modal system, as seen in the Kuḍumiyāmalai Inscription has been discussed most recently by Widdess (1980, pp. 21–5; 1995, pp. 104–24). Some features of svaraprastara (the note-permutation technique with which Widdess compared melodies from that inscription) seem to be present in surviving melodies for song-texts of the Shijing, preserved by Zhu Xi (Picken, 1956, 1957). See also this volume, p. 233.

[11] See translation by Gimm, 1966, p. 543, and reconstruction of the modal system (from data given in *YFZL*) by Picken (1969, pp. 92–100). Note corrections on p. 105, n. 1, of this volume.

118

but a negative pressure: a suction-force arising from a need that requires satisfaction.

We know that the Old Babylonians made use of *their* recognition of modal differences in the classification of songs into modal groups (Duchesne-Guillemin, 1969, pp. 3–11; for details see West, 1994, p. 170, and more recently Gurney, 1995, p. 101). It is here-and-now suggested that the suction-force that led to the sustained stimulus diffusion of the idea-system of the diatonic modes, westwards and eastwards from the Fertile Crescent, and later from Greece westwards, was a local need to classify tunes. The need was not peculiar to Europe; it was also conspicuous in the Middle-Eastern world.

Though there are no references to a relationship between string-length ratios and pitches in the early musical literature of South Asia, it is certain that songs (and later rāgas) were being classified already in the second half of the first millennium (private communication from Widdess, 1998). The need was scarcely less pressingly felt in East Asia. General familiarity on the part of song-poets (= lyricists) already in the Han (206–23 BC, AD 25–220) is demonstrated by designation of the mode to which lyrics were to be sung, as in the collection of popular songs and ballads of the Han dynasty [translated by Anne M. Birrell (1988) as *Popular Songs and Ballads of Han China*]. Though not shown by the translator, the texts in Chinese always display the mode to which they were to be sung. It is reasonable to suppose that melodies were freely devised by singers, given that information only, together with the rhythmic implications of the text itself.

The monograph entitled 'The Treasury of the Drum of the Jie' (perhaps a Turkic people) 羯 鼓 錄 *Jiegulu* (*JGL*), by Nan Zhuo 南 卓 (*fl.* 847), lists tunes by title under three pentatonic degrees (out of the five). This cataloguing-procedure would seem to imply discrimination of tunes that make use of three different pentatonic note-sets: 123.56; 23.56.1; 3.56.12. At the beginning of that monograph a statement about the pitch of the drum-sound is made: 'Its note's [or notes'] ruler is *Taicu*' 其 音 主 太 簇 – that is, the note that lies a tone (that is: two semitone degrees = 2 *lü* 律) above the fundamental of the entire system, the *Huangzhong* 黃 鐘 pitch.

If we accept a value of *D* for *Huangzhong* during the Tang, this statement implies that the initial of the *Gong* mode (123.56), starting on *Taicu*, would be *E*. The heptatonic form of this octave-species would then have been $E\ F^{\sharp}\ G^{\sharp}\ A^{\sharp}\ B\ c^{\sharp}\ d^{\sharp}$. If *Taicu* is 'to rule', to dominate in the Chinese hierarchical sense, *E* must have been the final of all three designated modes associated with the sound of this drum: *Gong*, *Shang* (23.56.1) and *Jiao* (3.56.12). The corresponding heptatonic series of the two latter would then be: $E\ F^{\sharp}\ G^{\sharp}\ A\ B\ c^{\sharp}\ d$ and $E\ F^{\sharp}\ G\ A\ B\ c\ d$. The three octave-species would correspond to Glarean Lydian, Mixo-Lydian and Aeolian on *E*. (The modal range of *Tōgaku* items is discussed later in Chapter 7.)

This same classificatory modal usage is also a feature of the musical traditions of the Middle Eastern and Islamic world in general.

The need of the Western Church for a classificatory basis on which to organise the vast body of liturgical music that had accumulated in the various centres of cultic evolution and development, seems to have reached a peak of urgency in the eighth or early ninth century.

Dom Jean Claire (1962, p. 196) commented (as did Higini Anglés) that the organisation of the repertory of Gregorian chant according to the Byzantine *Oktoechos* (see p. 107) was not a point of departure (in the history of the plainchant-tradition), but a conclusion. It marked 'the last and quasi-definitive formulation' (la dernière et quasi-définitive mise en forme) of melodies of the liturgical repertory. The idea of using the Byzantine system in classification is no older than the eighth or ninth century, as Anglés stated, even though that system itself was earlier . There is no possibility, then, that *composition* of Gregorian melodies (let us say between the sixth and the eighth centuries) was influenced by a scheme of systematisation adopted in the eighth or ninth century. The melodies had been composed, written down in one form or another, and collected together, centuries earlier.

In his study, just mentioned, Dom Jean Claire (*ibid.*, p. 198) summarised the chronology of the various surviving western chant-traditions as follows: Gallican (from the second half of the eighth century); Beneventan (from the beginning of the ninth century); Hispanic – in preference to the former term 'Mozarabic' – from the second half of the eleventh century. The strictly Gregorian Tradition – a tradition linked (in the light of surviving musical documents) with the expansion of the Roman liturgy in Frankish territory (stimulated by the coming to power of the Pepinids from 750 onwards) – successively overlaid, and virtually replaced, the other traditions in their native areas.

Again, according to Anglés, the chief object of the action of classifying the chant-repertories was: 'to settle the psalm-chant which follows the antiphon'. Certain modern authors seem at times to suppose that the only notion of importance, to be derived from the Roman Latin authors, was the demonstration of kinds of modal octave-species. Surely, however, what was already of importance, long before the eighth/ninth century, in the society of the learnèd, of those concerned with the music of the liturgy, of learnèd clerics speaking (as well as reading) Latin, was: first, the *technical vocabulary* transmitted in Latin forms from the Greeks, a vocabulary that permitted the naming of intervals; and, facilitated by this, the capacity to distinguish one kind of tetrachord or pentachord from another; the discrimination of *species* of tetrachords; and thence to the recognition of modal structures.

The absence from Western European musical cultures of variants in tetrachordal structure that correspond to the Ancient Greek *genera* (p. 230), so that only the diatonic genus was represented in the Western European area, meant that discrimination between *kinds* of tetrachordal structures was simplified in Europe. Long before octave-range structures were extensively developed in liturgical melodies, recognition of types of tetrachord: T T S, T S T, S T T, may well have sufficed for this discrimination, even before the time of Boëthius, who died in 425.

In second place in importance, among the gifts offered by the theoreticians of the Roman world, was the monochord which made possible the realisation, in concrete audible condition, of intervals discriminated and named in the sources from late Antiquity; it permitted the demonstration not merely of diatonic intervals of all sizes, but also of the various kinds of diatonic tetrachords. [We are henceforth avoiding (as far as possible) the terms *species* and *genus*, because the general reader may have no knowledge of their hierarchical relationship. After all, they are no more than kinds at two levels of organisation, the former reflecting dissimilarity, the latter similitude.]

As Dom Jean Claire has shown, the archaic melodies [corresponding to *do-*, *re-* and *mi-*nuclear structures (Dom Claire's 'cellules-mères') – called 'nuclear' because of their limited compass] in their psalm-tone condition display musical structures of extraordinarily limited range: a major third, a fourth, and again a fourth, in the three specimens he cites. These are, respectively, archaic *mi-*, *re-*, and *do-*modes. The intervallic structures are, respectively, T T, T S T, and T (S T) – where (S T) is a minor third.

In regard to modal structures of larger compass, Chailley refers to the existence in Martianus Capella of a list (= tableau) of the kinds of modal octaves and their tetrachordal constituents, in the ninth book of the latter's 'Marriage of Philology and Mercury'[12] [including under this heading (itself the title of the first two books) both the trivium: Grammar, Dialectic and Rhetoric, and the quadrivium: Geometry, Arithmetic, Astronomy and Harmony]. Of more immediate importance (we wish to argue) was the display by Martianus of the various structures of diatonic tetrachords (see text-sections [960, 961] in his work) as also of pentachords [962].

---

[12] Stahl, William Harris, and Johnson, Richard, with E.L. Burge (1977): *Martianus Capella and the Seven Liberal Arts*, 2 vols. See vol. 2 and pp. 359–71 ([930–63]).

All such information would have been seen, by clerical musicians, as far more relevant to their identificatory and classificatory needs than the Boethian exposition of Greek theory: a theoretical procedure through application of which all kinds of octave-sets could be displayed between the same pitch-limits (see p. 247). This latter theoretical procedure would have been of more interest in a musical culture dominated by the practices of kitharists than by those of clerks singing the daily Offices.

[For the future, an interpolation: the identification as *media*, of the note between lower and next higher tetrachord 'in all modes', was a further important structural feature, defined by Martianus.]

It is suggested then, that the conspicuous interest of Ancient Greece in tetrachordal structures did not render the transmission (by Latin authors) of aspects of Greek musical theory of lesser interest to the liturgical musicians of Western Europe, musicians who – as the earliest chant-specimens reveal – were themselves immersed, particularly during the early stages of chant-evolution, in musical structures of tetrachordal rather than octaval dimensions. This was certainly so throughout the period of 'modal evolution' in the Western Church, as discriminated by Dom Jean Claire, a period that occupied at least the three centuries between 'the last dissertations on Greek music (Boëthius) and the appearance of the eight modes/tones (of the *Oktoechos*) in Frankish territory (8th-9th century)' (les dernières dissertations sur la musique grecque… l'apparition du système des huit modes-ton (octoéchos) en pays francs…).

This then is our suggestion: that even the earlier summary statement of Martianus Capella, naming and defining tetrachords; supplying the Greek names of notes in latinised forms; naming, defining, and setting out the constitution (in terms of their string-length ratios) of the principal intervals (fourth, fifth, octave); listing – even before Boëthius – the principal *tropi* in the sequence: Lydian, Iastian, Aeolian, Phrygian and Dorian; all these things will have been seen as relevant by those already faced with the problem of classifying the music of the liturgy. Here was provided technical language in which to describe – to talk about – structures, and the means by which to discriminate between them.

It is worth noting that the *Dialogus* (no longer attributed to Odo of Cluny) attests the existence, in the tenth century, of vocal melodies of the range of a fourth or fifth. The Master-&-Pupil dialogue[13] runs thus:– Pupil: 'May there also be fewer notes [that is, less than eight] in a chant?' Master: 'There may certainly

---

[13] Let it be made plain from the start: all translations in this essay, and in particular those from medieval Latin texts, stay as close as possible to the original. An awkward and inelegant translation has throughout been preferred to a falsification, by some smooth paraphrase, of what the text says. French and Italian texts are cited in original spelling, with original diacritics.

be five or four; but in such wise that the five amount to a fifth, and the four to a fourth'. (p. 257: *D. Possunt esse & pauciores voces cantu? M. Possunt utique quinque vel quatuor; sed ita quidem, ut & quinque diapente, & quatuor diatessaron reddant.*)

That is to say, such melodies are either recognised tetrachords or pentachords, not any odd selection of four or five notes. By way of illustration, the Paternoster from the Hispanic repertory (p. 109, n. 6), thought to date from the fourth century, displays a compass of a fifth, constituted by a gapped-tetrachord (minor third + tone) with a tone added above: (*E.GA*) + *B*; the reciting-note and final is *A*.

It would seem then that the early Western-European chant-world, like the more easterly, Ancient-Greek musical world of the last centuries BC, was one in which, in the first half of the first millennium AD, the interval of a fourth, with one or two fillers and perhaps with a note added above or below, was a functional melodic unit. Any Church musician of that time would have recognised the relevance of Greek diatonic, tetrachordal types of melodic unit, to the music of chant in the liturgical use of his time. We have no reason to suppose, that in this earliest period of evolution of the music of the Western liturgy, the properties of octave-sets will have been of primary interest.

The Roman authors then had much of immediate relevance to offer, long before the appearance of the double-octave of Hucbald (p. 132). It is our view, that it was this interest of Latin-readers in the smaller structures of the Greek musical world that exerted 'the suction-force' – let us call it – (see p. 118), drawing in everything related to the needs of the West; everything that Martianus and Boëthius had to offer from the writings of the later Greeks.

Local musics and the phenomenon of modality

It is surely of significance that, in so many different cultures, the names of certain modes are tribal names, or names of localities associated with particular peoples or political entities, or names of divinities associated with particular territories. One may suppose that as soon as peripheral contacts led to the establishment of relatively stable and peaceful relationships between contiguous ethnic groups – contacts that afforded commercial and cultural interchange between communities of different (if only minimally different) ethnicity – the playing or accompanying of singers' tunes from one region by instrumentalists of another will have presented practical difficulties.

When one makes a pipe, fingerholes are inserted where they will yield notes for the tune or tunes one most wishes to play – as children may be observed to do in many a rural environment today. If an adult makes a lyre or harp, the number of strings will suffice for the number of different notes required, and the tuning of these will furnish the required pitches at a pitch-level suitable for the singer's voice. In early communities, this is likely (as in many such today) to have been the voice of the maker and instrumental performer.

For tunes by singers from different ethnic backgrounds, different pitches may well be required within the same comfortable vocal range. On a pipe, other fingerholes may then have to be made within the same length-limits; wide intervals may have to be subdivided, and the total number of fingerholes may need to be increased so as to make a pipe suitable for neighbours' tunes – tunes in the various 'manners' (= modes) of different adjoining ethnic groups.

On a lyre, within the same yoke, with one string yielding one note, new tunings – new degrees of tightening of existing strings – will be necessary; and there may be need to interpolate extra strings – if, for example, an archaic Dorian tetrachord, *E.GA*, needs to acquire a filler: *E F G A*; or (with a different filler) to become a Phrygian tetrachord at the same pitch: *E F♯ G A*: Phrygian tuning for Phrygian songs; Dorian, for Dorian.

Such discrimination between tunes, in terms of different regional tuning-practices, was surely a first practical recognition of the nature of what we understand by 'modality': a first recognition of musical 'manners' in the Graeco-Roman world. In the Greek world, nomenclature was embedded in practicalities: the modes were various sets of 'stretchings' = *tonos/tonoi* (to pull up strings to various pitches); or various sets of 'turnings'= *tropos/tropoi* of the tuning-mechanism (to achieve the same result: a stretching).

It is again surely significant that the Greek nomenclature, older than the Latin by a thousand years and more, refers to manipulations associated with a mechanical structure; the Latin term *modus*, however, is abstract, and of itself testifies to modification in transmission of a concept, through time as well as across space. Both groups of terms are metaphors; but the Greek terms are much closer to the concrete image of a structure.

Although we may no longer think of the ancient tribal names in the territory of mainland Greece, and in that of the Aegean coast of Anatolian Turkey, as relics of particular waves of 'Indo-European invaders' into those areas (Renfrew, 1989), it is still legitimate to regard such names as indicators of the presence of some degree of ethnic difference, if only in largely cultural (rather than genetic) terms, in regions so distinguished.

Conspicuously in the case of Greece we have reason to believe that tunes from the repertories of different ethnic groups, settled in different localities in the second millennium BC as Achaeans, Dorians, Aeolians and Ionians, were discriminated. The names of the Greek *harmoniai* (= modes) were of this kind;

and similar local names occasionally occur, as modal names, in Arabic, Turkish, and Persian, 'classical' musical traditions today.

The most copious repertory of local names (of peoples or places, functioning as modal names) comes, however, from South Asia and from the work of Widdess (1995). Already in the names of the seven primary jāti [the suddha (= pure) jāti], two names had regional significance. The jāti themselves were seven differing classes of modal segments from two scales, each of which consisted of a pair of disjunct tetrachords, with a tone of disjunction between the two. The jāti set of seven heptatonic diatonic modes did not survive in practical use beyond the middle of the first millennium AD (Widdess, 1995, p. 15). The first such local name, Gāndhārī (a Lydian note-set) specifies a region, Gandhāra: 'a channel of musical influences to and from Central Asia'; and it is not without interest that this name is cognate with Greek *kentauros* 'a celestial (or mortal) musician' and, of course, the musical centaurs of Greek legend.

Also among the primary jāti, Naiṣādī (an Ionian set) derives from the name of a ritually impure community in the Rajasthan region, the Niṣāda (Widdess, p. 23). Both Gandhāra and Niṣāda occur as regional names in the Vedas (c.1000 BC) and are among the most ancient ethnic and geographical Indian names. Again, among the 'hybrid' (saṃsargaja) jāti, three modal names, qualified by the ending -udīcya, refer to Northern areas, while a fourth, Āndhrī, refers to an area of South India.

While the names of the primary grāmarāgas (these had displaced the jāti by the middle of the seventh century AD) afford few clues to their origins, since none of the names 'denotes a regional or ethnic group' (Widdess, 1993, p. 39), names of the 'hybrid' (bhinna) and 'mixed' variant grāmarāgas, however, include a number of instances of regional or ethnic reference. Significantly, the term for a further group of rāgas, current at the end of the first millennium: bhāsā, itself means 'language' or 'dialect'. Strikingly, however, as Widdess (1993, p. 42) points out, all the regions and peoples to which 'hybrid' rāga-names refer lie at the periphery of the Ganges Valley; at the periphery of 'the centre of political power'.

He concludes that during the first millennium AD, 'rāgas were named after peoples and places on the margins of the civilised world'. While conceding that some may have been 'genuinely based on the melodies or musical styles of the regions or peoples after which they were named' – particularly where a primary rāga-name is prefixed with a regional name – it is improbable that rāgas 'named after tribes or low-caste social groups' imply interest of an urban élite in such musics; more probably such names are fictitious. As representative examples show, however, some 'ethnic' bhāsā-melodies exhibit clear musical relationship to a parent grāmarāga; others do not.

An instance of local tune/mode differentiation in a Papuan environment was observed by Feld (1990, pp. 35–7). In addition to their own tunes (based on the call of the muni-bird) the Kaluli people of Bosavi make use of differing pentatonic note-sets, borrowed from neighbours, each such set from a specific people. The high degree of musicality of the Kaluli is acknowledged by their neighbours.

Finally, regional names also occurred in China in the early medieval period. To those unacquainted with the history, world-wide, of melody as recorded in dated documents, or with the characteristics world-wide of existing folk-repertories, it may seem inconceivable that a single mode should represent the melodic habits of an entire population of a given area, as one is led to suppose Dorian, Phrygian, Lydian, and Ionian octave-sets once were for their eponymous ethnic groups; but this phenomenon is authenticated by historical sources from the other end of Eurasia.

We are told that the 'chamber-music' of the Gaodi 高帝 Emperor (206–194 BC) of Han consisted entirely of Chu 楚 tunes. The 'Chu-mode' was named after the kingdom of that name in the basin of the Yangzi River; its territory coincided in part with the modern provinces of Jiangxi, Anhui and Jiangnan. The mode was a Yu-mode 羽調, a 6.123.5-type mode in its pentatonic condition. In its heptatonic condition, the Yu-mode was a Glarean Dorian octave-set, to be represented by $D\ E\ F\ G\ A\ B\ c'$ perhaps pitched on C. 'Gaodi delighted in Chu tunes, and accordingly the chamber-music [= music played in the private apartments of the imperial family] consisted entirely of Chu tunes' 高帝樂楚聲，故房中樂皆楚聲也。(YFSJ 26, p. 376). This passage, from a preface to a first chapter entitled 'Words for Concerted Songs' Xianghege ci 相和歌詞 – a genre of song characteristic of the Han dynasty (see YFSJ), is also of interest in that it exhibits the lexigraph 樂 in use both as verb: 'to delight in' (le) and as noun: 'music with song' or 'music with dance' (yue).

Even today, in the region of Japan now known as Tokyo 東京, but formerly as Edo 江戶, hemitonic, pentatonic note-sets characteristic of the repertory of 'Edo Songs' Edobushi 江戶節 ('Songs of Edo-District') may be thought of as, at most, two principal modal types, in variant octave-sets that consist of two, congruent, hemitonic, gapped tetrachords (semitone + major third), either disjunct or conjunct. Of interest is the fact that the meaning of the Chinese lexigraph borrowed to represent the Japanese word for 'song' (fushi) in that phrase, is a bamboo-joint 節, hence 'a division of some kind', 'a section', 'a division of time', and by meaning-extension 'to keep time' in music. This Chinese character has no primary meaning linked with 'melody'.

In the embrace of the great Volga bend (as documented by Vikár, 1969), among the Votiak, speakers of a Uralian language, and one of the East Finnic

126

peoples living in the Udmurt Autonomous Republic, a trichord – to be represented as: *C D E* (final *C*) – suffices for their entire repertory of folk songs. A striking feature of these is their rhythmic complexity notwithstanding the limited compass of their scale.

Examination of laments from another Finno-Ugrian people, the Mordvin of the Mordva Republic (also undertaken by Vikár, 1989), revealed extended vocalisations constructed from a single, arched motive, like Votiak song largely trichordal, but of two types: do.re.mi, or la.ti.do.

Where modal names are not geographical or tribal in character, they may derive from the name of the particular degree (of an octave-set) on which the mode ends (and frequently the note which begins – as fundamental – the octave-set). The names of the modes, according to which Old Babylonian songs were classified, were of this kind; but these names were also linked, in some instances, with the names of local divinities.

The bulk of names in the Arabic, Persian and Turkish musical worlds are degree-names, with a sprinkling of place- and tribal-names. They are largely also names of standard note-sets, today aurally distinguished from scales of Western Europe by the distinction made between major and minor tones. While Winnington-Ingram was evidently reluctant to admit any Asian influence in Ancient Greek music, even he conceded the existence of Asiatic influence in the late eighth century BC in the names of 'Phrygian' and 'Lydian' *harmoniai*. Phrygia was a state with an Aegean coast-line extending from the Dardanelles to the Hermus River; Lydia lay between the Hermus and Maeander Rivers.

The earliest statements that relate to the Indian modal system, likewise define heptatonic sets by the name of the final note; and the earliest texts that speak of a system of mode-classes, seven of which were primary or 'pure', indicate that, already at the beginning of the first millennium AD, final-, sub-final, initial- and predominant-functions of particular degrees were discriminated.

It is to be noted (see p. 222) that the Persian tradition [as described by Farhat (1990) in his study of the dastgāh concept in Persian music] also discriminates such functions. To the note distinguished as shāhed/shāhid, to be used as intermediate cadence, he hesitates to apply the term 'dominant', holding the word to have harmonic implications. Unfortunately Farhat does not discuss the chronology of appearance of any of the Persian terms (see later).

In the Chinese modal system, at the time of its probable peak of development in the practice of the Tang period (618–906), 28 'modes' (*diao*) were discriminated, comprising only four, different, heptatonic, diatonic modes (in the sense of intervallically different heptatonic sets), each available in up to seven different keys.

It has been pointed out (Picken, 1975, pp. 607–8) that the last pitch-pipe to be generated by the cycle-of-fifths procedure (as used in theory by the Chinese in one formulation of that procedure) lies in such a position (namely, a fourth above the fundamental) that it would be central in a set of seven diatonic steps. Accordingly, it was suggested that the name of this pitch-pipe: 'Middle Pipe' *Zhonglü* 仲呂 may be an echo of ancient nomenclature (of the same kind as madhyama and mese) of Sumerian MURUB/Akkadian *qablī tum*: 'pertaining to the middle'.

Whether that be so or not, the strict intervallic relationship, between the Tang modal system, and that of China of the third century BC (when the pitch-pipes were reputedly devised), is indicated by the fact that the finals of the *Huangzhong Gong* octave-set of the Tang (in relative pitches, Lydian on $A^{\sharp}/B^{\flat}$), and of the *Zhonglü Gong* octave-set (Lydian on $D^{\sharp}/E^{\flat}$) were still a fourth apart in the Tang system. In the diatonic heptad of *Gongdiao*-finals, between the *Gongdiao*-octaves on the *Huangzhong* and *Yingzhong* 應鍾 pitches respectively, the Middle Pipe – *Zhonglü* 仲呂 – was still central. (See Picken, 1969, p. 98.)

The Chinese seem never to have felt the need to develop a set of words to define modal functions within heptatonic note-sets, a set of the kind developed at an early date by musicians of India and Iran; nevertheless, from early on they recognised a hierarchical order of potency among the five degrees of their primary pentatonic set: 123.56; and at a much later date the existence of a 'Ruler' *Zhu* 主 (a 'predominant', perhaps) was recognised, though not necessarily at a fifth above the final (Picken 1956, 1957, p. 162).

In the Tang system (Chapter 7) and in certain keys, all four modes were available at the same pitch. All four were available (for example) with *C*, *F*, or *G*, (relative pitches) as finals. In other keys, only two or three modes were available at the same pitch; and in one key, only a single mode (and that the basic Lydian note-set) was used. The original data are set out in *YFZL* (*c*.890). (See Picken 1969, p. 98ff. As already indicated in n. 1, p. 105, of this volume, three errors require correction in the Table shown.)

It is our contention that the problems of tune-classification in the 'high' musical cultures of Eurasia – all being musically literate cultures in their use of notations and/or tablatures – were similar. Given the first major impetus supplied by the generation (through a cycle-of-fifths procedure) of the seven possible heptatonic diatonic octave note-sets in Old Babylonia – an impetus, the effects of which reached China perhaps 2000 years later, and Japan a few centuries later still – all intervening cultures, in the path of transmission from the Fertile Crescent, manifest attempts to construct systems of classification appropriate to local conditions; and also (at times) similar attempts to define note-functions within each modal note-set.

Endings, Beginnings and Betweens

By no means was it the case (in the European area) that the discrimination of note-functions only acquired importance after the rise of the major/minor harmonic system of the West. The chronological sequence of treatises on music in the earlier and later medieval periods is (in part) a sequence marked by increasing awareness of modal structures and functions, and increasing precision in the naming of these.

As in all acts of classification, whether 'natural' or 'artificial' [in the sense given to these terms by Whewell (1840, 1847)], the structural features first discriminated by early medieval musicologists were 'coarse' rather than 'fine'. The terms that first appear suggest that it was the structure of 'simple' chant that first commanded attention, the type of chant associated with the delivery of prayers (*oratio*); with the recitation of the scriptures (*recitatio*); and with the projection of each verse of a psalm during the daily Offices. We are perhaps inclined to think of the more extended types of liturgical melody as typical of 'plainchant'; but the simple forms served (and serve) for the execution of the most important functions of any Office, and these are, in terms of functional needs, undoubtedly the most archaic forms.

Let it be stated immediately that the recitation-form – the largely monotone, and today largely equisyllabic, delivery of a 'sacred' text on a pitched, vocal sound – was not something unique to Christendom. It was and is a world-wide genre of speech-enhancement, of speech heightened in power and mystery by the use of the singing, rather than the speaking voice. The status of this process as a universal phenomenon (in the delivery of a text) was described, now many years ago, by Edith Gerson-Kiwi (1961).

As with any type of song, simple chant – a term conveniently adopted here because of the major importance of monotone recitation in its execution – manifested a beginning, a middle and an end; and it is plain that a first structural discrimination gave names to these markedly unequal segments of the chant-form, in such terms as *initio*, *medio* or *mediatio*, and *terminatio*. None of these were single musical sounds; and they were all in existence, as discriminated elements in chant-structure, by the date at which the earliest collections of chants of all kinds in notation became available – the 'tonaries' (*tonaria*) of the ninth and tenth centuries.

The term *initio* has been replaced by *incipit* ('it begins'); and this latter useful term has today received wide acceptance as a noun, in use as a borrowing in many languages, to signify a melodically-shaped, musical beginning. In the psalm-tones it frequently has the character of an ascending phrase of three or four notes.

129

The *medio, mediatio* – both are feminine nouns from the Latin adjective *medius* meaning 'middle' (or as a noun meaning 'the centre'); but its wide, general meaning is: that which exists between two defined limits. The *terminatio* signified a concluding phrase, not a mere final cadential note; and the musical texts reveal a number of set forms for such phrases, forms that acquired particular importance when each psalm-verse was answered by an antiphonal comment in an appropriate mode.

The shift from text-linked, musical phrases, to single, defined pitches that function as initial or cadential notes, was evidently complete by the date (between 1050 and 1100) at which the *Micrologus* of Guido of Arezzo appeared; but as late as the anonymous tenth-century *Dialogus* it is striking to find the author making use of the openings of chants of various kinds – that is, of word-borne, vocal melodies, familiar to his readers – in order to illustrate the nature of intervals of all sizes – semitone, tone, minor and major thirds, fourths, fifths. The interval in question was, in each instance, that between the first and second notes of the beginning of the chant cited, whether in ascending or descending sequence.

Where text was the all-important memory-aid towards the retention of the vast body of non-notated, or (later) imperfectly notated chant; where (in its early stages) neumatic notation was a visual reminder of melodic contour rather than a pitch-notation, it is understandable that the move towards identification of single vocal pitches – of discrete notes – could only occur following a very considerable advance in musical analysis. This advance will have been facilitated by knowledge of the technical, musical vocabulary made available in turn by Martianus and Boëthius, and above all by familiar use of the monochord.

As we now begin to examine the chronology of this evolutionary sequence of functional and locational terms – used in the description of degrees in modal octaves – an observation of general importance must first be made: a majority of translators and interpreters of the Latin works on musical theory have rarely observed strict standards of accuracy in their translations. Frequently they 'translate' Latin words either by words cognate in English or other European languages, or (in English) they merely anglicise a Latin word. The use of cognates, or of anglicised forms, may give a smooth surface to a translation, but this practice serves no useful purpose if the real meaning of the Latin text is not conveyed; yet worse, by such procedures, apparent technical terms, unknown to the original, may be created.

With some translators it is evident that the history of music, embedded in these earliest, Latin, European texts, is unimportant for their purpose. Particularly blameworthy is the practice of anticipating the appearance of a technical term in time, by translating its precursors as if the term itself had already emerged and received universal acceptance. The real history of the development of the

130

European technical vocabulary for the description of note-functions in modal structures is thus concealed.

The Double-Octave Series

At the beginning of this chapter, reference was made to the Old Babylonian tuning of strings (attached to the string-bar of a lyre or the arch of a harp) to seven different diatonic sets of notes, each set covering an octave + one note. [The theoretical method by which the Greeks generated seven *harmoniai* (octave-sets), within one and the same octave-range, will be described (for the sake of completeness) at the end of Chapter 5, p. 246.]

For the early medieval West, as has been argued here, it was not the generation of modal octaves within the same octave-range that was of interest, but a theoretical, continuous, diatonic note-set, laid out as a double-octave series, and analogous to The Greater Perfect System of the Greeks.

In its original Greek formulation, this consisted of two pairs of conjunct tetrachords, each pair being separated by a 'tone of disjunction'; this sequence, constituting a note-series of two octaves, was completed by adding a bottom note. The modal octaves in use in the liturgical music of the Christian Church were segments of such a note-sequence (see p. 133 onwards); and since they were first discriminated as aspects of a purely vocal music, it was unnecessary (in the West) for different octave-species to be realised within the same octave-limits.

When singers changed (or indeed change) from First Tone (Protus authenticus) to Seventh Tone (Tetrardus authenticus), the pitch of the final did (and does indeed) rise through the interval of a fourth (from *D* to *G*), for the Tones (or Church modes) are not sung within the same octave-range, save where convenience dictates transposition.

Of prime importance for the understanding of the later history of modal systems, and of musical theory in Europe, is the fact that the pseudo-Greek nomenclature (Hypo-Dorian, Dorian, etc.), applied by post-Carolingian writers to the Church tones/modes, did not imply any continuity in tradition or modal equivalence between the modal system of Ancient Greece and that of the Middle Ages.

How medieval usage came about is still matter for speculation. In Chailley's view (and words) it did so as a result of 'unskilful interpretation' (*exégèse maladroite*) of treatises on something that (in his view, and in a sense) had long been dead at the time when that interpretation took place. He suggests (1965, p. 54) that some unknown scholar, in the light of the eight octave-systems (segments of the double-octave-system of the Greeks, displayed by Martianus) ascribed one of these octaves to each of the Church Tones. The unknown may have obtained support in so doing from a synoptic Table, drawn up by Hucbald (d.930), in which the Greek system was related to the finals of the Church Tones.

The ambiguity in Greek nomenclature – where Dorian and Phrygian (for example) are both names of notes and names of octave-sets – was echoed in the naming of the Church Tones. The terms Protus, Deuterus, Tritus, Tetrardus (that is: 'first', 'second', 'third', 'fourth') were both names of notes – the successive degrees of the tetrachord of 'endings' (see later) discriminated by Hucbald, *D* to *G* – and names of Church Tones (paraphrasing Chailley, 1965, p. 51).

Nevertheless (and again we repeat our contention), it was surely the conspicuous tetrachordal organisation of early chant-melodies that will have made the discriminatory insights – afforded by Martianus – of such importance for those struggling to impose order on the liturgical repertory.

Endings and Tetrachords

The first step on the road to a Western functional and locational terminology for the degrees of heptatonic note-sets, was taken in the *De harmonica institutione* of Hucbald, born *c*.840. In this work, the degrees of a tetrachord *D E F G*, are for the first time named as 'endings' using the adjective *finalis* as a noun. The word plainly indicates an end, rather than a limit of range; and these four degrees were respectively the endings of the First, Second, Third and Fourth *Tones* – as originally named. When plagals came to be paired with their authentic forms, each of these original four Tones became divided into two, making a total of eight Church Tones or modes. Thus Protus (first) became Tones I and II; Deuterus (second), Tones III and IV; Tritus (third), Tones V and VI; and Tetrardus (fourth), Tones VII and VIII. (A 'plagal', it may be added, is a distribution of the octave-set of notes such that the *finalis* lies not in lowest, terminal position as first note of the octave, but internal in the set of seven notes, the set being extended downwards as far as the fourth below the *finalis*.)

Hucbald makes use of an equivalent of the double-octave of the Greek Greater Perfect System; but he begins to define successive tetrachords from the lowest note, rather than from the note above it. By this procedure he comes to adopt a different tetrachordal sequence from that of the Greeks.[14]

---

[14] Changes in scalar organisation involving change in tetrachordal disposition – for example, from a melodic organisation in conjunct, to one in disjunct, tetrachords – are known from other musical cultures. One such change occurred in Japan during modal revision of the practice of Buddhist cantillation in the twelfth and thirteenth centuries. (n.a.) This process seems to be reflected in the adaptation of an originally secular tune (from the *Tōgaku* repertory) for use as setting for a Buddhist Hymn of Praise: 'The Thirty-Two Manifestations' (of the primary physical attributes of the Buddha) (*Sanjuni-sō* 三 十 二 相) (n.b.).

(a) See W. Giesen, *Zur Geschichte der buddhistischen Ritualgesangs in Japan* (Kassel 1977), pp. 73–113.

```
|A  B  c  d|
    |d  e  f  g|
          |a  b  c'  d'|
                 |d'  e'  f'  g'|
|  Lows  |
    |Endings|
              |  Uppers  |
                   |  Highs  |
```

Each of these four scalar segments (upper sequence) is named in turn in the lower sequence, in Hucbald's diagram (*ad pag.122* in Gerbert *Scriptores*, I): Tetrachord of Lows (*Tetrachordum gravium*), Tetrachord of Endings (*Tetrachordum finalium*), Tetrachord of Uppers (*Tetrachordum superiorum*), Tetrachord of Highs (*Tetrachordum excellentium*). Only the word for 'ending' has any claim to being a precursor of a technical term, since in due course the 'endings' became the *finals* of the four primary Tones.

It seems to us, that the full implication of Hucbald's use of tetrachordal segments from chant, in exemplifying the properties of the double-octave, has not hitherto been fully appreciated. It is not merely that he is aware of the properties of the two-octave note-set as an assemblage of alternative tetrachordal sequences; but that (as will be shown) he plainly recognises the presence of scalar, tetrachordal, unit sequences of notes, in chant. It is also evident that such structures are abundantly present.

Whether filled or gapped, tetrachords are important building-units in the plainsong-melodies of the Christian Church; and this fact of itself explains the relevance of latinised Greek nomenclature, and of Greek emphasis on tetrachordal structures, to those concerned with the music of the daily Offices, and of the Mass, from earliest times onwards.

His first demonstration is one of maximal general interest for his readers, in that he displays the segmentation of the note-set in terms of a particular descending tetrachord, of intervallic structure T T S, which served (for those who heard it) to identify the first of the Church Tones, at the time when Hucbald may be assumed to have been writing. This demonstration is unfortunately made incomprehensible in Gerbert's printing, but becomes entirely meaningful in the version of the best manuscript (Codex Bruxell. 10078–95) as described by Weakland (1956).

(b) Markham, Elizabeth: 'Tunes from Tang China at Court and Temple in "medieval" Japan; first steps towards reading Japanese neumatic notation', *Trends and Perspectives in Musicology*, Publ. Roy. Soc. Swedish Academy Mus. No.48, 1985, pp. 117–39.

Hucbald equates a descending tetrachord derived from his Highs (together with the *a'* added to complete the double-octave) with one of the many intonation-formulae of the First Tone used in the West. In Hucbald's formulation, this is represented by the syllables NO-NE-NO-O.

He introduces his demonstration in this wise: 'However, the first four small notes from the melody of the Authentic Protus will serve as example of this tetrachord; they repeat regularly according to the following pattern: NO-NE-NO-O' (Gerbert I, p. 111: *Huius autem cuiusque tetrachordi exemplum primae quatuor voculae ex melodia autenti proti monstrabunt, quae ad hanc formulam se subinde subsequentur: NO-NE-NO-O*).

As shown by Bailey (1974, p. 48), *MSS.* in notation of the tenth and eleventh centuries, held in at least eleven libraries, reveal that this formula equates with the tetrachord *a' g' f' e'*.

The earliest writer to display such polysyllabic formulae, was Aurelian of Réôme (*fl.* 840–50) (Gushee, 1975). His *Musica disciplina* (Musical Knowledge & Training), probably written in the mid-ninth century, survives in a *MS.* of remarkably early date, the Valenciennes *MS.*: '850–950… with more speaking for the first half of that span' (Gushee, p. 25). Aurelian introduces such formulae in Chapters 8 (p. 82), 9 (p. 84), 19 (pp. 119–28). The beginning of Chapter 9 (transcribed on his pp. 83, 84) is shown in photographic facsimile (Gushee's Plate 1, 1) from the Valenciennes *MS.*. None of the formulae displayed by Aurelian is identical with Hucbald's NO-NE-NO-O; but formulae for First and Second Tones (NONANNOEANE and NOEANE, respectively) are shown with early neumatic notation above. As Aurelian observes: 'The Authentic Protus has many kinds' – presumably meaning 'of formulations'[15] (*Capitulum X: Autentus protus plures habet varietates*).

Hucbald's action, in equating the Tetrachord of the Highs + a' with NO-NE-NO-O is itself to be regarded as very early evidence of the musical character of one such polysyllabic formula, used to introduce the First Tone: a descending tetrachord with the intervallic structure: T T S.

From this most general tetrachordal example, Hucbald immediately proceeds to propose quite a different segmentation of the double-octave, starting (as he puts it) 'from the bottom' (*ab imis ordiri* – see below), proceeding in contrary ascending sense, through semitone, tone and tone, following the first four notes (according to his statement) of the responsorium: *Redimet Dominus populum suum*, and of the following phrase: *Et liberabit eos*.

---

[15] The lettering of the example from Aurelian in Powers [1980, p. 380 (i)] may confuse a reader since the lettering does not show the syllables used by Hucbald.

This responsory does not exist in the *Liber usualis* today; but pursuing a hint given by Weakland (1956), search in the thirteenth-century Worcester antiphonary (Codex F.160) brought to light a version with the tense of verbs changed from future to perfect,[16] in which the tetrachord on 'Et' is plainly: $e'\,f'\,g'\,a'$ (Example 1). The same tetrachord does indeed occur in the course of the first word: 'Redemit', but on the second syllable '-de-' rather than on 'Re-'. Hucbald is demonstrating, by this means, how the two-octave series could also be generated, starting not on his added low A, but on B, since $B\,c\,d\,e$ is intervallically S T T, as is $e'\,f'\,g'\,a'$. It is of course necessary to supply a tone of disjunction, following a sequence of two such tetrachords conjoined, in order to continue the scale. (Where Hucbald has 'eos' in the second phrase, the Worcester antiphonary has, more correctly, 'eum'.)

Example 1.

[*Palaeographie musicale/Les principaux manuscrits de chant grégorien, ambrosien, mozarabe, gallican, publiés en facsimile phototypique*, Dom André Moquéreau, moine de Solesmes, Tournay (1922), IX, 184 (Codex F.160 de la bibliothèque de la cathédrale de Worcester)]

Hucbald's account of his procedure is as follows: 'But if thou shouldst wish to begin this same series from the bottom – the first note accordingly being discarded [adopting Weakland's reading (his p. 80) of *ab imis ordiri* instead of *ab intus ordiri*], thou proceedest, for the rest, through semitone, tone, and tone – contrary to the above [that is contrary to the note-sequence of his original tetrachord: TTS] in the same way, accurately preserving the same places of conjunction and disjunction. And I submit examples: four of the first notes from the response: Redimet Dominus populum suum, the first syllable; or following in

---

[16] The change in tense was remarked by N.J.N. Hucbald has: *Redimet Dominus populum suum et liberabit eos*; while Codex F.160 has: *Redemit Dominus (dns) populum suum et liberavit eum*. The difference has not been explained. We are grateful to Father Tom Flick (Catholic Liturgical Commission, Brisbane) and Dom Barrett (Dean of Arts, University of Queensland) who confirmed these observations and discussed their significance. It is the case that the responses were not always biblical texts.

the same, Et liberabit eos, which are thus indicated. Re- and Et [namely, the notes to which these are sung] in suchwise rise above those notes through four tetrachords to generate the series itself.' (*Quod et hanc eandem seriem ab imis ordiri volueris, prima extrinsecus similiter relicta, in caeteris per semitonium, tonum & tonum ex contrario superioris procedis: ipsa duntaxat coniunctionis vel disjunctis loca diligenter eodem modo servans. Quatuorque primarum vocum exempla ex responsorio Redimet Dominus populum suum, prima syllaba vel subsequenti in eodem Et liberabit eos, submitto, quae sic pernotantur. Re.Et. quas voces ita sibi per quatuor tetrachorda rato ordine superat.*)

In effect, therefore, Hucbald demonstrates a quasi-Greek segmentation of the double-octave, starting with an S T T-type tetrachord, taken from a Western responsory and beginning one note above his lowest note when transposed down a fourth. Without a break in his text, however, he straightway goes on to demonstrate yet another, different, segmentation, using a T S T-type tetrachord, taken from a chant belonging to the Morning Office (*Ad matutinam* for Christmas Day); and this segmentation fits perfectly his double-octave, incorporating (as it does) the lowest note *A* when transposed down a fourth.

His example is the melisma on the syllable '*Ve-*' of *Venite*. The *invitatorium* (*Liber usualis*, 1960, p. 368) begins: *Christus natus est nobis: Venite adoremus.* On 'Ve-', the voice ascends through a T S T-type tetrachord. The half-verse may be transcribed:

Example 2.

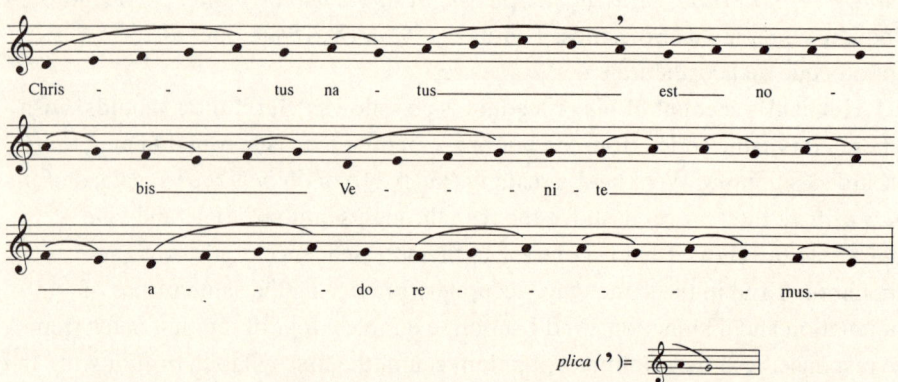

'If, however, thou shouldst desire to make an assemblage far removed from the same first chain of tetrachords, thou leadest forth, at the place "Venite" (taken from the invitatorium "Christus natus est nobis" as example), through tone, semitone and tone, up to the seventh; where, together with the disjunction of a

136

note placed above, thou orderest two tetrachords on the same course. On top, one more note is added according to the adjacent scheme.' (*Sin autem penitus ab ipse prima serie tetrachordorum cupias aggregare, sumpto ex invitatorio* Christus natus est *exemplo, ad id loci* Venite; *per tonum, semitonium & tonum usque ad septimam deducet, ubi cum disiunctione vocis superne exposita tenore eodem diriges tetrachorda: in supremo tamen una voce apposita ad subiectam formulam.*)

[Again the scheme is unintelligible in Gerbert.] As the transcription shows, 'Ve-' is sung to *d e f g* = T S T; and this is a transposed form of Hucbald's 'Tetrachord of the Lows': *A B c d*

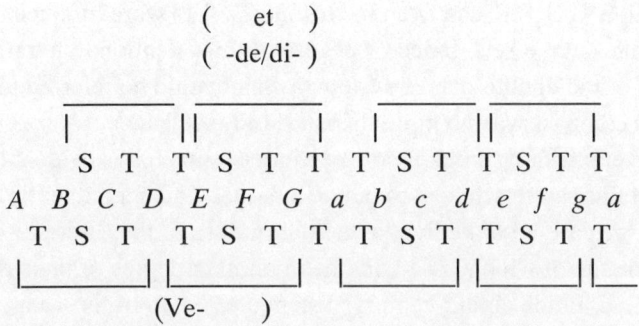

Can anyone doubt that those attempting to classify the chant-repertory had had their perceptions sharpened by the tetrachordal and intervallic nomenclature offered by late Latin authors? Can anyone doubt that tetrachordal structures are indeed self-sufficient melodic musical entities?

While Weakland most satisfactorily clarifies and rationalises Hucbald's text, he does not appear to be in any way interested in what Hucbald is doing or his reasons for doing it. He accepts, without comment, this interest in tetrachordal structures; and seems to find nothing remarkable in the fact that analysis has been stimulated by a vocabulary and insights that derive from structural discriminations first made in Ancient Greece. Why Hucbald should have chosen as tetrachordal unit of the double-octave the species: T S T, is not self-evident. The preferred Greek unit was S T T, which with a tone of disjunction, and the superposition of a symmetrical tetrachord of the same kind, yielded the Dorian octave-species: S T T (T) S T T.

In its pentatonic condition, as Baud-Bovy argued, the Dorian species on *E* would have yielded *E.GA, B.De*: two symmetrical fourths with a filler a minor third above the lower note. It is suggested by us that Hucbald chose a tetrachord of the form T S T because it was more useful in the context of Western European

137

chant. In its pentatonic condition, the First Tone yields *DE.G*, *AB.d* (eliminating the semitone-step); and a tetrachord of the form *de.g* is a frequent incipit in simple chant-melodies.

Perceiving the symmetrical relationship between the tetrachord of Endings and that of Uppers,[17] Hucbald also refers to the Uppers as *Affinales*, since by the operation of symmetry they are indeed linked 'to the Finals'. Because of the presence of a tone marking the disjunction of the two tetrachords, the *Affinales* are each a fifth above the corresponding *Finalis*, and three of them will (in due course) be recognised as serving a particular function in chant-organisation.

It should again be emphasised that the various intervallic constitutions (of the several types of tetrachord and pentachord) were what mattered, in the earliest stages of the identification of similar and dissimilar types of melodic organisation. T T S, T S T, S T T (and even the tritone: T T T) were of much greater importance than octave-sets. Indeed, because of this attention to tetra- and pentachordal aspects of the double-octave system, a chant could be referred to a Tone even though its compass was no more than a fourth (see later).

From Hucbald's exposition (probably of the ninth century), it is evident that the identification of a final was sufficient to define a mode, whether authentic or plagal.This was also the case with the five 'authentic' modes of the Chinese five-note system, each one of which ended on one or another degree of the basic, pentatonic scale: 123.56. In the eighth-century system of 28 *diao* of the Tang, however, each such modal octave-set, with its characteristic sequence of diatonic intervals, existed in seven different keys. The octave-sequences of the *key-notes/finals* of these seven keys, in ascending order, corresponded to Glarean Phrygian (for the set of *Gong* modes), Dorian (for *Shang* modes), Lydian (for *Jiao* modes), and Mixo-Lydian (for *Yu* modes).

As in Europe, so also in China [as shown by the lute-manuscript, Pelliot 3808 – see Picken (1971, pp. 113–18); Wolpert (1977, p. 113)], several terms are used in relation to 'end' and 'stop': 'the end' (*mo* 末); 'to stop', 'to cease' (*zhu* 住); 'to strike dead' (*sha* 殺 or *sha* 煞). The last idiom invites comparison with Western Turkish *karar*, where the expression *karar verildi* means 'he was condemned to death'. The word itself came into Turkish use from Persian. In modern Chinese the term is *zhong* 終, which also has 'death' as one of its meaning-extensions.

---

[17] The retention by Powers (1980, p. 380) of the Latin forms: *Graves* (Lows), *Superiores* (Uppers) and *Excellentes* (Highs) in his text, as if they were untranslatable technical terms, is unjustified. They are no more than noun-adjectives relating to height in pitch. English readers might wrongly suppose the two latter terms (*Superiores, Excellentes*) implied some judgement of quality other than relative pitch.

Hucbald's use of the term *Finales* for the final notes of the First to Fourth Tones did not suffice to establish this word as a technical term in future use. The *Dialogus* uses *finis* ('end') where it is quite certain that the term means not just a conclusion but a final note. The tenth section of that text begins, for example:

Pupil: 'Since thou hast demonstrated that melodies of all the modes take the pattern/rule [of the mode] from the end [-note], the time has come to say how many there are of these same modes or tones.' (p. 258: 10. *D. Quoniam probasti, omnium modorum cantus a fine regulam sumere, quot sint ipsi modi vel toni, tempus est dicere.*)

If melodies are to take 'the modal rule' from the end, this can only mean from a pitched note.

Three sentences later, the presence of the verb 'to end' in its passive form 'to be ended' establishes beyond doubt that this is the accepted idiom of the *Dialogus*. Responding to the statement: 'Some reckon there are four modes', the Pupil asks: 'Wherefore?' The reply given is: 'Because every typical chant may be ended on [one or other of] four notes of the monochord.' (p. 258: 10. *M. Quatuor esse modos (?) quidam putant. D. Quare? M. Quia omnis regularis cantus in quatuor monochordi vocibus finiri potest.*)

Even in the *Micrologus* (perhaps *c.*1040; Guido died *c.*1050), the term *finalis* has not yet established itself as the definitive technical term. Guido uses both *finis* ('end', 'limit') (as does *Dialogus*) and *finalis vox* ('last note'), where *finalis* is still used, evidently, as an adjective.

Although it was left to Aribo – who wrote a commentary on the *Micrologus* between 1070 and his death – to clarify many points in the earlier text, Guido himself at times achieves remarkable precision in describing what happens in the course of a chant:

'In addition, when we hear someone sing, we do not know of what mode his first note may be, because we do not know why tones, semitones and other kinds [of intervals] follow [as they do]. But in fact, with the song ended, we plainly recognise the mode of the last note from the previous [notes]. For when the song has begun, thou knowest not what is to follow; when ended, truly, thou perceivest what preceded. For that reason, the final note is that to which we pay better attention.' (Cap. XI, p. 144: *Praeterea cum aliquem cantare audimus, primam eius vocem cuius modi sit, ignoramus, quia utrum toni, semitonia reliquaeve species sequantur, nescimus. Finito vero cantu ultimae vocis modum ex praeteritis aperte cognoscimus. Incepto enim cantu, quid sequatur, ignoras: finito vero quid praecesserit, vides. Itaque finalis vox est quam melius intuemur.*)

This passage is surely remarkable for the perception revealed of the importance of musical memory in the recognition of modal identity. Guido conveys, succinctly, the progressive accumulation of musical information retained in the memory, and acquiring final confirmation, when the last note is reached – and not before! We note again that Guido writes of the 'last note' (both as *ultima vox* and as *finalis vox*). The adjective *finalis* has still not assumed, therefore, the status of noun and technical term. It is very clear, however, that it is as a pitched note, and not merely as an end – a point of temporal cut-off – that this note is of supreme importance.

By the time Aribo wrote his commentary on *Micrologus* (his death occurred at Liège in 1100), the *final* had been accepted as a standard, technical term. If indeed, as Anglés (1950, p. 101) stated, the *Micrologus* 'was the foundation of medieval music-teaching', Aribo's commentary made certain, and in great detail, what precisely every word, every phrase, every sentence, of that text meant to his contemporaries.

Aribo constantly uses the noun *finalis* as well as Guido's *vox finalis* or *finalis vox*, as (for example) in the phrase 'may lead the chant to the right final' (p. 132: *ducat cantum ad legitimam finalem*). He is still free to revert to Guido's idiom in commenting as follows (for example), where words taken from Guido's text are underlined:

'However, that <u>note which ends the chant holds chief place among others</u>' (p. 132: *tamen* illa <u>*vox obtinet principatum inter alias quae cantum terminat*</u>.)

At one point he expressly equates the two formulations, as in:
'<u>to the note that ends the chant</u>, that is to the final,...' (p. 133: <u>*voci quae cantum terminat*</u>, *id est finali...*)

His comment on the passage from Guido (previously translated) that begins 'In addition' (our third preceding paragraph) is of importance. Aribo takes up the sentence:

'<u>In addition</u>, that is, in addition to those reasons previously given, there is another reason why the last note should be the chief note in a chant.' (p. 134: <u>*Praeterea*</u>, *id est praeter illas rationes quas superius dedi, est alia ratio cur finalis vox ait principalis in cantu.*)

In the continuation of this passage, Aribo's citation re-emphasises the summation of musical experience in time that leads to the identification of a mode:

'For, <u>with the chant being ended, we plainly recognise the mode from the notes that have gone before</u>...' (p. 134: *Nam <u>finito cantu cognoscimus aperte modum ex praeteritis vocibus</u>,...*)

The quotation differs slightly from Guido's text as published today.

Finally, it is to be noted that by the date of appearance of the writings of John of Affligem (Johannis Affligemensis), in the early twelfth century (p. 160), 'final' and 'finals' (*finalis, finales*) are established terms; no longer is there merely an 'end' (*finis*) or a 'final note' (*finalis vox*).

It had taken perhaps a couple of centuries, from Hucbald to John, for *finalis* to establish itself, not as a final 'something', but as *the* final, in the sense of the last note of a chant.

The discrimination had been made, throughout this period, with ever increasing sharpness of insight into the parameters that define modal character.

The coupling of 'endings' and 'tetrachords', in the heading to this section of our survey, may well have appeared a *non sequitur*; but examination of Hucbald's text, and the step-by-step exposition of his material, reveal that the concept of tetrachordal structural units was integral and, in a sense, central to his recognition of the fact that the original finals of the primary Tones constituted a tetrachord, with the intervallic structure: T S T.

He was evidently aware that each of his Finales was both the last note of chants in a particular Tone, and a component of a structural, melodic unit of four notes, within the compass of a fourth, each note distant from its neighbours by the diatonic intervals of tone or semitone; a unit which, by transposition to the fifth and to the octave, would generate the two-octave note-set of the liturgical, musical world.

This conscious acceptance, in the post-Carolingian period, of the fundamental importance of tetrachordal units in the structure of Christian chant, may have been due (we now suggest) to the fact that the greater part of the population of Western Europe had acquired from the original Indo-European speakers not merely spoken language – susceptible of differentiation into the language-groups we know today in Europe – but also structural traits in musical language and dialects, traits common to the musical language and dialects of Ancient Greece, developed (in turn) by the Greeks, from those of the Indo-European-speaking population of the second millennium BC (p. 110).

Chailley (p. 108) was mistaken in insisting that Greek music had lived and died (and was no more), if by that he meant that its use of musical structures of the compass of a fourth, and its names for, and structural classification of intervals, had no relevance in the context of the music of the early Christian church (or, for that matter, in the context of Western and Eastern European folk-song); and he was, of course, ignorant of (or chose to ignore) the fact that many traces of Ancient Greek musical culture survive to this day, on the mainland of Greece and in regions that once formed part of the Ancient Greek empire – as repeatedly demonstrated by Baud-Bovy.

An Aside on Awareness of Tetrachords in Asia

Although awareness of the arithmetico-acoustic relationship between string-length ratios and musical intervals seems to have been transmitted eastwards to China by the third century BC at the latest, together with verbal reminiscences (in Greece, India and China) of ancient degree-locational nomenclature: *meson*, madhyama and *zhonglü*, there is no early evidence of Asian interest in the structure and variety of tetrachords, as elements in musical construction.

The small compass of Vedic chant is noted as indicative of the presence of small-scale structures; but such musical units have no wider recognition as constituents in more extended melody. As noted by Widdess (1995, pp. 368–9), the scales of the earlier period: of jāti and grāmarāga, 'appear more closely related to Sāmavedic chant than to the scales of later art-music…'. Since, however, Greek theory, with the recognition of the Greater Perfect System and all that flowed from it, was not elaborated until the fourth century BC, it is possible that the main transmission (if any such reached the South Asian environment) of string-ratio information had already occurred, perhaps eight centuries or more *before the codifications of the Greek musical theorists*, as a consequence of early contact between Kassites and Old Babylon (our p. 110). Certainly no Indian music exhibits anything resembling the use of tetrachordal structures in the manner of their use to be seen in ancient Greek music.

It is equally certain that, notwithstanding the importance of fourths as structural elements in Chinese melody, no verbal discrimination of any such unit occurred in China before the modern period. Similarly (as Dr Widdess informs us), in Indian music an octave or heptad is assumed for any mode, but is never explicitly stated in the earliest texts. With later definition of the mūrchanā by Śārṅgadeva, seven-note 'saptaka' (scalar units having modal properties) were specified. These are modal note-sets, established in descent from each degree of the (sa-ri-ga-ma-pa-da-ni)-set. Other than in Vedic chant, melodic units smaller than the saptaka have not been recognised as functional in Indian music, until the modern period. The essential point here, in contrasting the Indian with other systems, is the integrity of the saptaka (and hence of the octave) in theory and in practice.

Beginnings

The discrimination of tune-initials has occurred in the evolution of a majority (perhaps) of the 'high', literate musical cultures, sprung – to greater or lesser extent – (as we would argue) from information ultimately derived from the primary tuning-procedures of the Old Babylonians in the second millennium BC. In China, and for such ritual melodies as survive (reputedly) from the early eighth century AD, but in style reflecting Zhou ritual melodies of the fifth century BC at latest, tunes began on the final or on its upper octave (Picken, 1956, p. 160). By contrast, a tune that now appears almost certainly to be of the sixth century AD (the Broaching of *Ryō-ō*; see Volume 6, Appendix 5), begins on the seventh (*bian gong* 變 宮) of a heptatonic *Gongdiao* (Lydian) scale.

In Northern India (Widdess, 1980, p. 18), at least from the beginning of the first millennium AD, initials (grāha) were discriminated (as were finals); and the initial was usually the same scalar degree as the pre-dominant (aṃśa) – a note that occurs frequently throughout a given melody. The Western Turkish term (shared with the art-music traditions of Iran and of the Arab world): agaz (from Persian: 'beginning' āγāz) may be used; but a purely Turkish word for 'beginning' is more common in Turkey: giriş (= 'entrance', 'beginning'). This is a verbal noun, formed by adding the suffix -iş to the stem: gir- of the verb girmek (= 'to enter'). Yet another purely Turkish word is used for beginning: a deverbal substantive derived from the verb çıkmak (= 'to start', 'to come out'), namely çıkıcı (= 'starting'), where -ıcı, indicating regular activity, is added to the verb-stem (note: dotless 'i' in all derivatives of this last verb). The date at which these Turkish terms came into use has not been investigated.

At an early date, the term *qi* 起 (as in *qi diao* 起 調) appears in Chinese, where *qi*: 'to get up', 'to arise' is used in the extended sense of 'to start'. Here *qi diao* means 'to begin a' or 'the', 'tune' or 'mode'.

Dialogus (tenth century) uses *principium* (= 'a beginning', 'the origin') – derived from *princeps*, both in the sense of 'in first place' and in that of 'chief'. When it comes to the topic of where to begin a tune, this marvellous text supplies precious information in the most direct and simple manner:

'A tone or mode is a pattern/rule which, at the end of every chant, distinguishes [it]. For unless thou knowest the end, thou wilt not be able to decide where the chant is obliged to begin, or how far it is obliged to rise or fall [in pitch throughout its course].' (Gerbert, reprint 1931, D. ODDONIS DIALOG. DE MUSICA, p. 257: 8. *M. Tonus vel modus est regula quae de omni cantu in fine diiudicat. Nam nisi scieris finem, non poteris cognoscere, ubi incipi, vel quantum elevari vel deponi debeat cantus.*)

The pupil now asks the crucial question: 'What pattern/rule does the beginning take from the end?' (p. 257: *D. Quam regulam sumit principium a fine?*)

The answer is surely astonishing, but neither Strunk (1952), nor Powers (1980), have noticed anything astonishing about it:

'Every beginning is bound to agree with its end in accordance with the aforesaid six consonantia.' (p. 257. *M. Omne principium secundum praedictas sex consonantias suo fini concordare debet.*)

What these seeming 'consonances' are has been set out previously in section 5 of *Dialogus* (p. 255–6). They are 'conjunctions of notes' (*coniunctiones vocum*), 'which make different consonantia…' (5. p. 255. *M… quae consonantias faciunt diversas…*)

We would call them 'intervals', as becomes clear from what follows. Using terminology equivalent to that of the text, they are respectively: semitone, tone, tone + semitone (= minor third), two tones (= major third), a fourth, a fifth. In each case, an instance of the occurrence of that interval between the first and second notes of a known antiphon is given in alphabetical-notation, both ascending and descending. Gerbert's text is corrupt, but the correct quotations are given in staff-notation in Strunk (1952, p. 109).

In translating, Strunk chose to insert a sub-heading: '5. of the conjunctions of sounds', and this perhaps lessened the impact of the reply. (Properly, the two words he cites from *Dialogus* should be translated as 'conjunctions of notes'.) For whatever reason, the extraordinary implications of the statement that 'conjunctions of notes make different *consonantia*' was lost sight of. The use in *Dialogus* of this term *consonantia* – by implication translated by Strunk both for semitone and tone as 'consonance' – surely implies a very different notion of 'consonance' from that which we have in mind when speaking of consonant intervals today.

It is evident also that such 'conjunctions of notes' are not notes 'sounded together' in the sense of being sounded simultaneously, as later consonances tend to be thought of. They are notes sounded in sequence, and it is in this sense that they are 'conjunct' – 'conjoined'. The failure to draw attention to the anomalous sense in which *Dialogus* uses this term is the more remarkable since, both before and after the usage of *Dialogus*, 'consonance' (*consonantia*) carried the same sense of consonant intervals as discriminated by the Greeks and by us today.

The Master continues:

'No note is able to begin a chant unless the same be either the end-note, or agree with the end-note through one out of the six *consonantia*.' (p. 257. 8. *M.*

Nulla vox potest incipere cantum, nisi ipsa vel finalis sit, vel consonet finali per aliquam de sex consonantiis.)

It is to be noted that [*vox*] *finalis* and [*voce*] *finali* are to be understood because of the presence of '*ipsa*' immediately before '*finalis*'.

As already stated, displaying a remarkable degree of didactic flair, *Dialogus* illustrates each of these intervals, both in ascending and descending forms, by quoting beginnings (incipits) of twelve chant-melodies.[18] A single exception [to the rule that the initial note of a melody is in an intervallic relationship (with the final) of semitone, tone, minor third, major third, fourth or fifth] is mentioned: namely: that if the melody ends on the fifth note (counting upwards from $A = e$) – that is, it is a melody in the Third Mode/Tone –

'…it is frequently found to begin on the tenth note, *c* [counting from *A*], distant from the same fifth [note] (*e*) by the interval of a fifth and one semitone.' (p. 257. 8. *M …saepe invenitur incipere in voce decima c. quae ab eadem quinta E. uno diapente, unoque semitonio elongatur.*)

This sixth was not one of the recognised *consonantia*.

Betweens

We have seen how in time recognition came, not merely of the importance of the last note in a melody, as an ultimately declared determinant of all that goes before; but also of the need for greater precision in the language of description, from 'end', to 'last note', to 'final'. We have seen the birth of awareness of relationship between end and beginning.

As will be shown later, the development of an appropriate language (in which to talk about the structure of vocal melodies) shows that musicians thought of both liturgical chant and its associated, closely linked text, in the same way: as a flowing discourse.

We turn now to consideration of discriminations made – by early theorists – in their increasing insight into musical events between the beginning and end of a chant. In the development of an appropriate nomenclature, a major role was played (as already emphasised) by the Latin adjective *medius*. Translators have all too frequently seized on English derivatives, on cognates such as 'median' and 'medial'. In so doing, a technical term such as does not necessarily exist in the original text may be created. The mistake made is that of failing to recognise

---

[18] The correct forms of these, as opposed to their faulty presentation in Gerbert's text of *Dialogus*, were included by Strunk in his translation of a substantial portion of this anonymous text.

the range of meanings of the adjective. It is connected with Greek *mesos, -e, -on*; and its basic meanings are 'middle', 'midmost', 'midst'; but while its literal meanings relate to space, in a figurative sense it means 'between', 'intermediate', or 'intervening'.

The Latin readiness to make use of the adjective *medius* may, in some contexts, have been linked with knowledge of Greek *mese*, the fourth degree above the lower limit, *hypate*, of the Dorian scale-form (*mi'* – *mi*), the upper terminus of the tetrachord Meson; the descending structure of which may be represented as: *la so fa mi*.

In the Greek Greater Perfect System, this *mese* was not in the middle of anything.

In the Lesser Perfect System of three conjunct tetrachords, however, *mese* was indeed central in the set of seven, as (as we have seen) were madhyama in the Northern Indian heptad – the saptaka – and as was MURUB/qablītum – 'pertaining to the middle' (in some sense) in the heptatonic, diatonic set of the Old Babylonians in the second millennium BC.

In any case, quite apart from the attribute of being 'in the middle', it is understandable that as soon as upper and lower limits of a note-set had been defined, it became necessary to be able to recognise, and to speak of, what lay between those limits.

A group of words with meaning-extensions such as 'midmost', 'between', 'sub-dividing' – but never meaning action as a mediator, and only rarely with the arithmetical meaning of *proportio* – frequently appears in the history of modal note-sets. From *medius* a series of words derives, some known only to Late or Very Late Latin, but all with simple, non-technical meanings in English. Of this kind are: 'medial' – middle or intermediate in position, and 'median' – in the middle.

From Late Latin *mediare* 'to mediate', came meanings (1) to divide into two equal parts; (2) to be between; (3) to act as intermediary – in a process of reconciliation, for example.

'Mediant': present participle of mediare, meant and means no more than to be in the middle between two extremes.[19]

'Mediety', now obsolete, existed in Late Middle English and is an anglicised form of medietas – the quality of being a mean between two quantities, or an expression of proportion; in Law 'a moiety', etc.; in music, a monochordal sub-division. All the derivatives of medius employed in musical contexts refer merely to the subdivision of a musical space defined by specified pitch-limits.

[19] The meanings that follow are taken from *The Shorter Oxford English Dictionary* (1967).

The Between-String

An important further discrimination – to be added to those made by Hucbald (p. 132) in his *De Harmonica institutione* (p. 393) – occurs in the 'New Exposition' (*Nova Expositio*), written perhaps in 890 (Chailley, 1964, p. 60). In part repeating (though inaccurately) Hucbald's summary, the text states (Chailley, p. 199):

'There are, therefore, four Uppers indeed: *a b c'd'*, and four Lowers: *d e f g*. And the Uppers indeed, end the Hypo-Dorian, Hypo-Phrygian, Hypo-Lydian and Hypo-Mixo-Lydian [octave-sets] above, in the higher region. The Lowers, in truth, end the Dorian, Phrygian, Lydian, Mixo-Lydian [octave-sets] in the lower region. Hence they are also called "finals" [*finales*].' (Chailley, 1964, 138 a) *Sunt igitur quatuor superiores, id est* o, x, y, cc; *et quatuor inferiores, id est* e, h, i, m. *b). Et superiores quidem excellentiori parte finiunt, hypodorium, hypophrygium, hypolydium, hypomixolydium. inferiores vero finiunt ex graviore parte, dorium, phrygium, lydium, mixolydium, unde et finales dictae sunt.*)

Hucbald's 'Lows' were not, of course, his 'Finals'.

When the anonymous author moves on to describe the typical modal octave in terms of its constituent segments of fifth + fourth, a further discrimination appears, towards the understanding of which a prior word of explanation is necessary. In the description of the structure of the modal octave (both authentic and plagal), the text now makes use of numbers. Specifically: 6, 8, 9, 12; these are proportional string-lengths on the monochord in its early medieval, Western form (Adkins, 1967).

'And always, each and every principal trope [that is, an authentic mode] has below: a fifth from the midmost string [*chorda media*]; [and] above: a fourth, such that 8 is placed between 6 and 12.' [That is, the midmost string lies at the distance of 8 from the upper octave (6), namely, a fourth down, and a fifth up from the lower octave (12).]

Authentic

5th							4th
d	e	f	g	(a)	b	c	d'
12				8			6

chorda media

'Furthermore, each and every subjugate trope [plagal mode], [starting] from the final string, has a fifth above and a fourth below, indeed; such that 9 [the final] is placed between 6 [the fifth above] and 12 [the fourth below].' [That is, 9 (the final) lies a fifth down from the upper note (6) and a fourth up from the lower note (12).] These figures, 8 or 9, 6 and 12, are referred to as *medietates* (= 'proportions'). (Chailley, 1965, p. 200, paragraph 140, c): *Et semper unusquisque principalis tropus inferius habet diapente a chorda media, superius diatessaron, ac si 8 sint inter 6 et 12. d): Subjugalis vero unusquisque tropus a finali chorda superius habet diapente, inferius vero diatessaron, ac si 9 sint inter 6 et 12.*)[20]

Plagal

	4th							5th
A	B	C	(d)	e	f	g		a
12			9					6

chorda media

The author of the 'New Exposition' is pointing out that in an *authentic* mode, where the final is the lowest note, there is a 'between' or 'midmost string' lying a fifth above the final, separating lower pentachord from upper tetrachord. In *plagal* modes on the other hand (where the final is *not* the lowest note), the final itself bounds a pentachord that lies above it and a tetrachord that lies below it. In both authentic and plagal forms of the modes, a pentachord and a tetrachord are *conjunct*. For plagal modes, however, the conjoining note is the final; for authentic modes it is the between-string (*chorda media*). Clearly, in each of the four authentic modes there will be a between-string, and these four notes will be the same as Hucbald's Uppers.

This discrimination refers only to *location*. There is as yet no hint of recognition of *function* in defining the between-string. Nevertheless, from our position in time, we can see a locational term preceding a functional discrimination. The fifth degree above the final, in a majority of authentic modes,

[20] The continuation of this paragraph (d) has occasionally been misunderstood: *medietas* seems to have been confused with *chorda media*. We read: 'For this reason, if a note, whether higher or lower, is added, over and above the [limits of the] octave of any mode, it will not offend the ear if it be regarded as suitable for singing; namely, [if such a note] on either side of the aforesaid proportions [*medietates*], now here, now there, borders them, making a fifth + a tone, or a fourth + a tone.' (Chailley, 1965, p. 200, paragraph d) 141: *Quod si superius vel inferius alicui tropo extra speciem dupli tonus accesserit, non erit absurdum emmelim ponere, ut sit a praedicta medietatibus ubicumque tetigerit hinc vel inde, diapente et tonus, vel diatessaron et tonus.*)

There is no reference to the *chorda media* here. The Late Latin word *medietas* appears in Middle French and New French as médiété (n. a), with the meaning of 'proportion arithmétique ou géométrique dans laquelle se trouve une moyenne proportionelle.' This is precisely what the text is referring back to ('9 is placed between 6 and 12'). In Late Medieval English, mediety (from *medietas*) meant: 'the quality of being a mean between two quantities'. (n. b)

(a) Wartburg, W. von: *Französisches etymologisches Wörterbuch* (1969); (b) *The Shorter Oxford English Dictionary* (1967).

148

was destined for recognition as a landmark of very considerable functional importance in modal structure.

The Trumpet

When precisely any one of the technical terms for beginnings, betweens, and endings, first came into use (even in a preliminary form) is – as we have now seen – difficult to determine. Generally speaking, translators have tended to anticipate the emergence of later, established, terms. Our examination of early texts (undertaken as a preliminary study before the composition of this essay) has been far from comprehensive; and it is not as yet possible to furnish firm dates for the first appearance of this or that term. The most that can be done at this stage (and perhaps all that we can ever hope to do) is to locate a series of texts, often themselves not precisely dateable, in which such-and-such an expression is used.

The origin of some of the most important terms lies so far back in time, that they may well antedate (by some centuries) the earliest treatises; and one can only hope that future, informed examination of non-musical texts may reveal use of some of these terms, in their developed technical sense, by authors unaware of the historical importance of their testimony.

Reading general accounts of the historical development of the plainchant repertory, and of the large-scale evolution of the music of the Mass, and of the Offices of the Western Church, as well as of the music of the great Feasts of the Church Calendar, it is evident that interest tends to be focused on the larger-scale musical structures: the Antiphons, the Hymns, the Alleluias, the Sequences, the Tropes; but surely these were not, and are not, the most important structures, from the standpoint of the life of the Church. The daily, hourly, music of the Offices was, and remains, the heart of the religious life; and we may be certain that simple cantillation equates with the most essential and (as we have already suggested) the most archaic element in the didactic use of the singing voice by the Church, as it is for all other religions in which the chanting of established texts has become a perpetual duty for those consecrated to the life of the religious.

The simplest type of chant: the monotone recitation of syllables at a single pitch, delivered largely in units of equal duration, was an important musical invention, whenever in the History of Mankind it may have occurred. It made possible the clearly articulated delivery of a sacred text, not merely by a solo recitant, but also as a collective activity. It was, and is, a method of projection difficult for the spoken voice to equal in clarity – as made plain by the difficulty of training a verse-speaking chorus. It was, and is, a method by which the singing of relatively naïve and untrained singers can be co-ordinated through the imposition of the simplest possible, equal-pulsed metre. Delivered in this manner, a text acquires maximal comprehensibility thanks to the even-spacing of syllables; and thanks also to the added clarity of delivery obtained by suppressing individual pitch-variation, always present when readers or reciters use the speaking-voice.

In the first volume (on medieval music) of *A History of Hungarian Music* (1988)[21], the late Dr Benjamin Rajeczky and his collaborators set out in illuminating fashion specimens of the simplest cantillation taken from the Hungarian manuscript-tradition, as used in the three primary liturgical elements of any Office whatsoever: recitation of prayers (*oratio*), chanting of scriptures (*lectio*, *recitatio*), chanting of psalms (*psalmus*, *psalmodia*).

Not merely because these chant-forms are (musically speaking, and until today) the simplest types known, but also because they are of crucial importance in the daily sequence of Offices, it is reasonable to suppose that they were also the first types of chant to be developed in the Roman Church, using that designation in its widest European significance, embracing all regional differentiations, as well as the later dominant Gregorian tradition. (The remaining archaic types of Jubilus and Alleluia are excluded.)

The most obvious feature of such chants is the extended regular iteration of a note of constant pitch, the flow of pulses being interrupted from time to time. This structure it was (we suggest) that led to the recitation of simple chant being given the name: 'trumpet' (*tuba* – short 'u'). The chant-sound, in its syllabic delivery, resembled a tongue-articulated trumpet-call. We tend, perhaps, to think vaguely of a trumpet-call as a sustained blast; to suppose that no great difference in use existed between a Roman trumpet and a Roman horn (*cornu*). As described by Baines (1976, p. 63), the tuba was indeed a trumpet: a tube of narrow bore very gradually expanding, opening into a narrow bell, and fitted with a mouthpiece.

A late surviving tuba of the Gallo-Roman period – 'the Saumur tuba' – is illustrated by him (p. 64); its total length seems to have been about 160 cm. Presumably this instrument cannot be much later in date than the fifth century AD (p. 64).

It is certain, however, that the name tuba was transferred, following the Goth and Teuton incursions into the Gallo-Roman world, to 'curved instruments or horns of various shapes and sizes' (Baines, p. 67). Nevertheless, the straight trumpet reappears, in Western European use, from the eighth or ninth century onwards. There are tenth- or eleventh-century illustrations of such instruments,

---

[21] *Madyarország zenetörténete I. Középkor* (Budapest).

and twelfth-century silver trumpets were both given and received as gifts by the Popes, and were certainly played (p. 73). The fact that the sound of the tuba was higher in pitch than that of the cornu, perhaps invited comparison with the human voice; but it is surely the fact that it was tongue-articulated in playing, which led to comparison between a trumpet-call and simple chant. That such calls were indeed so articulated is made plain by the ancient transliteration of the trumpet's sound as 'taratantara'.

For this last, Baines (p. 63) refers us to Fragment 143 of the poet Ennius. Accepting the edition of Ethel Mary Steuart (1925)[22] – in which as far as possible fragments were allocated to the numbered books of the Annals of that author – the verse in question is Fragment 18 of Book II. Quintus Ennius (*b*. 239 BC; *d*. 169) created what Steuart called 'probably the boldest onomatopoeic coinage in Latin', in the line:

'But the trumpet with fearful sound sang: "taratantara" !' (*At tuba terribili sonitu taratantara dixit.*)

Steuart accepted that the verse refers to the destruction, by Tullus Hostilius, of Alba Longa, the oldest Latin town and mother-city of Rome.

This onomatopoeic representation of a tongue-articulated trumpet-call is important not merely for its revelation of articulation, but also because in context it discloses a rhythm. The verse is a dactylic hexameter. In Latin (and hence in this trumpet-call) all three of these consonants: t, r, n, were dental in articulation – that is, with the tip of the tongue applied to the base of the upper incisors and the front margin of the hard palate. The last metre (= the grammatical term for a foot) *'dixit'* is scanned as a spondee:| - - | (see later), the second syllable being counted as long by position. The normally short initial syllable (*'At'*) becomes long because followed by a consonant: the 't' of *tuba*. If we count units of duration (*morae*) – two for a long syllable (-), one for a short syllable (s), the rhythm of the sequence of syllables (the rhythm in which the verse was delivered in speech) becomes evident. The line may be 'barred' in units of two crotchets/quarter-notes.

At tu-ba ter -ri-bi- li so-ni- tu ta-ra-tan-ta-ra di-xit
|- s s |- s s|- s s | - s s |- s s|- -‖

This implies that, for the poet's ear, the trumpet-call was not merely articulated: it was rhythmically differentiated, in that the ear perceived syllables (both open and closed) initiated and closed by different consonants.

---

[22] *The Annals of Quintus Ennius* (1925).

The ear also perceived syllables of longer (-) and shorter (s) duration. A dental '*n*' at the conclusion of '*tan*' would occlude the mouth-cavity, interrupt the air-stream, and create a longer or shorter silence before a following -'*tara*'-. A rhythm such as: s s | - s s|, would be generated; and a helpful trumpeter tells us that the call would undoubtedly have been extended by repetition, and brought to a conclusion in a prolonged sound: on '*tān*'.

In the sequence shown by Ennius, the '*n*' is also a potential preparation for a dental '*t*', initial to the next '-*tara*-', giving added thrust to the sound generated. Tongue-tip on base of upper incisors is indeed the essential position. Moreover, the trumpeter consciously shapes the mouth-cavity for the production of a long '-*a*-' sound on: '*tān*'. The realisation that Ennius preserved a rhythmised trumpet-call for tuba prompts the question whether, originally, the simple chants of the Church, like the tuba-call, observed syllabic quantity, as known in classical Latin. As long as quantity was of importance in the Latin-speaking-and-writing world, the flow of simple chant will perhaps have been regulated by quantity:

|s   s   s   s | - s   s| -   - |
Pa-ter nos-ter qui es in coe-lis...

In churches of relatively long reverberation-period, the sounds of simple chant sung on a single reciting-note, would tend towards something resembling a trumpet-call. By the second or third century AD, however, there is evidence that observation of syllable-quantity in the Latin-speaking world was falling into desuetude, so that the suggested possible rhythmisation of '*Pater noster*' may well have been superseded by the rhythmically equisyllabic delivery heard today.

[It is to be noted that the consonant-clusters across word-boundaries did not usually lengthen a preceding vowel in Latin prose. Cicero's prose, exceptionally, was scanned like verse. In Greek, the pitch-level of long vowels was higher than that of short; but in Latin this differentiation is not known to have existed. Had it done so, the phrase 'taratantara', in this line of Ennius, might have exhibited pitch-differentiation of the syllables, with a shift to a higher harmonic on '-*tān*-'. (A reconstruction of Ennius's trumpet call, on a replica of a Roman *tuba* made of wood, with a metal mouthpiece, is to be heard in a recording by Lawson & Lawson, 1986.)]

It seems possible that the term '*tuba*' was first applied to the technique of recitation on a single pitch, and only subsequently to a reciting-note at a particular pitch. The earlier use might well go back to the days of Imperial Rome. The failure of the first Western-European Latin texts to say anything about either tuba or simple chant, as technical procedures, may imply that both were taken for granted.

We suppose, then, that use of *'tuba'* for a reciting-note in ecclesiastical use may belong to the early centuries AD rather than to the much later period (from the eighth or ninth century onwards) in which Roman-style, narrow-bored, straight trumpets were restored to musical favour, and to court-use in particular.

For the simplest chant of all: the strictly monotone syllabic recitation, without differentiated *initio* and *terminatio*, the reciting-note was both beginning and end; and in many cultures and communities of the world today, this practice still persists. With the expansion of simple-chant structures by the addition of *incipit* and *coda* (be it only to extend the compass to a tetra- or pentachord, gapped or entire), modal qualities emerged, even though the bulk of the associated text was still delivered through monotone recitation.

The later statements in the texts: that *tuba* and *tenor* are synonyms for the reciting-note; and that these terms were eventually transformed into dominant, indicate the extreme pitch-importance of the reciting-note in the context of particular chants. In relation to each Church mode/tone (whether in authentic or plagal form) the reciting-note was originally chosen – we may suppose – at a pitch comfortable from the singers' point of view: comfortable in its position within the range of the voice, comfortable in relation to the compass of the chant, and comfortable in relation to the position of the final – to the pitch-relationship between reciting-note and final.

Nor is it surprising that a fifth above the final should be the most common position for the reciting-note in authentic modes. Churches are resonant buildings, and the first four harmonics will have been evident to any singer with a good ear. Two and three will readily have been perceived in Church, as well as in the performance of harpers and lyrists outside. It should not surprise that the reciting-notes of authentic and plagal pairs are in simple harmonic relationship with each other and with their finals.

Stops or Pauses by the Way: Intermediate Cadences

A highly significant word that first appears in the evolving descriptive and technical vocabulary of the post-Carolingian, Latin-writing theorists is a technical term derived from the craft of the orator, from the Science of Rhetoric. It is this term, that by its use, plainly indicates that early writers on music thought of the complex: chant-melody+text as a type of discourse, as a monologue of a particular kind, with its own 'grammar' and 'syntax', subject to some at least of the limiting conditions that operate in verbal rhetorical statement.

In first place, the rhetorician – the orator – experiences, periodically, the need to stop: the need to take breath (of course), but also the need to give time for listeners to absorb, phrase by phrase, what is being stated. This is as true of delivery of a text through the medium of the singing voice, as it is of delivery through the declaiming, speaking voice.

The Latin technical term for such breaks – a term from the rhetorician's vocabulary – was *distinctio*. In rhetoric it meant 'a pause', 'a division'. The word derives from the verb *distinguo -stinxi -stinctum*: 'I separate, divide', used in grammar for punctuation. In a musical context, it is understandable that the term distinctio is used primarily for the punctuating cadences on certain lengthened notes at the ends of phrases, in the course of a liturgical melody.

It is surely blameworthy, in English-speaking translators of these early Latin texts, that they have been content to render this word, without comment, as 'distinction'. Given that the only commonly understood applications of this last word are: (1) 'to make a distinction' (that is, 'to distinguish', or 'to be separated from others by some quality or other'), and (2) 'to be distinguished', no student of music can have understood what was meant from the word alone, by reference to distinctions in the context of plainsong.

Its original rhetorical and grammatical usages in the Latin world make plain what was intended, namely, those notes on the path between beginning and ending, where the song/chant comes to rest; and (by extension) the musical and textual phrases that lead up to such a point of rest, to a cadence in fact. But for the abuse of the word 'medial' in other contexts, such phrases might be referred to as 'medial phrases'. To avoid that adjective, they will be referred to here as 'intermediate phrases' and 'intermediate cadences'.

These, then, are cadences or phrases that intervene between the opening phrase (or incipit – that itself may end in an intermediate cadence) and the phrase that concludes with the final. Already, and not later than the tenth century, *Dialogus* furnishes the gist of the matter:

'It is clear that the intermediate phrases also – that is, places in a chant at which we again stop [at an intermediate cadence], and at which we divide the chant – are bound to end on the same notes, in each and every mode, on which chants in that mode may begin.' (p. 257. 8. *M. Distinctiones quoque, id est loca, in quibus repausamus in cantu, & in quibus cantum dividimus, in eisdem vocibus debere finiri unoquoque modo, in quibus possunt incipere cantus eius modi manifestum est.*)

The text continues, and in so doing reveals much of the approach to melodic composition of a Church musician of the time:

'And where each and every mode begins the better and the more often, there it is customary, the better and the more suitably, to begin or end its intermediate phrases.' (p. 257. 8. *M. Et ubi melius & saepius incipit unusquisque modus, ibi melius & decentius suas distinctiones incipere vel finire consuevit.*)

The anonymous author well understood the consequences (for the listener's ability to recognise the mode of a chant) of the manner in which the pitches of intermediate cadences were chosen. He states:

'Moreover the Masters teach that more intermediate cadences should end on that note which ends the mode.' (p. 257. 8. *M. Plures autem distinctiones in eam vocem, quae modum terminat, debere finiri, magistri tradunt;...*)

The reason for this recommendation is, of course, that if some cadential note occurs more frequently than the final, the mode will be changed; moreover:

'the beginnings also are more frequently and more suitably effected on that same note which ends the chant.' (p. 258. 8. *M. Nam & principia saepius & decentius in eadem voce, quae cantum terminat, inveniuntur.*)

Dr Widdess (1995, pp. 257–9) has drawn our attention to the similarity between *distinctiones* and *vidari* (literally 'breaking' or 'cutting'). In early Indian musical theory these latter are phrases; and the note that concludes such a phrase is the *apanyāsa* or sub-final. In Indian theory, as expounded by Śārṅgadeva, a hierarchy of cadential pitches is defined, among which the apanyāsa holds the position of secondary (or sub-) final, acting (as it does) as section-final.

Let us recapitulate: in Beginnings (p. 143) we learned from *Dialogus*: 'every beginning is bound to agree with its end in accordance with' the intervals: semitone, tone, minor third, major third, fourth and fifth. We see now that the intermediate cadences are also required to stand in these same intervallic relationships with the last note of a chant; and we are advised to make more use (at intermediate cadences) of this same final than of other notes, so that the modality of a chant is preserved without ambiguity.

In *Micrologus*, Guido (writing perhaps a century later) re-iterates the principles formulated in *Dialogus*. His fourth chapter begins:

'Thou hast, therefore, six consonantia of notes, that is: tone, semitone, major third, minor third, fourth and fifth.' (*Habet itaque sex vocum consonantias, id est tonum, semitonium, ditonum, semiditonium, diatessaron et diapente.*)

Later he continues:

'Through the aforesaid six intervals [= *consonantia*], to be sure, the remaining notes [of a phrase] are bound to agree with the note that ends the phrase.' (*Capitulum xi*, p. 140: *Per supradictas nempe consonantias voci quae neumam terminat reliquae voces concordare debent.*)

(Note Guido's use of *neuma* for a phrase.)

This makes plain that, not merely are beginnings and intermediate cadences to be in the intervallic relationships of semitone, tone, minor or major third, fourth or fifth with the final of a chant, but every single note of every single phrase stands in those same relationships to the phrase-final.

By the middle of the eleventh century, therefore, it was understood that measurable intervallic relationships, measurable and definable on the monochord, existed between every note of a chant and the pitch of its final. And Guido continues:

'It is necessary that the beginning of a chant, and the ends (or, indeed, the beginnings) of all its intermediate phrases, cling to the note that ends the chant.' (Capitulum xi, p. 140: *Voci vero quae cantum terminat, principium eius cunctarumque distinctionum fines vel etiam principia opus est adhaerere.*)

Aribo (writing between 1070 and 1100, in his *Commentarius in Micrologum Guidonis Aretini*, p. 132) expands the first two paragraphs of Guido's *Micrologus* Chapter 11, p. 139. The chapter is entitled:

'Which note may obtain pre-eminence in a chant, and by what means?' (*Quae vox et quare in cantu obtineat principatum.*)

Guido himself had begun by stating that it is the note that ends the chant which does so; and he explains this achievement:

'For this sounds both longer and more frequently.' (*…ea enim et diutius et morosius sonat.*)

He continues:

'And the notes previously uttered are (as is apparent only to experts) so fitted to it that they seem, in remarkable fashion, to derive from it a sort of mood [= color] as it were.' (*Micrologus*, pp. 139, 140. *Et praemissae voces, quod tantum exercitatis patet, ita ad eam aptantur, ut mirum in modum quandam ab ea coloris faciem ducere videantur.*)

This word color (= literally 'colour') is again a term used in the description of oratory or speech; it signifies 'cast', 'character', or 'tone' (in the sense of 'manner'); and at the end of his commentary on the passage in Guido (p. 140) that begins: '*Voci vero quae cantum terminat*', Aribo offers a summary:

'In fact, the notes are fitted to the final in such a way, that they [1] both take their colour (or mood) from it in accordance with the Natural Law of what fits with what, and in addition [2] they owe their recognition to it: that is to say, you can discover from them to which [mode] they should be attributed, whether to the First [Mode] or to [one of] the others. For through the aforementioned intervals [consonantia] they agree with [any] intermediate cadence, and in truth, through these same intervals [any] intermediate cadence agrees with the final.' (p. 134: *Vere voces finali aptantur, ut ab ea et colorentur naturali lege proprietatum et habeant illam cognitionem ab ea, scilicet ut sciatur de eis cui debent attribui seu proto seu ceteris; nam per praedictas consonantias concordant distinctioni, distinctio vero per easdem consonantias finali.*)

[Smits van Waesbergh erred perhaps in supplying the marginal cue '*Micrologus Cap. viii*' on p. 133; the chapter-number appears to be *xi*.]

The implications (for the melodic structure of a chant) of this statement, are surely remarkable: any interval within and including a fifth (but excluding the tritone), lying to either side of the final, appears to be acceptable for use as an intermediate cadence. The only restraint is one of range rather than one of intervallic quality. Whether chants indeed display such structural features as here implied is a question for others to answer.

Echoes

Folk-etymology might suggest that a Latin word plausibly anglicised as 'repercuss' might mean 'to strike again'. This was not its original meaning, however: *percussio* (from *percutio -cussi -cussum*) could indeed mean 'a beating (of time)' and hence 'rhythm'; and the verb itself was used for 'to play' – a lyre, for example; but *repercussio* meant 'a rebounding', and in respect to sound the verb meant 'to echo' or 're-echo'. In its most general use it did not mean 'to strike again' but 'to strike back'.

In the form *repercussa* (where originally the adjective qualified the word *vox* ('note') or some other feminine noun, the word became important as a term for the reciting-note in simple chant. Early in the seventeenth century, and in the form *repercussio* (a feminine noun derived from the Past Participle of *percutere*) it was equated with the term dominant in its French form: *dominante* (p. 170).

Although the secondary sources for the history of liturgical music in the Western Church commonly allege that *tuba*, *tenor*, and *repercussa/repercussio* are synonyms, and that all three refer to the reciting-note of simple chant, no earliest date of use for any of these terms is ever mentioned. It has been argued (p. 150) that those features of simple chant, which invite comparison with a trumpet-call that consists of a single iterated pitch, led to application of the term '*tuba*' to chant; and that the term was first applied to the musical sound of simple chant, rather than to the procedure of syllabic iteration of the reciting-note. As to the use of *tenor*, it will be suggested in 'Holds' (p. 161) that the equation with *tuba* is a relatively late phenomenon, in this sense possibly later than *Micrologus*.

Again, notwithstanding the assumption of identity with the meaning of reciting-note, the texts suggest that *repercussa/repercussio* was also used (and may be first solely used) for relatively frequent returns to a particular pitch/note in the course of a chant, rather than repetition in continuous sequence.

An early instance in which the verb *repercutio -cussi -cussum* is evidently used for the re-echoing of a note – in the sense of singing it relatively frequently in the course of a plainsong-melody – occurs in *Dialogus* in part of the text not translated by Strunk. The author is concerned to inform the pupil how to decide whether a given chant is in the First Tone or in its plagal counterpart, the Second Tone. He sets out the two note-sets as follows [where (T) and (S) mark intervals of tone and semitone between degrees. Numerals in curved brackets are ordinal numbers of the successive degrees, counting upwards from *A*]:

First Tone: {8}   {9}   {10}   {11}
C (T) *D* (T) *E* (S) *F* (T) *G* (T) *a* (S) *b♭/b* (S) *c* (T) *d'*
(The author allows for a change from *b♭* to *b* and conversely; *D* is the final.)

Second Tone: {8}   {9}
G (T) *A* (T) *B* (S) *C* (T) *D* (T) *E* (S) *F* (T) *G* (T) *a* (T) *b*
(Again *D* is the final.)

Having made plain (*Dialogus*, p. 259.12) that chants in the Second Tone may ascend (like those in the First) to the ninth (= *b*) (counting upwards from *A*), but *not* to the tenth or eleventh (to the *c* or *d'*) to which First Tone items are permitted to ascend, the Master continues:

'And thus the Second Tone includes the *G*, and the first *A*, and the second *B* [first and second notes in the tetrachord below the final, *D*], which the First [Tone] does not include; and the First includes the tenth, *c*, and the eleventh, *d'* [counting from the low *A*], which the Second does not include. Of these [Tones], however, there are many chants that do *not* descend to *G*, and to the first *A*, and to the second *B*, [and] do *not* rise to the tenth or to the eleventh, regarding which [chants] it is uncertain whether they be of the First or Second Tone. The distinguishing difference between these is in such wise: If they do not rise to the eighth and ninth, they are most certainly of the Second Tone. So the eighth and ninth [notes] will be common to both [Tones]. When the chant ascends to these [notes], it will be of the First [Tone] if it stay on these for a long time, or *if it echo these for a third or fourth time* [our italics]. It will also be of the First Tone if it begin on the eighth [note].' (12. *M. Habet itaque secundus tonus G [the gamma is used for the low G] & primam A. & secundam B. quas non habet primus: & primus habet decimam c. & undecimam d. quas non habet secundus. Sunt autem*

158

horum [tonorum] plurimi cantus, qui ad G & primam A. & secundam B. non
deponuntur, ad decimam vel undecimam non elevantur, de quibus dubius est, an
primi, an secundi sint toni: quorum ita discretio est. Ad octavam & nonam si non
ascendunt, certissime de tono secundo sunt. Erunt itaque octava & nona
utriusque communes, ad quas dum cantus ascendit, et diu in eis permaneat, sive
tertio vel quarto eas repercutiat, aut si in octava incipiat, modi erit primi.)

In this illuminating passage from a work distinguished by its practical clarity, and
by direct and simple expression, we meet the verb *repercutere* itself in the
subjunctive mood; but it is plainly not describing the *repercussa* as it existed in
simple chant as a reciting-note. In a psalm-verse, for example, *that* note is not
iterated in sequence a mere three or four times, even though, indeed, all reciting-
notes in authentic modes are pitched at a fifth (or sixth) above the final. It seems
possible, then, that the later technical sense of *repercussa* had not developed
when *Dialogus* was written.

The use of the word *repercussa* in *Micrologus*, however, suggests a
reference to a reciting-note. We are told in Chapter 16 'On the manifold variety
of sounds and phrases' (p. 178, *Cap. xvi: De multiplici varietate sonorum et
neumarum*):

'Accordingly, the motion of notes (to be executed in six ways) [= the six
kinds of conjoining intervals – consonantia (our p. 144)] is done [as] arsis and
thesis, that is: rising and falling. Every phrase is fashioned from the two kinds of
motion – arsis and thesis – of these [intervals], apart from re-iterated and/or
simple [notes]' (p. 179: *Igitur motus vocum, qui sex modis fieri dictus est, fit arsis
et thesis, id est elevatio et depositio; quorum gemino motu, id est arsis et thesis,
omnis neuma formatur praeter repercussas aut simplices.*)

Since this passage concerns movement from note to note, it seems likely that
repercussa(s) are here 're-iterated notes'; that is, the behaviour of a note
sequentially repeated – a reciting-note – is being described. [The parallels
between this passage from Chapter 16 of *Micrologus* and the definitions of varna
(the act of singing) as displayed in Widdess (1995), in the Śaṅgītaratnākara (13th
century; 1. 6. 1–3) of Śārṅgadeva, are striking.]

The author of *Micrologus* is describing, note by note, the construction of
musical phrases: (a) by the movement of notes ascending or descending in pitch,
through one or other of the six specified intervals, and (b) by the use of repeated
or single notes. The chapter is concerned, as the title shows, with melody and –
more precisely in this context – with the movement of pitched notes associated
with the syllables of the text. Repeated notes are here an alternative to single
notes. This is not the 'echoing' of pitches as in *Dialogus*; here, surely, the

meaning is that of repetition of notes in sequence, and hence, that of a reciting-note.

In his review of criteria by which to identify the mode of a chant with precision, Johannis Affligemensis – John of Affligem – (author of *De musica cum tonario*) used a synonym of *repercutere* 'to strike back', 'to echo', as used in *Dialogus* and *Micrologus*. His synonym is *reverberare*, meaning 'to strike back', and presumably, like *repercutere* in regard to sound, also 'to echo'. The example he offers is as follows:

'Whence also, though this antiphon 'Ecce tu pulchra es' falls into the course of the Second Tone, nevertheless, because the upper [range] more often echoes the fifth from the final, it is to be reckoned as of the First Tone.' (*De musica...*, Capitulum xii, p. 92: *Unde et haec Antiphon: Ecce tu pulchra es quamquam in cursum secundi toni decidet, tamen quis superius quintam a finali saepius reverberat, primo tono deputator.*)

This is the phenomenon reported in *Dialogus*, and not an instance of a note sequentially repeated as a reciting-note, as in *Micrologus*.

Versions of this Antiphon survive in at least four *MSS.* consulted: two of the tenth (?) century (one in Lucca; one in Toledo); the 13th-century Worcester *MS.* already referred to; and the *Antiphonale Sarisburiense* (Frere, Volume 5 – examined by N.J.N.). The incipits of Lucca and Toledo are similar; and the opening 'Ecce tu pulchra es' in the Worcester *MS.* suggests that the later version is a variant of that current in the tenth century. The text is part of the Song of Songs, and but a tiny fraction of that text as it exists in the Vulgate. Already in the first verse: 'Ecce tu pulchra es amica mea ecce tu pulchra oculi tui columbarum' the fifth (a) above the final (d) is sounded five times. We have used the Old Sarum version.

Example 3.

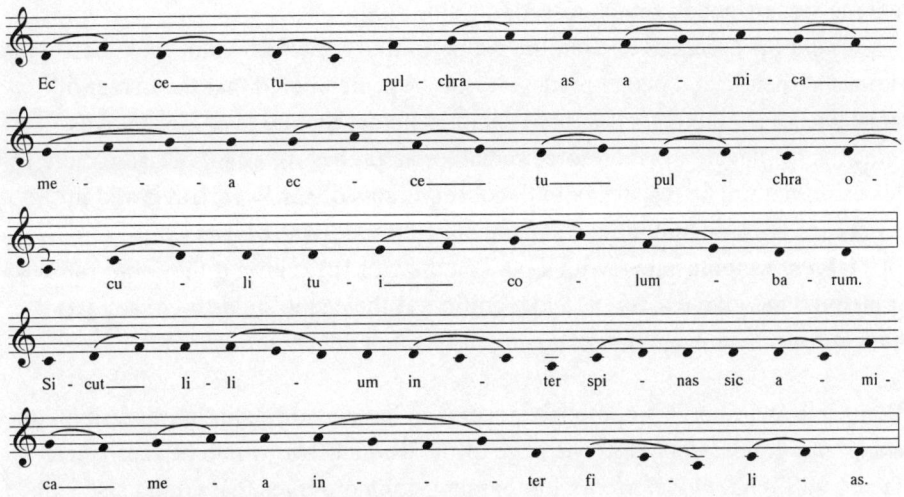

Ec- ce— tu— pul - chra— as a - mi - ca—
me - - a ec - ce— tu— pul - chra o -
cu - li tu - i— co - lum - ba - rum.
Si - cut— li - li - um in - ter spi - nas sic a - mi -
ca— me - a in - - - ter fi - li - as.

[Frere, Walter Howard, Bishop of Truro (1894), *Graduale Sarisburiense*.]

Holds

Another word that, like *repercussa* and *repercussio*, appears to have extended its technical meaning with the passage of time, is *tenor*. An early text, in which this word is evidently being used in a sharply formulated technical sense, is again the *De musica cum tonario* of Johannis Affligemensis, written between 1100 and 1121. The eleventh chapter of that work establishes two technical terms in their later accepted meanings by including both in its title:

'On the tenors of modes and on their finals' (*Cap. xi*, p. 82: *De tenoribus modorum et finalibus eorum*).

The author begins his account with a concise statement:

'Just as there are eight Tones, so also the tenors of the same are eight.' (*Sicut autem octo sunt toni, ita et octo eorundem sunt tenores.*)

He then pauses to derive the word from *teneo* 'I hold', as *nitor* derives from *niteo* 'I shine', or *splendor* from *splendeo* (with approximately the same literal and figurative meanings as *niteo*). While the primary meaning of the verb *tenere* is 'to hold', its meanings in classical Latin usage ranged from that literal meaning through 'to possess' to 'to master', 'to hold course' and 'to belong to'. The noun-derivative: *tenor* means principally a 'course' and an 'uninterrupted course' at that. In its musical use, from Guido (as we shall see later) to John, the term has

161

the meaning of 'holding on to', that is, sustaining a note. The meaning of
reciting-note is not as yet expressed.

John now proceeds to examine the permitted ranges of chant-melodies in the
various authentic and plagal modes. It is to be remembered that the matter of
range was crucial to any attempt to decide whether the mode of a chant was
authentic or plagal; and therefore crucial to the process of chant-classification. In
this examination, he restates both the observations of *Dialogus* [reviewed in
Echoes, p. 157], and Guido's restatement of these in *Micrologus* (xiii).

Of *tenors* John states (with a play on the word): 'It is as if they *hold* the keys
of melody and give us access to recognition of the chant.' (*Quasi enim claves
modulationis tenent, et ad cantum cognoscendum nobis aditum dant.*)

[Smits van Waesbergh's compositor seems to have made a slip in transcribing the
text as *claves modulationes.* The page of the Munich *MS.* which he reproduces
(facing p. 82) has *modulationis.*] In passing, John observes that Guido also calls
prolonging the last note 'tenor'. (*Sed et moram ultimae voci Guido tenorem
vocat.*) In fact, this seems to be the only express use by Guido of the term. In the
matter of permitted ranges of chant-melodies, Guido never once refers to the
word. As we follow John, it becomes plain that he is thinking in terms of
particular pitches:

'And in music, indeed, we call *tenors* when [and wherever] the first syllable
of *saeculorum amen* is begun, in any Tone whatsoever. (*Et tenores quidem in
musica vocamus, ubi prima syllaba saeculorum amen cuiuslibet toni incipitur.*)

His examples (p. 85) show that the first syllable of *saeculorum amen* is indeed
sung on a particular pitch, characteristic of each Tone.

Although it seems certain that John did not himself use the term 'tenor'
expressly in the sense of a reciting-note, it is evident that his list of tenors (in the
eight Tones/Modes) is that which has persisted to the present.

Re-arranging his concise statement in tabular form we have:

Tone	Authentic	Plagal	Tenor	Final
I	"		*a*	D
Protus				
II		"	*f*	D
III	"		*c*	E
Deuterus				
IV		"	*a*	E

V	"		c	F
Tritus				
VI		"	a	F
VII	"		d	G
Tetrardus				
VIII		"	c	G

This does not differ from the Table displayed (for example) by Reese (1940).

From this preliminary exposition, it is evident that John is primarily concerned with the 'holding'-meaning of *tenor*. *What* is held emerges from his list of tenors for the eight Tones/Modes. *Where* such holding occurs is plainly linked, for him, with the permitted *ranges* of authentic and plagal forms of the Tones. The sites of the tenors, and the permitted ranges, were therefore related.

The matter of range is taken up in the following chapter, where he comments:

'For also Odo [the monk of Cluny, formerly regarded as author of *Dialogus*] – who is very experienced in this art, and [is] approved by Guido at the end of his treatment [that is, in *Micrologus*, Chapter 13] – considers a chant to be in the authentic *Protus* if, rising from the final, it echoes the fifth three or four times'. (Capitulum xii, p. 92: *Nam et Odo huius artis experientissimus, et a Guidone in fine tractatus sui comprobatus, cantum qui a finali ascendens quintam ter vel quater repercutit autento deputat.*)

In this passage he misquotes [strictly speaking] both sources: it is *Dialogus* not *Micrologus* that refers to echoing the fifth three or four times; and *Dialogus* in fact speaks of echoing eighth and ninth (counting from *A*). Counting from the final, *D*, however, these would be fifth (*a*) and sixth (*b*) respectively. *Micrologus*, summarising the permitted range of initial and final notes of intermediate phrases, states that for authentic modes (apart from the *Deuterus* = Third Tone) it is least proper for them to extend to the sixth; that is to say, the fifth is acceptable. A reference to 'echoing' of fifth and sixth does not seem to occur in *Micrologus*.

The passage in *Micrologus* xiii – while appearing to be concerned with the maximal permissible interval between the final, and pitches on which chants may begin, or pitches at the beginnings and endings of intermediate phrases – in fact summarises virtually the same data (as are assembled by John) regarding tones and tenors. These same notes prescribed in *Micrologus* are both the permitted initials, and the permitted notes at beginnings and ends of intermediate phrases:

they are in the latter instance, therefore, tenors. The passage is telling us (among other things) that intermediate cadences are not permitted to be located on pitches higher (in relation to the final) than the pitch of the tenor characteristic of that mode.

The passage merits translation in full: 'In this matter then, it is foreseen on which notes of individual modes chants may more rarely or more often begin, and on which that may least be done. Thus in any plagals it is quite improper to range *either* the beginnings *or* the endings of intermediate phrases at the [distance of] fifths [above the respective finals], rarely it may happen to the fourth.' (p. 154: *Ibi enim praevidetur quibus in vocibus singulorum modorum cantus rarius saepius ve incipiant et in quibus minime id fiat, ut in plagis quidem minime licet vel principia vel fines distinctionum ad quintas intendere cum ad quartam perraro soleat avenire.*)

A glance at the Table of finals and tenors prepared from data presented by John (our p. 162) shows that no plagal mode exhibits a tenor distant by as much as a fifth from the final. Tones II and VI display tenors a third above the final; IV and VIII, tenors at the fourth above. Guido continues:

'In authentics, indeed, apart from the *Deuterus* [III], it is quite improper to range these same beginnings and endings of intermediate phrases to the sixths.' (p. 155: *In autentis vero, praeter deuterum, eadem principia et fines distinctionum minime licet ad sextas intendere;...*)

Again, the Table shows tenors at these positions, as previously stated. The sixth *is* the tenor of the authentic *Deuterus* /Third Tone; but it seems likely that this replacement of *b* by *c* arose from pre-occupation with the character of *b*, whether flattened or natural. I, V, and VII, all exhibit tenors at the fifth above the final in the data from John.

'But the plagals of the *Protus* [II] or *Tritus* [V] extend to the thirds; and the plagals of *Deuterus* [IV] or *Tetrardus* [VIII] extend, indeed, to the fourths.' (p. 155: *plagae autem proti vel triti ad tertias intendunt, et plagae siquidem deuteri vel tetrardi ad quartas intendunt.*)

Aribo comments on this passage, and in so doing refers to the *saeculorum amen*, as did (as we have seen) John. Words (in the translation) that derive from Guido's text in his Chapter 13, will be shown between single quotation-marks:

'There truly', that is, in these formulas, as in *saeculorum amen*, we see 'on which notes of the individual modes a chant may begin more often and more rarely, and on which it' – that is, the beginning – 'may least' occur. For every chant, whether plagal or authentic, can begin (or indeed any intermediate phrase

164

in a chant can begin or end) on that note higher than the final, by which the *saeculorum amen* stands higher [than the final], and [by which] the tenor of the entire psalm, appropriate to any authentic or plagal mode [stands higher than the final]. (*Micrologus*, Cap. xiii, p. 142) (Aribo, *Commentarius*, p. 142) (*Ibi enim, id est in illis formulis, sicut in 'Saeculorum amen' videmus in quibus vocibus singulorum modorum cantus saepius rariusve incipiant, et in quibus id*, scilicet inceptio, *minime fiat. Ibi enim altius potest omnis cantus tam plagalis quam authentus super finalem incipere, vel etiam incipere et finire quaelibet distinctio in cantu, ubi ascendit 'Saeculorum amen', et tenor totius psalmi aptati alicui modo authento vel plagali.*)

Again, slight differences between the accepted text of Guido, and Aribo's quotations therefrom, are to be noted.

Here it would seem that Aribo views the tenors not merely as sustained notes of a particular quality and position, but also as notes of a particular pitch in relation to the final; his reference to 'the entire psalm' perhaps implies that he is aware that tenors also function as reciting-notes.

It seems possible, then, that Aribo was aware (as Guido may have been) of the equivalence between tenor and reciting-note – a note pitched at a certain *maximal* height above the final, as were the sustained notes at the ends of intermediate cadences. Plainly, chants are permitted to begin *most frequently* on the tenor-pitch, or (what comes to the same thing) on the pitch of the first syllable of the formula *Saeculorum amen*; but other initials are not to be excluded. Whether this passage from Aribo implies a restriction, as compared with Guido's original formulation, has not been determined.

At the beginning of the twelfth century, therefore, tenors were notes judged most suitable for endings (or beginnings) of intermediate phrases; and since the end-notes of such phrases were prolonged as cadences they were properly called tenors. No one, so far as we are aware, has suggested a reason for this relationship between final and tenor in authentics and plagals. We suggest it is related to comfortable singing. With plagals descending at times not merely to a fourth, but even to a fifth, below the final, some balance between the excursions of the voice below and above the final was desirable, in evolved chant as well as in simple chant. That the chosen intervals between finals and tenors are fifths, fourths, thirds – and once a sixth – was due, it is suggested, to perception (perhaps unconscious) of 'consonances' in a resonant space.

Returning to the term *'tenor'*: this is evidently the functional precursor of the term *dominant* as used in the major/minor harmonic world of Western music, from the time of Rameau onwards (p. 175). It is worth mentioning that the word *dominus* (whence 'dominant') carried, among other meanings, those of 'owner' and 'possessor'; just as *teneo* 'I hold' also meant 'I possess'.

Interposed Betweens, and Mediants

With Tinctoris (1477) (*Johannis Tinctoris opera theoretica*, ed. Albertus Seay (1975) I, p. 7) – in service between 1472 and 1487 with Ferdinand I, King of Naples – the *consonantia*(s) of the eleventh century have become *concordantia*, and they are evidently simultaneous concords; *not* (as for *Dialogus*) intervals between consecutive notes. In his *Liber de arte contrapuncti*, II, p. 15, Tinctoris refers to the three concordances established 'before all other men by Pythagoras': fifth, fourth and octave; and from his list of eight different concords within the octave, the semitone and tone of the *consonantia* have disappeared, and minor and major sixths (*diapente cum semitonio* and *diapente cum tono*) are added. Distinction is made between perfect concords: unison, fourth, fifth, octave; and imperfect concords: minor and major thirds, minor and major sixths (p. 16); and perhaps for the first time, minor and major thirds are named as imperfect and perfect third, respectively (*tertia imperfecta* and *perfecta*).

Furthermore, in naming notes Tinctoris (p. 22) makes use not merely of functional names: 'initials' (*initiales*) and 'finals' (*finales*) but also of locational names: 'uppers' (*superiores*) and 'lowers' (*graviores*).

'Indeed we call them "uppers" if before, and immediately behind them, there is either a single note or several other notes [that are] one or more degrees lower; whereas so-called 'lowers' are those preceded or followed by one or several other notes, [that are] one or several degrees higher.' (II, p. 22: *Superiores vero illas appellamus quae unam aut multas alias ante se et post immediate habent uno gradu aut pluribus eis inferiores; et inferiores dictae sunt illae quae una aut multas aliae sive uno gradu sive pluribus altiores immediate praecedunt atque sequuntur.*)

Uppers and lowers, accordingly, are notes that mark upper and lower limits of compass; and now, for the first time, Tinctoris uses a term: 'between [-notes]' (*mediae*), for notes interpolated between initial, final, upper and lower:

'However, we call those "betweens" that are to be seen interposed here and there between the aforesaid, that is [the aforesaid] initials, finals, uppers and lowers'. (II. p. 22: *Medias autem illas vocamus quae praedictis, hoc est initialibus, finalibus, superioribus ac inferioribus passim interpositae conspiciuntur...*)

The following '*ut hic patet*' precedes an example.

166

Tinctoris' example shows that this judgement of locational character, and hence of name, is made sequentially, from note to note; and it is evident that the terms are purely locational and in this context in no way functional. Uppers and lowers define upper and lower limits of the scalar set of notes that comprise a melody. On this scale, in addition to upper and lower notes, the locations of final and initial are also marked.

Note that the adverb 'immediate', translated above as 'immediately' means literally 'without a "between" '.

This discrimination of 'betweens' becomes of even greater importance in the third part of Giuseppe Zarlino's *Le istitutioni harmoniche* (1558) [Third Part only translated by Guy A. Marco and Claude V. Palisca (1968); a facsimile of the entire work is available in the edition of 1575. (Gregg Press, 1966)]. In Chapters 6 and 7, using the term for simultaneous concords, Zarlino states that fifth and fourth are 'middles' (*mezana* – today *mezzana*) between the perfect and imperfect consonances (Facsimile: *Terza Parte*, pp. 178–9; translation: pp. 15–17). He recognises a series of diminishing consonantal perfection: octave, fifth, fourth. Between octave and fifth fall the sixths (minor and major) and between the fourth and the unison fall the thirds (minor and major). Again, the 'middles' are such by location; they may not be regarded as functionally mediating anything in any way.

Zarlino (Facsimile, Chapter 10, p. 182; translation: p. 21) uses the terms 'major' and 'minor', and expressly recognises the sad or cheerful character of thirds and sixths, in accordance with their major or minor character:

'All these have the power to change any melody and to make it sad or gay according to their nature.' (*Tutte queste hanno forza di mutare ogni cantilena & di farla mesta, ouero allegro secondo la sua natura.*)

Zarlino, too, is using the term *mezana* for the fifth degree above certain modal finals. That is to say, 'the middle string', the *chorda media* of *Nova Expositio* (our p. 147), the boundary between lower fifth and upper fourth, has become the *mezana* of Zarlino (Facsimile: p. 182; translation: p. 21).

He continues: 'The which we can see from this; that there are some melodies that are lively and full of gaiety; and some others, on the contrary, that are somewhat sad and lifeless. The reason is that in the former, the major imperfect consonances [that is, major thirds and minor sixths] are often heard on the last, final strings [= notes], or on the between-strings [= between-notes = intervening notes] of the Modes or Tones that are: the Ionian (I), the Hyper-Ionian (II), the Lydian (VII), the Hypo-Lydian (VIII), the Mixo-Lydian (IX) and the Hypo-Mixo-Lydian (X); as we shall see elsewhere: such modes are most gay and lively, because in them we hear, frequently sounded, consonances placed according to the character of the Harmonious Number: that is, the fifth: cut, or harmonically divided, into a major third and a minor [third]; the which is most delightful to "hearing".' (Facsimile: Chapter 10, p. 182; translation pp. 21, 22: *Il che posiamo uedere da questo; che sono alcune Cantilene, le quali sono uiue & piene di allegrezza; & alcune altre per il contrario, sono alquante meste, ouer languide. La cagione è, che nelle prime, spesso si odono le Maggiori consonanze imperfette sopra le chorde estreme finali, o mezane de i Modi, o Tuoni, che sono il Primo, il Secundo, il Settimo, l'Ottavo, il Nono, & il Decimo; come uederemo altroue: i quali Modi sono molto allegri & viui: conciosia che in essi udimo spesse fiate le Consonanze collocate secondo la natura del Numero sonoro: cio è la Quinta tramezata, o divisa harmonicamente in una Terza maggiore & in una minore; il [c]he molto diletta all 'Udito'.*)

As explained by Marco and Palisca (p. 22, n. 2), the consonances are arranged according to their 'harmonious numbers' in the sequence of their generation by successive divisions of a string into 2, 3, 4, 5 and 6 parts. Divisions 4, 5 and 6 yield a series of notes (forming a major triad) with major third below minor third. If the string-lengths are as 30 to 24 to 20, the fifth, C to G, is harmonically divided, and the middle term: E, is the 'harmonic mean'. For $A\ C\ E$, the fifth is divided by the 'arithmetic mean': C.

In either case we are back in the arithmetical world of Boëthius, and of the monochord; and the matter of the harmonic or arithmetic division of the interval of a fifth. What Zarlino says is: 'that is, the fifth: partitioned, or harmonically divided, into a major and a minor third'. (See preceding text.) His post-participle: *tramezata*, means no more than divided – as it were by a partition – by a note, the string-length of which is the harmonic mean between the lengths of two notes a fifth apart.

He goes on to consider the arithmetically divided fifths, where the intermediate note lies at a minor third above the lowest note, and a major third below the upper notes. We are plainly brought face to face with the future mediant and sub-mediant, though these terms are not as yet used. It is clear, however, that (whenever it was accepted) the term 'mediant' had no implication of a 'mediating' function; it was merely another 'between-note', discriminated in the centuries-long process of recognising note-locations and functions that required naming.

In his Chapter 12, Zarlino uses, for the first time, both the adjective *mezana* and the verb *mediare* with reference to the division of the octave-consonance into a sequence of notes. The fact that the adjective *mezana* is again being used is concealed by the translation of Marco and Palisca.

Zarlino refers to the consonance of the octave: 'when it is regarded by the musician simply and in general: that is, when its extremities are without any between-note, or other sound, and form a single interval, this [= the octave] is found to be of a single kind.' (Facsimile: Chapter 12, p. 184; translation p. 26: *Questa, quando è considerata dal Musico semplicemente & in generale: cio è quado [= quando] li suoi estremi sono senza alcuna voce mezana, ouero altro suono & fanno un solo intervallo, si ritrova hauere una sola specie.*) (Attention may be drawn to a degree of confusion in pagination in at least one copy of the Gregg Press edition of 1966.)

The condition of the intact octave is next contrasted with the subdivided octave. Zarlino continues:

'But when it [= the octave] is considered in detail, and according to its being diatonically divided into tones and semitones or divided into other intervals, then (I say) that its kinds are seven [in number], according to the ability of the intervals between the between-sounds to dispose themselves diversely in seven ways according to the character of the diatonic genus:....' (Facsimile: p. 184; translation p. 26:...*ma quando è considerata particolarmente, & secondo che ella è diuisa diatonicamente in Tuoni & in Semituoni; ouero mediata da altri interualli, allora dico, che le sue specie sono Sette, secondo che gli intervalli delli suoni mezani si possono diuersamente, secondo la natura del genere Diatonico ordinare in sette maniere:....*)

(Facsimile p. 185; translation p. 27) Marco and Palisca (translating from the edition of the text used by them) have: 'its intervening intervals'; we prefer (as here) 'the intervals between the between-sounds (*suoni mezani*)'. Their anglicisation of the participle *mediata* as 'mediated' – in translating the phrase *ouero mediata da altri intervalli* – is misleading, because English retains only the meaning of human action as mediator for the verb 'to mediate'. We suggest (as in the preceding paragraph): 'or divided into other intervals'.

It has been, perhaps, the continued use of such cognates that has encouraged belief that in some mysterious way the term 'mediant' encapsulated a kind of harmonic action. The only surviving touch of harmony here resides in mathematics, and in what Boëthius meant by harmonic and arithmetic division of the interval of a fifth.

A semantically interesting feature of Zarlino's text is the use of the past participle *mediata* in relation to the *G*-string (= note), between *C* and *c*, the octave bounding his First Mode. What Zarlino meant by this use is made evident by his adding the adverb 'harmonically' (*harmonicamente*); he is referring to the placing of 'the middle string' at the fifth above the lower note in the harmonic division of the octave – in the arithmetic division it would be located at the fourth above the lower note. That is to say, he is referring to the harmonic mean within the intervallic limits of the octave – hence his use of the participle *mediata*.

'I say then that the First Mode is such as I have shown, which arises from the first kind [= species] of the octave, *C* and *c*, of which the *G*-string is the harmonic mean.' (Literally, he says: 'harmonically meaned by the *G*-string'.) (*Dico adunque che'l Primo modo è quello, come hò mostrato; il quale nasce dalla Prima specie della Diapason, C & c, dalla Chorda G harmonicamente mediata.*)

Only the Third Part of Zarlino's work is translated by Marco and Palisca; but this passage (in Part IV) furnishes an instance where use of a cognate [frequently practised by these translators (see their Introduction, p. xxiii)] would be misleading to English readers. It is to be added that Zarlino's *Seconda Tavola* – a companion to the first *Tavola* (a list of chapter-headings in the four parts), arranged as an alphabetical index of topics – shows no 'dominant' entry, nor indeed any historically related term, such as repercussa, tenor or tuba.

In Zarlino's text, *mediata* means no more than sub-divided, as (for example) 'being in suchwise sub-divided' (*essendo in tal maniera mediata*); and this significance is conceded by Marco and Palisca themselves later in this same chapter. This use of *mediata* for 'sub-divided' was already accepted by Glareanus (*Dodecachordon*: Basle, 1547); but again Powers (1980, p. 408, Ex. 20) displays this latter author's 'mediated octaves' as if something fresh had been added to the vocabulary of modal description, necessitating a new and technical term.

Tenor, Repercussa, Dominant

Reference was made, in the Introduction to this chapter (p. 100), to Seidel's article on the concept of *dominant*. Pursuing certain of his references, particular importance attaches to Salomon de Caus, a Frenchman who served Prince Henry in London and dedicated his *Institution harmonique* (1615) to Queen Anne. His first reference to the *Note Dominante* states immediately that it is so-called 'by certain moderns'. This presumably implies that the usage was of recent date in his time:

'And as to the note contained within [the limits of] the octave, called the *dominant note* by certain moderns, one causes it to be heard frequently, so as to accord with the character of the mode in which the said note is, for it is usually that [note] which confers ornament on the mode one wishes to exhibit.' (Partie Deuxiesme, Chapitre X, p. 21: *Et quand à la note comprise entre le Diapason*

dite d'aucuns modernes NOTE DOMINANTE, on la fera ouir souuent, à celle fin
de suiure la nature de la Mode, ou la dite note sera. Car c'est celle qui donne
ordinairement l'ornement à la Mode, que l'on desire representer.)

(The word *ornement* may be equated with 'richness of expression'.)

To whom de Caus refers as 'aucuns modernes' is still unknown. His work appears to have been based, in part at least, on that of Zarlino (1558); but careful examination of Zarlino's text and in particular his fourth and last Part (devoted to 'the nature of mode and its kinds') (see Zarlino, p. 359), does not disclose any use of a term corresponding to *dominant*.

In his next chapter, de Caus begins an examination of the structure of all the modes, starting with the First Mode as it had become in his day, namely, the octave-set of *C* major. *G* is named as the dominant.

'On the first mode, called Authentic, and on its nature: The first mode, as may be seen in the preceding chapter, is contained within the octave of *C. sol, fa, ut,* so that the fifth on *C. sol, fa, ut,* which is G. *sol, re, ut,* will be the dominant note, and the two others together will be the rudder of all the others.' (Chapitre XI De la premiere mode dite Autentique, et de sa nature: *La Premiere Mode, comme se peut voir au chap. precedent, est comprise au Diapason de* C. sol, fa, ut, *en sorte que la quinte de* C. sol, fa, ut, *qui est* G. sol, ré, ut, *sera la note dominante, et les deux autres ensemblement seront le gouvernail de toutes les autres.*)

In the preceding chapter (X), de Caus has set out on a tenor-clef stave the structure of the First Mode: *C - G - c.* The 'two others together' (in relation to *G* in his statement in the preceding paragraph) are *C* and *c.* On p. 3 of the Partie Deuxiesme he supplies names of notes, in the *solfa* scale, as they occur on the clef-line (the line passing through a clef) in various clefs. This he now does in the preceding quotation, and by this means he defines notes in such a way that the principal notes of the First Authentic Mode are made plain, even to those familiar with a single clef only. Somewhat surprisingly he does not see fit to include his comments on 'dominante' in his index.

His remark regarding the dominant, that 'one causes it to be heard frequently' suggests that he regards repetition of the dominant as an essential feature of its behaviour in melodic exposition. From the chapter that follows concerning the Second (plagal) Mode, it is evident that he is using the term 'dominant' as the term 'tenor' was used by earlier writers; in his definition of the Second Mode, *C* is both final and dominant (Chapitre XII). That is to say, with an octave-set extending between *G* and *g*, *C* is not only the final but also (for him) the note that functions as a reciting-note in simple chant. Evidently, he is no longer defining a plagal dominant as a note at the interval of a third or fourth *above* the modal final.

Sebastian de Brossard in his justly famous *Dictionnaire* (1703) seems to imply that the term *dominante* in French had prior existence in Italian as 'dominante'. He continues:

'means *Dominante*. It is the sound that makes the perfect fifth with the final of Authentic Modes or Tones, and the third with the final, or the sixth with the lowest string, of Plagal Modes or Tones. See MODO.' (p. 31: DOMINANTE, Veut dire DOMINANTE. *C'est le Son que fait la 5te juste contre la finalle des* Modes *ou des* Tons Autentiques: *& la 3ce. contre la finalle ou la 6te. contre la plus basse corde des* Modes *ou* Tons Plagaux. *Voyez MODO*.)

(This late persistence of 'corde' for 'note' is striking.)

Interesting as are these statements regarding de Brossard's view of dominants in authentic and plagal modes, his comments under MODO (note use of Italian in an otherwise French text) are of still greater interest:

'In any melody whatsoever there are three principal strings [= notes]. The first is that one where one almost always begins, and where one must always end the melody; on this account one calls it *The Final*. The second is that which one *re-strikes*, which one repeats, and which one hears more often than any other; it is for that reason that one calls it, in Latin, *Repercussio* – as one might say *Re-striking* – and in French: *La Dominante*. The third is that which occupies the middle between the *Final* and the *Dominant*, and which usually is a third above the final; one calls it *The Mediant*. Otherwise one calls these three strings "essential sounds of the mode." ' (p. 61: 1. *Dans quelque Chant que ce soit, il y a trois cordes principalles. La premiere, est celle par où l'on commence presque toujours, & par où l'on doit toujours finir le Chant, c'est pour cela qu'on la nomme* La Finalle. *La 2de est celle, qu'on* rebat, *qu'on repette, & qu'on* entend plus souvent, *que pas un autre, c'est pour cela qu'on la nomme en Latin* Repercussio, *comme qui diroit* Rebattement, *& en François,* La Dominante. *La 3me est celle qui tient le milieu entre la* Finalle *& la* Dominante, *et qui pour l'ordinaire est une 3ce au dessus de la Finalle, on la nomme* La Médiante. *On nomme autrement ces trois Cordes*, 'Sons essentiels du Mode'.)

(Note that the word 'mode' is feminine for de Caus, but masculine – as today – for de Brossard.)

In this passage we see the re-striking meaning of *repercussio* fully accepted, together with an early use of the term 'mediant' (as *la mediante*). From other entries in the dictionary, however, it is plain that de Brossard felt it necessary to make a fuller statement regarding the significance of the dominant in the Church

172

modes, and again under an Italian term for mode: TUONO. He is concerned to show (once more!) how modality may be ascertained when a chant-specimen does not have the range of an entire modal octave. The problem was one (as we have seen) that had presented itself to would-be classifiers of the Gregorian *melodiarium* from the tenth and eleventh centuries onwards.

He observes (all italics original): 'But one often finds melodies lacking a range to fill out the octave of their modes. Such are the melodies of *Prefaces*, of many *Antiphons*, etc… Now in order to know from which Tone these fragments of modes have been derived, after having examined what is their *Final*, one must pay attention to what is their *Dominant*, that is to say, what is *the note most frequently repeated or re-struck in the course of these melodies.* For if this *dominant note* is the fifth or sixth degree *above* the *Final*, then the *Tone* will be *Authentic*; and if it is only the third or fourth degree higher than the *Final*, the tone will be *Plagal.*' [The ordinal number of the Tone would have been revealed (of course) by the note that functioned as final.] (p. 234:TUONO, IIIo. *Mais on trouve souvent des Chants qui n'ont pas assez d'étendue pour remplir toute l'Octave de leurs Modes, tels sont les Chants des* Prefaces, *de plusieurs* Antiennes, &c... *Or pour connoître de quel* Ton *ces* Portions de Modes *ont été tirées, après avoir examiné quelle est leur* Finalle, *il faut prendre garde quelle est leur* Dominante, *c'est à dire, quelle est* la Notte la plus souvent repetée ou rebattue dans la suite de ces Chants. *Car si cette* Notte Dominante *est 5. ou 6. degrez au* dessus *de la* Finalle, *pour lors le* Ton *sera* Autentique, & *si elle n'est que 3. ou 4. degrez plus haut que la* Finalle, *le* Ton *sera* Plagal.)

From this more lengthy and more detailed exposition, there can be no doubt that de Brossard, publishing at the very beginning of the eighteenth century, was still perfectly conscious of the essential practical problem that had evoked the continuous compilation, of résumés of modal theory from the time of Guido of Arezzo onwards: how to determine the modality of melodies; and (in particular) of those less than an octave in compass. De Brossard's summary statement of the height of the dominant above the final (in authentic and plagal forms of the modes) could serve in part as summary of the information given by John of Affligem (our p. 160) in his eleventh chapter (p. 82): 'On the Tenors of Modes and on their Finals'.

Furthermore, de Brossard is strictly concerned with modal *melodies* and primarily with ecclesiastical *chant*, in furnishing this summary for the purposes of modal classification. There can be no disputing that in this context, and for this author, the dominant had a *melodic* functional significance, as well as having particular locations in the various modes. His equating of the term with re-iteration, with the medieval *repercussio* (= *repercussa*) is particularly informative, since it is generally accepted that *Tenor, Repercussa* and *Tuba* were (among other things) synonyms for the reciting-note in simple psalmody.

Again, de Brossard's definition of the *mediant* as the third essential note of a mode, is made merely in terms of its occupying 'the middle' (*le milieu*) between final and dominant; it is a third above the final. His use of all these terms *still* (in 1703) in relation to chant-*melody* is surely related to the accepted usage (that continues in the French Gregorian-Tradition to this day) of the term 'dominant', freed from any major/minor harmonic prejudice. It is evident that de Brossard still accepted that, *in itself, the term 'dominant' had no built-in, fixed, intervallic significance.*

He ends his entry under TUONO with a statement (in abbreviated Latin) of finals and dominants for all modes, *not* of the Glarean system, but as set out by Hucbald, Guido, John of Affligem, and others.

'But in order to recognise immediately and without difficulty what are the *Final* and the *Dominant* of each *Tone*, here are two lines, easy to remember, and [also] understandable (the one and the other) according to the method of *Si*.' (*Mais afin de connoître tout d'un coup & sans peine quelles sont la* Finalle *& la* Dominante *de chaque* Ton. *Voicy deux vers aisez à retenir, et qui comprennent les unes et les autres selon la methode du Si.*)

In each line that follows, the ordinal number of the mode is followed by final and dominant, in that sequence. Odd numbers are those of authentic modes; even, of plagals – that is, of a mode with the same final but ranging from a fourth below to a fifth above the final.

'First: *d, a*; Second: *d, f*; Third: *e, c'*; Fourth also: *e, a*;
Fifth: *f, c '*; Sixth: *f, a*; Seventh: *g, d'*; Eighth also: *g, c'*.'

(Pri. *Re, La*: Sec. *Re, Fa*: Ter. *Mi, Ut*: Quart. Quoque *Mi, La*:
Quint. *Fa, Ut*: Sex. *Fa, La*: Sept. *Sol, Re*: Oct. Quoque *Sol, Ut*:)

De Brossard now makes plain the significance of each term of this summary (plainly intended to be learned by heart) by explaining the abbreviations (Pri., Sec., Ter., etc.) as standing for First, Second, Third – the ordinal numbers of the Tones – and by establishing that the first following letter is the Final; the second, the Dominant. In the case of Primus, for example: *Re* (*d*) is final; *La* (*a*) is dominant.

[His statement that the finals and dominants displayed are those 'according to the method of *Si* (*selon la methode du Si*) is a reference to potential transposition, whereby the essential identity of chants transposed up a fifth or down a fourth (his p. 231) is preserved. Transposed up a fifth, *Mi* (*e*) becomes *Si* (*b*). His range of alphabetical letters for notes shows that we are dealing with the untransposed modal octave on *d*.]

The dominants of this sequence of eight modes/tones are respectively at the following intervals above the finals: 5th, 3rd, 6th, 4th, 5th, 3rd, 5th, 4th. Plainly it was not necessary (in the view of this lexicographer, publishing in 1703) for a melodic dominant to lie, invariably, at a fifth above the modal final in the context of Gregorian melody. This is, of course, precisely what is to be observed in respect of other notes with dominant functions in quite other non-harmonic – let us call them 'anharmonic' – musical cultures.

Jean Philippe Rameau's formulations (offered at several points in his writings) of what constitutes the dominant – or, indeed, dominants – are by no means as clear-cut as those of de Brossard. Remembering that the *Nouveau système de musique théorique*, although published in 1726 (two years later than the *Traité de l'harmonie réduite à ses principes naturels*, 1724), was planned as (and indeed is stated to be) an introduction to the *Traité*, his definition of the dominant (in the *Table des Termes* p. 56) is essentially linked with the concept of 'fundamental sounds' that form a cadence.

'One calls *Cadence*, in musical terms, the cessation of movement [= *repos*] of which we wish to speak; and in order to distinguish between the fundamental Sounds, of which this repose is formed, one calls *Principal sound* – or *Tonic note* – the Principal Sound of the progression [= *modulation*]; its fifth above, *Dominant*, and its fifth below, *Sub-Dominant*.' (*Nouveau système*, Chapitre 7, p. 38. *On appelle* Cadence, *en termes de Musique, le repos dont nous voulons parler; & pour y distinguer les Sons fondamentaux, dont ce repos est formé, on appelle* Son principal *ou* Note tonique, *le Son principal de la modulation; sa Quinte au-dessus*, Dominante, *& sa Quinte au-dessous*, Sous-dominante.)

By his use of the expression 'fundamental sounds', rather than 'notes', he indicates that, in his view, and in harmonic music, the roots and the chords erected on them are inseparable in functional terms. His definition makes explicit the fact that the sub-dominant was not so-called as being a note one degree below the dominant, but rather that it was a note a *fifth below the tonic*. It is also plain that for Rameau, and in an harmonic context, the dominant is fixed in position at the interval of a fifth above the tonic. It no longer has the character of a tenor, variable in location in the different heptatonic, diatonic modes and in authentic and plagal forms of these.

In the *Traité* he narrows the *harmonic* concept of dominant still further: 'Above all it must be observed that we only apply the name of *Tonic* to notes that carry the Perfect Harmony [that is, a major triad], and that of *Dominant* to those

that carry the Harmony of the Seventh' [that is, a dominant seventh chord].
(*Traité…*, Livre second, p. 68: *Il faut remarquer avant toute chose, que nous ne donnons le nom de* Tonique *qu'aux Nottes qui portent l'Accord parfait, & celui de* Dominante *qu'à celles qui portent l'Accord de la Septiéme.*)

Indeed he goes much further than this, prescribing the term 'tonic dominant' (*dominante tonique*) for: 'a Dominant [in the sense of a chord of the seventh] of which the Third is major, and of which this Third makes the false-fifth [= a diminished fifth = tritone] with its Seventh'. (*…une Dominante dont la Tierce est majeure, & dont cette Tierce fait la fausse Quinte avec sa Septiéme…*)

Chords of the seventh – today's 'secondary sevenths' – in which the third above the fundamental is major but does not form a tritone with the seventh are, on his definition, to be called mere 'dominants': they cannot resolve directly in a major triad, but only through the intermediary of other sevenths followed ultimately by a dominant seventh – his 'tonic dominant'.

His view of the nature of dominance does not depend on frequent repetition; indeed it is in no sense a statistical concept in relation to the structure of a melodic line. It is a concept of dynamic function within a harmonic framework. 'One calls *Dominant* the first of two Notes which, in the bass, form the perfect cadence [see Example 4 below], because it should always precede the final Note and consequently "dominates" it.' (*Traité…*, Livre second, p. 56, voire *Table des Termes* (following the end of 'Livre quatrieme', p. 432): *On appelle Dominante, la première des deux Nottes qui dans la Basse, forment la cadence parfaite, parce qu'elle doit précéder toûjours la Notte finale, & par consequent la domine.*)

Example 4. *Cadence Parfaite dans la mode majeure* (from *Supplément*, p.464)

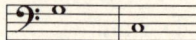

Nevertheless Rameau retains some trace of feeling for note-functions and locations in a purely melodic and anharmonic context, as shown by another of his definitions of 'tonic' in the *Traité*:

'The *tonic Note* is the name given to the one that concludes the perfect Cadence, in that it is with *it* that one begins and ends, and it is within the range of *its* Octave that all modulation [= melodic and harmonic progression] is decided.' [*it*, *its*, our italics] (Livre second, p. 56: *On appelle* Note tonique, *celle qui termine la Cadence parfaite, en ce que c'est par elle que l'on commence & que l'on finit, & que c'est dans l'étenduë de son Octave que se détermine toute la modulation.*)

It is probable that Rameau is not using the term *modulation* in the ancient sense of melodic movement – movement of intermediate phrases to permitted cadential notes – but rather, as suggested by our added parenthesis, in both a melodic and a harmonic sense. The primary meaning of *modulatio* in a Latin musical context, was the regular development of a melody, either in exposition during performance, or in exposition during the act of creation.

At what precise date, therefore, 'dominant' came to be substituted for tenor or repercussa or tuba – all three as 'reciting-note' – it has not proved possible to determine. Zarlino has no use for any of these terms in his index (p. 434), and it may be that a definitive and 'scientific' definition of dominant was first given by Hugo Riemann who, in 1893, established the term for the fifth above the final (by then, the tonic).

Riemann, however, was evidently thinking in terms of *note-locations*, not (as was Rameau) in terms of chords erected on roots. He does not have a special category of 'tonic dominants' although (of course) the importance of dominant-seventh chords is recognised; he is concerned only with intervallic relationships with the tonic; and he accepts Rameau's term 'sub-dominant' for the fifth below the tonic.

A similar relationship holds for 'sub-mediant' in respect to 'mediant'. The latter is the note that corresponds in pitch to the harmonic mean between tonic and dominant; it is a major third above the tonic. The sub-mediant is the third below the tonic – the third that is the harmonic mean between string-lengths that correspond to sub-dominant and tonic. It is necessarily a major third above the sub-dominant and a minor third below the tonic.

Apart from sub-final and super-final, we have arrived at the end of this winding trail through the discrimination and naming of degrees within modal note-sets. These last two are surely chiefly locational, rather than functional in their significance, though both sub- and super-finals may function as leading notes. In our Tang Chinese context, the super-final may function as leading note in descent; but even in heptatonic items of the Tang it is – with rare exceptions – the sub-mediant that performs this function in ascent.

'Pitch-Related Governance' (Powers, 1980, p. 427b) and 'Tonic' *versus* 'Final'
The preceding examination of locational and functional terms in modal note-sets and (in particular) of endings, beginnings and betweens, as elements in the structure of chant-melody, has revealed a hitherto unexpected degree of

conscious pitch-integration of that same chant-structure. This phenomenon is explicit in the *Dialogus* (see our pp. 144, 154), and in a passage from Chapter 11 (his p. 144) of the eleventh-century *Micrologus* of Guido of Arezzo. Since 1952, passages from the *Dialogus* translated by Strunk have been available to English readers having no Latin.

From *Micrologus* we have: 'With the note that ends a phrase, the remaining notes [of the phrase] are obliged to agree, through the aforesaid six *consonantia*. Indeed, it is the business of its beginning [= the beginning of the chant], and of the ends (and also indeed of the beginnings) of all the intermediate phrases, to cling to the note that ends a chant.' (*Per supradictas nempe sex consonantias voci quae neumam terminat reliquae voces concordare debent. Voci vero quae cantum terminat, principium eius cunctarumque distinctionum fines vel etiam principia opus est adhaerere.*)

This is surely a most remarkable statement. The six *consonantia*, as we have seen (p. 144), are the intervals of semitone, tone, minor and major thirds, fourth and fifth. Together, Guido's two sentences imply a conscious degree of pitch-relationship: (a) between all notes of an intermediate phrase of a chant and the cadential note on which the phrase ends; and (b) between the chant-final and the beginnings and endings of all intermediate phrases. Combining (a) and (b), it is plain that he is stating (as did *Dialogus* – our p. 144) that the pitch of every note of a chant should be determined by its final. It is no statistical 'predominance', no 'weight of recurrence' (Powers, 1980, p. 427), that determines this function of a chant-final; it is the necessary, precise, intervallic relationship between every note of the chant and its final that accounts for the all-controlling function of the final, in the evolution (from start to finish) of the individual chant-melody. Such intonational precision in pitch-relationships, between notes in a melodic line, is that which confers (and is perceived as) euphony.

Reference has several times been made to 'anharmonic' music – music without harmony in the Western sense – in relation to those musics, such as plainchant, such as the Tang-Court repertory, in which no phenomenon comparable with major/minor European harmony of the eighteenth and nineteenth centuries is to be observed. It is, however, only as an abstraction that such musics may be regarded as lacking in harmony, in the sense that the notes of such a linear melody never coincide in time with notes of different pitch.

Musical memory, however short-lived, always ensures that even an unaccompanied vocal line is heard as a sequence of notes in a harmonic context. In a building with any degree of reverberation, the successive sounds hang in the air, and if well sung in just intonation, their shifting combinations are harmonious. In many cultures, a drone – instrumental or vocal – supplies the ear with a continuous strand and standard of pitch-reference. The complex drone of the *tambura* in music of South Asia, or the vocal *ison* in the music of the Greek Orthodox Church, concretise the function of the final, so that euphony is both preserved and made more evident to the listening ear.

Powers (p. 427, Column B, below) stated that: 'The term "tonic" normally implies that the degree in question has some sort of pitch-related governance over other degrees, a governance that goes beyond mere weight of recurrence ("predominance") or temporal position ("finality").' Surely the passage from Guido, just now repeated, reveals 'pitch-related governance' in the highest degree, but exerted by a chant-final; a governance only related to temporal finality inasmuch as it is at the end that this pitch is to be identified.

In sum, therefore, the definition of 'tonic' offered by Powers is also a description of the relationship between a chant-final and every other note in a chant as perceived by ears of the eleventh century. If what Powers has said is all that can be said, then tonic and final are indistinguishable.

For Rameau, of course, they were clearly distinguishable since the tonic was the root, the fundamental, on which a final major triad was to be erected; and for Rameau, too, the dominant – his 'tonic dominant' that progresses to the tonic – was the root of a chord of the dominant seventh.

When we come to Riemann, however, writing in 1893, the dominant is again a single note of fixed intervallic distance from the tonic.

It was perhaps only the torrent of major/minor harmonic music, during the eighteenth and nineteenth centuries, that deleted all memory of, and use for, dominants other than that one at a distance of a fifth above the final. As in the world of plainchant, however, so also in other great traditions across Eurasia, such dominants are, or were, to be found. As shown by Signell (1977), in Turkish 'classical', 'art' music, the dominant: *güçlü* (= 'strong', 'violent', from *güç* = 'strength', 'force') is the fourth above the final in the modes (*makamlar*): *Kürdi*, *Uflflak*, *Neva*, etc., and the third above the final in *Segah*, *Saba*, etc.

In the rāgas defined by Śārṅgadeva (Widdess, 1980, pp. 124a, b), Predominants (*aṃśa*) may occur at a major second, a major third, a fifth and an octave *above* the final; and at a third, and an octave *below* the final.

Far from its having been perspicacious of Abraham and Hornbostel, and advantageous to their work in the field of ethnic musics, to reject the hitherto accepted vocabulary that provided locational and functional names for notes in modal note-sets in the Western tradition of plainchant, and of all later Western music until the time of Rameau, it might have been wiser to retain that vocabulary as it existed in the seventeenth century (and indeed until today, in the field of *Gregorianik*), making appropriate modifications where particular circumstances required it.

179

As the Gregorian-specialists have recognised all along, there is no need to avoid the terms 'tonic', 'dominant', 'mediant', etc., in reference to plainchant. No more is it necessary to avoid these terms in descriptions of the modal properties of music from the Tang Court.

Let us remember always that the term 'tonic', has descended to us from *tonus*, itself a descendant of *tonos* – a *stretching* of a lyre-string (a Grecian lyre-string, and before that of an Old Babylonian lyre- or harp-string) so as to obtain a desired pitch. A musical tradition as ancient as that of plainchant itself, in which (as in plainchant) tetrachordal structure is a dominant feature of melodic development, is not be denied access to that same ancestry. A tonic today is no more than a pitched note. In its original adjectival significance the word meant no more than 'of' or 'pertaining to' not just a 'note', but to a 'mode'= *tonus*.

There is indeed some interest in finding that the word that has displaced the ancient *finalis* from its status, is 'tonic' as defined by Powers. But that word *finalis* was, and is, precisely what has been stated to be a 'tonic'.

Surely, in view of Rameau's very precise statement as to what a 'tonic' is (p. 175), it is now improper for us to use that term (as redefined by Powers) in place of 'final'. We may no longer seek to justify such use by claiming that everything in our musical outlook changed with the definition (by Rameau in the early eighteenth century) of the European major/minor harmonic system.

Is there then *no* difference between the final in unaccompanied monody, and the tonic of a major/minor, harmonic ensemble-piece of the eighteenth or nineteenth century?

There is indeed a sense in which the two differ, namely, that the pitch of such an harmonic piece can only be maintained approximately constant if the performers, whether singers or players, neither sing nor play in tune. As demonstrated with compelling clarity by Nicolas Meeùs (1987, p. 28), voices or instruments have necessarily to perform at fluctuating pitch throughout a sequence even of five simple chords – in a progression (for example) from tonic major chord to the same tonic major chord – if the pitch of the tonic is not to fall by 22 cents. Meeùs's progression for string-quartet may be represented in figured-bass as follows:

$$| c \quad A \quad d \quad G | C$$
$$7$$
$$5$$

Neglecting octaves, and given the cents-value of $c' = 0$ (the logarithm of 1), then e' in the major triad on c (the interval of a just major third from c' – expressed as the ratio 5/4), will be 396 cents (ignoring fractions of cents in the first decimal place). With this e' being held through a minor triad on A, the a (in just-intonation) will be pitched at a perfect fifth of 884 cents below e'. Since just-intonation observes both major and minor tones, d and d' (in a minor triad on d) will next be spaced (by string-players observing perfect just-intonation) at a distance of 182 cents from e', rather than at the distance of a major tone of 204 cents therefrom. It follows that G and g (in the dominant-seventh chord on G) will differ from g in the first triad on c by a comma ($204 - 182 = 22$ cents). The g in the first triad was at 702 cents. Reduced by 22 cents, the g in the dominant-seventh chord will be 680 cents only. It follows that the perfect fifth below this, in the final tonic major triad (that is, c), will necessarily be a comma flat ($= -22$ cents). If the progression is repeated five times, in perfect just-intonation, an overall fall in pitch of the tonic chord of c, by $22 \times 5 = 110$ cents, will occur, as Meeùs demonstrated. 110 cents is almost a semitone.

By contrast, provided the ear of a leader/precentor is good enough to prevent drift in intonation (either upwards or downwards), plainchant can indeed be sung in tune.

Stimulus Diffusion yet again

Let us now return, briefly, to the process of stimulus diffusion in relation to theories of the generation of sounds, to the rationalisation of pitch-interrelationships, and to the classification of octave note-sets. It seems to us, looking once more at the history and distribution of modal systems, modal classification, modal nomenclature, throughout Eurasia, that two different categories of mental phenomena are to be distinguished.

These are:

First, far-reaching parallelism in nomenclature, in the use of *metaphor* in discriminating and naming note-functions and note-positions. Such parallel formations may indeed derive from the similar operation of the word-formation process in the brain – the poesis of etyma – throughout Eurasia.

Second, the presence of a common fund of arithmetico-acoustical knowledge – common from Europe in the West to the countries of Asia in the East; knowledge of a correlation between ratios of resonator-lengths and pitches generated when such a resonator is excited to resonance;

(a) this knowledge was first applied, in Old Babylonia and in the second millennium BC, to gut-strings under tension. Some 1200 years later it was applied, in China, to a very different resonating material: air in bamboo-tubes, for which the correlation between length and pitch was less perfect than for the original solid, in the configuration of a narrow, elongated cylinder under tension;

(b) from extant texts, this acoustical knowledge seems to have been acquired by the Chinese at a time later (by some centuries) than the period at which quite different, empirical, Chinese, technological procedures had made possible the tuning of sets of bells, at times in sequences of quasi-semitone steps over four octaves;

(c) the subsequent persistence and pervasiveness in China of an arithmetico-acoustical theory, based on knowledge of the relationship between length-ratios and musical pitches, is surely remarkable, since the process (the 'cycle of fifths' as we call it) was known to be *ineffective*, as a means of generating a continuum of perfectly tuned resonators, ascending in pitch by semitone-steps, repeating at each thirteenth step in a perfect octave above the initial and fundamental of the series;

(d) in China, that theory was eventually elaborated, in the late seventeenth century, into a theoretical process for generating an *equal-tempered sequence of semitone-steps* by operating with the twelfth root of 2: $^{12}\sqrt{2}$;

(e) though known to be insusceptible of practical fulfilment on pipes, this theory was propagated from China to Japan, Korea and Vietnam, with echoes in Kampuchea/Cambodia, Thailand and Burma. The arithmetical result perhaps reached Europe, in the seventeenth century, in the all-important recognition of the twelfth root of 2 as the key to equal temperament.

Regarding the *first* category of thought-processes – that of developments in vocabulary: when one considers the penetration over distance, and the persistence through time, of a word such as 'tone', in the Western-area of Indo-European languages, with meanings still today closely related to the original meanings of *tonos*, one is inclined to accept these two: *tonos* and tone, as cognates; to accept that 'tone' came into use in Western European languages as a loan, technical term, from an archaic vocabulary that had its origin, between West and East, in Ancient Greece.

On the other hand, parallel processes in the development of meaning-extensions may suffice to explain (for example) echoes of 'death' in terms for final cadences in a number of languages.

Regarding the *second* category of thought-processes – the common fund of arithmetico-acoustical knowledge: this is evidently an entirely different phenomenon from that inherent in the development of a parallel nomenclature. Here, evidence suggests, not parallel development, but rather the novel extension, of an arithmetico-acoustical relationship between string-lengths and pitches – a relationship rooted in observation and experiment – to a new environment, where the original, material basis was either unknown or of lesser cultural significance. The numerological element, present in the original idea-complex, became dissociated from its primary material substrate (strings of animal collagen); and the cyclical, arithmetical procedure itself was extrapolated far beyond the tonal limits of its original application.

It is of course the case that numbers, and those of their properties that relate to shapes, were the basis of a comprehensive view of the organisation of the Universe, in the science or proto-science of the Fertile Crescent, long before the rise of Ancient Greece; and it is certain that number was, for all ancient civilisations, a prime aspect of analytical technique, in the attempt to order, and to see the Natural World as ordered. In this context, one can understand the appeal of an imperfectly heard and imperfectly understood whisper from Old Babylon that seems to have reached China not later than the third century BC.

A singularity of the Chinese view of pitch-interrelationships is that, throughout history, save in the modern period, these have been defined exclusively as semitone-steps (*lü* 律). On into the nineteenth century, no larger interval was ever distinguished by a name; but the size of intervals could be expressed as a number of *lü* – that is, collectively, of pitch-pipes (*lülü* 呂律 – themselves distinguished by the numerical sequence of their generation). Materially, such pipes were one-note, stopped-flutes, made from bamboo-lengths of constant external and internal diameter. Their absolute pitches were maintained constant throughout a dynasty.

Even though it is now quite certain that sets of bells (with pitch-differences between adjacent bells of approximately equal-tempered semitones) existed in China at the end of the fifth century BC, it seems possible that the concept of measured and theoretically equal 'semitone'-steps was not fully developed until the arrival in China of knowledge of the acoustic significance of the ratio 1 : 2/3, and the extrapolation of this (by the 2/3 and 4/3 procedure) to fill out (theoretically) the musical space of an octave, indefinitely extended in either direction.

While the Old Babylonians made use of the 2/3 and 4/3-alternation method, in generating their diatonic octave, they did not extend the series beyond five operations. Their perfect octave was obtained by halving the initial string-length; and the missing central fourth of their octave was generated as the fifth, downwards, from the upper, perfect octave of the fundamental.

The appeal of Old Babylonian tuning-theory resided, surely, in its numerological character: in the bond that had been established between number and numerical relationships on the one hand, and the mystery of musical consonances on the other. Even where misapplied and misunderstood, its power to supply – in appearance at least – a means of dominating the universe of musical sounds, led (we suggest) to its being propagated from the Fertile

Crescent to Eastern Asia, and – through the monochord – to Western Europe also.

This idea-system was propagated throughout Eurasia in course of time because it offered (in theory) control of the sound-world of music, and of sounds in general, by an arithmetical series that was also an acoustic series: by a piece of information which (as Needham and Robinson saw, many years ago now) could have been expressed by an articulate traveller in a single sentence.

Chapter 5

Ancient China

As already outlined in brief (p. 114), views on the manner in which scales were generated in Ancient China have been transformed since the early 1980s, by studies of an astonishing array of tuned bronze bells, and slabs of lithophonic limestone, dedicated to the memory of Marquis Yi of Zeng 曾 侯 巳. A consequence of such studies has been the revelation that, already in the fifth century BC, Chinese musicians were defining pitches in relation to their function as scalar notes in different keys.

We are concerned with that period of the history of the Western Zhou dynasty (西 周) known as the 'Warring States' – from 475 BC until the enthronement of Shi Huangdi of the State of Qin 秦 始 皇 帝, with whose title this series: *Music from the Tang Court*, began.

In a sumptuous volume, Professor Lothar von Falkenhausen (1993) has furnished a major account of the history and technology of bell-fabrication; of the acoustic properties of Chinese bells; and the relevance of these to pitch-standards and to scalar structures already established in the fifth century BC. As he states, in regard to the naming of pitches in inscriptions on the bells, Chinese usage of that time is as if *we* referred to one-and-the-same pitched note as '*do* in the key of D, *re* in the key of C, *mi* in the key of B$^\flat$' and so on. The Chinese were evidently aware of key-relationships even before they had fully developed the nomenclature for fixed pitch-standards.

From intensive studies of cast bells (archaeological finds made between 1957 and 1978), it is now evident that while *sets* of bells of different sizes were undoubtedly assembled in the dynasty preceding the Zhou (the Shang: *Shang-Yin dai* 商 殷 代 *c.*1600 – *c.*1050 BC), these were never tuned as chimes. As reported by Falkenhausen, there is no evidence that any attempt was made in the Shang to produce bells that yielded any particular tonal pattern. Their merit may have been solely that they 'sang' at different pitches. It seems clear that bells were treated in the same way as drums: as percussion-instruments. One is reminded of the use, not merely of idiophones and membranophones, but also of horns and trumpets, in Tibetan Lamaist ensembles, as shown in particular by the studies of Mireille Helffer (1995). These reveal elaborate scoring of wind-instruments used in an entirely non-melodic, but nonetheless musically, highly organised fashion.

In the year 433 BC, King Hui of Chu 楚 惠 王 had caused ritual vessels to be made in honour of the deceased Marquis of Zeng, and the 64 bells unearthed from his tomb (Hubei Province, 1978) are probably of about the same date (see Falkenhausen, 1993, pp. 5–17). The pitches of these bells fall into sets corresponding to semitone-scales of twelve notes, in which the overlapping interdigitation of A- and B-tones (see our p. 115) furnishes twelve-note sets in various octaves, amounting to a continuous chromatic sequence of pitches through three octaves. Indeed the total pitch-range reaches five octaves (Falkenhausen, p. 25, Figure 126).

Though the two pitches yielded by such bells (see p. 199) were never entirely separated by technical means (both pitches remained to some extent simultaneously audible), the preferred practice of the founders and tuners came to be such that the pitch-difference – between the two notes yielded by one bell – was either a minor or a major third. The specific naming of the two striking-points on the bow of the bell makes certain that fabrication of two-pitched bells became a conscious goal; scalar chime-sets, consisting of chains of thirds, were available by Mid- to Late-Zhou.

It is the more remarkable, in view of the standard of bell-tuning already achieved in the fifth century BC, that knowledge and application of the 2/3 ratio to bamboo tubes appears to have made such an impact on the musical theoreticians of China whenever they received the information. The arithmetical procedure is first recorded in the third century BC (see *Lüshi chun-qiu* – preface dated 245 BC), and its influence has dominated Chinese musical theory down to today, as well as having dominated the view of Chinese musical theory that Westerners acquired in the time of Père Amiot (1779).

In the course of this essay we have been concerned, among other things, with phenomena of *convergence*: the appearance or the emergence of similarities or quasi-identities:

(a) for reasons of common habits of poesis in the shaping of languages, common not merely to Indo-European, but to Altaic and Sino-Tibetan also, and

(b) for reasons of historical linkage, brought about by the transmission of arithmetico-acoustical theory.

In this last section, a third type of convergence in modal phenomena will be described:

(c) convergence linked with the physical constitution of dominant musical instruments, and the manner in which modal attributes are displayed in pitch-space.

We have seen how, in Old Babylonia and Ancient Greece, the dominant role in the instrumental armoury of *lyres* (and/or *harps*), commonly with little more than an octave-set of tuned open-strings (and at times – for Greece in the archaic period, many less), seems to have led to the use of different modal octaves (or lesser pitch-sets) between the same pitch-limits.

Falkenhausen's study of bell-chimes of the Western Zhou has shown how the development of ideas of pitch-standards and their relationships to scalar 'notes' (and, we may suppose modes) became (astonishingly) intimately linked with idiophonic *bells*, apparently through the empirical discovery of the two-tone bell-shape (see later). That shape itself, he suggests, was a consequence of practical, geometrical restrictions in the earliest developments of the casting-process.

One of his more interesting observations is: that the favoured scalar set for bells of the fifth century BC (though not necessarily for other instruments) was one of four, rather than five, notes. He defines these as *do, re, sol, la,* equating them with four notes of the primary pentatonic set: 123.56, namely 12.56: *Gong, Shang, Zhi, Yu.*

The missing scalar degree-*name, Jue/Jiao* 角 was used on the Zeng Yi bells as a sharpening note-suffix, indicating a raising of the pitch by a major third. The missing degree itself (*mi*) was (in effect) the *Gong*-degree sharpened by a major third.

In Ancient China we find the same kind of octaval limitation of modal resources as that imposed by the lyre's yoke or the harp's bow, but associated in China with an entirely different class of stringed instrument – the zithers, where again a set of open-strings, limited in number, came to be tuned to a variety of different modal octaves within the same pitch-limits.

On a previous occasion (Picken, 1969i, pp. 103–4), it was argued that 'zithers (whole-tube or half-tube zithers – Hornbostel/Sachs 312.1 and 312.2) derive immediately from the intrinsic structure and natural properties of bamboo'; and in 1972 the making of a bamboo half-tube zither in a Thai village together with its use in accompanying the voice were witnessed, and later described (Picken, 1984, pp. 222–3).

The detachment of strips of the bamboo-cortex – using the tip of a knife-blade to obtain 'strings' for a two-stringed zither (for example) – may have arisen from seasonal observations, made by those living in so-called 'bamboo-cultural' areas, not merely in South-East Asia but anywhere in the world where giant grasses grow. (The genus *Bambusa* is by no means the sole such genus.) Idiochord tube-zithers extend into the European area, and their use there, both plucked and bowed, was reviewed in 1975 (Picken, pp. 173–82). As recorded in 1975, strips of cortex detach themselves spontaneously, when dead stems of bamboo undergo weathering.

It was argued (1969, p. 104) that the *zheng/sō* or *koto* 箏 is a more archaic instrument, historically and organologically speaking, than the more highly esteemed *qin/kin* 琴, since the former retains moveable bridges as on the simplest bamboo tube- or half-tube zithers. Such bridges serve to define the sounding length of a cortical 'string'. The *zheng* itself was once made from bamboo, and had five strings (as had the oldest *qin* – so we are told – in the time of the legendary Emperor Shun 舜). This is reported in the early Chinese dictionary: '*Commenting on the* wen, *Analysing the* zi' *Shuo wen jie zi* 説 文 解 字 (AD 121); see William G. Boltz (1993). Notwithstanding the simpler construction of the *zheng*, however, it is the *qin* that first appears (in Chinese texts of the last centuries BC) as an instrument used in the accompaniment of songs, both in court circles and elsewhere (Yang, Yinliu, 1980, pp. 78–9).

Liang Mingyue (1969, p. 158), seemingly following accepted Chinese opinion, has affirmed that a set of five arithmetico-acoustic statements, made in an early text, are a tuning for a five-stringed *qin*. The data are given in the 19th chapter of the *Guanzi* 管 子 book. This work is now regarded as a compilation of the late Warring States period (say, fourth century BC) rather than as a text written by the statesman, Guan Zhong 管 仲 who died in 645 BC. His personal name Zhong means that he was second in order of birth or younger of two. His family-name 'Guan', and his title 'zi' (the fourth grade of nobility; or the title 'philosopher') give the book *its* title (see Rickett, 1993, pp. 246–9). The title of Chapter 19 may be translated as 'Land Zones' (*Diyuan* 地 員), since *yuan* can mean an outer border – originally a circumference.

The chapter was examined in some detail from the standpoint of ecology and phyto-geography by Needham and his collaborators (1986, VI, 1, pp. 48–56); but their examination, while mentioning the first occurrence of a musical correlative – the emission of notes from soils in which the water-tables lay at increasing depths – omits all further musical data. Falkenhausen also has considered the connections between musical data in this chapter, and what the Zeng Yi bells disclose, in regard to a scalar set of pitches of the fifth century BC.

The chapter begins with a quasi-subtitle: 'Guan Zhong's setting the empire in order' 夫 管 仲 之 匡 天 下 . The alleged 'tuning instructions' (see Liang Mingyue) are not associated with the name of any instrument: the word *qin* does not occur anywhere in the chapter; and it is apparent that the 'tuning' is no such thing, but rather a piece of acoustical arithmetic: a specimen of numerological manipulation, sandwiched between other sequences of numbers, linked with quite different phenomena.

Some of these, indeed, are linked with the five sounds of the pentatonic sequence: 123.56 (though not necessarily in that order); some are not so linked. We have before us, therefore, a text that reflects the power of measurement, of number, and of musical pitch, to symbolise the order of the external world. We suggest that such a text itself reflects the same kind of proto-scientific attempt to establish order (and hence, in a sense, to control the universe) as we meet in the Ancient Greek world and, ancestral to that, in the world-view of the Ancient Fertile Crescent.

Only one passage in the chapter is arithmetico-acoustic in character; elsewhere, sounds are correlated with a series of numbers that relate to soil-properties and to the vegetation associated therewith. For example: soils where the water-table lies at a depth of 5 fathoms emit the sound *jiao/jue* 角, while for those with the water-table at successive depths of 4, 3, 2, and 1, fathoms, the notes are *shang* 商, *gong* 宮, *yu* 羽 and *zhi* 徵 in that order – say: $D c a g'$.

This first passage is followed by one that compares the five notes to animal sounds, linking the notes in opposite sequence: '*zhi* (G) – like a shackled hog, startled while being carried; *yu* (A) – like a horse neighing in open country; *gong* (C) – like an ox bellowing in a cellar; *shang* (D) – like a sheep separated from the flock; *jiao/jue* (E) – like a Ring-Necked Pheasant (*Phasianus torquatus G*m) that has climbed into a tree to call; the sound is shrill in its distress'. [Compare Śārṅgadeva's animal-note scale in *Saṅgītaratnākara* i.3. 48; but Śārṅgadeva was composing his great work more than fifteen centuries after the *Guanzi*.]

Without a break, there now follows a set of instructions for generating these same five notes, in a sequence such that the final ascending order is the same as in the last comparison. It begins: 'All starting-points for whenever one is about to generate the five notes.' 凡 將 起 五 音 凡 首. These stated five 'starting points' of the *Guanzi Book* reveal themselves as the actions that led, in the second millennium BC and in Old Babylonia, to the generation of the first five notes of what (on a harp or lyre) subsequently became a complete diatonic octave + one note.

The first five notes generated by the Old Babylonian procedure, starting (hypothetically) from C, would have been C - G - D - A - E; that is, the basic pentatonic set $CDE.GA$. In that procedure, if the C-string were given unit length = 1, the arithmetical operations could be represented as 1; 2/3; 4/3 x 2/3 = 8/9; 2/3 x 8/9 = 16/27; 4/3 x 16/27 = 64/81. Each of these five fractions of unity: 1, 2/3, 8/9, 16/27, 64/81, was a string-length – a fraction of the value in units of measurement (whatever it was) that had been given to the length of the C-string. The *Guanzi* text changes this only in so far as it provides for G and A to sound in the lower octave, so that *C* occupies a central position among the five pitches. The fractions yielded by this procedure are then: 1, 4/3, 8/9, 32/27, 64/81; and clearly 4/3 = 2 x 2/3; and 32/27 = 2 x 16/27, yielding the lower octaves of *G* and *A*, respectively. All these fractions are made immediately capable of realisation as lengths (in the exposition of the *Guanzi* text) by expressing the unit length in a number divisible without remainder by 3, 9, 27 and 81 – the number 81 itself.

The manner in which this sequence of arithmetical operations is set out is of interest. (Yang, Yinliu, 1969, omits 凡 首 from the opening statement about 'starting points'.) The text continues:

'First, making a unit: 1; divide it into three.' 先 生 一 而 三 之 (Yang substitutes 主; but this 'chief' or 'ruler' is surely a graphic corruption of *sheng* 生: 'to give birth to, to generate, to make.')

'Having four [threes] separated, together [make] 9 x 9 [= 3 x 3 x 3 x 3].' 四 開 以 合 九 九. [81]

'[This] suffices [to generate] the small original [that is, treble rather than bass] starting point of *Huangzhong*, wherewith to make *Gong*.' 以 是 生 黃 鍾 小 素 之 首 以 為 宮. (Yang has 'with which to achieve *Gong*' 以 成 宮.) [81]

'Being of three parts [81 = 3 x 27], increase it by one [part = 27] to make one hundred plus eight [108], making *Zhi*.' 三 分 而 益 之 以 一 為 百 有 八 為 徵.

'Evidently having three parts, discard its increase; this suffices adequately for it to generate *Shang*.' 不 無 有 三 分 而 去 其 乘 適 足 以 是 生 商. [81 – 27 = 54]

'Having three parts, again enlarge it by that with which it achieves *Yu* [72].' 有 三 分 而 復 於 其 承 以 是 成 羽. [54/3 = 18; 54 + 18 = 72]

'Having three parts, discard its increase; [this] suffices for it to achieve *Jiao* [48].' 有 三 分 去 其 乘 適 足 以 是 成 角. [72/3 = 24; 72 - 24 = 48]

It will have been noticed that this sequence of arithmetical operations is conducted throughout on a base of 3 which – since the all-important ratio is 2:3 or 3:2 – permits operation in units of length that remain whole numbers. There are no fractions in the final figures for relative lengths of the chosen resonator or resonating materials. With a *C* of 81 units, *G A C' D' E'* correspond to string-lengths of 108, 96, 81, 72 and 64 units (*cf.* Old Babylonian *CDE.GA*).

Falkenhausen (p. 305) also notes that the four 'simple' names of notes (*yin* 音) in the inscriptions on the Zeng Yi bells are those of the first four names of *yin* in the *Guanzi* passage.

While the proto-soil-science of this chapter from the *Guanzi* is in itself impressive, it should perhaps be emphasised that its genuine soil-science observations are set in an idealised arithmetical framework, such that depths of the water-table are defined (approximately) by a sequence of whole multiples of units of seven Chinese 'feet'. (This length-unit is the Chinese 'fathom' – *shi* 施.) To this extent, the entire chapter is structured in terms of the properties of numbers. In this context the acoustic properties of resonator-lengths find a rational place.

It is noteworthy that Yang Yinliu, like ourselves, and unlike Liang Mingyue, does not associate the length/note relationship with any instrument. Rather, he cites this passage as among the earliest examples of the calculation of relative lengths of a resonating material in relation to the five pitches. Liang (1969) was presumably led to equate the five pitches (in the sequence *GA.C'D'E'*) with a tuning because this note-set is the lower portion of the most common tuning for the 7-stringed zither: *GA.C'D'E.'G'A'* .

It must be stressed, however, that the data given by the *Guanzi* represent five different string-*lengths*; and the *qin*, as known at least since Wei 魏 times (AD 386–528), bore (and bears) strings of *equal* length that differed (and still differ) in weight and tension. (The measurements would also work, of course, on lengths of bamboo-pipe of constant bore, though not so well.)

The *Guanzi* formulae cannot, therefore, be interpreted as a *qin*-tuning. They are a prescription for generating a set of five pitches from precisely defined lengths of a resonating material; if strings, they must be of the same weight per unit length, same diameter, same tension, etc. Of course, *by ear*, a tuning-process might be undertaken, given the pitch-information afforded by the formulae. Having established a *Gong* note (*C'*), we tune down to the fourth below to consonance (*G*) with the *C'*, then up a fifth to *D'*, down a fourth to *A*, and up a fifth, to complete the set with *E'*.

A Chinese text of a somewhat later date (third century BC), 'The Spring and Autumn [Annals] of Mr Lü'(*Lüshi Chun-Qiu* 呂 氏 春 秋，季 春 紀，五 日), offers a different formulation, with the fundamental of the note-set in lowest position, so that generation of notes may proceed exactly as for the first five notes of the basic pentatonic octave: *CDE.GA*. From this, generating *C'* and *D'* as upper octaves of the low *C* and *D*, a seven-stringed tuning-system could readily be derived; and again it is striking that the Old Babylonians generated *their* octave of the starting-note and the next higher note by halving the length of the two lowest strings. More commonly, however, at this early stage in the history of the seven-stringed zither the strings seem to have been tuned *GA.C'D'E.'G'A'*, the upper octaves being tuned by ear.

Judging by later *qin*-practice the different modal possibilities of these two tunings were utilised without re-tuning; and the latter (*GA.C'D'E.'G' A'*) would have sufficed for the *Gong*, *Shang* and *Jiao* modes – the favourite modes of the Han, though known under the new names of 'Level Mode' *Pingdiao* 平 調, 'Clear' or 'Pure Mode' *Qingdiao* 清 調 and 'Great-Zither Mode' *Sediao* 瑟 調,

with finals at relative pitches C', D' and E', respectively. Song-texts of Han 漢 date (in *Yuefu shiji* 樂 府 詩 集) frequently specify one or other of these modes. In addition, use is made of the Chu mode, so highly regarded by the Gaodi Emperor of Han (p. 126).

This Han documentary evidence perhaps suggests that modal discrimination proceeded step by step following the degrees of the pentatonic set in ascending sequence. In later times, the *Zhidiao* seems to have been avoided because of potential confusion with the *Gongdiao*, as explained by Jiang Kui (Picken, 1966, pp. 157–8). From Han reports of the songs of Chu, we know that regional song-repertories could exhibit extreme restriction in their modal practice. In any case, since there existed no absolute pitch-standard in the tuning of the *qin*[1] (for example) the performer who sang to his own *qin*-playing, will have been free to adjust his overall pitch to suit his own voice.

The *qin* is unique among stringed instruments in marking the position of the acoustic nodes at all fractions of 1/2, 1/3, 1/4, 1/5, 1/6 and 1/8 of the string-length, by the insertion of thirteen countersunk circular markers, most commonly of mother-of-pearl: the *hui* 徽. The markers are distributed at the following fractional distances along the further side (from the player) of the string of lowest pitch: 7/8, 5/6, 4/5, 3/4, 2/3, 3/5, 1/2, 2/5, 1/3, 1/4, 1/5, 1/6, 1/8. In the reversed sequence of those fractions the *hui* are traditionally numbered from 1 to 13 (Picken, 1969, ii, Fig.1, p. 613).

As an instrument the *qin* is also unique in that stretching and turning occur as separate phases of the stringing and tuning operation. On the traditional instrument, the strings are pulled up to within about a semitone of their desired pitch by directly pulling on the string. Remarkably, the stretched string remains in that condition because of friction between the coils of its damped, non-sounding length, wound tightly round one of a pair of fixed pegs. The two pegs are shared between the garniture of strings, divided as 4 and 3. Only in the final fine-tuning-operation does a turning-operation occur, whereby the twist on a hank of silk (through the loop of which the string is passed and knotted) increases (or decreases – if turned in the opposite sense) tension in the sounding string-length.

Falkenhausen has drawn attention to the remarkable Han Chinese awareness of modal systems in states that were neighbours of the principality of Zeng, revealed by inscriptions on the Zeng Hou Yi bells. Chu in particular shared a wealth of equivalences with pitch-names of Zhou. These are set out on the bells themselves. They specify identities between pitches identified by two-lexigraph

---

[1] The lowest string was traditionally tuned to the first fully sonorous pitch obtained as string-tension increased.

(binomial) names. (See Falkenhausen, Table 16 and pp. 287–9, with a striking illustrative quotation at the top of his p. 289.)

Within the territory of the Middle Kingdom, however, from Antiquity to the first centuries AD, no ethnic diversity comparable with that in the Indo-European territory of Ancient Greece, seems to have existed, a diversity that led, seemingly, to discrimination of an entire heptad of diatonic modes on the basis of ethnicity.

In the Tang, the discrimination of at least four modal types: *Gong, Shang, Jiao/Jue* and *Yu*, is evident from data set out in *YFZL* (Picken, 1969, p. 97); and in the time of the Song 宋 poet, composer and musical theoretician, Jiang Kui 姜 夔 (1155–1221), five standard tunings for *qin* were recognised. These permitted playing on open strings of items in five different pentatonic modes. The tunings required the flattening or sharpening of four strings in all (discounting octaves), and only one such change occurred in each of four tunings. The metaphor that expresses flattening is 'slackening'; sharpening is 'clarifying' or 'purifying' (*man* 漫 and *qing* 清, respectively).

Some idea of Jiang Kui's detailed practical instructions for tuning the *qin*, and of the technical language in which these are expressed, may be gained from Picken (1971, ii, pp. 103–6). In Liang's account (1969, Table IX, p. 168), starting from Jiang Kui's accepted version of the pentatonic *Gongdiao* tuning: *CD.FGA.C'D'* (in relative pitches), he successively generates the *Gongdiao* in five keys: F, C, G, B^b and E^b. These are tunings in which the set *CD.FGA* is transposed, so that C (= *Gong*) becomes in turn F, C, G, B^b and E^b. All these changes are effected by 'slackening' or 'clarifying' – to be compared with Ancient Greek terms such as 'turning' (*tropos*) or 'stretching' (*tonos*).

The consequence of these transpositions is generation of five different *pentatonic* octaves+one note, in five different keys – modal octaves that correspond (starting from the lowest string) to the *Zhi, Gong, Jiao, Shang* and *Yu* modes, in which the string of lowest pitch acts as final. As on a Babylonian or Greek lyre, these are all available within the compass of one-and-the-same octave+one note (except for *Jiao*, where the set covers an octave+one-and-a-half-tones).

In the context of Jiang Kui's song in zither-tablature (Picken, 1971, p. 103, n. 11), standard tunings (which yield open-string modal sets corresponding to the five pentatonic modes) are termed 'correct playing' *zhengnong* 正 弄. These are contrasted with tunings for 'deviant modes' (as he understood the term): tunings in which the set of open strings included the auxiliaries, the *bian*-notes. His song: *Gu yuan* 古 怨 [a title to be paraphrased as 'Old resentment' (the real meaning is more complex – see Picken, p. 108)] makes use of a heptatonic set equivalent to a hexatonic version of the *Ichikotsu-chō/Yuediao* of the Tang: *C D E F♯ A B d*, where *D* is the final and *C* an auxiliary (the second auxiliary, *G*, is not available as an open-string sound in this tuning). Remarkably, the song displays modulation from *Shangdiao* to *Gongdiao* and back.

In 1969 (see Picken, 1969, i, pp. 104–5), attention was drawn to an observation from a greatly-missed musicologist, Robert Thurston Dart, that the so-called 'Confucian' type of *qin* – the *Zhong'ni-shi qin* 仲 尼 式 琴 – 'has the shape of an attenuated lyre'. The inclusive bridge simulates the yoke; and the indentation of the shoulders – 'Immortal's shoulders' *xianren jian* 仙 人 肩 – would seem to echo the incurving of the pillars that supported the yoke in certain types of lyres. This recognition (from a musician who was also a mathematician) of possible influence from kithara-morphology in the shaping precisely of that *qin*-type which, over the centuries, has become standard) is yet more suggestive today. Today we are aware of the possible impact, East and West, of knowledge not only of the Ancient Greek achievement, but also of that of the Old Babylonians, as a source of Chinese knowledge of string-length ratios.

Doubtless practical needs linked with vocal compass, in Asia as in Ancient Greece and the Fertile Crescent, led to the devising of tuning-procedures within the same octave; but why choose an overall compass of a ninth – in Old Babylonia on lyre or harp, and in China on the *qin* (see p. 193)? It is evident that on the *qin*, for whatever reason, it was convenient to use the same manner of displaying different modal octave-sets between the same pitch-limits, as on the lyre or on archaic harps – and for the same reason: the availability of a small number of open strings spanning an octave.

It is important to note that in the pre-Tang period *qin*-players most probably made use of open-string and harmonic sounds only. As R.H. van Gulik argued (1940, p. 185), in the developed finger-technique as we know it from Ming tablatures, 'a perfectly smooth and even surface [of the instrument] is necessary' for performance of 'the delicate movements of the left hand'. These movements relate immediately to the stopping of strings in a great variety of ways. The highly decorated inlaid surface of an instrument such as that surviving in the Shōsō-in (bearing a date in the Chinese Northern Wei 魏 dynasty, written in cyclical characters to be read as 435 or 495) would not have been suitable for movements of that kind. The posture of performers (to be seen in paintings) playing *al fresco* with the *qin* across the lap, would have been possible using open strings and harmonic sounds, but impossible for the left-hand techniques of the Ming – and, we may suppose of the Tang also, since dated Tang instruments are completely smooth. Like harps and lyres, therefore, the *qin*, too, made more use of open-string and harmonic sounds throughout its pre-Tang history.

It was the multiplication of strings on *zheng/koto* 箏-type-zithers, and the rise of fretted lutes, that released the modes of the Chinese system from the pitch-limits imposed by the *qin*. In the Tang, this is evident from the seven tunings (of the Japanese *gaku-sō* 樂 箏) that survive to the present in *Tōgaku* performance, with maximal pitch-differences of as much as a seventh (or a diminished octave) between strings of the same ordinal number, in different tunings. It may again be mentioned that, on the *piba/biwa* (p. 205), each of the four modes of the Tang could be played in seven different keys.

As set out in 'The Song History' *Songshi* 宋 史, it is a fact – if only an extraordinary coincidence – that the ascending sequence of pitches of their seven key-notes follows the intervallic sequence of the Greek Dorian heptatonic modal octave: S T T S T T (Picken, 1969, ii, p. 97). (In *YFZL*, this sequence is only followed by the keys of the heptatonic *Gong*-modes.) The advantage of this sequence is, that with this set of 'natural' notes, the number of degrees that require sharpening or flattening to effect transposition is minimal. In the Ancient Greek modal system also, the choice of the Dorian as *the* modal series, central to the entire system, minimised the number of operations required to obtain six other modal octaves, between the same pitch-limits (Henderson, 1957, p. 354).

Knowledge of the facts: that strings of the same weight per unit length, at equal tension, and of lengths in the ratios of 1 : 1/2, and 1 : 2/3, yield pitches at the intervals of an octave and of a fifth respectively, sufficed for the generation of the seven diatonic modes of the Old Babylonian System. Knowledge of the properties of the same ratios, applied to pipes cut from bamboo, sufficed for the theoretical generation (by the Chinese) of a complete universe of musical sounds, having the character of a dodecatonic octave, susceptible of continuous extension in musical space to higher and lower pitches.

Because of the end-effect – such that the acoustic length of pipes, as resonators, is lengthened by a factor related to the diameter of the pipe – any attempt by the Chinese to execute the cycle-of-fifths procedure using pipes, will soon have resulted in pitch-discrepancies between theory and the resulting set of pitches. These discrepancies would be far more considerable than that of the Pythagorean comma between the 13th-note of the cycle and the true octave of the fundamental.

This fact in itself suggests that the procedure, and the knowledge of the ratios, did not originate in China (no more than in Greece); but rather that the Chinese were making an attempt to apply arithmetical procedures that worked comparatively well for *strings* to *pipes* – of which (because of the abundance of the genus *Bambusa*) they had a copious supply, of diameter and internodal length appropriate to any such purpose.

The end-effect was indeed recognised by the Chinese, and an attempt to correct for its consequences was made by Prince Zhu Zaiyu at the beginning of the seventeenth century in his ideal procedure for the generation of an equal-tempered chromatic octave. (See Zhu Zaiyu 朱 載 育: *Lülü jingyi* 律 呂 精 義.)

In any case, as we have seen (p. 114), the Chinese seem to have developed empirical tuning-methods capable of generating a quasi-chromatic octave of tuned bells, without benefit of knowledge of string-length ratios and corresponding pitches. We have argued that Chinese attempts to apply quasi-Old Babylonian arithmetico-acoustic theories were due to the strong intellectual appeal of arithmetical theory. For practising musicians, however, such knowledge was superfluous. In Ancient Greece also (p. 247), the interests of practising musicians differed from those of theoreticians.

The apparent implication here: that the Chinese were intellectually attracted by the properties of arithmetico-acoustic theory, is supported by Falkenhausen's concise statement (his p. 309): 'The Zeng Yi bell-chimes and lithophone[s] were more than mere musical instruments; perhaps more importantly, they were tools with which the tonal realm could be measured. It did not matter that the inscriptions [on bells] were placed out of sight of the musicians; as far-flung connections and equivalences entailed by producing any tone, they were guideposts in the cosmic realm. The systematizing thrust of the Zeng inscriptions far transcends the scope of music.'

Being so much indebted to Professor Falkenhausen, it may appear churlish to object to his translation of the term *yue* 樂 as 'music' in the title of his historic study: 'Suspended Music'. As he displays so frequently throughout his text, *yue* was always much more than 'music' in our sense. It was a complex of instrumental music (in our sense), dance and song. In a sense comprehensible to us today it was 'ritual music', as set out most conclusively and emphatically in the *Yueji* 樂 記 'The Record of Ritual Music', now included in the 'Record of Rites' *Liji* 禮 記. The *Yueji* is believed to have been compiled from references to *yue* in texts that existed between 140 and 187 BC, and the definition of *yue* given there shows that the term embraced both the civil dances – in which dancers carried feathers and flutes, and the military dances – in which the dance-properties were shields and battle-axes; both were necessarily linked with instrumental 'music' in our sense, and at times with song. This was the very stuff of *yue*. The passage quoted here was translated previously in Fascicle 2, 1985, p. 108. The point is of such importance that the translation may be repeated here:

'Therefore bells, drums, reed-pipes,
lithophones, [pheasant-] feathers,
flutes, shields, battle-axes, are the

196

tools of *yue*;
crouching down, looking up, joining,
lining up, at ease, hastening, are the
patterns of *yue.*'

(Dr Michael Loewe helped in the translation in 1985.)

It is surely of enormous importance to maintain this profound distinction between
what we call 'music' and what the Ancient Chinese understood by *'yue'*.

There remains a further serious matter that leads us to reject 'Suspended Music'
as a translation of *Yuexuan* 樂 縣. Even for the sake of a *jeu de mots* one may not
ignore the force of word-order in Classical Chinese: the preceding lexigraph of
this pair must, in some sense, qualify what follows. The construction leads us to
expect a phrase with the general structure of 'the something of (or for) *yue*'. In
other contexts (pp. 32, 33) Falkenhausen translates *xuan* as 'suspensions'. This is
strictly speaking inadequate, since the term *xuan* is being used not merely for the
rack, but for the rack together with what is hanging from it: a bell- or stone-
chime. The term covers those musical entities that consisted of a rack supporting
suspended idiophones, of bronze or of lithophonic limestone.

In other contexts, however, Falkenhausen shows 'suspensions' properly
qualified by a preceding term. Accepting his use of 'suspension' – even though a
suspension (noun) is something that suspends rather than something suspended –
his 'palace-suspensions' of four racks for the Zhou king, 'awning-suspensions' of
three racks permitted to 'great lords', 'divided suspensions' of two racks for
ministers and magnates, and 'single suspensions' for knights, show the form that
a precise translation of *yuexuan* must take, namely: '*yue*-suspensions',
'suspensions for *yue*'. That is to say, the racks of idiophones to be employed in
the execution of *yue*.

One might invent a plural noun: 'suspends', to be used throughout, meaning
both the suspender and the thing suspended. *Music* was not suspended in any
sense, and the translation 'suspended music' is not consistent with translations
elsewhere in the text. The fact that, in the pre-classical language, the attribute
may follow the noun qualified may not be used to justify a construction such as
'suspended music'.

Falkenhausen's observation that there were relatively fewer bells in the bass
range of the Zeng Yi garniture, and the implied existence of a restricted 'ground
layer' of bell-notes is surely acceptable, particularly in the light of the pitch-
stratified structure composed of bronze idiophones in Balinese and Javanese
gamelan music today. One may agree with his statement that 'We do not know

exactly how the Eastern Zhou 'new music' differed from traditional ritual music', even though many would find the qualification 'exactly' misleading, since we know precisely nothing.

What we do know is: that the song-texts of Zheng 鄭 and Wei 魏 were heterometric, in contrast to the almost invariably isometric verse of the older stratum of 'The Book of Songs' *Shijing* 詩 經 (Picken, 1977, pp. 105–7). It was argued there, that it was the resulting *rhythmic interest* of any tunes (*yin* 音) of Zheng or Wei (to which such texts were set) that kept Marquis Wen of Wei (魏 文 侯) awake. The song-texts of Zheng exhibit the highest degree of irregularity of any song-texts in the *Shijing*, both in line-length and in stanza structure; these song-texts are also the shortest. It is probable – as a consequence of their rhythmic irregularity – that these songs 'exhibited rhythmic diversity within a fixed metrical framework', characteristic of all later Chinese song.

Furthermore, though no dialectal differences between the language of texts of the Zheng and Wei (and other) repertories now survive, the structure of their respective song-texts is specifically different (Picken, 1977).

A single cadential, musical and textual line may have survived from Zhou times, in the twelve tunes for the *Shi* preserved by Zhu Xi (for these see Picken, 1956, 1957). The text-line is: *Wan shou wu jiang* 萬 壽 無 疆 'A life-span of a myriad years without limit!' A musical setting is preserved, among Zhu Xi's twelve tunes, as the final line of Stanza 2 of '*Nan shan you tai*' 南 山 有 臺 (Mao 172). The same text-line also occurs in the song-texts: Mao 154, 209 and 211. Although it seems possible that these tunes were perhaps given a more topical modal flavour by being 'heptatonicised' in the *Kaiyuan* 開 元 reign-period (713–42), with auxiliaries (*biansheng* 變 聲) inserted to render them in part heptatonic, the tune for this line is tetratonic.

The same musical line, but with different textual underlay, occurs seven times in all, in three of the six *Huangzhong Qinggong* 黃 鍾 清 宮 song-melodies of Zhu Xi: twice as last line of a stanza; elsewhere as the second of a pair of musical lines in medial position (Picken, 1957, pp. 107, 108; see also Picken, 1969, iii, pp. 408–10).

The four notes of this syllabically-set line from one of the *Xiao Ya* 小 雅 may be represented, in terms of solfa, as: *sol la re do*. These are, of course, the first four notes generated by the *Guanzi* procedure (p. 190): fifth up, fourth down; fifth up, fourth down. They are also, however, the four scalar notes (*yin* 音) of the Zeng Yi bells and lithophones. If the set is written in the sequence: *sol la do re*, not only do we have the first four *Guanzi* notes, but octaval inversion would at once restore the four-membered set of the Zeng Yi *yin*: 音: *do re sol la*. What impresses here, and reinforces the argument for authenticity, is the sense of finality that this phrase (from a Zhu Xi melody): *sol la re do – G A d c* has for *our* ears. Musically it deserves to be, not merely a fragment of the music of Zhou, but a wish directed in sincerity towards Imperial Ears.

An immense gift from Falkenhausen's study is the sense of an evolutionary process in the history of Chinese music: from a percussive use of untuned bells, to the astonishing filling-out of musical space represented by the Zeng Yi bells, with four-note melodic structures at some stage perhaps antecedent to those of five notes.

We continue the sequence: from syllabic vocal setting in notes of equal duration in ritual texts of Shang and Zhou, to settings in terms of notes with durational ratios of 1:2 in folksong-like song-texts of the later Zhou. Thence to duration-ratios of 1:2:4, with occasional use of ligatures in settings of Tang and Song lyrics; and thence indeed to the beginnings of the melismatic-setting of song-texts in Yuan song, and its flowering in *Kunqu* 崑 曲 of the sixteenth century.

For the original use of Marquis Hou's bells in a *quasi*-polyphonic-harmonic musical texture there is no evidence. For their potential use in 'an inverted pyramid of rhythmic activity' – as in a Balinese Gamelan (Bakan, 1998, p. 446), argument might be advanced.

Bell-shapes
The preceding account of the significance (for the history of Chinese music) of chimes of two-note bells from the fifth century BC (as described by Falkenhausen) has thus far accepted the view – both of the Chinese and of Falkenhausen – that the two-note phenomenon depends on the leaf-like shape of these bells in cross-section.

In general, however, the phenomenon depends not on the particular leaf-like *shape* of the cross-section as such, but on any *departure from radial symmetry in distribution of the mass of the bell's substance about the vertical/central axis.*

The two-note phenomenon is also manifest in any handled-cup or mug, or in any bowl-shaped structure, circular in cross-section, made from a rigid but elastic substance, provided that a single handle, or two handles, or two decorative regions of high mass, are affixed to the vessel, so that distribution of mass in the wall is no longer radially symmetrical.

The attachment of even a single handle necessarily changes the radial symmetry in distribution of mass about the vertical axis of what had been a radially symmetrical, circular vessel. Attachment induces an acoustic node, matched by a node at the opposite end of a diameter. A plane exists about which the applied mass and the rest of the structure are bilaterally and symmetrically distributed. Though the cup be circular, on striking the rim (the 'sound-bow' of

199

this 'bell') at a point halfway between the ends of the diameter on which the handle lies, the note obtained will be lower in pitch than that obtained by striking the rim in one of the four intervening quadrants. With a pair of diametrally placed handles or lugs or decorative knobs, a ceramic vessel behaves as does a Chinese two-note bell. Striking in quadrants between the singular diameter and its 90°-counterpart yields notes higher in pitch than those from a points at either end of the counter-diameter. Fortuitously, the pitch-difference is approximately a major third for many vessels.

Variations in the distribution of mass around the circumference of a vessel can lead to variation in *stiffness* – to variation in resistance to deformation of the vessel wall in bending during vibration. In the case of the Marquis Yi bells, lune-shaped in transverse section, Falkenhausen's diagrams of sectioned bells show that differential thinning by the craftsmen has left the wall thicker in the quadrants that lie between nodes in the two modes of vibration (his Figures 40: displaying the two modes of vibration, and 41: with three examples from different bells). In the first vibration-mode (A-note) the ends of the longer diameter act as nodes because, since the metal is thinner there, elastic stiffness is relatively lower there. In the second vibration-mode (B-note), bending of the wall occurs predominantly in thicker portions, where stiffness is higher. For a cross-sectional representation of such a bell, see the diagram of a Lune shape [Chapter 4, Diagram 1, p. 115].

Yet again, the horned profile of the Zeng Hou Yi bells, even where the wall is of uniform thickness, confers a non-uniform distribution of mass around the periphery of the leaf-like figure of the cross-section.

Regarding the properties of the obliquely suspended type of bell known as *yongzhong* 甬 鍾 in the Zeng Hou Yi ensemble, it is of interest that even the miniaturised model – issued under the seal of Wuhan Conservatory of Music (武 漢 音 樂 學 院), measuring *c.*25 mm overall, from the tips of the 'horns' (*xian* 銑) to the flat top of the 'shank' (*yong* 甬) – yields two notes a major third apart, when struck (not too heavily) at the appropriate points, with a beater of small impact-area.

In this instance, though the wall appears to be of equal thickness throughout, the nodes of the A-resonance mode still lie at opposite ends of the longer bell-width. The combination of cross-sectional shape, and downwardly directed horns, confers bilateral acoustic symmetry.

The relative increase in the length of the 'handle' (*yong*) (historically surely a development from the shorter handle of the hand-held *nao* 譊, first developed as an army-signalling device) may perhaps have some acoustic significance, as well as its action as a counterpoise for bells so hung that the vertical axis of the bell is conveniently tilted in the rack.

200

Further to the diagram of a bronze clapper-bell *ling* 令 (Falkenhausen, Figure 54: 1800–1600 BC): the flange shown, whether single or double (as the text describes for later *ling*) is likely to have converted that bell-type also to a two-note bell.

Indeed, even a typical, modern, Swiss cow-bell – roughly elliptical in cross-section, in two halves (probably cold-dressed over a suitably shaped dolly), with brazed junctions down the sides – may yield two notes on striking, though with a much smaller pitch-interval between.

Also of interest, though not related to the two-note phenomenon, is the morphology of the beaters in use with the bell-ensemble for Marquis Yi of Zeng (Falkenhausen, Figure 107, p. 211). Their impact-surfaces of very small area – not more than a few square centimetres – will have guaranteed that most of the energy of the strike was dissipated in the elastic wave (the 'ring'), rather than in the surface 'clonk', thus improving the *tone-quality* of the sound generated.

There can be little doubt that the phenomenon of rigid, elastic vessels yielding two pitches will have been known to the Chinese from the world of ceramics, perhaps as early as the Shang period – say 1500–1050 BC – since occasional Shang stoneware vessels are to be found, fired at +1200 °C (Barnes, 1993, p. 120). These will have rung when struck.

In Later Zhou times (770–475), and in South-Central China, pots were regularly being fired at 1300°C. Two-handled, wide-mouthed bowls were present already among painted Yangshao forms (Barnes, p. 98; see her Box 6, f, Machang).

These facts imply that the two-note phenomenon may already have been experienced by the Chinese in ceramic vessels of the late Neolithic period.

In addition, it is now generally accepted that the bronze-casters took their moulding-procedures (including piece-moulding) from the Neolithic potters (Rawson ed., 1993, p. 230). It is probable, therefore, that the acoustic attributes of particular ceramic forms, attributes dependent on the elastic properties of clays fired at sufficiently high temperature, will have come to the notice of bronze-casters.

In sum, the phenomenon of Chinese two-note bells needs to be set in the wider context of empirical scientific knowledge derived from two crafts not usually regarded as interrelated.

Ancient and Modern India, and Persia

Looking at the musical systems of South Asia as reflected in Sanskrit handbooks from the first millennium AD (Widdess, 1980, 1995) it is perhaps not entirely fanciful to see, in turn in them, parallels with both aspects of those of Ancient

Greece: (1) modes (in India) as scalar note-sets; first, of two scales; later of a single extended scale, two octaves and more in pitch-length. (2) modes as variants of a sequence of pitches of ascending frequency, assembled in differing patterns of 'tone'- and 'semitone'- intervals, lying between the limits of a fixed pitch-range.

The use of single quotation-marks serves to remind: that Widdess (1993, ii) was the first to draw attention to the fact that, in terms of the number of theoretically equal microtonal *śrutis* in intervals between pitches, six of the seven ancient jāti (classes of modal note-sets) each included two weak notes. These could be omitted, so that the six scales were, effectively, pentatonic modes. Moreover, three of the Ṣaḍjagrāma jātis were of the type of Indonesian *pélog*, with their larger intervals-between-pitches more than three times the size of their smaller intervals. The three Madhyama-grāma jātis, on the other hand, correspond to the condition of Indonesian *sléndro* modes.To Widdess's further observations on the relationship between melodic and rhythmic systems of the modern gamelan and those of Ancient Indian music, we shall return later (Chapter 6).

In the earliest stage of the Indian theoretical system, we might seem at first sight to be concerned with modes as segments of scales of the same kind as those in the Systems of Hellenistic Greece, of the Middle-Eastern world of *makam/maqām*, and of East Asian *diaozi/chōshi* 調 子. As Widdess (1995, p. 48) makes plain, however, there are arguments for rejecting this view.

Let us examine briefly the structural features of Indian music in the period from 'the beginning of the Maurya to the end of the Gupta empires, a period of approximately 800 years from *c*.320 BC to *c*.AD 550' (Widdess, 1995, p. 22), a timespan to be equated in Chinese terms with the period from Late Zhou: King Shen Jing 慎 靚 (or Ding 定) 王 (320 BC), to the dynasties of Qi 齊 (Wen Xuan 文 宣), and Northern Zhou 周 (Ming 明).

The earliest source-texts of Indian musical theory are the Nātyaśāstra of Bharata and the Dattilam of Dattila. The text of the former (as we have it) dates from before *c*.AD 500, shaped between the fourth and the sixth centuries, but even so a compilation, the ingredients of which belong to the beginning of the millennium or yet earlier (Widdess, 1995, p. 4). What is most remarkable about the Indian system (and seemingly that of Iran – see p. 223) is already displayed here: it is the discrimination of functional note-names perhaps 1000 years before comparable discrimination is evident in the Western world, functional names such as 'start', 'the end', 'other ends', 'emphasized notes' – where (for temporary convenience) our non-standard paraphrases of the ancient terms are used for all four. What is extraordinary is that, notwithstanding the sophistication of the Indo-Iranian insights into musical structures, no reference to string-length ratios and their intervallic correlations occurs in early texts relating to scalar systems in the South-Asian world.

The reason for this seems to be that Indian musicians, much engaged as they were with stringed instruments, had, at an early stage, recognised a microtonal unit of pitch that could be generated at will. This microtone was used to define the pitch-value of all notes of the first preferred scales (the two grāmas) so that these too were reproducible at will, with their distinctive properties invariant. Semitones could be accurately divided into two; major and minor tones could be discriminated, and consonant pairings of fourths (two) and fifths (three) existed between notes within a scalar sequence. When the news from Old Babylonia arrived (as it might have done at least by 300 BC) musicians of South Asia seem to have had no need of nor use for it.

It is the case, however, that three fifths and two fourths were all the consonants required by the Old Babylonians in the generation of their octave of eight notes plus one.

The two scales of the earliest Indian modal system were, in Western modal terms, Dorian and Mixo-Lydian; the first note of the latter was the fourth note of the former. The names of the two grāmas, following the names of their initials and finals were Sadja-grāma and Madhyama-grāma.

There is no hint in any of the sources as to the origins of these scales, nor of the processes or standards that led to definition of pitch-relationships between notes in each octave-set. Definition seems to have depended on an observation that could only have been made after the pitch-standard for each note of both scales was fixed and reproducible by ear. Where there is no history, history must indeed be ancient.

That observation was: that having tuned two vīṇā (stringed instruments; but type not known) so that one carried the sa-grāma, the other the ma-grāma (the latter scale starting on the fourth note of the former), a pitch-difference existed between the fifth note of the sa-grāma: 'pa', and the second note of the ma-grāma, also 'pa'. Such was the capacity for pitch-discrimination among South-Asian musicians in the first half of the first millennium, that this pitch-difference came to serve as a pitch-unit of smallest dimensions. A whole number of these defined different intervallic-distances between notes in the two scales: 4, 3, 2. This primary unit of pitch-measurement was the śruti. It may be observed, that this quasi-quartertone was precisely the vocal step undertaken by singers of the Euripidean detached enharmonic pyknon in the surviving fragment of Orestes, for example (see West, 1992; 1994, p. 284).

Concepts as refined and precise as these do not spring into existence fully fledged (like Athene from the head of Zeus) without antecedents. What we are told is to be regarded as a sequence of observations, themselves the consequences of a history as yet unknown. It is to be concluded that we know little of the most remote stages in the development of Indian music. We must perhaps take much more seriously the implications of the music and traditions of the Sāmaveda, the tradition of chanting verses from the Vedas, if this matter is to be pursued.

As Widdess states, however (n. 3, p. 207): 'The *śruti*-measurements [measurements of interval sizes in *śrutis*] thus give a good approximation of the consonant intervals [fourths and fifths – respectively nine and thirteen *śruti*] and distinguish clearly between consonant and non-consonant intervals.' Just so; but are we to suppose that musical memory for interval-sizes in the two grāmas was so perfect that the unitary *śruti* – the quasi-quartertone – could be guaranteed to result each time from the two-vīṇā experiment?

Let us return to the known. We are concerned with the concepts of jāti, grāma and grāmarāga. The jātis were and are classes; the word itself means 'class'.

A jāti was a class of tunes, all of which belonged to the same mode. The first attribute of this class – and we would argue the <u>first</u> attribute to be recognised in time, in the earliest stage of the system – was that all tunes belonging to the class could be regarded as composed of pitch-components from one or other of two scales: grāma. Of these, one was equivalent to church-Dorian on *C* (with sharpened fourth), the other to Glarean Mixo-Lydian on *F* (with flattened seventh). It is surely of interest that this pair of heptatonic modal note-sets, in two keys, were what the entire modal system of Tang China was reduced to in the last years of the ninth century (this volume, Chapter 1, pp. 6–7).

The most important structural feature of each class of tunes, of each jāti, recognised at latest by about AD 500, was the discrimination of note-functions, revealed in the application of functional and/or locational names to certain pitches. Only one of these functional terms was applied at a constant location. This was the note on which the tune ended: nyāsa, the Final. If it is permissible to regard the sequence: from 'pure' (śuddha) jāti to 'modified' (vikṛta) jāti, as reflecting a sequence in time, it was the case that the final pitch – the nyāsa – was recognised (in the earlier phase of discrimination of each jāti) as functioning also as a 'predominant': amśa, a note much emphasised; today's Predominant. The nyāsa (final) itself could also function as apanyāsa: a 'Sub-Final', closing intermediate phrases (as used by Widdess). [This corresponds to what we have elsewhere termed an intermediate or phrase-final.]

The 'modified jāti' in their turn disclose a further increase in the number of functions discriminated, and a wider range of distribution of these among the notes of the grāma note-sets. It was perhaps, at this point in evolution, that tunes of the same jāti could properly be regarded as members of different classes of rāga.

While similarity – in these very general respects – between scalar and modal systems may be recognised over a vast geographical area, in one respect there exists a profound difference between Indian music and the rest, in that the notation of music in India has always been (as expressed by Widdess, 1980, p. 6) oral in origin and mnemonic, rather than visual and prescriptive as in the West. The use of syllables from the spoken language 'is one of the most ancient features of the Indian musical tradition'. Unlike the Indian syllables, most of the widely used graphic symbols of the West are not themselves susceptible of oral articulation. Not until the coming of solmization did the West make use of anything comparable with the Indian system.

In India, mnemonic instrumental notation precedes the traditional sa-ri-ga (sārgam) notation, itself stemming from the middle of the first millennium AD. In contrast to mnemonic instrumental systems for percussion and chordophones, the syllables of the sārgam each denote one, single, musical pitch. In the sārgam of today (unlike the system of the jāti), the pitch-set syllables define a single heptatonic octave-set comparable, say, with a scale of C-minor, in the sense that each syllable (and pitch) occupies a specific location in the pitch-set. The sārgam are locational names of *notes*, in the sense of relative pitches, but not of *pitches* in an absolute sense.

By AD 500 the grāmarāga system had replaced the jāti, and note-functions, too, had changed. In the jātis, alternative notes might function as Initial or Predominant. In the grāmarāgas, however, only a single note functioned in this way. Furthermore, whereas each jāti exhibited a different note as final, within the set of grāmarāgas only two finals occurred: ma and pa.

As will be shown later, it seems likely that discrimination of note-functions existed at an early date in Persia/Iran also, and indeed may go back to the epoch of a common Indo-Iranian language, parent not only to Vedic and Sanskrit, but also to Old Iranian: the language of the hymns of the *Avesta* and of Persian cuneiform inscriptions.

It is reported that sometime between AD 568 and 578 a musician from Kuchā (an oasis-state on the Northern rim of the Takla Makam Depression), at the court of the Wu-*di* Emperor of the Northern Zhou dynasty (北 周, 561–81) demonstrated by means of a 'foreign lute' (*Hu piba* 胡 琵 琶) (1) scales in octave-sets of seven differently pitched notes (*sheng* 聲); (2) seven different scales/modes (*diao* 調).

[Kuchā was subsequently captured by the Chinese in 648, and was the seat of the Anxi 安 西 Protectorate from 649 onwards. Of the kingdoms in the Tarim Basin (the fertile margin of the Takla Makam), Kuchā was the one most strongly under Indo-European cultural influence (Wechsler, 1979, pp. 214ff). The language of Kuchā in the sixth century was an Indo-European language: Tokharian (private communication from Professor Nicolas Sims-Williams, School of Oriental and African Studies, University of London)].

The Kuchean musician's name, as recorded in the *Sui History* (*SS Suishu* 隋書, 14, p. 345) sounded something like 'Sujiva'. The meaning of this name: 'Easy Life' is possible; but 'Sujivha' = 'Sweet tongued', would suit a musician. The phonetic transcription in Chinese (蘇 祇 婆) yields 'Suo-tśi-b'uâ' in the dialect of Chang'an 長 安 (*c*.AD 600) (Karlgren, 1957: **67c**; **590 p**; **25 q**).

A full account of this incident was given by Professor R.F. Wolpert in 1975 in his Dissertation for the Ph.D. Degree (University of Cambridge, No.9447): *Lute Music and Tablatures in the Tang Period*. References to earlier examinations of the Chinese text, and to probable Sanskrit equivalents of the sounds represented by the Chinese phonetic transcriptions, may be found (perhaps more conveniently than in his Dissertation) in his paper of 1981, p. 100, n. 26 (see later). The substance of this account was reconsidered, after discussion *viva voce* with Wolpert, in 1980, by Dr D.R. Widdess, in his Dissertation: *Early Indian Musical Forms* (University of Cambridge, No.11727) and more recently in his book: *The Rāgas of Early India*, 1995.

The incident is re-described in detail here, not merely because the account documents an outstanding example of direct 'diffusionist' transmission of musical knowledge across cultures, and in a West-to-East direction, but also since (in certain respects) a little more may now be contributed to the discussion, and because it is in any case useful for the reader to have opportunity to look at the content of so remarkable a text from differing standpoints. It also confirms the historical priority of Indian musical theory.

Our presentation of the text differs from those of Paul Pelliot (1931) and Liu Maocai (1969) (see Wolpert, 1975, 1981) in that we have made use of Karlgren's reconstruction of the sounds of his 'Ancient' Chinese (as opposed to the 'Archaic' language of Chinese texts such as the *Shijing* 詩 經).

Sujivha had come to the Court of the Wu-*di* Emperor of Northern Zhou (who died in 578) in the train of a Turkic princess, married to the emperor in 568 (see Wolpert, 1975, p. 106, n. 27). His 'foreign lute' has been plausibly equated [by Wolpert (p. 102) and others] with the 5-stringed lute (*Wuxian piba* 五 弦 琵琶) (Wolpert, 1981, pp. 97ff). The demonstration itself is described in a word-of-mouth report made to the Wen-*di* Emperor of Sui in AD 587 – judging from the date of an expression of anger by the Emperor – on a day when (as he states) he has borne the Mandate of Heaven for seven years since enthronement in 581.

The Emperor's anger arose from failure of the musically learnèd to restore the music of ritual. Earlier, in 582, he had scornfully rejected a suggestion that the repertory of Liang (502–50) (a state on the Southern border of Sui) be considered as possible source. He affirmed *that* to be 'a music apt to destroy a State'. The phrase goes back to the hair-raising story of Duke Ling of Wei (534–493 BC) who heard ghostly zither-music when encamped by night (R.H. van Gulik, 1940, pp. 136–7).

The description of Sujivha's demonstration was made by Zheng Yi, Duke of Pei 沛 公 鄭 譯, a distinguished statesman and 'knower of music' (*zhiyinzhe* 知 音 者) who had companioned the Wen-*di* emperor in his youthful studies. As a musician he spoke with authority and (as emerges from the text) he was also a skilled performer on the lute. He it was who not merely reported what Sujivha said and demonstrated, but also (it would appear) himself repeated Sujivha's demonstration. The text reports what Zheng Yi observed and what he later demonstrated; but Zheng Yi does not give explicit expression to the conclusions to be drawn from what was observed. These we are left to infer. Moreover, even his observations are clouded by the ambiguity of some of the technical terms employed.

The account begins: 'Listening to what he [Sujivha] played, in the space of one scale there were seven notes. Subsequently, on questioning him about it, he replied saying: "In the Western Region my Father was praised as one who knew about music. As transmitted and practised through generations there were seven kinds of mode." 聽 其 所 奏 ， 一 均 之 中 間 有 七 聲 。 因 而 問 之 ， 答 云 ： 父 在 西 域 ， 稱 相 知 音 。 代 相 傳 習 ， 調 有 七 種 。

'Taking these seven modes [of Sujivha's demonstration] and carefully comparing them with the seven *notes*, they fitted each other like matching tallies.' 以 其 七 調 ， 勘 校 七 聲 ， 冥 若 合 符 。 The use of the word *fu* 符, originally the half of a split bamboo-tally, to be matched with its partner as evidence of identity at source, signified the closest possible match between items compared; and the word *ming* 冥 is here used in the ancient sense of 'to cover' – said of one thing that conforms completely to another.

What precisely this statement means, however, in terms of detailed actions in sequence, is more difficult to determine. It is here suggested that the meaning is at least an expression of identity between the *content*, in relatively pitched *notes*, of each of the Kuchean seven-note octaves, and that of the different *octave-sets* of the seven Chinese heptatonic modes. The observation would seem to have been of maximal importance for Zheng Yi.

We infer that it alerted him to the possibility of *initiating* modal note-sets on the two auxiliary notes that transformed pentatonic to heptatonic scales. In the Chinese modal system, we infer that possibility had not hitherto been explored. The version of the modal system from Kuchā, presented by Sujivha, revealed a musical world in which not merely did the note-set of a diatonic mode comprise seven rather than five notes, but a world in which a different mode might originate on each of those seven notes.

The ambiguity that has to be addressed in interpreting this passage lies in the meaning of the word '*sheng*' (translated above as 'notes'). In the *Shuo wen* 説 文 dictionary of the early second century AD (see Cumulative bibliography) two words for 'sound' are equated in their lexical definitions: *sheng* and *yin* (聲, 音). On the whole, as the practice of the dictionary shows, *sheng* is the term for sounds in general; *yin* that for musical sounds; but the entry under *yin* continues: '*doh, re, mi, so* and *la* are *sheng*' (Picken, 1962, p. 40). In that earlier paper it was concluded that *sheng* only means the five notes in a musical context and when contrasted with *yin*.

The passage in the *Suishu* that now follows relates Kuchean to Chinese <u>modes</u> and will be discussed later. At this point what is important is that the Kuchean modal octaves appear at first sight to be equated with Chinese 'notes'; both the note-names of the five-note modes, and the names of the auxiliary notes, are used in these equations. It seems highly probable, then, that the term '*Gong-note*' (*Gong sheng* 宮 聲), for example, is here to be understood in the sense of the *Gongdiao* note-set: *gong, shang, jiao, bianzhi, zhi, yu, biangong* – the seven-note set; indeed, as already noted, the *Shuo wen* (*Shuo wen jie zi, di san, shang*) lists the set of pentatonic note-names in sequence as *sheng*. The text runs as follows; first, identity is established between *yin* and *sheng*: 音 聲 也. Having stated this identity, however, the text continues, giving examples of both: 生 於 心 有 節 於 外 謂 之 音 'Born in the mind, having categories without, these are called *yin*'; 宮 商 角 徵 羽 聲 '*Gong, Shang, Jiao, Zhi, Yu* [that is the five notes of music] are *Sheng*; 絲 竹 金 石 匏 土 革 木 音 也 '*Silk, Bamboo, Bronze, Stone, Gourd, Crock, Hide, Wood* [that is the eight timbres of musical instruments] are *Yin*.' *Sheng*, therefore, appear to be musical notes of relative pitch; *Yin* appear to be more or less complex sounds, differing in timbre; pitch is not a factor in their discrimination.

In the light of the *Suishu* text it appears that, from Sujivha's demonstration, Zheng Yi came to realise that both auxiliaries might be included among the *sheng*: *bianzhi* and *biangong*. If we accept that anciently, therefore, '*sheng*' meant not only 'note' but also 'mode', we might translate (see p. 207): 'taking these seven modes (*diao*) and comparing them with the seven ancient Chinese modes' etc., etc. *Diao* in the meaning of 'mode' may have replaced *sheng* with that meaning; the word *diao*, of course, originally carried the meaning of 'tune'.

Continuing: 'Yi, therefore, with practice played these, only then acquiring the correct [rules] for the seven notes' 譯 因 習 而 彈 之， 始 得 七 聲 之 正 'But these [= notes], when they complete these seven modes (*diao*), also bear the names of five scales [*dan* = 且], and a *dan* makes seven modes.' 然 其 就 此 七

調，又 有 五 旦 之 名，且 作 七 調. 'Translating it by a Chinese word, *dan*
is what we call *yun/jun* [= scale]'. 以 華 言 譯 之 ，且 者 則 謂 均 也 。

[In a private communication, Dr Widdess suggests that the word *dan* may be
a Chinese 'spelling' of Sanskrit tāna. The *d* of Chinese *dan* stands for a dental
unaspirated unvoiced *t*, corresponding precisely with the *t* of tāna. This Sanskrit
term is used in the Nātyaśāstra for a transilient scale of five or six notes
(Widdess, 1995, p. 275) and so would be appropriate for pentatonic forms of the
five Chinese modes.]

The Chinese word *yun* or *jun* (均) is again an ambiguous word with a long
history of musical use. From an original meaning 'to measure off', 'to strike', 'to
tune', it became, by meaning-extension, the name of a stringed instrument used
in refining the tuning of bells; and thence to a scale in which the note *Gong* was
tuned to a specific pitch-pipe from among the twelve. Each such scale was, in
effect, a heptatonic *Gong* mode-key on that pitch-pipe.

In the sense of 'scale', and read as *yun*, the term may have existed already in
the *Guo yu* / *Kuo yü* 國 語 ('Dialogues of the State') from *c*.425 BC. Nowadays
the term *yun* is understood as a scalar set of the pitches of the pitch-pipes, starting
on a particular *lü*. Within such a set, seven different mode-sets are available,
starting each on a different *lü*. In the compass-limits of a single octave, inversion
of a portion of the set will be necessary, if the entire set is to be displayed in
pitch-sequence.

Zheng Yi continues in regard to these five *yun*: 'Their notes (*sheng*) also
correspond to [the pitch-pipes] *Huangzhong, Taicu, Linzhong, Nanlu, Guxian*,
five scales. The seven pitch-pipes other than these have no notes for modes.' 其
聲 亦 應 黃 中 ， 太 簇 ， 林 鍾 ， 南 呂 ， 姑 洗 五 均 ， 已 外 七
律 ， 更 無 調 聲 。 The notes of these pitch-pipes as specified here (with
Huangzhong as C) are D, G, A, E.

It is to be noted that these five notes ('their notes') can only be the initial
pitches on which each of the five *yun* begins. Furthermore, it is remarkable that
the names of the five pitch-pipes in this passage are cited in the relative sequence
of the notes *Gong, Shang, Zhi, Yu, Jiao*. This is the pentatonic *Gongdiao* note-set
as it would have been written in the fifth century BC, where as yet only four *yin*
音 were established as notes, and *jiao* was *Gong* raised in pitch by a major third
(see p. 187).

And now comes Zheng Yi's crucial demonstration of the consequences of
Sujivha's original demonstration. Unfortunately the text is corrupt.

'Yi next, in accordance with his fingering of the lute-strings… made
[further] scales, added to their notes, and thus established seven scales [on the
seven hitherto rejected pitch-pipes]. In all they amounted to twelve, corresponding to the twelve pitch-pipes. One pitch-pipe had seven pitch-degrees

(*yin*).' [That is to say, a single pitch-pipe could function as any one of the seven notes in a heptatonic modal octave, and starting from any pitch-pipe a seven-note modal octave could be generated.] 'Each pitch-degree established one mode. Therefore having completed the seven modes [on each of the] twelve pitch-pipes, in all there were 84 modes, revolving in their association, every one of them in harmonious accord [with the rest].' 譯 遂 因 其 所 捻 琵 琶 弦 柱 相 飲 為 均 ， 推 演 其 聲 ， 更 立 七 均 。 合 成 十 二 ， 以 應 十 二 律 。 律 有 七 音 ， 音 立 一 調 ， 故 成 七 調 十 二 律 ， 合 八 十 四 調 ， 旋 轉 相 交 ， 盡 皆 合 。

The translation of the beginning of this passage departs from that of Professor Wolpert. When he wrote, not later than 1975, our knowledge of the vocabulary of *piba*-technique (in the Tang and pre-Tang periods) was limited. His suggestion that the apparent binomial term 'string-posts' *xianzhu* 弦 柱 might mean 'tuning-pegs' seemed reasonable, since such pegs are indeed post-like (while 'frets' *zhu* 柱 never are).

With the passage of time has come further knowledge, such that in the Tang period tuning-pegs are similarly *xianzhu* 弦 軸, where *zhu* (by itself) means 'a pivot'. The uncertainty in the passage is not exhausted by *piba xianzhu*, however. The two lexigraphs *xiangyin* 相 飲 are incomprehensible in this context. *Xiang* might be construed as 'mutually', but *yin* is 'to drink, to swallow'. *Yin* however – as suggested by Dr Marnix StJohn Wells (School of Oriental and African Studies) – might be regarded as an error for the same-sounding lexigraph: 引, originally 'to draw a bow-string' and hence, figuratively, 'to extend'.

What might have been a sensible action would have been to re-tune the five strings, so as to obtain perhaps an interval of as much as a fourth between each pair. In this way the total compass of the instrument would have been greatly increased.

In order to display every mode with its final as lowest pitch, he would need to have at his disposal at least 14 notes of heptatonic *Gongdiao* mode in an ascending sequence; but that condition is not essential, since notes do not necessarily have to be presented in octave-sequence. Were such a demonstration practicable, the meaning of Zheng Yi's statement (already cited) might well have been that the substance of the seven notes was indeed, comprehensively, the substance of the seven diatonic modes.

Modern editions of the *Sui History* show Sujivha's words as speech – as indeed the formula in the text: 'replying said' 答 云 would lead one to understand. The preamble that leads to quotation of the words of Sujivha is also shown as direct speech from Zheng Yi. The statement that follows (of correspondences between Kuchean and Chinese terms, see later) is shown as a continuation of the speech of Zheng Yi himself. At the end of this statement, direct speech ceases, and the text becomes narrative. It seems clear that Zheng Yi sought to be in a position to repeat both aspects of Sujivha's demonstration: (a) the display of a seven-note octave; (b) the display of each of the seven diatonic modes of the Kuchean System. This use of 'correct' (*zheng* 正) in relation to 'mode' parallels Latin use of 'regula' (see p. 143).

Returning to the second part of that demonstration, the text perhaps implies that it was made easier for Chinese listeners to follow what was happening by *first* setting out the notes of a scale in the Chinese basic Lydian heptatonic octave of the *Gongdiao*, and only then making comparison between Kuchean and Chinese modes. We make this suggestion, because the first mode demonstrated was (in fact) the Kuchean *equivalent* of the *Gongdiao* itself.

As already stated, it has been supposed that the lute used in Sujivha's demonstration (perhaps also in that of Zheng Yi in his repeat-performance) was the five-stringed *piba*. The demonstration might have been facilitated, however, if the lute in question had been of the type described in the surviving fragments of the poetical essay by Fu Hsüan (Fu Xuan – 3rd century AD) on a *piba* with twelve frets and four strings, to be identified with the type known as *Ruanxian/Genkan* 阮 弦 after its maker/player (see Picken, 1955). On such a relatively long-necked instrument, chromatic scaling, with a fret for each semitonal degree, equating with the twelve pitch-pipes, may have been available.

Happily, less ambiguous than the matter of what precisely Sujivha *did* – in the sense of exactly how he did it – are the names of the Kuchean modes and their Chinese equivalents in terms of the five-note Chinese scale. Zheng Yi, having ended the statement regarding concordance between the seven modes of Sujivha and the seven notes of his scale, proceeds: 'The first is called...' – where one expects the ordinal numeral to indicate: 'the first of his seven modes'. Nevertheless – as already disclosed – he ends the equation with the name of a note, a scalar degree of relative pitch-value, not the name of a mode. This continues throughout the set of word-equations; the word for 'mode' is never used. He equates what appear to be Sanskrit names of 'modes/scales' with single 'notes'. As argued earlier, however (p. 208), it seems probable that the names of *notes*, that functioned as finals and initials of the five pentatonic modes, were used also as names of modal note-sets, from the first century AD onwards, until a new term '*diao*' (previously meaning a tune), came to be used in the sense of 'mode'.

A most striking feature of the Sanskrit names of modes/scales given by Sujivha is that they are the names of the Indian grāmarāgas. In the Ancient Indian context, however, the finals of the grāmarāgas *did not form a diatonic octave* – as do the finals of Sujivha's modes; the finals of the grāmarāgas were restricted to two pitches (see p. 214). The sequence of finals of the seven jātis, on the other hand, constituted a diatonic octave.

The Chinese 'spellings' of the grāmarāga-names (in meaningless sequences of two or more Chinese monosyllabic words), together with their probable Sanskrit equivalents, are set out here in the sequence of Sujivha's demonstration, using Karlgren's sixth-century, Chang'an-dialect values as an approximation to the sounds of Chinese lexigraphs in the Sui dynasty.

GRĀMARĀGA			Karlgren (1957) references:[2]
Sādhārita	Sâ-t'â-liək	娑 拖 力	**(16e, 4f, 928a)**
Kaiśika	Kiei-śiək	雞 識	**(876n, 920k)**
Ṣaḍjika	Ṣa-śiək	沙 識	**(16a, 920k)**
Ṣaḍjagrāma	Ṣa-dź'i-ka-lam	沙 俟 加 濫	**(16a, 976m, 15a, 609j)**
Ṣaḍava	Ṣa-lâp	沙 臘	**(16a, 637j)**
Pañcama	B'uân-źiäm	般 贍	**(182a, 619f)**
Vṛṣabha Ārṣabha	Γəu-lji-dz'iäp	侯 利 捷[3]	**(113a, 519a, 636b)**

Regarding the name vṛṣabha: Dr Widdess notes that ārṣabha and vṛṣabha, though not certainly cognate, both have the primary meaning of 'male animal, bull', hence also 'the best of any [kind or race]'. Perhaps Zheng Yi was intending to spell vṛṣabha rather than ārṣabha. It is also possible, however, that confusion began with Sujivha.

As already perceived by Widdess (1995), this agreement between Chinese spellings (of names of the grāmarāgas) and their Sanskrit spellings is linked with a far-reaching correspondence between the scalar structures of the modes equated, as now shown here.

---

[2] The more recent work of E.G. Pulleyblank, *Middle Chinese: a Study in Historical Phonology* (1984), has been consulted, but does not yield reconstructions of the Sanskrit terms more obviously satisfactory than those of Karlgren.

[3] The last character should properly be written with the bamboo-determinative: 竹.

Sāt'āliək	T T T S T T S	
(1)		Gongsheng / Satuodiao
Sādhārita	T T T S T T S	

Kieśiək	T T S T T S T	
(2)		Shangsheng / Yuediao
Kaiśika	T T S T T S T	

Ṣaśiək	T S T T S T T	
(3)		Jiaosheng / Pingdiao
Ṣaḍjī[4]	T S T T T S T	

Ṣadź'ikalām	S T T S T T T	
(4)		Bianzhisheng
Ṣaḍjagrāma[4]	T T S T T S T	

Ṣalāp	T T S T T T S	
(5)		Zhisheng / Shuangdiao
Ṣāḍava	T T S T T T S	

B'uanźiäm	T S T T T S T	
(6)		Yusheng / Banshediao
Pañcama	T S T T T S T	

Ґəuljidźiäp	S T T T S T T	
(7)		Biangongsheng
Ārṣabhī	S T T T S T T	

Evidently, as observed by Widdess (1980), in five of these pairs out of seven (numbers 1, 2, 5, 6, 7) the Sui-dynasty *sheng* exhibit intervallic sequences of tone

---

[4] *Ṣaḍjīka is unattested but plausible in the opinion of Widdess.

and semitone identical with those of the corresponding grāmarāga. The correspondence claimed by Zheng Yi may surely be accepted as valid.

A very remarkable feature of the demonstration is: that Sujivha chose to illustrate the correspondence of Chinese modes with the set of seven grāmarāgas (we infer from the majority of names), even though the grāmarāgas were rāga-like variants of heptatonic note-sets. The grāmarāgas did *not* begin (as the jāti did) each on a different degree of the Ṣaḍjagrāma or Madhyamagrāma note-set. As the Kuḍumiyāmalai inscription shows (Widdess, 1979, 1980, 1995), five of the seven grāmarāgas exhibited cadences on *F*, two on *G*: ma and pa respectively.

That inscription itself may plausibly be dated to the seventh century; but clearly we must accept that the names of five of the seven grāmarāgas were already known to Sujivha, when he made his demonstration in the sixth century. His quasi-grāmarāga set was displayed in a sequence that equated each mode *either* with one of the five Chinese heptatonic modes, *or* with one of the two (for the Chinese hypothetical) modes on the auxiliaries; he was not displaying the grāmarāgas as set out in the Kuḍumiyāmalai inscription (Widdess, 1979, pp. 144–50). In that inscription, Madhyamagrāma (not used by Sujivha) and Ṣaḍjagrāma are rāga-variants of the same note-set; Ṣaḍava shares the same final with the two previous grāmarāgas but its note-set differs from these. Sādhārita is indeed a Lydian octave-species, but its final is the same as that of Madhyamagrāma, Ṣaḍjagrāma and Ṣaḍava.

In the light of the demonstration, however, we can only accept that, for Sujivha, modal sets that bore the names of gramarāgas could still be thought of as top-tail inversions of Ṣaḍjagrāma and Madhyamagrāma; as yet (for him) members of the gramarāga-set did not need to have, exclusively, the character of rāga-variants of the same octave note-set.

What Sujivha appears to have done was to display seven heptatonic diatonic modes in a sequence that imitated that of the finals of the older jāti-set; and he began with the modal octave that equated with Chinese *Gongdiao*. Members of the jāti-set were, indeed, defined by different finals, namely the notes sa, ri, ga, ma, pa, dha and ni.

It is of interest to examine what might have been the consequences of such a demonstration, following the sequence of the jāti and beginning from Gāndhāri, the jāti that corresponds to *Gongdiao*.

Sheng / Diao		**hypothetical JĀTI-equivalent**
Gongdiao	$E^b\ F\ G\ A\ B^b\ c\ d$	Gāndhārī
Shangdiao	$F\ G\ A\ B^b\ c\ d\ e^b$	Madhyama
Jiaodiao	$G\ A\ B^b\ c\ d\ e^b\ f\ g$	Pañcamī
Bianzhi-diao	$A\ B^b\ c\ d\ e^b\ f\ g$	Dhaivatī
Zhidiao	$B^b\ c\ d\ e^b\ f\ g\ a$	Naiṣādī
Yudiao	$c\ d\ e^b\ f\ g\ a\ b^b$	Ṣāḍjī
Biangong-diao	$d\ e^b\ f\ g\ a\ b^b\ c$	Ārṣabhī

Sujivha is plainly using grāmarāgas as interval-sets, not as grāmarāgas. He ignores the fact that their note-sets do not begin on different initials/finals.

In this sequence, however, Pañcamī would not have the structure of the *Banshediao* ($G\ A\ B^b\ c\ d\ e\ f$). In fact, it equates with the structure of the *Jiaodiao* ($G\ A\ B^b\ c\ d\ e^b\ f$); the structure of Pañcamī appears under *Yudiao*. Indeed, in this display *Yudiao* and *Jiaodiao* would need to change places if the note-sets are to agree with those of the jāti at the same locus. As shown by Widdess, however (1995, p. 48), while the jāti-Pañcamī may have exhibited either a natural or a sharpened sixth above the final, in the grāmarāga-Pañcama, the sixth was certainly major (antara ga), so that correspondence between Pañcama and *Banshediao* did indeed exist, as demonstrated by the man from Kuchā.

As already indicated, the Chinese text equates, not Kuchean modal names with Chinese modal names (= *diao*), but Kuchean modal names 'spelled' in Chinese syllables, with Chinese note-names (= *sheng*). There is no Indian evidence, however, that the names of the grāmarāga were ever used as names for their initials in a jāti-like sequence. The jāti-names were also names of notes however. Perhaps, then, since he was using grāmarāga names *as if* they were jāti names, Sujivha expressed himself correspondingly in Chinese, using 'note' (= *sheng*) instead of 'mode'/*diao*.

Again, a feature of Zheng Yi's exposition is that he offers a Chinese translation of each grāmarāga's name. The statements of equivalence are all structured in the same way, and in five out of seven instances they are untrue, in the sense that the Chinese is not a translation of the Sanskrit name:

'The first is called Sātjāliək; in Chinese words: "level sound"; that is the Gong-sound.' 一 曰 沙 妥 力，華 言 平 聲，即 宮 聲 也。

That is to say, the Sanskrit term Sādhārita is said to mean 'level sound' (*pingsheng*) and is immediately equated with 'the *Gong*-sound' using the copula *ye* 也. The lexigraph *ping* may also mean 'to control or regulate', 'pacified', 'peaceful, tranquil', etc..

If we proceed through the set of equations, but substitute the Sanskrit equivalents for their Chinese spellings, the second, Kaiśika, is said to mean 'long sound' (*Chang sheng* 長 聲).

The third, Ṣaḍjī, means 'sound of an upright disposition' or perhaps 'true sound' (*Zhizhi sheng* 質 直 聲).

The fourth, Ṣaḍjagrāma, means 'responding sound' (*Yingsheng* 應 聲), where *ying* may also mean 'suitable, right, proper, necessary' if read in the First Tone; but 'to reply or to echo', as well as to respond, if read in the Fourth Tone.

The fifth, Ṣaḍava, means 'echoing harmonious sound' (*Ying he sheng* 應 合 聲).

The sixth, Pañcama, means 'Fifth sound' (*wu sheng* 五 聲).

The seventh, Ārṣabha/Ṛṣabha/Vṛṣabha means 'long-horned-ox sound' (accepting the correction of *hu* 斛 to *qiu* 觓, as adopted by Wolpert (1975, p. 109, following a suggestion from Liu Mau-tsai). *Qiu* means horns of a particular configuration: long, curved or crumpled.

This set of equations shows that, in two instances only, are the 'Chinese words' indeed a translation of the Sanskrit: *wu* of *wusheng*, is indeed 'fifth', corresponding to Pañcama; and the 'ox' of the seventh sentence corresponds to Vṛṣabha (or something similar) meaning 'ox'. Sujhiva was only aware, presumably, that there was a mode of some such name, and of this structure. The meanings of the Sanskrit names of the grāmarāgas in Chinese translation are not given by Sujivha.

When questioned about his demonstration (perhaps by Zheng Yi himself), Sujivha answers first by mentioning the status of his 'father in the Western Region, praised on account of his knowledge of music' 父 在 西 域 稱 為 知 音. He does so, presumably, to enhance his own authority in making a musical demonstration so novel to a Chinese musical audience. [The term: 'knowing music' *zhiyin* 知 音 existed also in Sanskrit as a term of esteem, applied to a musician or to a musically knowledgeable person. His reference to the Western Region does not, however, carry us much closer (geographically speaking) to the North-West of the Indian sub-continent, a region influential in the development of both jāti- and grāmarāga-systems, though possibly the Ganges valley was the homeland of both (Widdess, 1995).]

To the Chinese, the 'Western Region' meant different things at different times; but at no time did it imply much more than the states of the Tarim Basin – today's Xinjiang Province and the Uygur Autonomous Region. Both Sujivha from Kuchā, and his father (with a wider acquaintance – one may assume – with states of the Tarim Basin), were inhabitants of cultural colonies distant from the home of that culture – the Indian sub-continent.

Of additional importance in Sujivha's demonstration is the implied fact that the seven named modes of the Kuchean system were heptatonic and diatonic; and that they included two modes of which the initial notes had hitherto been regarded merely as auxiliaries in the Chinese system.

As indicated by Widdess (private communication, 1995), at least four of the note/jāti names are ethnic/regional: Ṛṣabha/Ārṣabhī, Gāndhāra/ī, Dhaivata/ī, Niṣada/Naiṣadī. Originally these may have indicated *melodic* differences, not mere pitch differences. Perhaps, as with Chinese Chu (p. 126), these were *the* modes of particular regions.

[Dr M. StJ. Wells (School of Oriental and African Studies) has drawn our attention to the fact that the incident reported in *Suishu* is again described, with discussion of foreign modes and pieces, in the *Yueshu* (*c*.1000) of Chen Yang: 陳陽 樂 書 164 卷 胡 曲 調. Dr Wells would also emphasise that while this demonstration (of equivalence between Indian and Chinese heptatonic modal note-sets) is important for us, what was of maximal importance for Duke Zheng Yi of Pei was: that the *Gongdiao* note-set, in its Lydian form, with sharpened fourth and seventh, should be accepted as the basic mode-key of the Chinese system.]

Turning to the grāmarāga-set as displayed in the Kuḍumiyāmalai inscription, however, it is evident that grāmarāgas therein are indeed rāgas, in that identical note-sets are used in entirely different melodic ways to construct different melodies. The didactic grāmarāga-specimens of the Kuḍumiyāmalai inscription demonstrate in exemplary fashion the nature of rāga-variants of one-and-the-same note-set.

In this connection it may be mentioned that attention was drawn, in 1956, to the different skeletal schemes displaying relative pitch-durations, and movements between pitches, in six *Qingshang* melodies for song-texts from *The Book of Songs* (*Shihjing* 詩 經), preserved by Zhu Xi 朱 熹(Picken, 1956, 1957, p. 166); the comment was made: 'the mode evidently embraces a number of rāga-like variants.' Had any one of these served as model for other tunes, with the same note-set and the same internal dynamics of note-functions, the Chinese system would have developed such variants.

If no other materials existed, the different grāmarāgas of the Kuḍumiyāmalai inscription, fashioned from identical note-sets, would surely have the status of different *tunes*, of different compositions using the same note-set; but this surely is what rāga was in origin: a local tune. We must suppose – and it is not a foolish supposition – that some regions made use, not just of a single mode, but of a single tune and its variants.

Attractive though this idea might appear, there is little to support the view that grāma (in the word grāmarāga) retains its meaning of 'locality', 'village'. The technical names of the grāmarāgas would seem rather to be using the 'collection', or 'assembly' meaning of grāma – equated in usage with 'scale'. Nevertheless, the original supposition was not foolish, nor is it foolish to ask: Does evidence exist anywhere of regional dependence on a repertory that consists of a single tune ?

It does.

In the Provinces of Eastern Turkey – Rize and Erzurum – as observed and recorded in 1952 (Picken 1953/4, p. 76; 1975, p. 549), and in the repertory of performers on the double-chanter, droneless, Eastern Turkish bagpipe: *tulum* (Picken, 1975, pp. 528ff), all six dance-tunes recorded were named by place-names; and each place was represented by a single, named tune, each tune consisting of a phrase (maximum compass a sixth), usually not more than one or two measures in length, subject to small-scale rhythmic and melodic variation.

At that time the bagpipers were *the* musicians (the *only* musicians) of the stockmen and lumbermen of the forest-zone. Tunes for the closed- or open-circle dance: *horon*, were played and recorded on 8 August, 1952, in Hemşin (now known as Çamlı Hemşin) by a group of pipers assembled through the kind intervention of the District Magistrate, Bucakmüdürü Nuri Trabzonluoğlu. All players either named *regional* tunes: Rize *horon havası*, Hemşin *horon havası*, or specifically named village-tunes: Papilat (off the road up to Hemşin from Pazar), Çariska (above Fındıklı) in the Province of Rize; and Mehmetina and Hevek (villages in the Province of Erzurum, above İspir). All these tunes were known to all the assembled pipers, themselves from different villages near Hemşin; and each tune was the only *horon*-tune of the village or district named.

The Turkish word *hava* is precisely 'air' in its most general sense – the air, weather, wind, atmosphere, climate – but also 'tune' as in Shakespeare's English. The 'mode' of all these bagpipe-tunes is no more than a descending trichord or tetrachord, commonly graced by a descending major second or third, extending the compass to a fifth or sixth.

[Recordings by Saygun and Reinhard (see Picken, 1975, p. 536) showed a different structure for bagpipe-tunes from the Province of Artvin/Çoruh: a very

218

short tune supported by a sustained drone. Whether, in that province also, a village may be represented by a single bagpipe-tune is not known.]

This phenomenon may be regarded as too local, and too specialised in character to have wider significance. Nevertheless it illustrates the possible validity of the hypothesis just advanced: that not only a single *mode* may characterise a region, but a single *tune* and its variants (in a highly specialised instrumental tradition) may perform that function.

The demonstration by Sujivha testifies to his awareness, in the sixth century, of seven modal octave-sets, starting on different finals, themselves in the sequence of a heptatonic octave. What was it that happened, that led to different *interval sets* being referred to the same final (in the Kuḍumiyamalai inscription: Madhyamagrāma and Ṣaḍava, for example)?

We suggest that the passage from the jāti-system to the grāmarāga-system may have been correlated with the replacement of harps by gourd-resonated stick-zithers (Marcel-Dubois, 1941).

The earliest iconographical evidence for the presence of harps (horizontal arched-harps) in the sub-continent, dates from the Śunga period (second to first centuries BC), following the post-Alexandrine Maurya dynasty (322–185 BC). Harps continued in use, in the North-West, during the Mathura period (first to fourth centuries AD), and were in favour also in South India between those dates. In the South, one type of harp continued in use until the seventh century; but following the end of the Gupta period (at the end of the fifth century, say) harps disappear from the North.

Widdess (1980, 1995) accepts that the jāti-system was in existence before the fourth or fifth century AD; and the primary grāmarāga-system by the seventh century. The correlation between the appearance in time of the latter and the first iconographical evidence (1): for the use of stick-zithers; and (2): for the ending of the use (in ensemble) of arched harps, is surely sufficiently striking for us to ask what this replacement of one instrument by the other may have meant in practical, musical terms.

In images of arched harps shown in Marcel-Dubois' figures, the accepted normal number of strings is seven and never more than ten strings save in Central Asia. Iconography, and surviving ancient harps, suggest that the string-attachment to the arch was like that on the modern Burmese harp. Literary evidence (but no iconographic evidence) exists for harps with 14 strings in South India. On such instruments, each of the jāti-classes could have been displayed at its proper relative pitch in the basic gamuts (Ṣaḍjagrāma and Madhyamagrāma). With fewer strings, the quasi-Burmese tuning-mechanism would have been available to facilitate re-tuning within the octave range, and re-tuning is attested in the theoretical literature. (Incidentally, as Marcel-Dubois emphasised, the lyre

219

is only represented in the art of Gāndhāra in the extreme North-West; and this was the region of Graeco-Buddhist art, with all that that may imply for a potential, eastwards propagation of musical ideas from the Ancient Middle East.)

The apparently sudden disappearance of harps, and their replacement by stick-zithers, might seem to imply a change in ethnic balance, as yet not examined. What is certain, however, is: that a change in musical capability would be inevitable in exchanging a polychordal harp for a stick-zither with but one string.

Marcel-Dubois, examining representations of stick-zithers, stated that a fretted 'stick' is not represented until the fourteenth century, but earlier examples can be cited, and the Saṅgītaratnākara (13th century) describes frets on the kinnari vīṇā. She accepted as probable that the earliest 'stick-zithers' were bamboo tube-zithers perhaps of the simplest kind, with a cortical ribbon, lifted from the surface to form a 'string', as described for a two-stringed half-tube zither from rural Thailand, made as a child's toy, seen in 1972 (Picken, 1984).

In Thailand today, however, this bichord was used as a fixed-pitch drone; and it is not impossible that the earliest gourd-resonated, bamboo, single-stringed tube-zithers in India were used in the same way. Widdess (personal communication) describes having seen frets on monochord stick-zithers at Borobudur (c. 800).

In his 'Grove' account of vīṇā (1984) Widdess described the technique of playing a monochord stick-zither in harmonics, as recounted in the 13th-century Saṅgītaratnākara. The technique is also used today on other instruments of South-East Asia. It is the case, however, that a plucked string – 'gut, sinew, silk, cotton, metal' are mentioned as possible materials – will not yield a harmonic (if plucked while an acoustic node is lightly stopped), unless the string is under tension. Furthermore it is essential that it be mounted raised clear of the surface of the tube – if it is a stick-zither string. Both ends must be firmly attached to a rigid support on the resonant body, and at one end there must be a tuning mechanism.

The mounting of the string has to be of sufficient rigidity for it to be tensioned enough to yield the desired pitch. With a violin G-string (G below middle C), one might expect to apply a tension of between 20 and 40 newtons ($\approx$ two to four kilogrammes) to yield a pitch, such that the first harmonic (the octave of the open string) lies comfortably in the vocal range of a female singer. (Tension figures kindly supplied by Dr James Woodhouse, Department of Engineering, University of Cambridge.)

It is unlikely that the idiochordal 'string' of a monochordal stick-zither of bamboo (for example) could be brought to a comparable tension. The mechanical requirements for a highly crafted stick-zither might well have been met by

Śārngadeva's time; but such an instrument may not be equated with an idiochordal stick-zither.

As Benade (1960, p. 113) put it, concisely and comprehensibly: 'A good musical string is... one in which the tension contributes as much (and stiffness as little) as possible to the forces which make it vibrate. Other things being equal, we want to use as thin and flexible strings as possible, and at the highest possible tension.' It is inconceivable that a monochordal, idiochordal, stringed instrument could comply with those conditions.

On the other hand, it is well possible that a fretted, monochordal zither, but again with a thin string, under adequate tension, plucked with the left hand while the right passed a smooth cylinder as a moving bridge, from point to point along the string, would be capable of yielding any modal octave whatsoever. Even for this system, however, the string would require secure mounting and the tension would need to be high enough for the previously stipulated conditions to be met.

It is questionable, therefore, whether any 'primitive' resonated stick-zither could have been applied to a *melodic* use, and it is doubtful that the monochord stick-zither of Sarasvatī (who decorated wrapper and p. 171 of Dr Widdess's noble book) could have been played in harmonics.

The monochord lutes (*yaktaro*) of Pakistan are held in a position not far removed from that of the single-string stick-zithers, and are used exclusively by a singer as a drone-instrument to accompany his own singing (Baloch, 1973). Such a zither might yet, in time, have been the origin of the characteristically Indian practice of string-drone accompaniment – for which, however, there is no evidence before the fifteenth century (Widdess, 1995, p. 7). In performance, the Thai villager who made the bichordal half-tube zither (Picken, 1984, p. 223), pitched his own voice in relation to that of the bichord and (as the transcription shows) that pitch became the mediant in his vocal improvisation (compass: 123.5.). The structural and technical sophistication of performance possible on later, Indian stick-zithers should not encourage us to hypothesise melodic use of the earliest examples.

The use of a sliding-stick as moveable fret on a stick-zither, fretted or unfretted, parallels that on Japanese one- or two-stringed zithers (*ichi-gen-kin* 一弦琴, and *ni-gen-kin* 二弦琴), still in use in the nineteenth century.

It has been suggested that the practice (of sitar-players) of playing the melody primarily on the top string, while simultaneously striking the second string as an intermittent drone (Widdess, 1995, p. 7, n. 2), may reflect the continuation of a melody+drone practice, on transfer from stick-zither to polychord lutes, when the Delhi Sultanate was established in the 12th century. It should be remembered, however, that this manner of playing lutes is widely traditional and exists today in virtually every area where plucked lutes are in use, whether long- or short-necked.

What happened in the course of time in Indian music may perhaps be regarded as no more than what tended to happen on lyres in Ancient Greece, and on polychord zithers in Ancient China: the restriction of all modes, including rāga-type variants, to a limited pitch-range. In a sense, perhaps, it was the mechanical impossibility of achieving perfectly tuned modal alternatives, at a particular point in time, that encouraged the exploration of rāga-variants.

Such may have been the impact of stick-zithers on the Indian concept of music (it would appear), that when importation of polychord lutes to the sub-continent would have permitted return to a quasi-jāti-like, quasi-Middle-Eastern, modal system, that return did not occur. Even when the fretting of those highly-developed tube-zither lutes known as vīṇā [adopting the ancient name of the arched harp and before that of a bamboo pipe (see Widdess, 1984)] afforded extended use of octaves with continuous semitone-frets, such a return did not occur.

The music remains confined, notwithstanding a range of several octaves, to a single, octave note-set, with its own tonic/final. We name the ending-note in this way since, as we have shown, a final was, and is always, a tonic.

Privately Widdess has raised with us the question whether it is proper (as implied here when we drew attention to the complex drone of the tambura) to refer to any pitched note, present in that drone throughout a performance, as 'a final'. The final (it may well function also as initial) is always and necessarily present, in some sense, to the inner ear of the musician, whether a drone is present or not. It is that 'one far off divine event' to which the whole created musical work moves in any culture.

Transposition of all rāgas to the same 'tonic' had already occurred by the 15th or 16th century, and it has been suggested that one should not imply a direct connection between the modern drone-tonic and the ancient final. 'Because of the drone and changes in both melodic and rhythmic structure, the sense of a final as the degree on which one must end has been dissipated' (Widdess, 1995).

A music that is not going anywhere from the outset, would seem to challenge our concept of 'music'.

Reference has already been made to the existence of Persian terms for the discrimination of note-functions, terms that closely parallel discriminations in Sanskrit from the first centuries of the first millennium. Such observations as are presented here are deeply indebted to the scholarship of Dr Ilya Gershevitch (Emeritus Reader in Iranian Studies, University of Cambridge). Our attention had first been drawn to the set of terms displayed (without comment) by Hormoz Farhat (1990) in his monograph on the Dastgāh concept in Persian music:

	Persian	Sanskrit
Initial	āγāz	graha
Final	forūd	nyāsa
Intermediate Stop	ist	apanyāsa
Dominant/Predominant	šāhid ('witness')	aṃśa ('denominator')

One of these Persian words: forūd, has the general meaning of 'down' with no intrinsic implication of musical use. Its musical expression, however, is as an ultimately descending, melodic passage that ends on the final of the mode. Remarkably, Sanskrit nyāsa, too, means 'throwing or casting or laying *down*' [*ni* (plus root *as-*)].

The Sanskrit for 'initial' graha (cognate with English 'grab'), again means simply 'to seize', where Persian āγāz (Turkish āgāz – a loan from Persian) means 'beginning'. In the Sanskrit, the section-finals or intermediate cadences in a musical structure are termed 'away "downs" ' = apanyāsa, coined secondarily from nyāsa by combining with apa = 'away', and meaning, presumably, 'stops' *away from* the final 'down-falling' cadence.

Unlike the graphic and dramatic initial 'seizing' (graha), or the final descending 'down' (nyāsa), the fourth functional discrimination in Sanskrit is metaphorical. This, the 'predominant' – 'the note or notes most emphasised throughout the melody' (Widdess, 1995, p. 7) – is the word aṃśa, the compound aṃśa-svara being defined as 'key-note' or 'chief-note in music', hence 'predominant' (Widdess).

The range of meanings of aṃśa [Monier-Williams, *Dictionary of Sanskrit* (p. 1, col. a)] is considerable: 'a share, portion, part, party; partition, inheritance; a part of booty; earnest money; stake (in betting); a lot; the denominator of a fraction; a degree of latitude or longitude'. The musical meaning occurs under compounds formed with aṃśa. The meaning 'denominator' perhaps offers the strongest clue to the choice of this term in its musical usage. With all three other functions defined, the 'predominant' (using Widdess' term) is the note that is decisive as an indicator of character.

Of these four Sanskrit words: graha, nyāsa, apanyāsa and aṃśa, musical meanings are given only for graha, nyāsa and aṃśa in the St Petersburg *Dictionary of Sanskrit*, or in that of Monier-Williams. Apanyāsa does not appear at all.

While 'seizing', 'beginning', 'casting down' and 'down' – that is to say graha/āγ āz and nyāsa/forūd – are realistically descriptive terms, the remaining terms: aṃśa/'denominator' and šāhid/'witness' seem to be figurative. In the case of the last pair: Sanskrit apanyāsa presupposes the existence of nyāsa; and Persian ist, as 'stop', suggests awareness that a finalis = forūd will follow at a later stage.

In frequency of occurrence aṃśa may seem to be a sort of 'dominant', and its role may seem to equate in this respect with that of a Dominant in Europe from the seventeenth century onwards. But a dominant that is not always numerically dominating suggests to us a need to look for some attribute other than frequency of occurrence as the essential characteristic. Conceivably the Sanskrit term may have been modelled on the meaning of Persian šāhid = 'witness'. But to what does the šāhid 'bear witness'? Surely to the essential character of the mode. In Europe too (if šāhid and aṃśa are to be equated in some degree with 'dominant'), as in Ancient Iran and Ancient India, the notes so named do indeed 'bear witness' to the essential character of a mode. They also have in this sense a 'denominating' character, remembering the 'denominator' meaning of aṃśa.

One begins to wonder whether 'Denominator' might not be a better general translation for aṃśa. It must be remembered that we are encountering the meanings of these Sanskrit words as memories from Śārṅgadeva's musical world of the thirteenth century, not necessarily their musical meaning at the beginning of the first millennium AD in the time of Bharata's *Nāṭyaśāstra*, or yet earlier.

Rameau in fact remained fully aware (our p. 176) of the tonic character of 'la Notte finale' in its melodic operations. He did so, notwithstanding his chordal definition of that note: 'nous ne donnons le nom de *Tonique* qu'aux Nottes qui portent l'Accord parfait'. Of the *Note tonique* he states: 'it is with *it* that one begins and ends…' (Livre second, p. 56: *On appelle* Note tonique, *celle qui termine la Cadence parfaite, en ce que c'est par elle que l'on commence & que l'on finit, & que c'est dans l'étenduë de son Octave que se détermine toute la modulation.*)

For Rameau of course 'tonique' – still with its adjectival force – denoted a note appertaining to the mode: *le ton*; and in its terminal, 'final', noun-sense it carried all the force of 'pitch-related governance' inherent in the conception of 'tonic' proffered by Powers.

All items of music that are complete – that is to say, they are of more than motival, gestural dimensions – result from a process of creative composition through time. Works of plainsong are frequently works of a high degree of structural complexity and musical sophistication. They are compositions developed in ways that share some structural features with the development of modal expositions in other cultures.

Of great importance is the observation that, over time, Indian perceptions of the rhythmic structure of measured music 'in the modern performing traditions of North and South India' (Widdess 1995, p. 263) have brought with them a shift such that 'it is the first beat of the rhythmic cycle that is the point of greatest interest'. This, in a sense, happened also in the music of China between, say, the Tang and the rise of *Kunqu* in the seventeenth century. Invariably, in the banquet-entertainment music of the Tang Court, the heaviest rhythmic event, in measures of 4, 6, 8, beats to the measure, falls not in the first beat, but on later beats within the bar. A single item among items in measures of six beats to the bar in the *Dunhuang yuepu MS.* exhibits a principal drum-beat on the first beat of six. The repertory of this collection of melodies show signs of Persian influence (see Rockwell/Picken 1998). Conceivably, changes in India came about under influences arising from the military incursions of the Ghaznavids in the twelfth century.

The great variety in pitch-distances between aṃśa and nyāsa in different rāgas of the grāmarāga series makes one wonder whether any word reminiscent of 'dominant' is suitable as a translation of aṃśa.

The difference in character – descriptive *versus* metaphorical – common to different pairs of the four functional terms, both in Sanskrit and in Persian, suggests:

first, that both sets are historically related in the two languages;

secondly, that in Persia (as in India) functional discrimination was made in two stages. In the first stage, possibly still Indo-Iranian, only 'the beginning' and 'the end' were analytically acknowledged. By the second stage, both Indians and Iranians had identified notes with intermediate functions. Furthermore, this identification was done by both peoples *paripassu* and interdependently. In the case of the Sanskrit terms, these are in use already in the *Nātyasāstra* of Bharata [first centuries AD, before about AD 500 (Widdess, 1995, p. 4)].

As a process involving both discrimination of functions, and word-creation, it is plain that what happened (in the Indo-Iranian context) parallels (in some degree) what happened, much later in time, and over centuries, in Western Europe. In this instance, there are no grounds for postulating transmission of information between two so widely separated cultural centres. The metaphors employed with reference to derivative discriminations in the two centres have no point of contact, either in meaning or in etymology; they are representative of parallel word-formations.

Ancient Greece

In the wake of such substantial and authoritative recent accounts of Ancient Greek Music as those of Barker (1984, 1989) and West (1992), it may well be regarded as the height of folly and impertinence to comment here. It seems to us, however, that viewed from the perspective of this survey, there are things to be said that have not been said hitherto.

In regard to the Ancient Greek tradition, it is important always to remember not merely how late are the fragmentary surviving musical documents, but also how late are the theoretical texts. For knowledge of the former we are greatly indebted to West for publication in transcription of so generous a proportion of all that survives, together with detailed annotations making plain his interpretation of the modal properties disclosed. In addition he offers both a translation of the original text-underlay and a discussion of the organisation of the various fragments.

In that [as Farhat (1990, p. 16) states]: 'Most Persian modes, in their elemental forms, can be expressed within a tetrachord or a pentachord', there is (to a degree) a parallel with the overwhelming emphasis laid on the tetrachord as the primary melodic unit in Ancient Greek music. While later Greek theoreticians were fully cognisant of filled, non-transilient, octaval structures, the stress still laid on the importance of tetrachordal structures in the classification of the *genera* in the last centuries BC, and the use of such structures by the voice in the earliest surviving musical fragments – from early dated copies onwards – characterises (as it seems to us) a unique musical world, the strangeness of which has perhaps not been sufficiently emphasised.

The earliest note-names of the Greeks appear to have been string-names on a seven-stringed lyre. On a lyre held tilted away from the player's body, the string in lowest position – 'bottom' (*netē*) – was the highest in pitch (West, p. 64) – as to this day on lutes worldwide. The kithara might indeed be tilted so far in performance that the axis of the instrument became horizontal. All names of strings were locational; and only one: *mesē*, seems also to have acquired functional significance. This string ('middle') appears to have acted as tonal centre, and from here the voice not infrequently descended to a final cadential note a fourth below, as demonstrated by surviving musical examples (West, p. 193). In West's survey, no instances appear of obvious functional names for particular strings/notes. Since such names are conspicuous both in Ancient Indian and in Persian/Iranian music, their absence perhaps implies that the Greek system reflects a more archaic musical world, in which functional discrimination had scarcely begun. The striking emphasis on, and pre-occupation with, tetrachordal structures, evinced by the Greeks, is also, perhaps, suggestive of this.

Whether of seven or eight notes, their scalar set included two tetrachords. These were conjunct in the earlier seven-note form, defined by *Netē*, *Mesē* and *Hypatē* ('topmost'); disjunct in the eight-note form (from the Pythagorean, Philolaus): *Netē -Tritē* ('third'), and *Mesē-Hypatē*.

Although the cultured world of Greek music seems scarcely to have known flutes before the Hellenistic period (West, p. 112), it seems highly unlikely that the Greeks did not, at a rural, folk level, make use of the widely-distributed, long, slender, avian bone-flutes (ulnae of Cranes, Herons and Swans) with three fingerholes towards their distal end. Writing subsequent to West's extended description of the instrument (pp. 81–107), and his vehement castigation (p. 1) of the 'deplorable habit' of calling an *'aulos'* a 'flute', there can scarcely be need to emphasise that in this present paragraph the word 'flute' does indeed mean 'flute', and not a pipe excited to resonance by a reed that may be either a single-reed (a tongue lifted by a cut from the surface of a cylinder), or a double-reed (formed in the simplest case by compressing a cylinder).

Dr Graeme Lawson (Macdonald Institute for Archaeological Research, Cambridge) has drawn our attention to the fact that fragments of bird-bone flutes have been recorded from the Upper Palaeolithic in Western Europe, including ulnae from the Gryphon Vulture, both from France and from the territory of the former Czechoslovak Republic in Eastern Europe.

In bone-flutes of the tenth to twelfth centuries AD from Northern Europe (Swan and Crane bones), the three fingerholes commonly yield a variety of quasi-tetrachordal note-sets with intervals of varied size between pitches. In practice, and for the sake of improved tonal quality, such a flute will usually have been overblown to the first harmonic (the octave). If, following the first tetrachord, such a flute is overblown to the second harmonic (at the fifth), the same flute will yield an octave that consists of two such 'tetrachordal' structures, separated by a 'tone of disjunction'. This means that any single tetrachord, of any structure, may have been converted to an octaval note-set by the physical properties of the flute. A pipe with a beating reed, whether single or double, would not in this way generate an octave from a single tetrachord.

Because of their small diameter, it will often have been possible to over-blow bone-flutes to yet higher harmonic levels, thus obtaining experimental information regarding other types of octaval sets. Today, the 'tabor-pipe' of the Anglo-Saxon world may be regarded as a descendant of such long, narrow pipes: a simple, end-blown, duct-flute; played and fully supported by one hand only, leaving the other free for manifold operations. It is perhaps important to stress again that end-blown bone-flutes (and indeed comparable flutes made from the reed *Phragmites*) will have belonged, if they existed in the ancient Greek world, to the instrumental armoury of the simplest of country folk.

Not only are we ignorant of that armoury among ordinary and country-folk in Ancient Greece; we are supremely ignorant of the musics of the non-Greek, non-Indo-European-speaking former inhabitants of that territory, as well as of the musics of non-Greek neighbouring states. It is important to remember that the oldest bronze lurs of Scandinavia and Ireland, outstanding in the craftsmanship of their metalwork and in their musical properties, are of about the same date as the earliest Minoan finds. Ancient Greece was not, musically speaking, a unique 'European', cultural lighthouse in a sea of 'barbarism'.

Again, the Etruscans were no Indo-Europeans, yet Etruscan frescoes from central Italy reveal all the principal instruments of classical Greek musical culture. What linked the two? Were the instruments that we associate with the Ancient Greeks in fact part of the patrimony (perhaps even, as we shall see, 'matrimony') of non-Indo-European Western Eurasia?

The *auloi* and aulos-fragments of the world's museums are instruments of sophisticated performers and their audiences. They are not the sound-producers of the beautiful Alexis for whom Shepherd Corydon burned. The former's oaten-pipe was (indeed today may still be) a remarkably effective musical instrument, in shade, under a hedge, on a dreamy summer's afternoon.

It is disturbing – in regard to the question of their 'Grecian' origins – that the Greeks seem to have made conspicuous use of imported instruments, from Phrygia, from Libya. Even more disturbing, perhaps is the fact that the etymology of *phorminx* – their most ancient lyre – *salpinx* (trumpet) and *syrinx* (panpipe) is unknown; yet again, *lyrā* and *kitharā* appear to be loan-words from an unidentified foreign language (West, p. 50, n. 5). All such words may have belonged to the pre-Greek population, or have been borrowed from eastern neighbours.

Such considerations make yet more important the observations of the late Samuel Baud-Bovy (on the folk music, folk-instruments, and folk-dances of present-day Greece) as a supplement to what Antiquity reports. We know too little of the folk-culture of Ancient Greece to be certain what was indigenous and what acquired from neighbours.

Although the properties of long-forgotten and discounted, folk bone-flutes might, hypothetically, have opened the way in Greek musical culture to an early experience of different types of tetrachordal and octaval structures, it was evidently the performance-mechanics of lyres that led the Greeks to a relative pitch-nomenclature. Even in regard to the hypothesized flutes, however, we would still require explanation (see later) of the choice of a particular type of tetrachord as a musical unit. That historical texts did not record, and would never have recorded, a possible 'folk-flute' origin of scales in Ancient Greece is understandable. In Anatolia today, it is the case that a village lute-player takes precedence, both social and musical, over the shepherd who plays an eagle-bone flute (Picken, 1975, p. 389).

Turning now to the historical record, and to the lateness of theoretical texts, Aristoxenus (a pupil of Aristotle, *c.*384–22 BC) is known through his *Elementa Harmonica* (*c.*320 BC) (see Barker, 1989, p. 119) and from citations in works perhaps 500 years later in date. Ptolemy – the hero (as will become evident) of this present section – does not appear until the first half of the second century AD.

Although Pythagoras of Samos (*c.*570–500 BC) was credited (from the fourth century BC onwards) with knowledge of the string-length ratios that correspond each to a given musical interval, the stories of Pythagoras studying in Babylon (in the sixth century BC) are no older than Iamblichus (*c.* AD 330), himself a pupil of Porphyry (AD 233–300), biographer of Pythagoras. Both were Neo-Platonists from Alexandria, settled in Rome (Abraham, 1979, p. 50).

From their evident awareness of the sound-world of seven-note scales of multiple octaval compass – already in the fourth century BC, and from then onwards until the writings of that great scientist, Claudius Ptolemaius, and in particular of his *Harmonics* (Barker, 1989, pp. 275–391) – there can be no doubt that the Greeks were entirely at home in that world. Yet they were also – and we return to harp on the fact – the first people of any culture to discriminate, and emphasise the musical importance of tetrachords in the structure of musical discourse.

The originality of Aristoxenus in his aggressive rejection of all that the Pythagoreans upheld – in special, the close-coupling of music, physics and mathematics – is generally recognised. To us, however, it seems that his musical individuality and distinction lay in a persistent focusing of attention on tretrachordal structures, notwithstanding the impact of Pythagorean ideas and the accepted generation of the octave by cycle-of-fifths operations.

Tetrachords

West has properly stressed the importance, in the musics of many peoples, of 'tetrachords' in the sense of intervals of a fourth with one or more infixes. We suggest, in addition, that the reason for this discrimination of a particular musical unit by the Ancient Greeks, as well as by other peoples of Eurasia, needs to be inquired into, even though explanation is likely to remain highly speculative.

Aristoxenus recognised the importance of a musical unit: the tetrachord; but neither Pythagorean conceptions of scalar organisation, nor the procedures of the Old Babylonians in the second millennium BC in the generation of scales, explain the discrimination, as a melodic unit, of the interval of a fourth: the third in order of 'perfection' as a consonance; the third in order of generation in the sequence of harmonics of a given fundamental.

Not only does the focus of attention impress; so also does Aristoxenus' insistence on the limitations of the human voice, and on its incapacity to sing more than two microtones in sequence with accuracy of intonation. If indeed he was mistaken in insisting that the diatonic tetrachord: *e f g a* was the source of the trichord of Olympus: *e f a* (rather than the converse), he was surely correct in holding fast to the notion that what was singable was probably a necessary precondition for the development of such a refinement as the *enharmonic* tetrachord with its divided semitone.

It is perhaps worth reminding the reader that, while Ancient Indian discrimination of the śruti (a quasi-quartertone) reveals an awareness of the possibility of microtonal subdivision (made concrete for the Greeks by their use of the monochord), no Indian voice ever sang through, no Indian instrument ever played through, a series of śruti in sequence. The śruti measured intervals and served to change the size of intervals, between notes enlarged or reduced in pitch by one or more śruti. In the enharmonic genus, on the other hand, a musical reality for Euripides, the smallest pitch-step was to be sung through in sequence.

As it seems to us, however, we do not even know what the original meaning of the term: *tetrachordon* was, other than the inescapable meaning of 'four strings'. That it also implied four pitches seems certain; but may we with certainty assume that, in remote antiquity, these were notes *within* the compass of a fourth? Granting the importance of the interval, and the reality of a range of possible infixes, 'four strings' might once have meant pitches spaced as *E - A - d - g* or *A - d - e - a* (the latter a standard tuning for the Chinese lute: *piba*); both are sequences of fourths.

The cantillation of Japanese *Nō*-performance today frequently moves from pitch to pitch through two steps of a fourth, between the 'Low, Middle and High nuclear tones' (Kishibe, 1981, p. 51–3). More extensive information is available from the account of the music of *Nō* in the encyclopaedia: *Nihon Ongaku Daijiten* (1989); see 'Scales & Melody-Types' *Onkai to senritsu kei* 音 階 と 旋 律 型 pp. 461, 462.) The steps of a fourth, defined as *b - e - a* (ascending), in the cantillation-tradition of the mid-Edo-period were *geon* 下 音, *chūon* 中 音, *jōon* 上 音; but in the *yowagin* よ わ 吟 ('weak/soft singing') scale, an infix a tone below the upper note was inserted into the second tetrachord, and the series could be extended upwards by two tones.

In Japanese cantillation practice today, notes of a single fourth may be repeated in the pattern: *e'- e'- b - b - e'- e'- b - b -* ('weak/soft singing, middle nuclear-note melody' *yowagin chūge senritsu* よ わ 吟 中 下 旋 律).

Comparison of mid-Edo and contemporary practice suggests that the 'chain of fourths' structure was more clearly defined in the earlier period.

Again, on the three-stringed, long-necked, Japanese lute *shamisen*, in the tuning known as *san-sagari* 三下り ('three descending'), the three strings are tuned to a sequence of fourths: $b^{\flat}$ - *f* - *c*, for example.

These are mentioned here as possible examples of 'tetrachordal' musical organisation in general terms, and in a very different culture, at a very different time. We recognise, however, that the surviving Ancient-Greek tradition knew only that the three *genera* of tetrachords were three different ways of placing one or two infixes *within* the limits of a fourth, which (in diatonic terms) could be regarded as composed of two tones and a semitone.

It is further to be noted that with a single infix added, the tetrachord remained a particular type of *melodic* unit: the interval between the upper limit and the infix (in descent) was always the larger interval in the tetrachord; and by the Greeks the tetrachord as a unit seems to have been more commonly used in descent.

This constancy of structure is something different from (for example) the structure of the strictly anhemitonic tetrachords in Chinese music, where tritonic (that is: 3-note) tetrachords may assume forms with the minor third above or below: *de-g*; *d-fg*. Furthermore, within a given pentatonic set, traditional Chinese melody appears largely free to explore all possible, different, tetrachordal segmentations of the set; free also to move through the degrees of any tetrachord either in descent or ascent.

Reading through the rich collection of transcribed Greek examples (West, pp. 284–325), ranging in date of copying, and (at times) of origin, from *c.*300 BC to the third century AD, the changes in melodic style through time are striking. Even in the earliest examples, however, the feeling of major 3rd+semitone tetrachordal structure is nothing like as strong as in, say, the melodic line of a Japanese folk song in *Edo-bushi* 江戸節 modality, or in a *Pélog* melody from Bali.

Indeed, in the space of the Euripides *Orestes*-fragment 3 (West, p. 284), the lower tetrachord *a - e* , is sketched out once only, in reverse order: *e - f^- f - a* (where *f -f^* represents the divided semitone). In fragment 4 (p. 296: *Iphigenia*), the sub-unit – *pyknon* (the pair of conjunct microtones together with the *f* of the major third) – *f - ê - e* (where *ê* halves the semitone between *f* and *e*), and its inverse: *e - ê - f* is present, as also is a *pyknon* at the fourth above, ascending. In both fragments (and strikingly) much detached use is made of this unit. In the former extract, the *pyknon* from both inverted tetrachords is used; in the latter, that of the lower only.

This is very different from Japanese use of this type of tetrachord. In Greek use, the third – if present – is more frequently above (West, p. 192): 'a descending motion through the tetrachord is more harmonious than an ascending one'; 'a tetrachord begins at its top note and ends at the bottom'; 'low notes after higher ones are nobler and more expressive than the opposite'. These observations on the use of the *pyknon* show plainly that, although detachable in sources as late as the works of Euripides, there was no doubt whatsoever that the *pyknon* was part of the tetrachord.

We suggest the fact that, in general, descending musical gestures have a re-assuring effect (Fernald, 1992, pp. 262–82) may have helped to favour retention of this sequence of the components of the tetrachord in Greek use, as it appears to have done in so many cultures (see Picken, p. 10, in Fletcher, 1999). 'Nobility' and 'expressiveness' are both attributes likely to induce feelings of re-assurance.

In the matter of orientation, in Japanese use one frequently finds alternation in sequence of the elements of the tetrachord: ascent followed by descent; for example: e - f - a - f - e; or the same with decorative extension to the fifth, as in: e - f - a - b - a - f - e. On the other hand, modulation between the use of disjunct and conjunct tetrachords is perhaps as frequent in the Japanese context as in the Greek.

The vocal use of the *pyknon* – so striking in the earlier, more 'archaic' Greek fragments – may have been due to its expressive, dramatic quality, linked with the sliding use, by the voice, of pitch-change through pitches not sharply defined, and to that extent simulating an aspect of the weeping voice (Picken, in Fletcher, 1999).

For that matter, the musical singularity of a majority of these fragments of the most ancient Greek music needs stressing in another respect. In their 'chromaticism' – whether as in the chromatic genus; or in that of the microtonal enharmonic, or in the use of notes outside the ostensible note-set – they are almost without parallel in other musical cultures. There is nothing comparable (in our experience) with any other music in the melodic line of much of the first Delphic paean (127 BC) of Athenaeus (West, pp. 288–92). Rare instances of superficial similarity that occur to us from distant memory are the Turkish early-morning *makam*: *Saba*, or the Hindustani *rāga*: Purya Kalyan and other *rāgas* of the Kalyan group. West himself (p. 196) comments on such chromaticism, but not, perhaps, with the emphasis that might be anticipated.

The question remains, in regard to the Greeks, to the Japanese and others, whence came discrimination of this type of fourth as a melodic unit? It is indeed widespread, as West has noted. Unlike the Greeks, the Japanese (like the Chinese, the Mongolians, and many others) have had nothing to say about the

232

unit until modern times. In the Greek environment, and centuries after complete octave-sets had become the standard musical resource for Greek melody, Ptolemy still discussed 'the division of the tetrachords by genus, according to what is rational and evident to perception' (Barker, p. 275: *Harmonics* Chapter 15).

The scale-generating procedure of the Old Babylonians, extended to nine notes, discloses three possible tetrachordal, diatonic units of minor third and tone, arranged in two different ways, and one such tetrachord consisting of major third and semitone in descent. It would seem, however, that it was the filled octave, generated either by the procedure of the Old Babylonians, or by that of the later 'Pythagoreans', which came to dominate the musical, scalar outlook of the art-music world of antiquity in the Eastern Mediterranean.

The segmentation of the infilled octave – as we see it today in the Turco-Arabic art-music world – reveals both fourth+fifth and fifth+fourth organisation of heptatonic octave-sets. Such segmentation does not draw attention to any particular type of tetrachord. For chains of fourths – of tetrachords – independent of octaval segmentation, we have to look further East, to Turkish and Turkic folk-song styles, for example. There, indeed, fourths are to be observed in use as melodic units, as for example in the dramatic descent of the male voice, beginning in highest tessitura, from tetrachord to tetrachord in many an Anatolian Turkish 'long song' (*uzun hava*).

The sources of a melodic tetrachordal unit

We are aware of only two possible sources from which this musical idea of the tetrachords might have been derived:

(1) as imitation of a bird-call, such as that which accounts for the ritual song of the Kaluli people Bosavi (Papua, New Guinea) (Feld, 1990, and our p. 126). In the Papuan instance, four notes in descent cover a fifth, consisting of a tetrachord (tone + minor third in sequence) + a tone. The Kaluli choice of a dove's call is understandable, since many doves tend to call in clearly pitched notes, delivered sufficiently slowly for humans to grasp and imitate them, delivered moreover at pitches within the range of the human singing voice. Avian musical utterances with these attributes are not restricted to doves, however. In Greece three possible avian candidates susceptible of human imitation have been known since ancient times: the cuckoo, the hoopoe and the hoopoe lark.

The calls of the hoopoe (*Upupa epops*) and of the hoopoe lark (*Alaemon alaudipes*) are arresting and remarkable in their purity of tone and low-pitched, far-carrying quality. The former iterates notes of equal pitch in pairs: 'oo…oo…oo'. First and second repeats may occur on slightly rising pitch-levels.

The hoopoe lark has a similar, precisely pitched song, but of much greater duration (12 minutes in one recording), with considerable variation in the duration of the (usually repeated) constituent notes. The quality of sound from both birds has been likened to that produced by blowing across the top of a bottle – that is to say, consists largely of fundamental tone. Neither of these two species ventures into conspicuous, wide-pitch intervals [private communication from Joan Hall-Craggs (1995) Sub-Department of Animal Behaviour, Madingley, Cambridge]. While Armstrong noted (1958, p. 207) that the hoopoe is still 'a sacred bird in Egypt', it is certain that the cuckoo, if not sacred, nevertheless occupied an immensely important place in the folklore of Ancient Greece.

The song of *Cuculus canorus* (Laurence Picken & David Hindley)
Cuculus canorus '... breeds in all climatic zones of the West Palaearctic except arctic tundra and desert' (*Birds of the Western Palaearctic*, Volume IV; see Cramp, 1960). The call with which it is chiefly associated (though by no means its only type of vocal expression) is arresting, muted in quality and far-carrying. What is spectacularly unusual in cuckoo-biology is the vast area of the earth's surface over which it and its two sub-species are to be found. *C. canorus* and the sub-species *telephonus* and *bakeri*, as shown (*ibid.*, Map, p. 404) extend virtually throughout the Eurasian landmass; only the Holarctic and the Tropics are excluded. If the sub-species are included, the range extends over West China, East to North China and Japan.

As to its vocalisations, these have been examined in detail by Glutz von Boltzheim and Bauer (1980, 1984) and most recently by Hindley (1996).

The last employs a unique method of study that goes beyond the traditionally used sonographic representation of bird-song. *Signalyze*, a signal-analysis programme, is used to extract data (frequency, amplitude and time-into-the-signal) from finely-selected spectra within a bird-song signal. The programme converts this data into MIDI-data (pitch, key velocities, note-durations, etc.) appropriate to the computer music-programme *Finale*; fashions a multi-staved 'score' (involving several 'windows') that facilitates precise, graphic representation of the microtonal movement of sound in all parameters, and generates a synthesized 'performance' of the score (by means of a *Yamaha SY77* synthesizer), that closely simulates the original bird-song, both in sound and sonographic representation. Through such processes a coherent and meaningful analysis, using both acoustical and musical terminology, can be applied.

Below are three sonograms prepared by D.H.. Figure 1 is a set of three sonograms based on a single recording of three cuckoo calls. 1a & 1b reveal the general 'visual' characteristics of the twin-syllable calls. 1c shows how the first

234

syllable of the first strophe changes dramatically in pitch and amplitude through its length, and within a very short period of time. (The units of the time-scale are milliseconds.)

Figure 1a. Three Cuckoo calls (strophes) at original pitch and speed

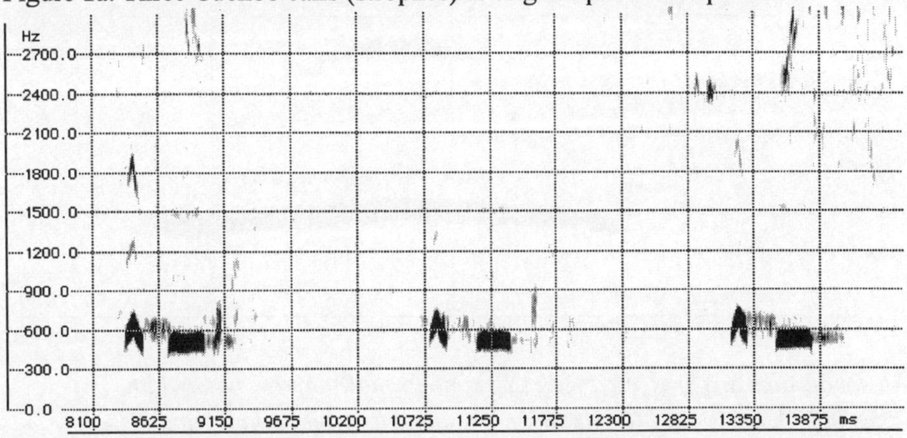

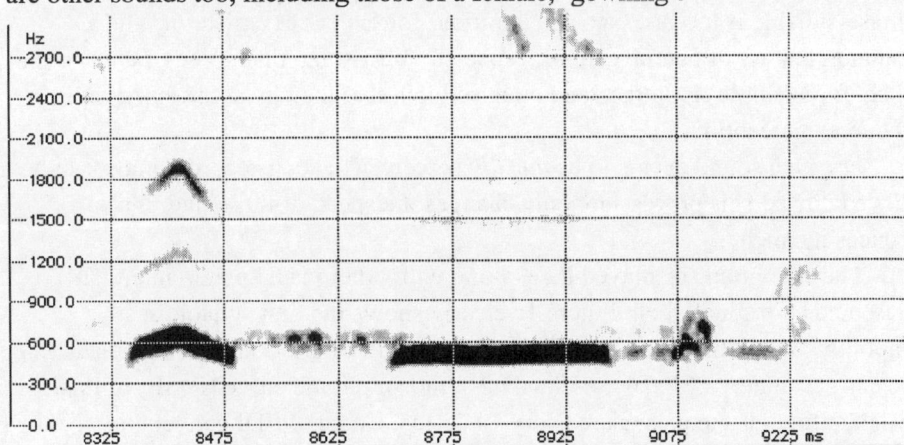

Figure 1b. Strophe 1, now 'zoomed-in', showing the distinctive characteristics of the two syllables. The shadow following each syllable is reverberation, but there are other sounds too, including those of a female, 'gowking'.

Figure 1c. First syllable of strophe 1, at greater 'zoom', showing the strong fundamental, and the weaker partials at the 8ve and 15th

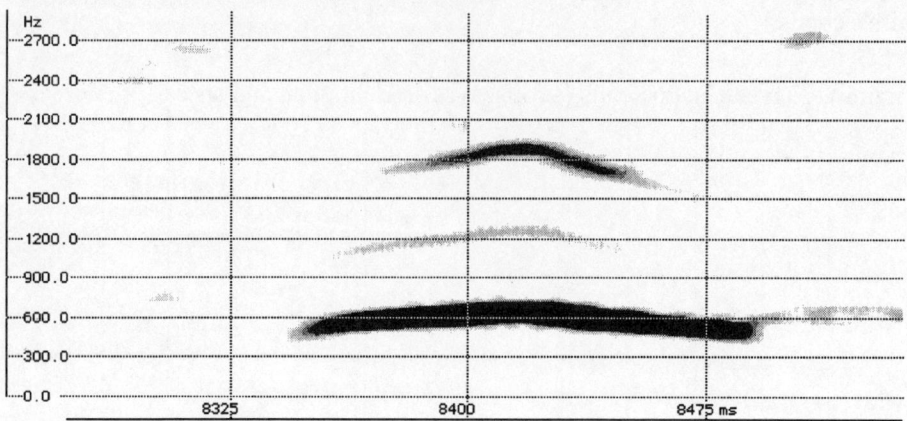

(All sonograms are presented with the same format: narrow bandwidth (25ms/40Hz), half range (0–3000Hz), pre-emphasis, smoothing, and 88% darkness.)

Though the pitch-range of the cuckoo-calls generally falls within human range of perception, the movement of the sound through the inverted 'V'-shape of the first phrase-syllable is too fast (short in duration) for the ear to register it. It is a common feature of natural sounds, especially bird-song, that speed of change (in pitch, for example) is so fast, and pitch so high, that they lie at the extreme limit of human perception.

For such sound events to be *aurally* perceived, a song-recording needs to be slowed down. This process not only changes the speed of the sound, it also reduces its pitch.[5]

The sonograms displayed here, along with other visual material, are all presented at original pitch. Figure 1c clearly shows the first syllable as a smoothly articulating sound. In Figure 2 below, the Data Conversion spreadsheet, we can see under ' "Signalyze" Analysis', the amplitude curve (in dB) of this syllable through samples taken every 14/15 ms. Under 'MIDI conversion', Note

---

[5] In his preparation of a bird-song for analysis, D.H. usually slows down the original recording, not just to make the sound-events audible, but also for technical reasons: (i) to place the song in a frequency-range that suits the application default FFT-Comb Routine for the generation of reliable data, and (ii) to enable the accurate processing of MIDI data within its sound-parameter 31.25 kilobaud. For MIDI performance these cuckoo-calls needed to be slowed down four times.

236

Pitch, the pitch-curve, moves from A4$^\sharp$/4 to D5$^\sharp$/4, the highest (and loudest) pitch, and falls through the intervening pitches back to A4$^\sharp$/4.

Figure 2. Data-conversion spreadsheet for cuckoo call, Strophe 1, at original speed.

Spectra have been taken at c.15ms intervals that provide frequency (shown to the left of the spreadsheet), along with amplitude and time-into-the-signal; their conversion into MIDI musical-data follows through the centre of the sheet. The extreme right column, under Time Conversion, lists 64th-notes (traditionally the shortest note-value) against the spectra-samples at a metronome-speed (MM) of 144 1/2-notes per min. At this speed there are 4608 64th-notes per min, or 76.8 per sec. One 1/64th-note lasts 0.013sec. These are the values of the notation in Figure 4. The twin-syllabled cuckoo-call (without its reverberation) lasts about 2/3rd sec.

TITLE: Cuckoo strophe - limited sampling					MIDI CONVERSION						
		"SIGNALYZE" ANALYSIS 23/4/96 (A4=440Hz)			FREQ'Y CONV	AMPLITUDE CONVERSION Continuous Data		TIME CONVERSION MM set @ 144 1/2 notes per minute.				
No:	Sect'n	Freq'ncy:	Time:	Amp'de	Note Pitch	Main Volume value 1 6/64	control value 2 3/64	1/8 0.104	1/16 0.052	1/32 0.026	1/64 0.013	1/64 0.013
	Cu---	f	oT	dB								
1		f 464	oT 8338	dB 17	A4#/4	13	14	1	1	1	1	1
2		f 533	oT 8352	dB 35	C5	33	36			2	2	2
3		f 563	oT 8367	dB 44	C5#	54	57				3	3
4		f 583	oT 8381	dB 48	C5#3/4	67	72		2	3	4	4
5		f 618	oT 8402	dB 50	D5#/4	73	80				5	5
6		f 616	oT 8417	dB 50	D5#/4	73	80			4	7	7
7		f 578	oT 8432	dB 49	C5#3/4	71	76	2	3	5	8	8
8		f 546	oT 8447	dB 46	C5#/4	62	66				9	9
9		f 521	oT 8459	dB 43	B4#/4	53	55			6	10	10
10		f 498	oT 8474	dB 39	B4	43	45				11	11
11		f 464	oT 8483	dB 29	A4#/4	25	27				12	12
	ckoo----											
12		f 473	oT 8701	dB 37	A4#	40	42	1	1	1	1	28
13		f 491	oT 8722	dB 43	A4#3/4	54	60			2	2	30
14		f 496	oT 8742	dB 45	B4	61	64		2		4	32
15		f 493	oT 8757	dB 45	A4#3/4	61	67			3	5	33
16		f 491	oT 8775	dB 45	A4#3/4	61	67			4	6	34
17		f 483	oT 8790	dB 44	A4#3/4	58	63	2	3		7	35
18		f 483	oT 8808	dB 43	A4#3/4	54	60			5	9	37
19		f 483	oT 8826	dB 43	A4#3/4	54	60			6	10	38
20		f 486	oT 8841	dB 44	A4#3/4	58	63		4		11	39
21		f 488	oT 8859	dB 44	A4#3/4	58	63			7	13	41
22		f 491	oT 8877	dB 44	A4#3/4	58	63			8	14	42
23		f 493	oT 8892	dB 44	A4#3/4	58	63				15	43
24		f 496	oT 8909	dB 45	B4	61	64	3	5	9	16	44
25		f 498	oT 8927	dB 45	B4	61	64				18	46
26		f 496	oT 8942	dB 44	B4	57	59			10	19	47
27		f 493	oT 8957	dB 42	A4#3/4	51	56		6	11	20	48
28		f 491	oT 8972	dB 36	A4#3/4	37	39				21	49
29		f 456	oT 8984	dB 24	A4#/4	20	20				22	50

The Pitch Score (Figure 3) shows the musical transcription for all three strophes seen as sonograms in Figure 1a, and based on the full Data Conversion sheet. Though it would appear that the notation here is composed of discrete pitches, in reality these are simply reference pitch-points in a continuum of pitch-movement. Between the highest and loudest points of the first syllable and those of the second syllable, D5$^\sharp$/4 and B4, the intervallic distance is just over a minor third. However, the intervals of the second and third strophes: D5$^\sharp$3/4 to B4, and E5 to

B4 show a movement widening to a perfect 4th – the golden tetrachord. In regard to the extra visible traces of sound that follow the first call (Figure 1b), the background 'gowking' call of the female, the cuckoo in question was perhaps in the middle of his annual visit. The pitch-range of the three calls accords with the view of Glutz von Boltzheim and Bauer (1984, Volume IV, Voice: pp. 412, 413) that characteristic two-note calls 'may span various pitch-intervals from a 2nd to a 5th, most frequently a minor 3rd'. Joan Hall-Craggs (from private communications (1995), Cambridge) is of the same opinion. The cuckoo on its arrival in the United Kingdom, commonly begins its season of song with a call of a descending minor 3rd. On the Isle of Sark, a cuckoo has been heard to begin its dawn-song at a minor 3rd and gradually to 'warm up', on the spot, to a major third; in South Oxfordshire, cuckoos have been heard calling in perfect fourths.

Figure 3. The three strophes of the cuckoo's calls in pitch-notation
This notation represents an early sketch in the creation of a musical score for the generation of a close sound-simulation of the cuckoo's song. Here we see only the fundamental line of sound – in tone-quality the sound is sinusoidal; but the cuckoo's song is enriched by timbre – the simultaneous addition of other sinusoidal sounds at different pitches above the fundamental. To provide this vital dimension, the data from these sounds are similarly extracted through spectral analysis. They are then converted into notation and set out on independent staves above the music shown here. Much later, when all these lines of sinusoidal sound (and amplitude-change) are mixed and played simultaneously, the unique 'colour' of the song comes to life. However, from what can be seen already in Figure 3, it is evident that all three strophes follow closely the same form, even to the twin amplitude-peaks in the 2nd phrase-syllable. There are also differences between the strophes. Most noticeable is the upward movement in pitch: in the 2nd strophe by 1/4 tone, in the 3rd, by 1/2 tone.

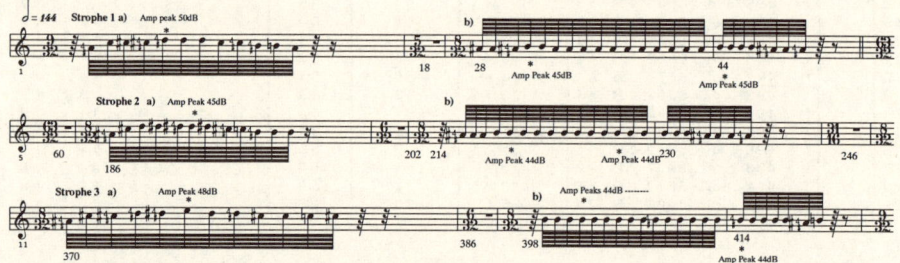

We call the bird 'cuckoo' presumably because this is the sound we hear it make. How far does acoustical analysis of the sound support this onomatopoeic imitation? The character of any sound is largely determined by its timbre – the admixture of partials with the fundamental – and the way timbre subtly changes through time. *Saying* 'cuckoo' involves three components: the two different vowel sounds, and the /k/, a consonant having a transient source, with a plosive release-burst that initiates both vowel sounds.

238

The vowel of the first syllable is very similar to the neutral human phonetic vowel, the 'schwa' [ə]: the sound of the un-accented indefinite article '*a*' in the command 'bake me *a* cake!', or of the final 'e' in German *Knabe*. It is a pure vowel and can be sustained in speech, since the human vocal tract can be held in a constant shape during its production. According to Rosen and Howell (1991), the fundamental sound of [ə] is overlaid by 'odd integer multiples (3x, 5x, and so on)'.

In Figure 1c, traces of partials can be seen moving in parallel above the strong fundamental of the first syllable. If the fundamental is roughly centred around 600 Hz, the next strongest trace is centred around 1800 Hz – one of the odd integer multiples – or, in pitch, a 15th (2 octaves) higher. A fainter third trace centres around 1200 Hz – an octave higher. If we were to produce a sonogram at full range to 7000 Hz, however, we would not find a partial of 3000 Hz (5x). Even so, the first vowel-sound of 'cuckoo', articulated briefly (and without the consonant supplied in this and every other human simulation throughout Eurasia – though not always the same consonant, see later) seems an appropriate onomatopoeic imitation of the first syllable.

If the second syllable is articulated as 'oo' – that is as /u/ – the simulation is very far from convincing. We are in trouble because the shape of the human vowel-tract for this sound is more complex (according to Rosen and Howell) than it is for /ə/. It is 'narrower at the lips, wider further in, and then narrower again at the velum'. /u/, then, generates more harmonics. In fact, as the sonogram shows (Figure 1b), the second syllable has only the slightest of harmonic traces above the fundamental. Here (to all intents and purposes) is a 'pure' sinusoidal sound generated by the cuckoo. (Traces in the sonogram above 2400 Hz belong to other sources – some of it to the 'gowking' female.)

It may surprise the reader to learn that neither syllable of the cuckoo's song shows any trace of an initial consonant, whether a fricative or plosive release-burst. Nevertheless, peoples of other cultures also hear initial consonants to both syllables. Frequently, however, the consonants are other than the 'C', 'K' and 'G' sounds heard by Europeans.

Athanasius Kircher (*Musurgia universalis*, 1650) represented the vocalisation of the cuckoo as a falling minor third ($E^{\flat}/C$), with syllables 'gucu, gucu' as underlay. We do not know how Kircher would have pronounced this, however; but if the vowels were the reverse of today's spelling, '(c)oo(ck)u', that would be more correct in respect of vowel-quality, and would account for the greater number of harmonics visible in the sonogram of the first syllable.

As to how different peoples have heard and hear the cuckoo: Ancient Greeks heard κόκκῦ; today's Swedish is gök; Dano-Norwegian, gjøk.

Slavonic names include Russian *kukovat, kukushka*; Slovene *kukavica* (f.), *kukanje* 'the cry of the cuckoo', *kukati* 'to cry like the cuckoo'; but *kukavica* also means 'a coward' and is a component of a number of plant names; the adjective *kukast* = 'sad', 'gloomy'. The Serbo-Croat names display the same range of meanings as the Slovene, and the cuckoo name is again feminine.

The Hungarian: *kakuk* is interesting for the short 'o' character of the 'a' in the first syllable – a different hearing of the /ə/ of the first syllable. Anatolian Turkish has *guguk kuşu*: 'the cuckoo-bird'.

In French, *coucou*; in Italian, *cuculo*. The different vowels chosen to simulate the cuckoo's 'vowels' are striking, and surely in themselves witnesses to the strangeness of these components of the distrophic song.

Chinese has several terms for the Cuculidae *Dujuanke* 杜鵑科 where 'Dujuan', however, is zoologically the name of *Cuculus poliocephalus*, one of the Japanese species, but not of course *canorus* and not calling 'cuckoo'. Both *Guogong* 郭公 and *Bugu* 布穀 are used in China for *Cuculus canorus* Linn. For the first *guo*, Karlgren [(1957): **774 a** 郭] shows phonetic values of *kwâk /*kwâk* /kuo for the three periods: Archaic (for the earliest Chinese texts), Ancient (for the values of the *Qieyun* Dictionary of *c.*600 AD) and lastly for Modern Chinese in the Beijing dialect (see later).

These disyllabic compounds in Chinese are purely onomatopoeic; the meaning of the monosyllabic words is unimportant. (For those, however, irritated by inscrutable Chinese characters: *Guogong* 郭公 might be translated, improbably as 'Lord of the Twin-Towered City'; the phonetic history of the second syllable is given by Karlgren's **1173 a** 公: *kung / *kung* / kung; its meanings extend from 'father' through 'prince' to 'palace' and 'just'. *Bugu* 布穀 may mean: 'Spread grain!'.)

A famous line from a yet more famous poem by the late Tang poet: Bai Juyi 白居易, namely: 'Lute Prelude' '*Piba-yin*' 琵琶引. [The *Yin* musical form was an unmeasured prelude, the first movement of the 'Large Piece' (*Daqu* 大曲) of the Han dynasty (Picken and Nickson, 1999).] The line in question is: 杜鵑啼血猿哀鳴: to be translated, all too crudely, as 'The cuckoo cries "Blood!"; the lemur weeps and wails!' It is doubtful, however, that the bird referred to is truly the 'cuckoo'. For some listeners, the cuckoo (*Cuculus canorus*) may well 'cry of blood', so unearthly does the disyllabic strophe at times appear. We have no reason to believe that Wordsworth found the call unearthly (see 'To the cuckoo'), but even he enquires:

'O cuckoo, shall I call thee bird
Or but a wandering voice?'

The bird known to the Chinese as *Dujuan* 杜鵑 is *Cuculus poliocephalus*, however, and is regarded by the Japanese as a particularly sweet singer. The two birds may have been confused. The cuckoo-family is indeed called 杜鵑科 'the *Dujuan* Class' in Chinese, and the family includes not only *C.canorus* and *C.poliocephalus*, but a number of other species as well. Only *canorus* and the sub-species *canorus telephonus* call 'Cuckoo!', however.

Shijiu 鳲鳩 is at times used for Cuckoo, but more frequently, for Turtledove or Woodpigeon. The lexigraph for 'corpse', or for one who impersonates the dead at a sacrifice, *shi* 尸, appears not only in the first lexigraph of that binome, but may also appear, solitarily, in place of 鳲 in the term *Shijiu* 尸鳩. Evidently the call of the cuckoo has something sinister for many listeners. The vowel sound of this lexigraph: *shi*, is described as an 'apical vowel', in character somewhat similar to the schwa /ə/ previously mentioned.

For the name of the Japanese sub-species *canorus*: *Cuculus canorus telephonus* the same lexigraphs are used as for the Chinese *Guogong* 郭公. In Japanese, the duplet is pronounced as *kakkō* (written かつこう in the *hiragana* syllabary). The pronunciation of the two lexigraphs today, when spoken separately, however, is: *kaku* and *kō*. The doubling of the consonant: '*kk*' in the compound reflects the presence of a second 'k' in *kaku*. As Karlgren's values show, *kwâk* (as pronunciation of 郭 in Northern Chinese) goes back at least to the fifth-to-seventh centuries BC. [His sound-values derive, in the case of his 'Archaic' readings, from rhyme-tables for 'The Book of Songs' *Shijing* in particular, compiled by scholars in the Song dynasty.]

Another species of Cuckoo that occurs in Japan, *Cuculus poliocephalus*, the *Dujuan* 杜鵑 of China, becomes *Token* in Sino-Japanese, but its familiar Japanese name is *Hototogisu* ほととじす. Its song is much appreciated, but is quite different from that of *Cuculus canorus*.

The commonest cuckoo-name current in Korea, and kindly supplied to us (by Ms Inok Paek) in *hangul*, is *ppokkugi* in standard romanisation. Of particular interest is the short 'o' of the first syllable again equating with a schwa /ə/. As in the Chinese name *Bugou*, the imagined consonants are voiceless.

Dr Jonathan Condit has drawn our attention to the song 'Cuckoo', scored for voice with hour-glass drum and clapper accompaniment, the earliest known such popular song in Korea (Condit, 1984, pp. 59, 321), perhaps the oldest Korean tune for which a date (early twelfth century) can be established. The tune exhibits both open fourths in descent, and descending fourths with a minor-third filler. In this text the cuckoo is named as 'pegok': a form of the name 'ppokkugi' without the terminal '-gi' where the -i- is a nominalising ending; the -g- derives from the -k- of a non-nominalised form (Note from Condit, 15.1.99). Of interest is the fact that the melody descends through a major second only over the name, from 'pe-'

to '-gok', not through a tetrachord. However, the duration of 'pe' (an eighth-note/quaver) is half that of 'gok' (a quarter-note/crotchet). In this respect the song reproduces quite accurately the relative lengths of the two syllables of the cuckoo's strophe. The notation thus imitates the real length of the vowel in the two syllables, setting the two syllables to a falling major second, the two notes being an eighth-note/quaver and a quarter-note/crotchet respectively. Dr Condit informs us that there is uncertainty about the pronunciation of the -e- in his spelling of 'pegok'. Some hold the fifteenth-century sound to have been that of Modern Korean ō (close to the schwa). He favours an Italian 'e' and a 'pure' -o-, like Italian 'o'.

Subsequently, the descending vocal line falls through an open fourth from the pitch of '-gok' (b^b), and ends the line and the song on a further falling fourth with an infix: e^b- c - b^b. The bird is both named, and its characteristic tetrachords illustrated, in the setting of a text-line of eight syllables.

Perhaps the most remarkable name for the cuckoo is that among the Halk – the larger 'half' of Mongolian territory to the East of the Zhungaria/Halk Divide. Dr Andrea Nixon informs us that the name, written in old Mongolian script,[6] is read today as '*kököge*', where '*ge*' is a suffix (comparable, perhaps (?) with the Korean '*-gi*'; but the bird is *called* 'xөxөө'). For both syllables the vowel is represented by a schwa, but lengthened in the second syllable so that the duration-ratio of the two equates with that of the two syllables of the cuckoo's call (as in Korean 'pegok'). The 'x' consonant is a voiceless guttural, closer to the sound in 'ich' rather than that in 'Ach!'. In this onomatopoea, in its modern Halk form, therefore, the consonants have almost entirely disappeared. Both vowels have assumed the schwa-character, but their relative durations relate to those of the cuckoo's two strophes.

The syllable-forms of the Old Mongolian writing are of interest in that they appear in other musical contexts, even though their ancient pronunciation is unknown. The term for 'mode' is '*kög*' as in *kököge*; music in general is '*kögçim*'. Links seem possible with Iranian '*kuk*' ('to tune an instrument') and/or Chinese 曲 [Karlgren: Archaic *$k'iuk$ / Ancient *kiwok* / Modern *kü* (*pinyin* qu3)], translated by us as 'piece', in the sense of a 'piece of music'.

In all these names (with the exception of those from Scandinavian countries) the morphology of the various onomatopoeas is of the same kind: voiced or unvoiced consonants (labials or gutturals) are followed, in two syllables, by

---

[6] The script is said to derive from forms of the Nestorian-Christian alphabet, but written vertically instead of horizontally, in imitation of the Chinese orientation of lexigraphs in vertical columns.

vowels from an ə-a-o-u series. The Scandinavian names are presumably derived from the 'harsh repeated Gowk' previously referred to.

The song of *Cuculus canorus* and Mahler's simulation

The first movement of the *First Symphony* of Gustav Mahler (Opus 20) in *D*, opens with a sequence of fourth-calling 'cuckoos' from flute, piccolo and oboe, with the instruction: *'Wie ein Naturlaut'*. At bar 30, a solo clarinet repeats four times the figure of a falling fourth with the express injunction: *'Der Ruf eines Kuckucks nachzuahmen'*. This is surely firm evidence that the falling fourth of the Cuckoo's call has musical implication for a musician's ear. There is no reason to doubt the reality of this fourth as a significant musical unit, perceived as a fourth by Man, sung by a commonly unseen bird.

As they reach the human ear, coming from this potential singing-teacher of humans, it is not solely the clarity of the pitches uttered, nor their common pitch-invariance (to human ears) over a short time interval, that attract musical attention, but the fact that, for any 'musical ear' they exhibit, during the season, a step-wise increase in the size of the interval generated. Overall, the most common perception of the song is of a two-note utterance in which the interval between the two notes increases from minor third, to major third, to fourth, over time. Few of us have heard a Cuckoo calling a second or a fifth (though these occur); many of us have heard the three intervals just named.

Again, Mahler too confirms the depth of human perception of the advent of the Cuckoo as harbinger of Spring: in his description of the symphony, the first movement bears the expressive title *Frühling und kein Ende*.

If a particular bird may have led Greek musical minds to the concept of a fourth, reached progressively by intervallic steps evident to humans, it is surely the Cuckoo. Through the season his descending vocal gesture is extended for human ears from minor third to major third to perfect fourth, say: *c - a - a♭ - g*: a chromatic tetrachord; indeed, the chromatic genus itself.

If it was the Cuckoo who conferred such a gift on the Ancient Greeks, may it not have done so more generally throughout that vast region of temperate Eurasia, where the melodic importance of tetrachords as musical building units is generally acknowledged? One might argue that Chinese and Mongolian listeners focused attention on the 'initial minor third+fourth a tone below' forms of the Cuckoo's call, whereas the Japanese noted those forms as well as the 'major third+fourth a semitone below' descents. In their perception of the latter they would then have shared Ancient Greek sensibilities.

Perhaps only the Ancient Greeks came near to retaining memory of this indebtedness, in their conspicuous focusing on tri- or tetrachordal structures – the overall compass of which is a tetrachord – as the prime unit of melodic architecture. That even they have forgotten the origin – if indeed it was in this wise – might mean that the memory lies at least six millennia before their earliest records.

That the overlapping memories of natural events, shared by successive generations, may extend back at least that far, was suggested by the observations of Kinnier-Wilson (1979) on what appear to be reflections, in Mesopotamian mythology, of natural phenomena linked with a vast landslip in the Zagros Mountains of South-Western Iran – the Saidmarreh landslip. This occurred as the result of an earthquake in about 9500 BC. Like the Great Wall of China, this immense scar is visible today from the Moon. Deaths from releases of carbon-monoxide and/or hydrogen-sulphide occurred over ensuing millennia, and appalling visible and audible natural phenomena were linked with such releases, such as the 'great Snakes' – rivers of heavy oil, and 'lion-headed' columns of burning gas, coupled with the roaring of the 'Bull of Heaven'. Sumerian and Akkadian documents from the third millennium onwards appear to reflect these phenomena, seen as punishment for having incited the anger of the gods.

Was there any natural event that suddenly brought with it the Cuckoo? There was indeed a prodigious natural event; but not sudden in its manifestation. It cannot be that the end of the last Ice Age led to an overwhelming first experience of vernalisation, associated with the appearance of this and other birds. The climatic change was gradual; it will have ended about 12,000 years ago. Flooding of coastal areas is more likely to have impressed the inhabitants than hitherto unheard calls of the Cuckoo, or the advent of dancing Cranes and the wise-eyed Owls of Minerva, in Greece in particular.

Armstrong (1958) examined the folklore of the Cuckoo throughout temperate Eurasia, noting (for example) the perching of a Cuckoo on the head-dress of Numinchen shaman in Manchuria; the placing of a wooden model of a Cuckoo above the effigy that represents the dead man in a Gilyak cremation; the Ainu belief that the imitator of the Cuckoo's call risks enchantment – to mention only instances of cuckoo-beliefs from regions most remote from Greece.

It was in Ancient Greece, however, that 'the cuckoo came nearest to apotheosis' (Armstrong, p. 207), for Zeus 'wooed Hera in the guise of a storm-driven cuckoo on Mount Kokkygia in Argos'. There is no need to repeat here instances of belief in the Cuckoo as harbinger of Spring, beliefs so widespread that even Siberian tribes 'date their spring ceremonies by its call' (Armstrong, p. 198). As Armstrong's account shows, the range and variety of magical properties associated with this bird is unusually extensive.

It is also evident, in the Greek environment, that the Cuckoo was known to the non-Indo-European-speaking substrate of the population before ever speakers of Proto-Indo-European began to penetrate into the Balkans and Eastern Europe between 4500 and *c.*2000 BC (Mallory, 1989). The story of Zeus's wooing Hera is a symbolic representation of the accomplished ascendancy of an intruding male god over a resident female divinity: 'The Great Mother' of the Mediterranean Basin and the ancient world of Western Asia.

The rape, subsumed in the myth of courtship on Cuckoo-Mountain, was paralleled elsewhere in the Indo-European world, where Indra (in the Ramayana) wooed a nymph as *cuculus/kokila.* The outstanding attribute of this avian divinity would seem to have been *laziness.* 'Cuckoo-Mountain', according to Pausanias, the 2nd-century-AD traveller (2. 36. 1) also had the name: Thornax. It may be significant that Hesychius the lexicographer (5/6th century AD) notes: 'Thrōnax: kephen [both 'e' long ='drone']: Laconian' (the metathesis of a vowel and r is common in ancient Greek, as here between thornax/thronax). That is to say: 'Cuckoo Mountain' was also known as 'Drone Mountain'. 'Drone' is indeed a term of disapproval applied to the Cuckoo by country-folk in many areas of Eurasia.

There is reason to accept, then, that the Cuckoo had made its impact as avian visitor long before the arrival of the speakers of Proto-Indo-European; indeed we may properly suppose it to have been a spring-visitor ever since climatic change permitted regular annual vernalisation of the countryside, with all the consequences for Man, for animals, and for plants, associated therewith.

There is, however, a further possible source of tetrachordal melodic units to be considered:

(2) Maceda (1990, i) has shown how pentatonic anhemitonic scales, as well as pentatonic hemitonic scales, may both be generated on flutes of large 'scale' in the organ-pipe sense, on which the first finger-hole lies at the midpoint of the length; and on which subsequent finger-holes are drilled at specified multiples of the circumference (for further details see Maceda's paper). Under certain conditions hemitonic pentatonic flutes may be made, and these include tetrachords that consist of major third + semitone. The generation of a note-set that includes one or more such tetrachords does not, of course, explain the choice of such a tetrachord as a melodic unit.

Maceda reminds readers that Curt Sachs (1943, pp. 73–4) noted the presence (in the Cairo Museum) of two flutes of *c.*2000 BC (from a tomb of the Middle Kingdom) with the first finger-hole at the mid-point. Sachs notes that the scaling of one of these approximates 'theoretically' (presumably because calculated from measurements) to 248–289–165 cents – a quasi-Japanese major-third+semitone tetrachord. Again the configuration of the tetrachord is a matter for the maker's choice, and that remains unexplained.

It is perhaps important to stress again that European archaeological evidence establishes that end-blown bone flutes (and indeed we must suppose any reed-flutes) from the Upper Palaeolithic onwards, belonged to the musical armoury of the simplest of folk. It may be coincidental that the first fingerhole of the *aulos* itself, seems invariably to have been situated at the halfway mark. Was this a reminiscence of the structure of a Maceda-like divisive type of flute that offered a major-third+semitone tetrachord, using the circumference or half-circumference as a measure in spacing fingerholes?

Imitation of the cuckoo is one possible source of the tetrachordal melodic units so conspicuous in the vestiges of the music of Ancient Greece, and perhaps of that unit throughout Eurasia; but this is speculation only. The work of Feld has shown undeniably, however, that Man does learn music, on occasion, from birds.

It remains to display one last brilliant insight of the Greeks, profoundly satisfying to a musicologist; of no practical use whatsoever.

From recent surveys of the history of the music of Greece in Antiquity it is evident that what Boëthius and Martianus Capella transmitted (through the vehicle of Latin) represented the latest Hellenistic views on scalar structure, as rationalised by Ptolemy. The enormously useful vocabulary for the naming of filled tetrachords and pentachords no longer carried any trace of the subtleties of the *genera*, as set out by Aristoxenus. This vocabulary had little to do with the Ancient Greek music of the earliest surviving fragments.

The Old Babylonians recorded not only knowledge of the relationship between string-length ratios and intervals between pitches, but also a practical *retuning-procedure* (see later) for the generation of the seven kinds of modal octave from any one kind to any another (Gurney, 1994). From the Greeks (who traditionally received knowledge of the ratios from Babylonia *via* Pythagoras) we have received knowledge *not* of what their instrumentalists (lyrists, kitharists) did in practice in tuning from one diatonic mode to another (that we can guess in general terms), but rather a group of theoretical constructs. Two of these are scalar systems extensible upwardly to the highest useful pitch. Ultimately, the two systems provided a standard nomenclature for a sequence of ascending pitches, separated one from another by intervals of approximate tones or semitones (West, 1992, p. 166).

It was argued by the late Dr Marcelle Duchesne-Guillemin (1967, pp. 233–46) that the remarkable nomenclature of these sequences of degrees, in the two systems (Old Babylonian and Ancient Greek) are related to the tuning of strings from both ends of the lyre-yoke as practised on Sumerian and Babylonian lyres. West (1993/4, p. 162), while acknowledging the justness of that observation, did not wish to accept such an historical connection.

A third theoretical construct of the Greeks was surely intended to supply a rational explanation of, and justification for, the intuitive and empirical tuning procedures of lyrists and kitharists – those procedures that any string-player could devise for himself, procedures that the Greek theorists never bothered to record. What the practising musicians were capable of, and that which so evidently intrigued the theoreticians, was their ability to generate, at will, seven different diatonic heptachords (or octachords) within a pitch-range of an octave suited to the singer's voice.

How Greek theory achieved this last theoretical construct is difficult to grasp from the expositions of Henderson (1957), Winnington-Ingram (1980), or Powers (1980). Here an attempt will be made to explain what was done in practice; why this procedure called for theoretical explanation; and the ingenuity of that explanation.

The Old Babylonian process of tuning from one diatonic, heptatonic mode to another (by operating on the tritone) is concisely set out on a surviving cuneiform tablet from Ur (see Gurney, 1994). No Greek text reflects this. In the absence of testimony from Greek written sources, we must suppose that the kitharists proceeded empirically, making the relatively few adjustments of string-tensions (by means of the tuning-mechanisms on the yoke), sharpening or flattening particular strings, as their ears dictated.

By the time of Aristoxenus (4th century BC) a set of *harmoniai* – heptatonic modal segments of the continuum of the Greater Perfect System – were discriminated. These were octave-sets delimited by beginning each set on a different degree of the System.

For the Western Church, the concept of a linear set of pitches, at intervals that were precisely defined in terms of semitones and tones, was entirely adequate for the naming of the characteristic scales of the four original 'tones' in their authentic (= descent below the final not permitted) and plagal (= descent below the final to the fourth permitted) forms; but it is evident that, for the Greeks, this summary, linear sequence of pitches, was intellectually inadequate.

Dissatisfaction was implied by a further development in theoretical exposition. Wedded (as they largely were) to melodic, stringed instruments of the lyre-type, it seems to have been felt essential to furnish a rational procedure for what performing musicians did, by ear and instinctively, in tuning their instruments to any required modal note-set *within the same pitch-range*. As West (1992, p. 229) states, the concern of Aristoxenus in his display of the sequence of *keys* (synonymous with the *modes* or *tonoi*) 'was to provide for and account for every kind of modulation'.

The diagram adopted by Barker (1989, ii, p. 20) – a simplification of Ptolemy's data – crystallises Ptolemy's main aim: to display the *tonoi* in such a way that each *tonos* projects 'onto a specified octave range a different species of the octave' (Barker, p. 19). The version of this diagram in staff-notation, provided by Henderson (1957, p. 354), is perhaps more readily understood.

One can imagine the satisfaction of that moment when it was realised that a modal note-set, beginning (in the Greater Perfect System) on a degree one tone *below* the first note of the Dorian octave, could be brought to lie *between* the same pitch-limits as the Dorian octave, by transposing the entire linear system *up* a tone (see later). All seven different modal octaves could then be obtained by theoretical transpositions, up or down.

This procedure had no practical use; it was without interest for the practising musician; but it will have satisfied minds interested not so much in physics and acoustics as in a conceptual problem in the geometry of musical space. It was, surely, enormously satisfying to a theoretician to be able to explain how all the different octave-sets (between the same, fixed pitch-limits) could be derived by displacement in a plane of a continuous linear sequence of symbols – in other words: by transposition – so that different segments of the Greater Perfect System, lying between *different* pitch-limits, could be brought to lie between *the same* pitch-limits.

Barker was perhaps the first to express Ptolemy's purpose plainly and precisely. It must be stressed, however, that this result was also in the mind of Aristoxenus. At the risk of repetition and stating the obvious, it remains to say what the procedure was intended to achieve, theoretically speaking, and how this theoretical construction was simply related (1) to the structure of lyres and kitharas, and (2) to the needs of performers on these instruments as accompanists to singers who would wish, at all times, to sing – no matter what the mode of the song – within the compass of the octave best suited to the singer's voice.

Summarising and recapitulating: the Old Babylonians reduced all modal octaves to the same pitch-range by an explicit retuning-sequence operating on the tritone. What the Greeks did in practice, the historical texts do not seem to tell us; what they did in theory was to devise an imaginary process of transposition of the Dorian octave, both upwards and downwards. If we imagine the *E*-string of that octave tuned up by a tone to $F^\sharp$, and all other notes similarly raised in pitch, the Dorian octave *E F G a b c d e*, becomes $F^\sharp G a b c^\sharp d e f^\sharp$. Extending the series to the left by one note, *E*, we have now, between *E* and *e* a new intervallic sequence: $E F^\sharp G a b c^\sharp d e$ – the Phrygian octave-species.

In order to obtain all *tonoi* in pitches that lie between the same octave-limits, the theoretical transpositions from the pitches of the Dorian set, *E* to *e*, are: *upwards*, successively, by T, T, and S, yielding in sequence Phrygian, Lydian and Mixo-Lydian octave-sets; *downwards*, by S, T and T, yielding in sequence:

Hypo-Lydian, Hypo-Phrygian and Hypo-Dorian octave-sets. (It is again, and always, to be emphasised that these are not any like-named Church-tone octaves.)

One might, of course, begin with any particular octave-set as central to the theoretical, transposition-scheme; but there would only be one octave-set in which all the notes within that octave range were 'natural'. It is again to be stressed that this was a theoretical scheme for generating the seven kinds of octave-sets by transposition of a single octave-set – though Henderson would seem to deny this purpose.

Let us return to the preceding *theoretical* procedure of hypothetically raising the pitch of the Dorian-set by one tone throughout, and see how different was the situation of the kitharist-*musician*. The latter will have known that, in order to change from the Dorian set to the Phrygian *within the same octave range*, he had only to sharpen his second and sixth strings – supposing his instrument had at least seven strings. In respect of other octave-sets, changes would be of the same kind: slackening or tightening a small number of strings. Notwithstanding contrary views in some quarters, Winnington-Ingram (1980, p. 666a) urged that the word *harmonia* 'meant among other things a tuning'. Moreover it was a tuning 'which provided the notes required for a particular type of melody associated originally with a particular people, Hellenic or Asiatic'. Just so.

To claim (as did Henderson) that all this had nothing to do with music and the practice of music is both true and untrue. It is *true* in the sense that no kitharist or lyrist had any need to think of his sharpenings or flattenings of strings in terms of the infinitely extensible Greater Perfect System being shifted, entire, by prescribed intervallic steps, through imaginary musical space, so that the required modal note-set lay between the ends of the yoke of his kithara. It is *untrue*, because there was indeed a purely intellectual need to rationalise that which lyrists and kitharists achieved spontaneously in their music-making, innocent of any theory.

It need hardly be stressed that there was no need for any concept of *absolute* pitch in this system, no more than in the Indian system. Keys existed, theoretically, in the potential transposability of the system; and we have reason to believe that a small number of keys were recognised and used in practice – transposition of a given *tonos* to several pitch-levels, for the convenience of singers of different age and sex, was recognised and practised.

The importance of string-tension changes in the tuning-process probably accounts for the several meanings of, and confusion between, the Greek words *tonos* and *tropos*, and their Latin 'equivalents' (*tonus* and *tropus*) at various times, and the spread of meanings of *modus*, used for both of these. *Tonos*: 'a stretching', plainly refers to the tensioning of a string to convert it to a resonant material and to bring it to a desired pitch. So also, however, is the reference implicit in *tropos*: 'a turning', for what was turned was the tuning-device associated – for the purpose of pitch-adjustment – with the attachment of each string to the yoke of a lyre or kithara. It is easy to see how the plural *tonoi* could eventually come to stand for continuous double-octave scales: the *harmoniai*, generated from a set of strings by differential stretching of individual strings, each such scale being initiated from successive degrees of a given, basic note-series – a *systema* or System.

To Aristoxenus, *tropos* (like *genos* = *genus* = kind, linked to other kinds by similarity) meant both a *tuning* and a *musical style*, perhaps both a specific sort of note-set (*eidos* = *species*, or *aspect* = sort, separated from other sorts by dissimilarity) and a body of melodic formulae appropriate to that sort.

The fact that it was the Dorian octave-set that constituted the central *tonos* from which, by transposition up and down, six other octave-sets were generated within the compass of one and the same octave, was no accident. As Baud-Bovy (1978) reminded us, Plato, writing in the post-classical period, regarded the *Doric* as the only truly Greek mode. Its perfection was perhaps linked with an original *absence* of semitone intervals in the pentatonic condition: *E G A B D*. Sparta and Argos were indeed opposed to any increase in the number of strings on the lyre. Such opposition was justified, if this increase led to a change in *ethos* of the music performed; and a change from pentatonic, anhemitonic tuning, to heptatonic, would indeed have brought about such a modification.

As Baud-Bovy demonstrated, it is precisely in Thessaly and Epirus, where Herodotus locates the origin of the Dorians, that anhemitonic melodies exist today. This would argue for an original pentatonic condition of the 'natural' Dorian octave – the octave that occupies the central range of the Greater Perfect System. In the pre-classical period it might, however, have been hemitonic pentatonic: *E F A B C e* – as 'Japanese' as could be (as West, 1992, p. 389, has pointed out).

...and yet further East?

In East Asia, and on zithers evolved along lines of morphological descent very different from those followed by harps and lyres, we observe an extraordinary convergence of tunings, due to built-in dimensional constraints. A number of different, alternative, modal note-sets come to be presented to the performer between the limits of a single octave, analogous to what has been observed in the Fertile Crescent and in the Mediterranean Basin.

With the *zithers*, as with the lyres – since in the East as in the Ancient West the resonating medium is a string in its conformation, whether it be of animal *collagen* (gut in the West) or *keratin* (horse-hair in Central Asia) or twisted strands of silk-*fibroin* (the silk of *Bombyx mori*, in East Asia) – the *vocabulary of the tuning-process* in modulating from one modal set to another, employs terms relating to *stretching* (metaphorically 'clarifying' *qing* 清), or *slackening* (metaphorically 'slowing' *man* 漫) and, on Asian lutes (as on lyres and harps) terms relating to *turning* (*nian* 捻), and specifically of turning 'pivots' = *zhu* 軸 = tuning-pegs. The parallels in technical nomenclature between Chinese and Greek stringed instruments may well be due to convergence; but it is worth recalling that a Greek colony, and the remnants of a Roman legion, survived respectively on the edge of, and within, the borders of the Empire of Han.

'When in 327 BC Alexander set forth from Bactria to conquer India, he left behind him, north of the Hindu Kush, the nucleus of a central Asian Greece' (Bernard, 1967, p. 71). The initial discovery of the site of Ai Khanoum ('Moon Lady') in Afghanistan was made (in modern times) by His Majesty, King Mohamed Zaher Shah; and the first campaign of excavation was directed by Bernard in 1965. The city was destroyed by fire around 100 BC; but the ruins are 'those of a great Hellenistic city of central Asia' (Bernard, p. 77). Certainly in the first half of the third century BC 'the official language, the literary culture, and the educational system were all exclusively Greek' (Bernard, p. 88). The traditional year-date of the city's destruction (according to *The Historical Records*, *Shiji* 史 紀) is 129 BC; but Bernard argues that since *Shiji* records that Bactria 'kept its own capital and could receive foreign ambassadors', the city retained a degree of autonomy. Numismatic evidence suggests that 'the Graeco-Bactrian presence maintained itself, in certain parts of Bactria, at least down to *c.*100 BC' (Bernard, p. 94). By this date, the empire of the Han extended to the very borders of what remained of Bactria.

Regarding Rome, it is reported that the remnants of a Roman Legion defended a Hun city against the army of Han (even displaying the characteristic *testudo*-formation of their interlocked shields) until their defeat in 36 BC, as described in *The History of the Former Han* (*Hanshu* 漢 書 17, p. 3013); and there is a tradition that by AD 5 a band of survivors from this heroic defence had established a city, near modern Yongchang 永 昌 (38'10" North; 101'55" East) and the Great Wall, in Gansu Province not far from Lan'zhou 蘭 州.This city survived in name as 'Ligan' or (almost incredibly) 'Lijian' 驪 革干, until overrun by Tibetans in AD 746. The probable site was visited by David Harris, first in 1988 (see Harris, 1989, 1991). It is likely, therefore, that lyres/kitharas came rather closer to physical contact with the Seres, the inhabitants of the land of China, than we have hitherto thought possible. The Seres/Chinese were minimally known to Pliny the Elder (*Historia Naturalis*, Book VI, xx) for their 'wool from woods' (cotton?), but famous to other Romans for their silken garments: *serica*.

Chapter 6

The Modal System of *Tōgaku* as a Vestige of the 28 Mode-Keys of the Tang Inheritance: Different Modes with Like Finals; Like Modes with Different Finals (L.E.R.P.)

Of the 28 mode-key systems (*diao* 調) of the Tang, but a handful survive among items of the *Tōgaku* repertory, even if we include items no longer performed and known solely from manuscripts in tablature. This chapter offers a preliminary sketch of the relationship between the 28 systems of the Tang, and the 9 or so that persisted in use in Japan in manuscripts from the eighth to the thirteenth centuries and onwards.

It is important to note that no previous authors have been in a position to know precisely what the octave note-sets for any item of the Tang-Music originally were. Our certainty of the primary status to be accorded to the mouth-organ tablatures means that we, now and for the first time, have direct detailed knowledge of the note-series used in any piece in mouth-organ tablature, in a particular mode-key group – knowledge independent of any historic modal association, linked with the original Chinese modal name of that group.

In reading the tablatures for *stringed* instruments it is always necessary to be aware of possible confusion between a tuning and a mode or mode-key (as R.F.W. first emphasised). There is no such danger where mouth-organ tablatures are available, since each lexigraph has an invariant, absolute-pitch significance.

As pointed out by Traynor and Kishibe (1951) (see also Marett, 1977, p. 8), the absence of an *F*-pipe on the standard mouth-organ in use in Japan, led to the Chinese *Shuangdiao* 雙 調 (a Mixo-Lydian series on *G*, with *F*$^\sharp$) being transformed in Japan to an Ionian series – *Sōjō* – (with *F*$^\sharp$). This substitution apart, the remaining octave-sets are mostly stable, with minimal application of accidentals.

Two mode-keys, however, exhibit conspicuous use of accidentals: *Sada-chō* and *Taishiki-chō*. In the light of Fujiwara no Moronaga's careful description (Fascicle 5, p. xii), the former was a Lydian series with *D* as final: *d e f*$^\sharp$ *g*$^\sharp$ *a b c*$^{\sharp\prime}$. The condition of the eight *Sada-chō* items (Fascicle 5 and Volume 6) shows that modal revision has occurred – to greater or lesser extent – in all but one item. This revision may have occurred already in China before transmission to Japan. The nature of this revision is: firstly, change of the sharpened fourth to the natural fourth; secondly, change of the sharpened seventh to the natural.

By these changes, the modal condition of the pieces becomes *Ichikotsu-chō* as exhibited in mouth-organ tablature. Removal of the sharpened fourth at once

252

removes the possibility of tritonic leaps, so conspicuous (in Tang *Yayue* 雅 樂) in what Zhu Xi called the *Huangzhong qinggong* mode 黃 鍾 清 宮 (Picken, 1956, 1957), so popular (we have reason to believe) in the music of Western Liangzhou 西 涼 州, as used in the construction of the melody for the Taizong Emperor's birthplace-ode (Volume 6, 1997, p. 12).

The other conspicuously-unstable mode-key is *Taishiki-chō* (*Dashidiao* 太 食 調 or 大 石 調). Originally, this was a Mixo-Lydian note-set: T T ST T ST, with final, *E*, lying a tone above the fundamental of the entire musical system: *D*. The epithet *Dashi* (deriving from 'Tajik') was used during the Tang as a designation for the Empire of the Caliphs – the entire area of Arab conquest and control – with which the Tang Chinese were in contact through *their* control (at that time) of the peripheral oasis-states surrounding the Takla Makam Depression. [The Japanese 'spelling' (in Chinese lexigraphs) of the adjective *Dashi* differs from the Chinese; but the sound-values of the two forms were similar in the Tang. Both these contemporary phonetic spellings of a non-Chinese place-name reproduce the final 'k' of Tajik. The Japanese version is: 太 Karlgren-Ancient – 317**d** *t'âi* -; 食 921**a** *dziǝk*; the Chinese version: 大 317**a** *d'âi*-; 石 795**a** *ziâk*. These are then respectively T'aidziǝk or D'âiziâk = Tajik.]

From the data supplied in *YFZL*, it is evident that the qualification 'Dashi' was also applied to two *Jiao* (= Aeolian) mode-keys of intervallic structure: T S T T S T T, with finals on *E* and *F*ᵇ. This suggests that mode-key variants in this range were particularly popular with performers.

Without exception, melodies in *Taishiki-chō* exhibit instability of the mediant, of the sub-mediant, and of the sub-final; that is to say, we meet with alternative use of *g*ᵇ/*g*; *c*ᵇ/*c*; *d*ᵇ/*d*. The octave-set may thus be regarded as fluctuating between Ionian (*Zhi* 徵); Mixo-Lydian (*Dashidiao*); Dorian /*Yu* 羽 (T S T T T S T) and Aeolian /*Jiao* 角 (T S T T S T T).

The finals of the entire set of surviving modal octaves of *Tōgaku*, set out in ascending order of pitch-sequence, with *D* (*Huangzhong/Kōshō)* as fundamental, constitute a major sixth: *D E F*ᵇ *G A B* (See Table 1: for convenience, the character of the mediant, whether minor or major third, is shown in the rightmost column). Excluding *G*, five of these are in the intervallic relationship: T T 1ᵇT T, to be obtained through the Old Babylonian tuning-procedure, by a sequence of fifth-up, fourth-down, twice repeated, starting from *D*. (The missing *G*, as with *F* in the Old Babylonian sequence, could be obtained from the octave of *D* by tuning down a fifth.)

Table 1. The finals and note-sets of surviving modal octaves of Tōgaku
Fifth-dominants in square-bracketed italics

Type	Gong	Shang	Shang	Yu	Jiao	Shang	Shang	Yu	Yu	Mediant
Japanese Name	Sadachō	Ichikotsu-chō	Taishiki-chō	Hyō-jō	Banshiki no Kaku-chō	Sō-jō	Sui-chō	Ōshiki-chō	Banshiki-chō	
										−
										−
										+
										+
										−
										−
										+/−
										+
										+

Note-sets (reading from the linked columns):

bc♯def♯g♯a Banshe diao: TSTTTST [*f♯*]

abcdef♯g Huangzhong diao: TSTTTST [*e*]

abc♯def♯g Xiashi diao: TTSTTST [*e*]

gabcdef♯ Shuang diao: TTSTTTS [*d*]

f♯g♯abc♯de Dashi diao: TSTTTST [*c♯*]

ef♯gabc♯d Zhengping diao: TSTTTST [*b*]

ef♯g♯abc♯d♯d
ef♯g♯abc♯d♯ } Dashi diao: TTSTTST[*b*]
ef♯gabc♯d

ef♯g♯abc♯d♯d♯e Yue diao: TTSTTST [*a*]

def♯gabc Yue diao: TTSTTST [*a*]

def♯g♯abc♯ Taicou gong (transposed down e →d): TTTSTTS [*a*]

This does not, of course, imply any conscious echo of such procedures, two millennia after they were first practised in the Fertile Crescent. Nevertheless, the musical importance of this region of the Tang gamut is no co-incidence: it is rooted in relationships between diatonic modal note-sets as strong in eighth-century China as they were in Europe in the same period. What early medieval music of East Asia (1), the music of Old Babylon in the West (2), and the ecclesiastical music of medieval Europe (3), had in common was: that all three operated within the framework of a diatonic heptatonic modal octave within the comfortable compass of the singing voice.

In East Asia, the development of terms for note-functions advanced to the discrimination of 'final' and 'dominant' functions, and of a set of fixed-pitchnames (the *lü*4/ *lü*3 律 呂). Another series of note-names, independent of absolute pitch, but in fixed relative-pitch relationship among themselves (*Gong* 宮, *Shang* 商, *Jiao* 角, *Zhi* 徵, *Yu* 羽) was in existence in China during the last centuries BC (but not, as we have seen in Chapter 6, prior to the bells of Marquis Yi of Zeng); and to each individual note of the set of five was ascribed a degree of hierarchical potency within the set, and within the sequence of notes in a tune. In this EastAsian system, then, locational names were allotted relative functional importance in the constitution of a given melody. Such theoretical concepts seem to have applied, however, to the First Mode only – to the *Gong*-mode: 123.56.

From the weighted-scale analyses of melodies (N.J.N., 1998, Appendix 3, p. 203), it is evident that the heptatonic character of the *Ichikotsu/Yiyue* mode may be regarded as superimposed on a pentatonic *Gong*-nucleus. *Ichikotsu-chō* behaves like a heptatonic *Gong*-mode with changed auxiliaries. The locational Western terms are as useful here, however, as in writing or speaking about plainsong-melodies, since they have no harmonic significance and – unlike the *Gongdiao* note-names – no implications of relative potency.

It seems to us, as argued in Chapter 4, permissible to use Western locational terms in the description of Chinese heptatonic melodies. For that matter, the terms may surely be applied also to the components of hexatonic or indeed pentatonic note-sets, as here for the pentatonic *Gongdiao*, for example:

Final   Super-Final   Mediant   Dominant   Sub-Mediant

C   *D*   *E*   *G*   *A*
         (Sub-Final and Sub-Dominant lacking.)

Finally, it might not be unreasonable to apply the locational terms even where, say, a note-set is irrational in terms of ratios between pitch-frequencies.

At the time when the 28 Tang mode-keys were first reconstructed from data given in *YFZL* (Picken, 1969, pp. 92–100), it was not known that the *Tōgaku* repertory establishes beyond doubt that the *Huangzhong/Kōshō* pitch of the Tang was *D*. Further important acoustic data had earlier been made known by Shiba (1955), however, when he described iron plates of a keyed metallophone: *hōkyō/fangxiang* 方 響 (also known as *hōkyōban* 方 響 板: 'rectangular sounding-plates'). Nine such plates from an original set of 16 survive in the *Shōsō-in* 正 倉 院 – the Imperial Treasure-House – established in AD 756. Investigation of these showed they had been tuned 'rigorously to an exact system of sounds. The frequency of the sound corresponding to the Western "*a* " was 440 vibrations per second.'

Yang Yinliu (1980, p. 163) allocated emergence of the *fangxiang* of 16 iron plates to the time of the Northern Zhou 北 周 dynasty (AD 561–81). According to the *Yueshu* 樂 書 (*c.*1101), the plates were 8 x 2 'inches' (*cun* 寸) in area, the upper ends being rounded and the lower ends squared off. The *fangxiang* used in the *Qingyue* 清 樂 'Clear, or Pure, Music' of Western Liang (*Music from the Tang Court*, Volume 6, p. 20) had 16 plates tuned to *Gong* scales (based on the pitch-pipes *Huangzhong* and *Dalu* 大 呂 – a semitone apart) distributed one above the other in a rectangular frame. This statement implies the presence of two sets of 8 plates: *d e f♯ g♯ a b c♯'d'* and *d♯ f g a a♯ c' d' d♯'*.

This same pitch of *a* = 440 cycles per sec. is also the pitch-value of *a* in surviving members of an original set of twelve flutes (each corresponding (in fundamental pitch) to one of the 'pitch-pipes': *lülü*) and also, arguably, of six mouth-organs (all in the *Shōsō-in* – three each, of two sizes), the brass reeds of which had perished. The position of the fingerholes (closure of which induces the reed to speak – because the impedance of the pipe is increased when the air-pressure is raised or lowered), and the position of the vents (that determine the acoustic length of each pipe) show that they too probably sounded virtually at Modern Concert Pitch.

In the modern mouth-organ of the *Gagaku*-ensemble, *a* sounds at 438 c.p.s.. It seems probable, then, that the *a* of the ensemble for *Kangen* 管 弦 (the 'Pipes and Strings' of *Gagaku*) and *Tōgaku*, has remained virtually unchanged for the past 1200 years. The music of Tang was played virtually at the same pitch as 'concert pitch' in world-music today.

In the Table given here, the mode-keys are arranged in ascending sequence according to their finals. A column at the extreme right-hand edge shows whether the mediant is a major (+) or a minor (-) third above the final. Mode-key names are shown in sequence from left to right at the head of columns over the final of each mode-key. Chinese pentatonic modal names are placed above the specific Japanese name.

256

Of the four modes: *Gong, Shang, Jiao* and *Yu*, the *Shang* exists in three Japanese, and four Chinese keys; the *Yu* in three keys; and *Jiao* and *Gong* each in a single key. *Shang* and *Yu* modes occur on the same finals, *E* and *A*; each mode in each key.

Thus the system shows some resemblance to the *qin*-condition, as set out by Jiang Kui (our p. 193), in the sense that some, unlike modal octaves, occur between the same pitch-limits. The system also reveals the range of keys made possible by the development of the *piba* (and other lutes) with four strings and four frets.

The Table shows that the heart of *FBBF* – the two pairs of *Yu* and *Shang* mode-keys on finals *A* and *E* – find their place here (see Chapter 1, p. 7). *Fengxiang Diao* and *Fan Fengxiang Diao* on *A* (alternatively described in *FBBF* as *Fengxiang Diao* in 律 and 呂 forms) reappear as *Ōshikichō* 黃 鍾 調 and *Sui-chō* 水 調.

Huangzhong Diao and *Fan Huangzhong Diao* on *E* – alternatively *Huangzhong Diao* in 律 and 呂 forms – re-appear as *Hyō-jō* 平 調 and *Taishiki-chō* 太 食 調.

Conceivably *Banshiki-chō* 盤 涉 調 on *B* might be related to *Qing Diao* 清 調. Both will have ended on the same final. Perhaps the former survives as a vestige of the 律 form of *FBBF*'s indexed pair: 清 調 and 反 清 調, of which the 呂 form, though named there, is not even represented by a tuning-testing piece in *FBBF*.

Given more recent knowledge that the pitch of the *Huangzhong*-fundamental in the Tang was *D*, an earlier Table (Picken, 1969, p. 98) requires raising in pitch by a tone throughout from *C* to *D*. If this is done, all the observed mode-keys of *Tōgaku* find their place there, as the following survey demonstrates:

If *Banshiki/Banshe* (today on *B*) is the sixth in ascending order in the *Yu* group of keys in the Table of 1969, then the *Yu*-mode of which the final lies a tone below that of *Banshiki* can only be *Ōshiki*, that is, the *Huangzhong diao* on *A* – and this is indeed so.

And what of the *Yu*-mode of which the final lies a fourth below *A*, on *E*? From the Table of 1969, Japanese *Hyō-jō* equates with the *Zhengpingdiao* 正 平 調; and, very satisfactorily, that Chinese modal title includes the *hyō* (= *ping* 平) of *Hyō-jō*.

Among the *Shang* modes in different keys, the transformation of *Sōjō* to the *Zhi* condition in *Tōgaku* performance (because of the absence of an $F^\sharp$ pipe on the modern *shō*) has already been mentioned (p. 252).

In the Table of 1969, the *Shuangdiao* starts from *F*. Transposed up a tone, it becomes identical in final with *Sōjō* (*G*) as exhibited in the Tang-Music repertory.

The *Shang* mode with final a tone above that of *Shuangdiao*, namely *A*, Japanese *Sui-chō*, equates with the *Xiaoshidiao* of the Table of 1969.

A minor third down from the *G* of *Sōjō* brings us to *E*, the final of *Taishiki-chō*. Correspondingly (in the Table of 1969) a minor third below the *Shuangdiao* is the *Dashidiao* on *E*.

Finally, the first *Shang* mode of the Table of 1969 is the *Yuediao*, a fourth below the *Shuangdiao* on *G*.

On *D* in the Japanese system, we have *Ichikotsu-chō*. We interpret this title as 'the first *Yuediao*', and would explain the addition of *ichi* to the modal name as having arisen because the *Yuediao* was indeed the first *Shang* mode of the set of such modes, in seven different keys, in the Tang system of 28 mode-keys.

In this mode-key name, the word *kotsu/yue* 越 is perhaps the State-name: Khotan in an early Chinese 'spelling' – as suggested by Professor E.G. Pulleyblank (see Picken, 1974, p. 12, n. 10).

Thus the *Shang* group of mode-keys may include two regional names for that mode in different keys: the Khotan mode (*Yuediao*) and the Tajik mode (*Dashidiao*). As shown elsewhere (Fascicle 5, p. 121), the original mode-key of *Etenraku* (= 'Music of Khotan') may have been *Taicu Shang*: *e f♯ g♯ a b (c♯) d*; that is, a hexatonic form of the *Dashidiao/Taishiki-chō*.

Thus all the surviving mode-keys (*chōshi/diaozi* 調子) encountered in *Tōgaku* items, find their places in the Table as reconstructed from *YFZL* in 1969. Even the *Kaku/Jiao* mode has its place there. This is a variant of *Banshiki-chō* to which Marett drew attention (1977, pp. 11, 59; also pp. 51–55, 57 – though these latter items were not labelled as *Kaku* in *HFF*). The single instance of this modal variant in the surviving performed repertory, *Kenki-kodatsu* (Shiba, 2, pp. 163–5) finds its place in the *Dashijiao* group, with final *f♯*: *f♯ g♯ a b c♯' d' e'*. (It is to be noted that this item does *not* resemble the pieces of the same name in *HFF*.)

The only heptatonic *Gong* mode represented by pieces in the *Tōgaku* repertory is the *Taizoku/Taicu Gong* mode, transposed down a tone from *E* to *D*, and known as *Sada-chō* (Fascicle 5, p. xii).

The title *Huangzhongdiao* for the *Ōshiki-chō* of *Tōgaku* is misleading. The so-called *Huangzhongdiao* on *A* (such as the Table of 1969 shows when transposed up a tone) is in fact a *Yu* mode, derived from a *Gongdiao* series, based on a *Huangzhong Gongdiao* in which *Gong* is pitched on *C*.

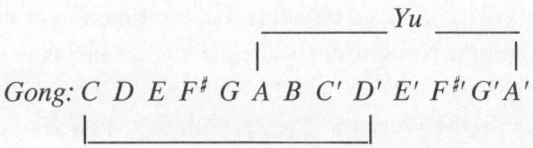

Gong: C D E F♯ G A B C' D' E' F♯'G'A'

The origin of those mode-key names in the Table of 1969 that do not appear in Japan (or do so very rarely), is not a matter to be pursued on this occasion. The Table perhaps implies encroachment of popular names – some place-related (such as *Yue* and *Dashi*) – on mode-key areas once occupied by two-element names of the *Yayue* system, in which the absolute pitch (in pitch-pipe terms) of the *Gong*-degree was named first, followed by the particular modal series to be extracted from (originally) a *Gongdiao* set that started on that pitch.

Some names in the Table seem to have developed as word-plays on a regional name – such as *Xiaoshi* ('Small Stone') as opposed to *Dashi* (= 'Large Stone'); some are based on pitch-changes in the final – sharpening (by a semitone) to yield: 'high' (高) versions, such as *Gao Dashidiao*, with final a semitone higher than that of *Dashidiao*.

From the practice of contemporary Tang-Chinese texts it is evident that, from a Chinese standpoint, the mode-key name alone conveyed all necessary musical information. The Tang name implies not merely modal character in terms of the intervallic sequence of degrees, but also the pitch of the final in absolute terms – absolute at least for the duration of the dynasty. No further specification of a 'mode-pattern' was necessary, though such a term is available in modern Chinese: *diaoshi* 調 式. If required, the intervallic structure could be set out as a linear sequence of notes expressed by pitch-pipe names of absolute value; or it could be stated relatively in terms of the monosyllabic names of notes in the 5-note set, each one of which was sufficient to specify a mode.

The pieces that survive (as the *Tōgaku* repertory) show that the pitch of the initial note, sometimes described as 'starting the tune or mode' (*qidiao* 起 調; p. 143) is not necessarily the final; and indeed inspection of the 31 items comprised in the groups *Ichikotsu-chō* and *Sada-chō* reveals that any degree other than the sub-dominant (the fourth above the final) may act as initial. It is to be noted, however, that the ritual tunes of Tang-Chinese *Yayue*, preserved by Zhu Xi and attributed to the Kaiyuan reign-period (six items in each of two heptatonic modes, *Gong* and *Shang*, respectively), invariably begin on the final or its upper octave (Picken, 1956, 1957).

The condition of the secular *Tōgaku* items so far examined bears witness to a degree of awareness of modality no more structured by the use of a technical vocabulary than was the contemporary world of eighth- or ninth-century Western, ecclesiastical chant. In China, as in the situation revealed by the

259

Dialogus (p. 144), no *finalis* is discriminated by name, but the function of the last note as a determinant of modality is recognised, in the China of Tang as in Carolingian Europe.

In contrast to the position in the Western Church (both Roman and Orthodox) the intervallic structure of a Chinese mode in a particular key could be defined precisely, acoustically, in terms of standard pitch-pipes, as well as in terms of a standard, scalar, locational terminology and its inversions. In China, while 'starting' and 'ruling' functions were recognised, there was also (as previously mentioned) ancient recognition of a hierarchy of importance among the notes of the pentatonic set (Picken, 1966, p. 157; please read 'the *Dasheng* Office', rather than 'Prefect Ta-sheng' – *mea culpa!*).

This according of status to notes in a hierarchical sequence implies the overriding importance of the final; but Jiang Kui (Picken, 1966, p. 157), quoting a musician of the Sui dynasty (sixth century) adds: 'those distant from the Palace being subordinate'; that is to say, in his own song-melody, as he listened to its being played, there was (we may suppose) a balance – in both frequency of occurrence and duration – between notes immediately relating to the final, and those of secondary importance. This recalls the cautionary comment of *Dialogus* in advising economical use of intermediate cadences on notes other than the final. Without sparing use of these, the distinctive character of *modus/diao* will be destroyed.

Not until the nineteenth century (perhaps) does the notion of a *dominant*, as a recognised function, become explicit in a Chinese source. Zhu Xi (twelfth and early thirteenth century) had stated that, in *Yayue* items, while beginning and ending on *Gong*, one may stop (in between) on any of the five degrees (Picken, 1956, 1957, p. 162, n. 22).

Although the functions of *tenor* or *dominant* were not discriminated through use of technical terms, by musicians of Tang, N.J.N.'s analyses have shown beyond question that in pieces in the *Ichikotsu-chō* mode-key group the note at the interval of a fifth above the final frequently functions as a *dominant*; and this note also functions as a *tenor* in its frequent occupation of the position of sustained cadence at the ends of intermediate phrases. Inspection of the scores – or more readily of the conflations (N.J.N.) – shows at once that the note *a* occurs frequently as a phrase-cadence. In its use of four different heptatonic modes corresponding to Lydian, Mixo-Lydian, Dorian and Aeolian (in their tone and semitone sequences), each in seven keys, Tang China enjoyed a more richly prescribed world of instrumental and vocal mode-keys than did seventh- and eighth-century Europe.

Pieces in *Ichikotsu-chō* never present us with plagal forms of the Mixo-Lydian octave-set. This perhaps supports our earlier suggestion that the

260

development of plagal forms is predominantly linked with vocal performance; if the real pitch of the mode final is relatively high, some voices may have found it easier to use the plagal form rather than the authentic. Instruments came first in importance in *Tōgaku*, even though many – if not originally all – items may have been associated with texted songs.

As yet the weighted-scale statistics recorded by N.J.N. relate only to pieces in the *Ichikotsu-chō* and *Sada-chō* mode-keys. In both groups, as stated, the fifth above the final functions (in many instances, though not in all) as a statistical dominant, in terms of duration and frequency of occurrence.

In *Kaibairaku/Huibei yue* 'The Eddying Bowl' (Fascicle 3, p. 49; Fascicle 5, p. 55), while the structural role of the fifth is evident, it is the mediant that by a narrow margin functions as principal intermediate cadence at the end of two-measure phrases.

The 'Way-Walking' of *Katen* [a movement from *Tori* (Fascicle 4, pp. 38ff)] illustrates how intermediate cadential function can switch from dominant, to final, to mediant, and back to final, in the course of a single movement. Indeed, there is great variety in the structures to be observed. For example, in the anomalous *Bosatsu* (Fascicle 4, p. 86) dominant and final 'amount to 50 percent or more of the tonal weight' (N.J.N.) and 'the strongest single note in each piece is the dominant' (N.J.N.). By way of contrast, the mediant 'overshadows dominant and final' (N.J.N.) in *Sukoshi* (Fascicle 4, p. 91).

In the *Ichikotsu* and *Sada* mode-keys, no instance of a functional, statistical dominant at any interval above the final, other than fifth or major third has been encountered. In an extended movement, such as the Prelude to *Ōdai-hajinraku / Huang-di pozhenyue* (Fascicle 1; Fascicle 2, pp. 76, 77) every note of the Mixo-Lydian note-set occasionally functions as intermediate cadence *with the exception of the mediant*. In the entire movement, the sub-mediant (by a small margin) has a higher weighted-scale value than has the dominant; but in the first half of the Prelude, the fifth above the final functions overwhelmingly as most-favoured intermediate cadence.

In order to obtain at least a glimpse of conditions in other mode-keys, a summary scrutiny of 26 of the 'small pieces' (*shōkyoku* 小 曲) from among the *Tōgaku* scores prepared by Shiba (1969, 2) was undertaken, reading the roots of the *shō* cluster-chords (*aitake* 合 竹) in order to determine the plainest form of the *canto fermo* (as opposed to the *canto figurato* of the *hichiriki*, for example). In addition, our own complete set of transcriptions of the 60 items available in Meiji or Shōwa printed editions (see Fascicle 1, p. 6, n. 4), was re-examined. This inspection has shown that while the fifth above the final functions as the most frequent intermediary cadence in a majority of items, and in a majority of the mode-keys represented, in Shiba's material as in ours, this is by no means invariably the case.

In *Hyō-jō* (final *E*), for example, occurrences of the final at intermediary cadences may outnumber those of the fifth, *B*; or the fifth may occur more frequently than the final; or the fifth and other modal degrees may all occur at such cadential points. *Etenraku* 越 殿 樂 in its *Hyō-jō* version is remarkable in that its phrases end invariably on the final, except for the third phrase that ends on the sub-dominant, *A*.

'Chicken's Virtue' *Keitoku/Jide* 雞 德 (Jones & Picken, 1987) is exceptional in its construction: with five phrases in all; first and last end on the final, *B*; the other three on *B*, *A* and *F*$^{\sharp}$, in descending order of frequency. No note functions conspicuously as a tenor. (For a possible association between this last title and a scandal of the reign of Tang Xuanzong, see Eide, 1983, concerning 'Precious Chicken' and 'Heavenly Treasure', pp. 8–20.)

On the other hand, items in *Taishiki-chō* (same final: *E*) exhibit the fifth, *B*, as the dominant cadence. Items in *Sō-jō* (final *G*) make use both of *D* and *B* as intermediate cadences. In *Ōshiki-chō* (final *A*), *E* is the most frequent cadence-note, other than the final. *Banshiki-chō* (final *B*) makes use for the most part of the fifth, *F*$^{\sharp}$, at intermediate cadences; but *Seigaiha* 'Waves of Qinghai/Kokonor' (Xinjiang Province) is anomalous in that intermediate cadences are located *either* on the mediant, *D*, *or* on the final, *B*.

The *Kaku/Jiao* form of *Banshiki*, represented by the surviving *Kenki-kodatsu* 劍 氣 渾 脫 (final *F*$^{\sharp}$) exhibits *A* as intermediate cadence; but other *Kaku* items in Marett (1977) show *C*$^{\sharp}$ as the most frequent cadence – again, this is the fifth above the final, *F*$^{\sharp}$.

Summarising these observations, it is plain that, regardless of the character of the four different kinds of modal octave represented in the Tang, the fifth above the final acts as a preferred cadence at the end of intermediate phrases in many of the items examined. Bearing in mind, however, the great variety, in pitch and frequency of use of notes placed at the ends of phrases in *Ichikotsu-chō* and *Sada-chō* repertories (as revealed by the analyses of N.J.N.), this present summary is only to be regarded as preliminary. It awaits elaboration and detailed scrutiny, as study of the repertory is extended to other mode-keys. For the present it may suffice to have demonstrated that throughout the *Tōgaku* repertory, the fifth above the final frequently performs the function of a dominant, and frequently also that of a tenor in its use as cadence at the ends of intermediate phrases.

Chapter 7

Parallels in the Organization of Music in Time in Indonesia, Ancient India and Ancient China (L.E.R.P., Nicholas Gray and Robert Walker)

If it may be argued that the most archaic Dorian octave was quite possibly composed of two, disjunct, major-third + semitone tetrachords (West, 1992, p. 389), it is to be remembered (see our p. 192) that Widdess (1993, ii) has shown that such transilient scales also existed in early forms of the Ancient Indian modal system. In addition to the presence in that system of scalings to be regarded as analogues of Indonesian *Pélog* and *Sléndro* scales, the organization of *rhythm* also, in early Indian music, was similar in three respects (as also shown by Widdess) to that of the modern gamelan of Java and Bali.

First: in the ancient music of India and the music of Indonesia – let us say both that of Java and of Bali since the fifteenth century – the sum of beats (Sanskrit mātrā) in a musical structure was always a sum divisible by two at all levels, down to an ultimate unit-structure of two-beats duration: the kalā (Sanskrit). The kalā of higher order – binary multiples of this unit: x2, x4, etc. – are always divisible by 2.

Secondly, early Indian music and the music of the gamelan in Java and Bali are also similar in that kalā are assembled into larger units of time-measurement. In gamelan music, units of four beats (*gatra*) are grouped into the *gongan* unit-segments of gamelan music. In both Java and Bali the minimal size of a *gongan* is eight beats; but the *gongan* itself may comprise 2x that figure, or 4x, or 8x, up to 32x in the *gendhing agung* of 256 *gongan* beats (Maceda, 1995, ii, p. 109). The last note of such a *gongan* is marked by the largest hanging gong: the *gong ageng*. In the music of the early Indian tradition, a clap, or a small-cymbals' clash, marked either the beginning or the end of the metrical pattern (Sanskrit tāla).

The melodic line of gamelan music (Maceda, 1995, ii, p. 109) is divisible 'in phrases of four beats *gatra* [Indonesian]'. Pieces of music are classified in length-forms from shortest to longest, each divisible by four. From the shortest of 8 beats the size-sequence continues with 16, 32, 64, 128 and 256 beats to the single *gongan*. All these are divisible by four. That is to say, the number of *gongan*-units of 8 in the sequence increases x2, x4, x8, x16, x32. It is the case, however, as pointed out by Nicholas Gray, that *Gendér Wayang*, one of the oldest forms, does not always obey this rule. Phrases are often of uneven length, and there are numerous units of 1, 3, or 5. This may be related to providing a more flexible melodic line more suitable for the delivery of words.

Widdess (1993, p. 466), while not wishing to argue that his observations –
on the presence in Ancient India of pentatonicity of two quasi-Indonesian types,
as well as the presence there of conspicuously binary-unit-based, rhythmic
organisation – *proved* origination of these features of the musics of Indonesia in
India, offered that possibility as an interpretation of the historical and musical
evidence. This present chapter will perhaps persuade that such caution is
unnecessary, and that these similarities in rhythmic and other organisation go
back in time much further than may have been supposed, and may have far wider
geographical relevance.

Ancient Chinese music in the light of parallels between ancient Indian and Indonesian musics

In this context, it is surely appropriate to mention, first, the pronounced
importance of the binary-beat-unit, in the rhythmic organisation of both measured
and unmeasured movements, in the *Tōgaku / Tangyue* Tang Music repertory also;
and secondly, the terminal (or occasionally mid-point) position of the postponed,
cadential bassdrum-stroke in every measure in the Tang Music, and at the end of
every unmeasured 'drum-beat period', in that same repertory. It is evident,
moreover, that the concept of the binary-beat is still today deeply embedded in
Chinese ideas of rhythmic organisation. The famous *baban* type-tune is most
simply defined in terms of 'eight beats', where each 'beat' is in fact a binary unit
of two eighth-notes/quavers (Stephen Jones, 1995, p. 145).

Nor is the archaic musical treatment of the prosodic unit-line of four
monosyllabic Chinese words to be forgotten. This verse structure is characteristic
of the vast bulk of song-texts in 'The Book of Songs' *Shijing* 詩 經 (Picken,
1977). In the twelve settings of song-texts of the Zhou period or earlier,
preserved by Zhu Xi from a source of the Tang, in a text printed between 1217
and 1232 (*Yili jingzhuan tongjie*), each such text-line is treated as a musical
measure of four notes of equal duration, musically grouped as two binary beats.
The first of these ends on what were conveniently distinguished on analysis as
'half-line finals', the second on 'line-finals'. In fact, the half-lines end (with few
exceptions) on the same few notes that occur as 'line-finals'. Within each binary
beat, therefore, there is musical movement from a note of quasi-'initial' character
to one of more 'final' character (Picken, 1956, 1957, i, pp. 151–3, p. 161).
Although Chinese have always thought in terms of an archaic verse-line of four
monosyllabic words, the use of rhyme and archaic musical treatment of the set of
four, suggest that the structure is properly to be regarded as one of eight unit
beats.

The present rhythmic organisation of traditional measured Chinese music, with the principal percussion-event on the first beat of a measure, did not exist in the entertainment music of the Tang Court. Indeed, as late as the popular-encyclopaedia: *Shilin guangji* 事 林 廣 記 (1100–1250, perhaps first printed in 1325), a song-tune score (in tablature) shows 'drum-beats' as hollow circles (as in some Sino-Japanese scores of the Tang Music), on both long and short notes, in a rhythm that might occur in a Tang tune, in bars of four beats. That is to say, a drum-beat is marked on the third beat in each measure (Picken, 1969, ii, p. 611, 願 成 雙 令). [Dr Widdess comments on the fact that circles are also used to denote drum-beats in Tibetan scores of ritual music (Helffer, 1995).]

In a private communication (letter of 21 October, 1995), Dr Stephen Jones drew our attention to the fact that in pieces for a percussion-ensemble from Hebei Province, as well as in the pure percussion-repertory of the Southern *Shifan luogu* (Jones, 1995, p. 260), the 'strong beat falls on the end of the phrase' – as so frequently occurs in eight-beat measures of the *Tangyue/Tōgaku*. This implies that some forms of Chinese music of today still preserve this feature of Chinese music from earlier periods.

Even in regard to the respected repertory of the 7-stringed zither (*guqin* 古琴), it has been argued (Picken, 1969, ii) that the small hollow circles – that marked (until 50 years ago) the ends of phrases in scores in tablature – may derive from terminal drum-beat symbols that served to delimit measures, even though no drum was actually beaten in the execution of such pieces. (Nowadays these circles are frequently – and regrettably – omitted when printing items transcribed in staff-notation.) This would imply that even when the great book of tablatures: *Quxian shenqi mipu* 膠 仙 神 奇 秘 譜 was printed in 1425, a relic of Tang rhythmic notation of eight-beat measures survived, with a measure-end ictus to be compared with Indonesian (Javanese and Balinese) and Ancient Indian rhythmic organisation.

Again, of course, the music of China today might be regarded as a type of gamelan *sléndro* in the extensive use of the 123.56-*scale*. Auxiliary notes seem now to be less generally acceptable to the Chinese public at large than they appear to have been in the Tang dynasty. The disappearance of so many aspects of the musical life of the Tang, Song, and Ming dynasties, from Chinese music as we hear it today, suggests perhaps that the rise to power of the Manchu in the Qing dynasty had a far greater musical impact than has hitherto been recognised.

The special case of the repertory from Tang
In a sequence of publications, Maceda (1990–5) has charted the emergence of a 'bipolarity' between fifth and final, both in early European, and in Asian musical

forms. He has also drawn attention (Maceda, 1995, ii) to parallels in rhythmic organisation between the 'measured music' of Tang 'Entertainment Music' (as transcribed by us) and the rhythmic organisation of music for gamelan. He indicates the importance of the cadential role of the fifth note above the final in the two traditions, and in this context has made a detailed analysis of the suite *Toraden/Tuanluanxuan* 'The Whirl-Around' 團 亂 旋 (*Music from the Tang Court*, Fascicles 2, 3), in terms of pitches at bassdrum-beats on a binary beat at the end of measures of eight beats. These minim/half-note-pitches, in counts of four, are comparable with what happens, melodically speaking, in the 'cantifermi', or 'core-melodies', or 'Fixed Melodies'(Hood, 1967), of the *gongan* in gamelan pieces.

Our studies of tunes from the Tang repertory have shown that melodic bipolarity (between alternating occurrences of fifth and final at the ends of intermediate phrases) is not infrequent. In his examination of what happens in gamelan music, in both the *Sléndro* and *Pélog* scales of Java and Bali, Maceda has described the strict segmentation of melody as 'counts of four' in equal notes. For the first sixteen, quasi-eight-beat measures, in the first Section of the Prelude of the Tang suite:*Toraden*, Maceda shows (his p. 118) that bassdrum-notes of minim/quarter-note value constitute the following sequence:

Section 1   *B B B E A D E A*
                        A D D A A D B D
where each pitch is to be thought of as the last minim/half-note of a measure of eight quarter-notes: (a)   1   2   3   4   5   6   7   8   (beats of an 8-beat
                                                        B   measure)
                                                        B
                                                        B
                                                        E

If we define the scale (with auxiliaries added) as:
                        I   II III IV V VI VII
                        D E F# G A B   C

Sections 2 and 3 of the Prelude (Maceda, pp. 119, 120) may be represented as

Section 2   *C C D C A E D C*
                        B D G A A D B D

Section 3:   *F#C D C A E D C*
                        B D G A A D B D

Each section amounts to a sequence of sixteen measures of 8.

In a letter to Professor Maceda (dated 5 June, 1996) thanking him for the gift of his paper, 'A Logic in Court Music of the Tang Dynasty', Professor Noël Nickson observes, however, that he is 'not completely confident that pieces other than those of 8, 16 and 32 drum-beats duration "may be considered as emendations, deviations or incomplete versions of a standard or a majority preference for pieces exactly divisible by four" '. He goes on to mention certain short pieces from the Tang-Music repertory that are 'quite naturally balanced in their 14-measure forms' (see our p. 284).

Traditions of Java and Bali

In the Javanese tradition, the fourth note of each of *three* such segments of four pitches in sequence is marked by a punctuating gong: *Kenong*; and the fourth note of the *fourth* such segment, by the gong: *Gongan*. Pitches in the relationship of a fifth or its inversion tend to appear in alternation, as final notes that delimit sections of four counts of four.

As an example, a *Sléndro* unit-set [compare Section 1 (a) p. 266] may be represented as 6 5 3 2 – these being pitch-components from a hypothetical 123.56 pentatonic set. Within this set, 2' is the inverted fifth of 5; 3', that of 6:

$$(1\ 2\ 3.5\ 6.\ 1'\ 2'\ 3'.\ 5'\ 6'.\ \text{etc.})$$

In an example cited by Maceda, the regular musical structure displays alternation of 5 ('final') and 2 ('fifth') occurrences. These pitches demarcate sections, the lengths of which (in beats) are multiples of 2. For example (and substituting *C*-based pitches for numerals from the 123.56-set):

PITCHES on ‖: (4th- 8th- 12th- 16th-beat) x 3 :‖ (4th- 8th- 12th- 16th-beat) x 1‖
              d   d   e   d   *c   d   g   g*

              ‖   ‖
punctuating
gong: ^*Kenong*   ^*Gongan*

where *Gongan* is the large hanging Javanese gong of lowest pitch.

A feature of performance-practice in Java (as in Bali) that tends to be overlooked in descriptions of performance, is the invariable presence of introductory material before the statement of a first complete *gongan*. In Bali, and in the special case of the peripatetic *Gamelan Belaganjur*, this introduction may amount to no more than a species of 'anacrusis'. More general perhaps is the prefacing of a piece by an introduction, as described by Mantle Hood and Hardja Susilo (1967, pp. 16–17) where the largest gong – *gong ageng* – that ends the 16-beat *gongan* of the Fixed Melody: *Gondjang Gandjing*, is sounded on the last note of the solo-gendér introduction, as if that note were the last note of a precedent statement of the *gongan* that follows.

In the Balinese context, and in the light of observations made by the composer, Robert Walker, who has lived in the Karangasem district of Bali for seven years and performs as a member of the gamelan of his village, there is always – in the most general terms – an 'anacrusis' preceding the first statement by all performers of the complete *gongan* of *Gamelan Belaganjur*.

The recent study of this gamelan by Michael Bakan (1998) does not reveal what actually happens in any performance. In the village (Figure 1 from Robert Walker), exposition of the *gongan* begins with a stroke on a (more or less) $D^\sharp$ gong *Lanang*, followed in that measure by two syncopated strokes on *Kempur*. A stroke on *Wadon* (on E) starts the second measure of four beats; and now *Ponggang* (two groups) enter on beats three and four. The entire *gongan* (as thus far stated) repeats (with the *Ponggang* melody now complete) over eight beats. This unit is repeated at will and indefinitely.

Example 1. *Gamelan Belaganjur*, heard in the village; transcribed by Robert Walker

In the next version of the *gongan*, *Reyong* (in two groups) are added, making a colotomic score of three staves; this again may be repeated indefinitely. In the last repeat (that it *is* the last is decided by the players of the *Kendang* drums who initiate a fusillade of activity), players of the *Cengceng* [saucer-cymbals (one pair per player, one cymbal posed and struck; a striker worn on the palm)] are induced to enter on three, last quarter-note beats, in the second four-beat bar of a *gongan*. From then onwards, *Cengceng* continue in sixteenth notes, until all end together on the first beat of the second half of the final *gongan*, sustained by *Wadon*, *Ponggang*, *Reyong*, and all portable drums.

In a second transcription (Example 2) of a version of the same piece played by a gamelan heard at a distance, performance begins with a form of the *gongan* presented by *Ponggang* (two groups), *Kempur* and *Lanang* alone (*Wadon* being absent or inaudible because of being at the same pitch as *Lanang*, but in an octave too low to be heard at a distance), with *Ponggang* supplying the first half-note (of the hocket between its members) against the bass (here imperfect) of *Lanang* (and *Wadon*). After repeated statements of the minimal *gongan*, rapid figuration from two groups of *Reyong* over the *gongan* is repeated through

269

several cycles until, in the last repeat of the second half of a cycle, and presumably signalled by the *Kendang*, the *Cengceng* sound (as in the village) on the last, three, quarter-note beats of the cycle; whereupon all metallophones and membranophones enter in full chorus. (Mr Walker also reports that at times the three quarter-note beats may be halved to three eighthnote beats, in the latter half of a measure of four quarter notes.)

Thereafter, the full chorus repeats through several presentations of the complete *gongan*, at the end of which the four common-time bars between repeating double-bar-lines are repeated, *dal segno*, with *Cengceng* repeating its previous signal over the last three beats of the latter half of the *gongan*.

Example 2. *Gamelan Belaganjur*, heard in the distance; transcribed by Robert Walker

270

These two versions of the *Belaganjur* performance display the same kind of anacrusis: postponement of the entry of the *gongan* in full colotomic chorus. The absence of *Wadon* here was due (as later confirmed by Mr Walker in conversation with one of the group) to the fact that their *Wadon* is too heavy to carry over long distances.

In Java there can be no doubt that the *gong ageng* is sounded on the last pitch of the *gongan*. In Bali, and in the singular instance of the minimal *gongan* of *Belaganjur*, the *gongan* may appear to be reversed, in respect to the gong-sequence, with *Wadon* initiating the sequence, while *Lanang* of the second half of the cycle ends it. This alternation does not, however, modify insertion of the *Cengceng* in the second half of the last *gongan*, before entry of the complete gamelan. This apparent reversal in structure comes from listening in the Western way, accepting that: where an accent falls, a measure necessarily begins.

A gamelan-player from Ubud pointed out, however, that in a dance-piece (*Belaganjur* has no dancers), a dancer would begin a pattern of steps from the Balinese fourth beat, and continue through *their* eighth beat, in a *gongan* of eight beats. This is why the Balinese fourth and eighth beats tend to be regarded by Westerners as first and fourth beats: because both carry an accent. A shift in Mr Walker's barlines, by three quarter-notes/crotchets to the left would restore beats 1 and 5 to behaving as beats 8 and 4.

Gamelan Belaganjur is peculiar in being a processional gamelan; but what these Examples 1 and 2 display seems to happen, in a sense, in the presentation of other gamelan pieces as well. As we have already learned from Hood's account of the recorded performance of *Gondjang-Gandjing*, 'the last note of the introduction (played by solo gendèr) sounds with the *gong ageng* that ends the *gongan* of that piece.

We suggest that, in the matter of a postponement of the beginning of the work proper in Indonesian music, there is a parallel with what is to be observed in the performance of each 'small piece' that survives in the 'Tang Music' repertory of the Japanese Court. Unfortunately, no Large Piece survives in today's performance, so we do not know what happened at the outset, when such pieces were played at the Japanese court in the seventh to ninth centuries.

There is, nevertheless (we suggest) a resemblance to what happens in Java and Bali, in what happens today in the performance of *Tōgaku* items in the 'Quick 8 beats' category, such as 'Waves of Kokonor' (*Seigaiha/Qinghaibo* 青海波) – see Shiba (1969, Volume 2, p. 76). A solo-flute begins the melody, and the first bassdrum-beat occurs on what was originally the fifth beat of a measure of eight. This *taikō*-beat initiates a staggered entry of the other instruments, with the solo zither (*gakusō*) being the last instrument to play (on the equivalent of beat 5 of the second measure of the original). 'Shiba takes until the third *taikō*-

beat to have everybody *tutti*' as Dr Elizabeth Markham points out. The original condition of this melody, with its twelve drum-beats, distributed on the fifth beat of twelve bars of eight beats, is shown in the transcription by Marett (1997, p. 55) from the most important early flute manuscript of the 'Tang Music', completed in 966. It is to be observed that – as in the *Gamelan Belaganjur* performance – all remaining melodic instruments have joined the ensemble by beat 5 of the eight-beat bar, as do all colotomic instruments, both idiophonic (the *shōko*) and membranophonic (*taiko* and *kakko*).

There is yet another parallel delay in the entrance of percussion, in the performance of the *Processional* (遊 聲) in the Large Piece: 'The Emperor Destroys the Formations', where musicians and dancers ascend to the dance-terrace together, with winds playing the piece while processing; other instruments join the ensemble when the musicians are seated. When all have taken their places on the terrace – and only then – a single stroke, with upbeat, on the bass drum (*taiko*) signifies the beginning of the piece proper with the *Prelude*. The same manner of performance is followed in the *Processional* of 'The Singing of Spring Warblers' (*Music from the Tang Court* 2, p. 52).

The phenomenon of tetratonicity in the oldest Chinese music

One undoubtedly archaic feature that links gamelan and ancient Chinese musics is the tendency to employ principally only tetratonic tune-segments, and to use the major third pitch of a 123.56 pentatonic set (roughly corresponding to the *Sléndro*-scale) sparingly or not at all in such segments. In Java, and in one mode, *Pélog Patet Barang*, as Hood (1967, pp. 16, 29) described, the third may at least occasionally be given the unexplained name: 'enemy tone'. Hood's analysis shows how the note 'is "captured" and given melodic prominence'. This striking name for the major-third is only mentioned here as indicative of occasional antagonism in character, in what is for us a unique context.

In China, in song-tunes probably dating at least from the fourth century BC (our p. 276), the third was not a member of a Chinese tetratonic note-set of which use is made in some of the 12 songs for lyrics from 'The Book of Songs' *Shijing* 詩 經 (*c*.7th century BC).

In his admirable survey of Chinese bells, Falkenhausen (1995) writes (p. 284): 'At that stage of the Zeng inscriptions (see our p. 187), the "Five Notes" do not yet seem to have formed a closed set;…' It is evident that an abundance of names, with many alternatives, was already available for all pitches and for all notes, in China of the fifth century BC. The implication that an archaic tetratonicism may have existed at one time is surely important, and such note-sets are present indeed in Zhu Xi's melodies for song-texts of The Book of Songs.

272

From the listing of the 12 note-names of the Zeng inscriptions it is certain that those who composed the inscriptions were aware of the 12 intervals of a fifth, from an initial *Gong* necessary for the generation of a *C* to *C'* octave. In listing the sharpened degrees, Falkenhausen prefers to read 角 as *jue*; as one of the five *yin* 音 it is perhaps more normally read as *jiao2* or 3. Its first meaning is that of an animal horn – the graph appears to derive from the appearance of a horn with a central cavity, in longitudinal section. Read as *jue2* the meaning is 'to compete, to wrestle' [Note a possible link with 'the enemy' as name for the major-third degree in one Javanese mode (our p. 272)] or: 'a corner'.

Falkenhausen himself (his p. 305) stresses 'that the four "simple" names of notes (*yin*) in the nomenclature documented by the Zeng inscriptions – *do, sol, re* and *la* – coincide with the first four notes obtained by the *san fen sun yi fa*[1] 三 分 損 益 法,' …as used in the *Guanzi* book: 管 子 卷 第 十 九 地 員 第 五 十 八, for generating the set of twelve pitch-pipes, the *Lü4 Lü3* 律 呂 . He continues: 'the generation of the eight remaining notes in the set of twelve *yin* involved steps of a major third, precisely the interval between *do* and *mi*, the next following note obtained by the *san fen sun yi fa*.' His plural 'steps' suggest he has in mind the thirds C-E', $C^{\sharp}$-$E^{\sharp}$, D-$F^{\sharp}$, $D^{\sharp}$-G, E-$G^{\sharp}$, F-A, $F^{\sharp}$-$A^{\sharp}$, G-B, $G^{\sharp}$-C'. These are of course inevitably generated by the sequence of fifths from the fourth fifth onwards.

We can be certain, however, from these inscriptions on the bells of Zeng, that the Chinese were aware of the cycle of fifths before ever they came to exploit the virtues of two-pitched bells.

The existence of a tetratonic final, or medial (but never initial) musical line, making use of the degrees: *Doh, Re, So, La*, was recorded in Picken, 1956 (reprinted in 1957), but its significance was not appreciated at that time. The set of four notes already specified: *Gong Shang Zhi Yu*, is that of a stanza-final line, or that of the last musical line of a song, preserved in a chapter from a work by the Song philosopher Zhu Xi: 'A Comprehensive Elucidation of the Canon of Rites and Ceremonies and its Commentaries'(see Picken, 1969, p. 410). The form of the musical line, with *f* as mode-final, is *c d' g' f*. [Recent re-examination of details set out in that paper (in the light of the original text of Zhu Xi, posthumously printed in the early thirteenth century), has shown two errors in the list of line-repeats of a different line in Song 6 (Mao 172) namely: I.3 (that is line 3 of stanza (*zhang* 章) I) repeats as III.3 and V.3.]

To indicate precisely the position of the musical line *c d' g' f '* in the stanza, the number of lines in the stanza must also be recorded. In the case of Mao 172, the stanzas are each of six lines. Each such six-line stanza consists of three

[1] This phrase may be translated 'The procedure: of three parts, destroy one [or] add one.'

couplets and, for the important occurrences of *c d′ g′ f′*, position is clear if the line-number is expressed as a fraction of the total number of lines in the stanza, namely: II.6/6; III.2/6; IV.4/6. The use of this formula, either in stanza-terminal position, or as second term in a couplet, then becomes obvious to the eye.

The final *text*-line 'A myriad longevities without boundaries' *Wan shou wu jiang* 萬 壽 無 疆, with its overwhelming longevity-wish, was shown to occur also in Mao nos.154, 209, 210, 211; in each instance in final position, and usually at the end of a song (Picken, 1969, p. 410, righthand column, 172 *Wan shou wu jiang: c d′ g′ f ′*; see also Picken, 1977, p. 107).

In the twelve melodies for song-texts from the *Shijing* 詩 經, preserved in pitch-pipe notation (*Lü4 Lü3* 律 呂) in the work of Zhu Xi, the musical line to which this text was at times sung occurs in stanza-final position in Mao 162, III.5 and Mao 172.II.6, but in medial positions too, as III.2/6, IV.4/6.

In all medial positions, however, the formula is the second member of a linked pair of 4+4 lexigraphs. This accords with the view (Picken, 1977, pp. 88, 89, 107, 108) that the text-line of eight-lexigraphs is the basic unit of Chinese archaic verse, as it is (in terms of syllables) for Sanskrit verse, the Avestan *Hymn to Mithras*, ancient Christian hymns and certain Hungarian folk songs, as well as folk songs of the Bedouin (Picken, 1977, p. 89).

Mao 161 also provides two stanza-terminal instances (stanzas II and III) in which the four-note formula is distended, by the interpolation of the *Mi* degree and repetitions of *Re* and *Doh*, to accommodate more monosyllabic words to the measure, as in the final line of the song: 'wherewith at the banquet to delight the hearts of my elegant guests' *Yi yan le jia bin zhi xin* 以 燕 樂 嘉 賓 之 心: *c d′ f′ e′ d′ g′ f′*, where the final *f′* is to be lengthened to twice the duration of each of the preceding notes in this measure.

This re-examination of musical lines in relation to text-lines suggests that a more extensive examination of the settings of *all* lines in their various contexts in these twelve notated specimens, preserved at latest from the Tang, may throw yet more light on composition-methods in the late Zhou period.

In Mao 172, for example, while II.6/6 sets *Wan shou wu jiang* to *c d′ g′ f′*, III.2/6 shows a sub-medial use of the same musical formula for an innocuous 'There are pears on north mountain' *Bei shan you li* 北 山 有 李 in response to the preceding 'On south mountain there are medlars' *Nan shan you qi* 南 山 有 杞.

On the other hand I.6, that ends with 'A myriad longevities without time-limit' *Wan shou wu qi* 萬 壽 無 期 – another longevity-wish, almost equal to 'without boundaries' – is set to a pentatonic fragment that includes the *Mi* degree: *f′ a g′ f′*.

In Mao 172.IV.4/6, *c d′ g′ f′* is the setting for yet another longevity-reference: 'Why no eyebrow-longevity?' (presumably: 'Why do your eyebrows show no sign of age?' *Xia bu mei shou* 遐 不 眉 壽. In the final cadential line, V.6/6, 'Guard and nurture your posterity' *Bao ai er hou* 保 艾 爾 候: *f′ d′ c f′*, the *g′* is discarded.

Notable stanza-final lines of the *c d′ g′ f′* formula occur in Mao 161 '*You, you*, the stags roar', I.8/8: 'Making known to me the works of Zhou' *Shi wo Zhou xing* 示 我 周 行; and in Mao 162 'My four steeds are weary', III.5/5: 'No time to care for my father' *Bu huang jiang fu* 不 遑 將 父. The respective stanza-lengths in lines are eight and five, respectively, and the numbers of stanzas are three and five.

The association between 'A myriad longevities without boundaries!' and the cadential formula *c d′ g′ f′* is not inevitable; but the finality of this musical formula, as stanza-final and in medial couplets, is supported by several tunes from the *Huangzhong qinggong* (黃 鍾 清 宮)-six of the 'Twelve Songs', with texts from the *Zhou Nan* 周 南 of the Zhou tradition. As already noted, the favoured terminal position of the text-line *Wan shou wu jiang* itself, is also displayed in Dobson's record of occurrences and their positioning (Picken, 1969); but it may not be assumed that these lines were always sung to the same musical formula, even when in terminal position.

The preservation of these tunes in pitch-pipe notation, printed as underlay to the song-texts, was attributed by Zhu Xi to the Song authority on ritual, Zhao Yansu (see Picken, 1956, 1957, p. 149). The same source reveals Zhu Xi himself commenting that 'as if preserved in the bosom by a sage, the Jin Monograph [on music?] 晉 志 recorded that at the end of the Han, Gang Kui 扛 夔 transmitted four pieces [*qu3* 曲] of ancient *Yayue* 雅 樂. The first was called "The Stags Roar" [previously mentioned].' The Western Jin dynasty lasted from AD 265 to 313 so that at least one of the Twelve Songs existed in pitch-pipe notation some three centuries before the Tang.

Persistence of a tendency towards tetratonicity (with minimal use of the major third) in later music of Han and Tang

Earlier, reference was made to Falkenhausen's comments on inscriptions on bell-sets from the tomb of Marquis Yi of Zeng (*Zeng Hou Yi* 曾 侯 乙) dating from the fifth century BC (Falkenhausen, 1993, p. 283). These show that the pentatonic series of that time lacked a unique name for the degree that corresponds to *Mi*; to the major third in relation to *Doh = Gong*. The names of notes in these inscriptions reflect, therefore, a tetratonic note-set consisting of *Gong, Shang, Zhi* and *Yü* [that is (in Falkenhausen's spelling) *Do, Re, So, La*].

When *Mi* was added, it was referred to (in our terms) as '*Do* sharpened by a major third'. The graph to indicate this degree of sharpening was *jue / jiao* 角. What would later be the major third above *gong* 宮 was written as 宮 角. This lexigraph *jue/jiao* could be added to any of the four notes (*yin*) to indicate sharpening by a major third.

In the past year, it has come as a great surprise (to Noël Nickson and Laurence Picken) to find what appears to be a surviving *yan* 豔 movement from Han 'Large Pieces', as well as two movements from musical suites of the Tang, all three of which exhibit relatively little use of the major third above the mode-final. The data are set out in a paper to be published (*Acta Iranica*, 2000) in a volume dedicated to the memory of Mme Marcelle Duchesne-Guillemin. N.J.N. has shown that the first four most frequently occurring notes in (1) the Prelude of the 'Large Piece' from the Sino-Japanese repertory of *Tōgaku*: 'The Emperor Destroys the Formations'; in (2) the 'Wild Prelude' of the quasi-Large-Piece: *Ryō-ō* from the same repertory; and in (3) a supposed *Yan* 豔, the 'piece' *Soramitsu / Suluomi* from the Sino-Japanese *MS.* known as *Gogen kinfu* 五 弦 琴 譜, amount respectively to the following percentages of their tonal structure:

1. d + a + b + e = 75 per cent
2. a + d + b + e = 74 per cent
3. e + d + b + a = 81 per cent

That is to say: these same four notes dominate the structure of each item:

d, a, e, b = $(d\text{-}e\text{-}a\text{-}b)$

This implies that three hundred and more years after the Han dynasty, there was still a reluctance to use the major third above the mode-final, just as there seems to have been in the fourth century BC.

Maceda's counts of four notes already link the music of Indonesia with that of Ancient and not-so-ancient China, while the *Sléndro*-like and *Pélog*-like ancient scales of early Indic music also establish a morphological link with Indonesian music.

Tetratonicity without the Mi degree

Mr Nicholas Gray drew attention to the fact that the ancient Balinese *kekawin* chant is extraordinary in its melodic structure. The word *kekawin* derives from Old Javanese *kawi* 'a poem' (from Sanskrit kāvya). It refers to the chanting of old Javanese poetic texts in a variety of Sanskrit-derived metres, based on a series of longs (*guru*) and shorts (*laghu*). In approximate transcription he shows here (Example 3) the first verse of *kekawin Ramayana* in the metre *wirama sronca*. The four principal notes of the chant, in ascending order: $E, F^\sharp, B, C^\sharp$ are the sequence of three fifths from E, with $F^\sharp$ doubled in length so as to confine the set of four within the space of an octave from the initial E. In the sequence of generation the notes are $E, B, F^\sharp, C^\sharp$. Mr Gray comments: 'I think it is particularly significant that the melodic outlines of many *kekawin* songs, presumably handed down in an unbroken oral tradition – since the 9th century in the case of the *kekawin Ramayana*, have a melodic shape based on notes 1, 2, 5 and 6 of the pentatonic series.'

Example 3. First stanza of the *kekawin Ramayana*, from a private recording made, and transcribed, by Nicholas Gray. The *kekawin* is sung by the *dalang* Pak Kaca Winaya.)

'Once there lived a noble king – listen and you'll hear him.
He was renowned throughout the world, the lord of all his enemies.
Glorious, learned in all fields of knowledge.
King Dasaratha was his name, and no mortal man excelled him.'
[Translation taken from: *Kekawin Ramayana*, Volume 1, translated by Widia (1984).]

This is the earliest *kekawin* known and the text has been dated (mainly on linguistic evidence) to the ninth or possibly early tenth century. As in this stanza, the third line often contrasts in structure with the rest. The effect of the oscillation between $f^\sharp$ and a in the melody of line 3 is properly represented by Mr Gray's notation, though worthy of finer structural analysis. To the ear it seems plain that there is no tendency for the missing major third ($G^\sharp$ in relation to E) to be interpolated.

In the Chinese context, we can now be certain that the tetratonic musical lines [that lack the major third from the fundamental (*Gong* 宮)] date from before the Han systematisation of cosmological order; they date indeed even from before the establishment of the sequence of numbers in the domain of music. Part of that numerical sequence may conveniently be taken from its statement by Sima Qian 司 馬 遷 in his 'Record of History' *Shiji* 史 記 from 90 BC; but the origin of the complete sequence lies much further back in the history of China.

Counts of four in other genres of Balinese music

The strict, major-third free, tetratonicity of *kekawin*-chant is at present a unique phenomenon. The four notes of *Gamelan Belaganjur*, for example, are from the *Pélog* set:

2	3	5	6
dong	*deng*	*dung*	*dang*;

while the four *Gamelan Anklung* notes are *Sléndro*:

3	5	6	1'
deng	*dung*	*dang*	*ding* (pitch-names);

in both cases notes are consecutive. In *Sléndro* modes, both in Java and Bali, relative importance of notes seems to be determined by fifth-relationships; for example:

1'	5	2	6	3
ding	*dung*	*dong*	*dang*	*deng*
less so	secondary	most important	secondary	less so

As a Javanese example, the Fixed Melody: *Gondjang Gandjing* (Hood, 1967, p. 17) runs through the first *gongan*:

2 1 6 5, 2 5 2 1, 2 1 2 1, 2 1 6 5
Gong Ageng

In their demonstrable relationships of the distance of a fifth between most important and secondary notes, in counts of four, these sets confirm the similarity

278

between Indonesian musical structures and that of the Tang Music examples analysed by Maceda.

The history of note-set names in dateable Chinese sources from the first millennium BC

Statements of the names of musical notes, the pitch-sets used in song-melodies, first appear in philosophical works of the Western Han (206–6 BC) that seek to display the composition of the ordered whole that constitutes the universe. To that end, they define multiple correlations between numbers, the organs of the body, points of the compass, the sequence of the seasons, the musical notes and other attributes: colours, tastes, odours, etc., etc.. Marcel Granet's *La Pensée Chinoise* (1950) still affords the most remarkable introduction to a vision of the universe so vastly different from any Indo-European or Judaeo-Christian outlook.

An assemblage in tabular form, presented by Granet (his p. 376), and deriving from 'The Seasons' *Yueling* 月令, illustrates the nature of the correlations established between items from the various categories listed above. That work was incorporated in 'Mr Lu's Spring & Autumn [Annals]' *Lu-shi Chun-qiu* 呂氏春秋, compiled about 239 BC, from an earlier work of the late 4th or early 3rd century BC, from which it has since disappeared. From the *Yueling* (a treatise on the calendar) three sets of correlations may be set out here:

Compass Points:	East	South	Centre	West	North
Numbers:	8	7	5	9	6
Notes:	*Jiao* 角	*Zhi* 徵	*Gong* 宮	*Shang* 商	*Yu* 羽
(Equivalent relative pitches:	*E*	*G*	*C*	*D*	*A*)

[It may be added that the ancient texts do not display these correlations in the tabular form used by Granet, but rather assemble them in sequence following the name of a month. For example:

'The First Winter Month, *Mengdong*;
the sun is in [Lunar Lodge] *Wei* ('tail');
at dusk [Lunar Lodge] *Wei* is centred;
at dawn [the asterism] Seven Stars is centred;
its day is *Reng'gui*;
its divinity is *Zhuanxu*;
its spirit is *Xuanming*;
its worm is scaly;
its note is *Yu*;

among the *Lu*4 it is *Yingzhong*;

its number is 6;

its taste is salt;

its smell is a stink;

its sacrifice to the dead is virtuous.'

('The Seasons' *Yueling*月 令, 5, 22)

The term 'centred' signifies that the Ruler, looking due South to the horizon at dusk or dawn, sees the particular astronomical object in the centre of his field of view. See: Needham, *Science and Civilisation in China*, Volume 3, pp. 229ff, especially 234–7.]

Such correlations were extended to the Five Viscera; and again according to the 'Record of History' *Shiji* 史 記 of Sima Qian: 'The *Jiao*-note (= East- Spring = Wood) stirs the liver and establishes harmony twixt man and perfect goodness." In the correlations as displayed by Sima Qian himself, the numbers attributed to the notes *D* and *A* are changed to 8 and 9 respectively. In any case these numbers require comment.

They derive from the work known as 'Zuo's *Record*' *Zuo zhuan* 左 傳 perhaps better named 'Mr Zuo' *Zuoshi* 左 氏. Ostensibly this is a commentary on the 'Spring & Autumn', a chronicle of the State of Lu [see Anne Cheng (Loewe, 1993, p. 67)], and it is the longest of three commentaries associated with the 'Spring & Autumn'. The commentary itself is 'mainly concerned with rites and ethics' but is partnered by 'a long, purely historical chronicle that originally had nothing to do with the *Ch'un ch'iu* or even with the State of Lu' (Anne Cheng). Karlgren's conclusion was that the *Zuoshi* was 'probably to be dated between 468 and 300 BC' (A.C.). It would seem to have preceded *Shiji*.

The numerals paired with the Notes are the latter part of a sequence from 1 to 9, the centre point of which is '5'. The set, through the sequence of its terms, creates a vision of universal harmony. The numbers of the Notes are the last five numbers of the set of 9, and the entire set centres on 5: the fundamental of the set of musical notes. We proceed as Granet so sensitively describes from One: not merely 'the unit', and 'a unit', or the 'one', but also 'the Breath' (*qi*4 氣), pitch of the voice falling as air is expelled. The sound *yi*1, with the voice pitched relatively high and level, is indeed '1' (一).

Our reason for pausing to specify the distribution of numbers to names of the 5 *yin* is that the numerical sequence set out on p. 279 seems to have been determined by intervallic relationships established in the generation of the pentatonic set from the *Gong*-note, where letters with a superscript – for example *E'* – indicate notes in the octave starting on *C*.

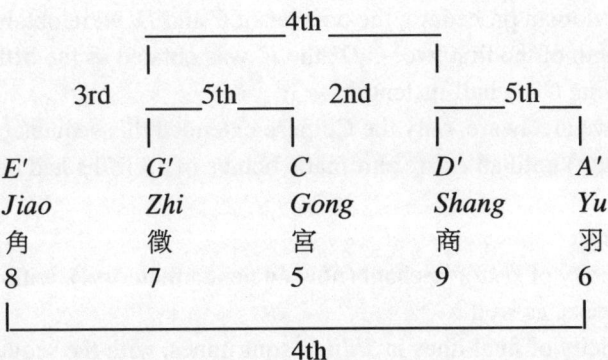

Since this sequence of numerals, correlated with the pitches of the five musical notes, is as that set out in the *Zuo Shi*, this may imply that the *Jiao*-note, at the distance of a major third from the *Gong*-note, was already one of the *yin* in the fourth century BC. This in turn might imply musical use of tetratonic sets that *lack* the major third before the fifth century BC, when the Zeng Hou Yi bells were dedicated.

In any case, consideration of note-sets brings into view another periodicity, that of the fifth-cycles. The four-note set of the *kekawin*-chant required three fifths – as can be seen immediately from the diagram above, remembering that D'' has to be doubled in length to yield D' within the octave.

> $C - G'$,
> D' (D'' doubled in length to bring within the octave),
> $D' - A''$
> A' (A'' doubled)

required three fifths
> $= C\,D'\,G'\,A'$

The 5-note set of the *Zuo Shi*- and *Shiji*-Tables:
> $C - G'$,
> $G' - D''$,
> $D' - A''$ (A'' doubled $= A'$),
> $A' - E''$ (E'' doubled $= E'$)

required 4 fifths
> $= C\,D'\,E'.\,G'\,A'$

The six-note set of Old Babylonia, obtained by the cyclical procedure, required five fifths
> $= C\,D'\,E'.\,G'\,A'\,B'$.

In the Old Babylonian procedure, the octaves of C and D' were obtained by halving the length of the first two: C D'; the F' was obtaied as the fifth down from C', by lengthening C' by half its length.

So far as we are aware, only the Chinese extended this sequence of fifths (at least theoretically) until an entire chromatic octave of 13 fifths had been generated.

The fact that:

(1) the tetratonicity of *kekawin*-chant (how ancient a memory!), with the fifths in root position exists, as well as

(2) the tetratonicity of final lines in *Shijing* song-tunes, with the sequence of notes changed so that, in the course of the phrase, movement occurs between fifth and final, as well as

(3) the pentatonic form of the note-set of *Zuo Shi* and *Shiji*, and

(4) the hexatonic set generated by cyclical procedures in Old Babylonia exist,

all suggest the possibility that this sequence follows an evolutionary series in historical time.

In China there can be little doubt that the use of tetratonic melody-lines of type (2) preceded in time that of pentatonic lines of type (3). The constitution of the tetratonic nucleus, as well as the sequence of potency in the *Gongdiao* pentatonic set [as stated in the 'Record of Music' *Yueji* 樂 記, 第 十 九, Chapter 19 (at latest 100 BC)], both bear witness to the primary character of the *Gongdiao* in the Chinese modal system. Only in the *Gongdiao* note-set is it possible, in terms of musical function, for *Gong* to 'act as Lord'.

It is surely worthwhile to set out, complete, that extraordinary summary of serially diminishing potency, with all its implications for musical awareness, at a time so distant from our own:

'Record of Music'
Do (*Gong*) acts as Lord: 宮 為 君 。
Re (*Shang*) acts as Minister: 商 為 臣 。
Mi (*Jiao*) acts as People: 角 為 民 。
So (*Zhi*) acts as Affairs: 徵 為 事 。
La (*Yu*) acts as Things: 羽 為 物 。

If the Five are not ordered, song-notes are inharmonious.
五 者 不 亂 。 則 無 帖 滯/忄心 之 音 矣 。
If *Do* is disordered, then the arrogance of that Lord is excessive.
宮 亂 則 荒 。 其 君 驕 。

282

If *Re* is disordered, then the undoing of that Official is dismissal.

商 亂 則 破 。 其 官 壞 。　　(官 / 臣)
　　　　　　　　　　　　　　(of that Minister)

If *Mi* is disordered, then the resentment of that People is grievous.

角 亂 則 憂 。 其 事 怨 。

If *So* is disordered, then the toil of those Affairs is pitiful.

徵 亂 則 哀 。 其 事 動 。

If *La* is disordered, then the lack of that Wealth is hasardous.

羽 亂 則 危 。 其 財 匱 。 (財 / 物)
　　　　　　　　　　　　(those Things)

If all Five are disordered, mutual hostility is frequent. This is called negligence.
When thus, destruction of that State cannot be delayed for one day.

五 者 皆 亂 。 迭 相 陵 。 謂 之 慢 。 如 此 。 則 國 之 滅 亡 無 一
日 矣 。

The song-notes of [the States] of Zheng and Wei are indeed notes of a disordered generation. They are to be likened to neglectfulness.

鄭 衛 之 音 。 亂 世 之 音 也 。 比 於 慢 矣 。

Form and number

In general terms, both Nickson and Maceda have commented on a possible relationship of design correlated with number, in two areas of cultural life. Nickson (1990, Fascicle 5, p. 83) commented on a 'feeling for a balanced structural design' in musical organisation of items of music from Tang, and 'the urban landscape of the imperial capital, Changan, with its vast streets and immense squares'. Maceda (1995, p. 137) commented: 'In gamelan, lengths of pieces of music based on four counts and layers of counts of four represented in square forms of terraces in Borobudur do not seem to be mere coincidences, when other examples of square forms are found in the Angkor Wat and in other temples in Thailand, Burma, China, Japan and India. Where does the concept of the square come from, and how did squares come to be symbols of religious principles in buddhist temples? Or, to ask the question differently, where do counts of four come from, and how did they become basic structures in music in Asia?' Maceda writes sympathetic to, and cites, Nickson's comment (Maceda, p. 140).

Such cycles as: 2, 4, 8, 16 are named [and described by James Gleik, 1988, p. 215] as 'Feigenbaum sequences' after their first observer. Bifurcations of this kind arise in biological systems at all levels of complexity, as well as in the worlds of fluid motion; cycles in ecology, in economics; circadian rhythms in man and other animals, and in plants; in the morphology of clouds, of rivers; in meteorology as in schizophrenia.

An elementary mathematical procedure that affords a glimpse of their genesis, relates to changes in numbers of a growing population. If, for instance, we draw the graph (generated by a modified, linear Malthusian equation) that displays growth of a population of fish (let us say):

$$x_{next} = rx$$

where x is the original size of the population, and r is the rate of its growth.

Since in an environment where the supply of food is limited, growth must inevitably diminish as the population increases in size, Robert May (a biologist) and George F. Oster (1976) (see Gleik, p. 69) – in an attempt to bring greater realism to the equation – added a term allowing for modification in the size of x over time, so that the equation became:

$$x_{next} = rx\,(1 - x).$$

They then proceeded to plot a graph, with increasing values of the parameter r along the X-axis, and with population-size increasing, from zero at the origin, up the Y-axis.

When the value of the parameter reaches 3.0, the curve divides into 2, and thence successively into 4, 8, 16 branches. Thereafter there follows a chaotic region, with points distributed, densely and at random, throughout the entire area of the graph.

On continuing to increase the value of r, however, stable cycles were occasionally found to return. These were followed by a further chaotic region, out of which a further cycle of bifurcations emerged, passing rapidly through cycles such as 3, 6, 12…, and 7, 14, 28…: further examples of 'Feigenbaum sequences'. It may be noted that Nickson's Tang tunes of 14 measures (p. 267) might find their place in this later development.

All that can be said of the phenomenon at this stage is: that living systems are subject to the emergence of such regularities whenever some constraint on their rate of growth, itself increases continuously in numerical value through time.

A striking instance of the emergence of cycles of bifurcations was observed in the work of Guevara, Glass and Mackay (1979) on the behaviour of microscopic aggregations of living heart-cells from seven-day-old chick-embryos, dissociated in a suitable saline. After shaking, such dissociated cells form aggregates, little more than a tenth of a millimetre in diameter. On further shaking together, such aggregates began to beat spontaneously at a frequency of about one per second. When an external, pulsed, electrical rhythm was applied to the suspension (by means of a micro-electrode inserted into a single cell of an aggregate) – frequency and intensity of the stimulus being controllable – beat-patterns of period-doubling were observed (see Gleik, p. 290). Such patterns would bifurcate and bifurcate again, as the stimulus was changed. 'Using nonlinear mathematics, we can understand quite well the different rhythms and their orderings.' (Leon Glass)

Such doublings of periodicities occur in biological systems, when these are under pressure of some kind. To know more, we need to understand 'the flowing geometries that sustain complex systems like the mind' (Arnold Mandell, 1985 – see Gleik, p. 298). To that domain belong also, seemingly, the periodicities of musics and of architecture.

Envoi

The surprise of this volume (for those contributing to it) has been the inescapable manner in which the contents have led us to recognise the importance (for the West) of relationships between sounds and the dimensions of resonators – relationships established in a cultural region rarely thought, by those in the West, to be of importance to the culture of its musical world.

In the third volume of his gigantic enterprise, Joseph Needham's *Science and Civilisation in China*: Mathematics and the Science of the Heavens and the Earth (1959, p. 82), he observes that, 'Sumerian and Babylonian arithmetic was essentially sexagesimal, and there can be little doubt the sexagesimal fractions of the Greeks and Alexandrians, together with the division of the circle into 360°, were derived from there…', 'Sexagesimal fractions… never played any part in Chinese calculations. An argument against strong Babylonian influence [on Chinese arithmetic] may be drawn from the fact that Chinese never contains a philologically unitary symbol for 2/3, that fraction so important in Mesopotamia.'

Nevertheless, the earliest Chinese source that describes the attributes, and the making, of the pitch-pipes (the 'Spring & Autumn Annals' of Mr Lü, *Lü Shi Chunqiu*) would seem to reflect the 'two-thirds ratio' in two ways.

First, the fundamental pitch-pipe of the Chinese system of pitches – the *do* of *Yellow Bell* (*Huangzhong Gong*) is stated (*Lü Shi Chunqiu*) to be a bamboo-pipe 'of uniform bore and thickness', 'three inches and nine-tenths' [of an inch] in length (Picken, 1957, iii, p. 94). That is to say, the numbers 3 and 9 are mentioned in the Chinese text, even though there is no fraction there.

Secondly, in order to generate the octave-set of the cycle of fifths, one is instructed (*Lü Shi Chunqiu*, 6. *Yin lü*), 'To the three parts of the generator add one part, making the superior generation. From the three parts of the generator reject one part, making the inferior generation.' Starting from a pipe of pitch C, two-thirds of this yields G. This two-thirds pipe, doubled in length, yields a note a fourth down from $G = D$; and the set becomes CGD. Starting again from D, these operations would be repeated, resulting in pitches, $CGDAEB$; overall, therefore, $CDEGAB$ – to be continued.

'Rejecting one third' of a pipe leaves us with two-thirds: the Babylonian fraction. We return to arithmetic to the base 60 rather than arithmetic to the base 10. We are in the Old Babylonian world of the mid-second millennium BC. For the future, we have need to discover why the primarily sexagesimal world of Babylonian astronomy was also the world of harmonic ratios.

286

Nevertheless, the recent discovery of a group of avian-ulnae flutes (*Grus japonensis* Millen) from 7000 to 5700 B.C. (Juzhong Zhang and others, 1999), each with seven finger-holes, surely demonstrates that such a set from that time can have owed nothing to knowledge of the harmonic ratios. As yet the cent-values of the pitches thus obtained have not been published in their entirety. Those that have show a minor third (hole 1 to 2); hole 3, slightly larger than a major second, and hole 7 to the end of the pipe, slightly smaller than a minor third. The small, circular, approximately equal, finger-holes suggest that maker(s) were aware of the kind of pitch-relationships they desired to establish between the sequence of pitches. Some notion other than that of harmonic ratios must have determined the laying-out of sets of seven. May it have been a consequence of laying eight adult fingers, side-by-side, along a length of tubular hollow bone, and drilling finger-holes beneath the tips of seven fingers? Such a set will surely have covered an approximate octave, and in due course the taste of the maker will have determined the temperament of the set.

Cumulative bibliography

Abraham, Gerald (1979) *The Concise Oxford History of Music*, Oxford University Press, London

Abraham, O. and Hornbostel, E.M. (1903-4) 'Phonographierte indische Melodien', *Sammelbände der Internationalen Musikgesellschaft* 5, pp. 348–401, Leipzig

Adkins, Cecil (1967) 'The technique of the monochord', *Acta Musicologica* 39, pp. 34–43, Basel

Adriaansz, William (1973) *The Kumiuta and Danmono Traditions of Japanese Koto Music*, University of California Press

Affligemensis, Johannis (*c.* 1100–21) *De musica cum tonario*, ed. Joseph Maria Antonius Frans Smits van Waesberghe, *Corpus scriptorum de musica*, 1, 1950/1, Rome

Amiot, Père Joseph Marie (1779) *Mémoire sur la musique des Chinois, tant anciens que modernes*, à Paris

Anglés, Monsignore Higini (1954) 'Latin chant before St Gregory', Early Medieval Music up to 1300, *The New Oxford History of Music* III, pp. 58–127, London, New York, Toronto

Antiphonale Sarisburiense (see Frere)

Arai, Hakuseki 新 井 白 石(1964) *The Armour Book in Honchōgunkikō* (本 朝 軍 記 考) translated by Y. Ōtsuka, ed. H. Russell Robinson, Rutland (Vermont), Tokyo

Aribo, Scholasticus (*fl.*? Freising *c.* 1068–78); see *Expositiones in Micrologum Guidonis Aretini* (1050–1100)

Armstrong, E.A. (1943c) 'The crane dance in east and west', *Antiquity* 17, pp. 71–6
(1958) *The Folklore of Birds: an Enquiry into the Origin & Distribution of some Magico-Religious Traditions*, London

Arsunar, Ferruh (1962) *Gaziantep Folkloru*, Istanbul

Aurelian of Réôme (Aurelianus, Reomensis monachus) (859): *Musica Disciplina*, ed Lawrence Gushee, *Corpus Scriptorum de Musica 21*, American Institute of Musicology, 1975

Bailey, Terence (1974) *The Intonation Formulas of Western Chant*, Pontifical Institute of Mediaeval Studies, Toronto. See pp. 5, 12, 48 Mode 1

Bakan, Michael B. (1998) 'Walking Warriors: Battles of Culture and Ideology in the Balinese Gamelan Belaganjur World', *Ethnomusicology* 42, pp. 441–84, University of Illinois Press

Bake, A.A. (1957) 'The Music of India', *The New Oxford History of Music*, Vol. I, Oxford

Baloch, N.A. (1973) *Development of Music in Sind*, Hydarabad, Sind Pakistan, Sind University Press

Baqiong shi jinshi buzheng 八 瓊 室 金 石 補 正 (Lu Zengxiang 陸 增 祥, 1924); reprint 1967, Taipei

Barker, A. (1984-9) *Greek Musical Writings*, 2 vols., Cambridge

Barnes, Gina L. (1993) *China, Korea and Japan, The Rise of Civilization in East Asia*, Thames & Hudson, London

Baud-Bovy, Samuel (1967) 'L'accord de la lyre antique et la musique populaire de la Grèce moderne', *Revue de musicologie*, 53, pp. 3–20
(1978) 'Le dorien était-il un mode pentatonique', *Revue de musicologie*, 64, pp. 153–80

Bäumker, W. (1886) *Das katholische deutsche Kirchenlied in seinen Singweisen* (Freiburg i.B.), I, 252, 1, No.7; reference from Dr Rajeczky

Bei Qi shu 北 齊 書 (Li Baiyao 李 百 藥, 565–640), Zhenghua shuju 1972, Beijing

Beishi 北 史 (Li Tingshou 李 廷 壽, 7th century), Zhenghua shuju 1972, Beijing

Benade, Arthur H. (1960) *Horns, Strings & Harmony*, Anchor Books Doubleday & Company, Inc. Garden City, New York

Bernard, Paul (1965, 1966, 1967, 1968, 1973) *Fouilles d'Aï Khanoum, campagnes 1965–69; rapport préliminaire publié sous la direction de P. Bernard*, 2 volumes
(1967) 'Aï Khanum on the Oxus: a Hellenistic city in Central Asia' in *Proceedings of the British Academy* Volume 53, pp. 71–95, Oxford

Biji manzhi 碧 雞 漫 志 (Wang Shuo 王 火勺 1149) Zhongguo wenxue cankao ziliao xiao congshu, I, 6 1957

Birrell, Anne (1982) *New Songs from a Jade Terrace*, George Allen and Unwin, London
(1988) *Popular Songs and Ballads of Han China*, Unwin Hyman Limited, London

Boëthius, Anicius Manlius Torquatus *De institutione musica* (ed. Godofredus Friedlein, 1867), Leipzig. (See Bower, 1938)

Boltz, William G. (1993) *Shuo wen chieh tzu* 説 文 解 字 in Loewe, Michael (1993)

Bower, Colvin Martin (1938) *Boethius* The Principles of Music, *an introduction, translation, and commentary*, University Microfilms, Inc., Ann Arbor, Michigan. See in particular Books II and IV.

Bronson, B.H. (1959–72) *The Traditional Tunes of the Child Ballads*, Princeton, N.J.

(1980) 'Folk and popular balladry', *The New Grove Dictionary of Music and Musicians*, ed. Stanley Sadie, vol. 2, p. 73b, London

Brossard, Sebastian de (1703) *Dictionnaire de musique, contenant une explication des terms Grecs, Latins, Italiens et François, les plus usitez dans la musique.* 6e ed., Amsterdam

Bunting, Edward (1840) *The Ancient Music of Ireland, arranged for the Pianoforte. To which is prefixed a dissertation on the Irish harp and harpers, including an account of the Old Melodies of Ireland*, Hodges and Smith, Dublin. Also Donal O'Sullivan (1983) *Bunting's Ancient Music of Ireland* with Mícheál Ó Súilleabháin, Cork University Press. See *Fada an lá gan clann Uisneach*, p. 209: *d e g | a (b) c d*, and *Argan mór*, p. 212: *d f g | a c d*, for Bunting's original transcriptions.

Caus, Salomon de (1615) *Institution harmonique divisée en deux parties*, Francfort. See Partie Deuxieme, p. 3.

Cefu yuangui 冊 府 元 龜 (between 998 and 1023; Wang Qinruo 王 欽 若 and others), Zhonghua shuju, 1960, Beijing

Chailley, Jacques (1965) *Alia musica* – traité de musique due IXe siècle éd. critique commentée avec une introduction sur l'origine de la nomenclature modale pseudo-grecque au Moyen-Âge, par J. Chailley. Publication de l'Institut de Musicologie de l'Université de Paris, 6

Chavannes, Edouard (1895, 1905) *Les Mémoires historiques de Se-Ma Ts'ien* 5, p. 398, n. 4, Paris

Chen, Yingshi 陳 應 時 (1990) '*Dunhuang yuepu xin jie* 燉 煌 樂 譜 新 解 和 燉 煌 樂 譜 的 譯 譜'. See Rao Zongyi 饒 宗 頤 (1990) '*Dunhuang pibapu*' 燉 煌 琵 琶 譜, p.104, 新 文 豐 出 版 公 司 Xinwenfeng chuban gongsi, Taipei

(1993) '*Dunhuang yuepu "chepai" zai zheng*' 燉 煌 樂 譜 掣 拍 趷再証, Yinyue yishu 音 樂 藝 術, 上 海 音 樂 學 院 Shanghai yinyue xueyuan, Shanghai

Chian, Lezhi 錢 樂 之 (*fl.* AD 450). See Needham, III, pp. 346, 384, etc.

Chuci 楚 辭 (attributed in part to Qu Yuan 屈 原, 400 BC). Wang Yi 王 逸, first editor of the *Quci zhangzhu* 楚 辭 章 句, early second century AD. This is usually incorporated with the 'amplification' by Hong Xingzu 洪 興 租 (1090–1155) and other Song scholars, and may be found in both the *Sibu congkan* 四 部 叢 刊 and *Sibu beiyao* 四 部 備 要 series.

Chū Ōga ryūteki yōroku-fu 註 [注] 大 神 龍 笛 要 錄 譜, Tenri Library *MS*. See Marett, 1988

Claire, Dom Jean (1962) 'L'évolution modale dans les répertoires liturgiques occidentales', *Revue Grégorienne*, pp. 196–211; (*suite*) II 'La méthode d'observation de l'évolution modale', 1963, pp. 229–45, Paris

Coedès, G. (1948) *Les Etats hindouisés d'Indochine et d'Indonésie*, Paris

Commentarius in Micrologum Guidonis Aretini – see *Expositiones in Micrologum Guidonis Aretini*

Condit, Jonathan (1976) 'Differing transcriptions from the twelfth-century koto manuscript *Jinchi-yōroku*', *Ethnomusicology* 20, (1) pp. 87–95, Ann Arbor, Michigan

(1984) *Music of the Korean Renaissance*, Cambridge University Press

Cooper, Arthur R.V. (1973, 1986) *Li Po and Tu Fu*, London

(1985) 'Exploring etymographic origins of Chinese characters', Paper for 'British Association for Chinese Studies Conference', Durham, 21 September

Couvreur, S., *S.J.* (1896, 1926) *Cheu King* Texte chinois avec une double traduction en français et en latin (Sien Hien imprimérie de la mission catholique); see pp. 5, 6.

Covell, J. C. & Covell, A. (1984) *Korean Impact on Japanese Culture*, Hollym

Cramp, Stanley *Chief Editor*, *Handbook of the Birds of Europe the Middle East and North America: The Birds of the Western Palaearctic*,
Volume 1 (1977), *Ostrich to Ducks*, Oxford. For sonograms from Sture Palmér and S. Wahlstrom, see p. 395.
Volume 4 (1960, 1977, 1984), *Terns to Woodpeckers*; for voice of *Cuculus canorus* see pp. 412, 413.

Crawcour, Sydney (1965) *An Introduction to Kambun*, Ann Arbor, Michigan

Curzon, L.B. (1979) *A Dictionary of Law*, Estover: Macdonald and Evans; many editions

Dai jimmei jiten 大 人 名 辭 典 (1953) Heibonsha, Tokyo

Dainihonshi 大 日 本 史 Tokugawa Mitsukuni 德 川 光 國 and others (1810–51, 1928–9) 卷 之 三 百 四 十 七, 志 五, 禮 樂 十 四, 樂 曲 一, 左 部 樂 *Ichikotsu-chō* 壹 樂 調 二 十 五 曲, pp. 215–21, *Sada-chō* 沙 陀 調, pp. 221–4, Tokyo

[*Da*] *Tang Liu Dian* (*DTLD*) [大] 唐 六 典 (completed in 738; compiled by Li Linfu 李 林 甫, Wenhai chuban she, Taipei; reprinted in 1962. See p. 287.

The text corrects a mis-writing of *zhen* 陣. For a further note on this work, and on Li Linfu, see P.A. Herbert: '"A Hawk among Rabbits": an appraisal of the T'ang Chief Minister, Li Lin-fu' in 布 目 潮 渢 博 士 古 稀 記 念 論 集, 東 ア シ ア の 法 社 會 1990 年 5 月, 汲 古 書 院 刊.

Demiéville, P. (1925) 'La Musique Čame au Japon', *Etudes Asiatiques*, *Publications de l'Ecole française d'extrême-orient*, Nos. xix, xx, Paris, G. van Oest, t. 1, pp. 199–226

Dialogus de musica (*c.*935). See: *Incipit musica Domni Oddonis* in Gerbert *Scriptores* (q.v.) pp. 252–65. For Strunk's translation of the passage on 'the conjunctions of sounds', see Strunk (1950) pp. 109, 110.

Dobson, W.A.C.H. (1968, i) *The Language of the Book of Songs*, Toronto (1968, ii) 'The Origin and Development of Prosody in Early Chinese Poetry', *T'oung Pao* 54, pp. 231–50

Duchesne-Guillemin, Marcelle (1963) 'Découverte d'une gamme babylonienne', *Revue de musicologie* 49, pp. 3–17, Paris
(1969) 'La théorie babylonienne des métaboles musicales', *Revue de musicologie* 55, pp. 3–11, Paris

Eckardt, Hans (1952) '*Ryō-ō*', *Sinologica*, Zeitschrift für chinesische Kultur und Wissenschaft, III, 2, pp. 110–28, Basel; '*Somakusa*', *Sinologica*, III, 3, pp. 174–89
(1956) *Das Kokonchomonshū* 古 今 著 聞 集 *des Tachibana Narisue* 橘 成 季 *als musikgeschichtliche Quelle*, Wiesbaden

Eide, Elling O.(1982) 'Li Po's riddle naming Cloud-ritual Hsü in relation to the Feng Sacrifice of 742 and the Great Heavenly Treasure scandal to which is appended a note on the Stamping Songs and a Sino-Turkish name for the Huns', *Tang Studies*, Number One, pp. 8–20, Wisconsin

Enchiridion musices (see *Dialogus de musica*)

Expositiones in Micrologum Guidonis Aretini (1050–1100), *Commentarius in Micrologum Guidonis Aretini*, Aribo ed. Jos. Smits van Waesberghe (1957), Amsterdam

Falkenhausen, Lothar von (1993) *Suspended Music: Chime-bells in the culture of Bronze Age China*, University of California Press Ltd

Farhat, Hormoz (1965) Ph.D. Thesis, University of California at Los Angeles (1973) *The Traditional Art Music of Iran* (High Council of Culture & Art, Center for Research & Cultural Co-ordination, Publication 16, Teheran (1990) *The Dastgāh Concept in Persian Music*, Cambridge University Press, Cambridge

Feld, Steven (1982, 1990) *Sound and Sentiment: Birds, Weeping, Poetics, and Song in Kaluli Expression*, Second Edition, University of Pennsylvania Press, Philadelphia

Fernald, Anne (1992) 'Meaningful melodies in mother speech to infants', ed. Uwe Jorgens & Mechthild Papusek, *Non-Verbal Vocal Communication: Comparative and Developmental Approaches*, Cambridge University Press, Cambridge

Frere, Walter Howard, Bishop of Truro (1894), *Graduale Sarisburiense*. A reproduction in facsimile of a manuscript of the thirteenth century, with a dissertation and historical index illustrating its development from the Gregorian *Antiphonale Missarum* by W.H. Frere, Plainsong & Medieval Music Soc. London. *Graduale*, ibid. 24. Facsimile 1966

Fu, Yunzi 傅 芸 子 (1940) *'Wuyue Lanling wang kao'* 舞 樂 蘭 陵 王 考, *Tōhō-gakuhō* 東 方 學 報 10, pp. 85–93, Kyoto

Fujiie, Reinosuke 藤 家 禮 之 助 (1988) 日 中 交 流 二 千 年, Tōkai daigaku, Tokyo

Fukushima, Kazuo and Nelson, Steven G. (1983) *Descriptive Catalogue of the Eighth Exhibition* 'Musical Notations of Japan' Research Archives for Japanese Music, Ueno Gakuen College, Tokyo

Fushimi no Miya bon biwa-fu 伏 見 宮 本 琵 琶 譜, copy of an original manuscript completed in 920/921 by Prince Sadayasu (Fujiwara no Sadayasu 藤 原 貞 保 (新 王) (Facsimile published by Kunaichō Shoryōbu in 1962, Tokyo)

Gakkaroku 樂 家 錄, Abe Suehisa 安 倍 季 尚 (1690); ed. Masamune Atsuo 正 徠 敦 夫 and others (1935–6), 5 volumes (*Nihon Koten Zenshū* 日 本 古 典 全 集 edn.), Tokyo

Gakukō mokuroku 樂 考 目 錄; see *Gakkaroku* pp. 964–94 卷 之 三 十 二, *Ichikotsu-chō* pp. 967–72, *Sada-chō* pp. 973–4

Gamō Mitsuko 蒲 生 美 津 (1986) 'A study of Ranjō (*Ranj ō skōkō* 亂 聲 小 考)', *Shominzoku no oto* 諸 民 族 の 音 Collected memorial essays for Koizumi Fumio (小 泉 文 夫 先 生 追 倬 論 文 集, pp. 237–56) (summary pp. 818–19), Tokyo

Garfias, R. (1964) *Music of a Thousand Autumns*, Berkeley, Los Angeles, London

Genji monogatari no ongaku – see Yamada, Yoshio

Gerbert, Martin, Freiherr von Hornau (1784) *Scriptores ecclesiastici de musica sacra potissimum*, 3 volumes, San Blasius (Reprint 1931)

Gerson-Kiwi, (Esther) Edith (1961) 'Religious chant: a pan-asiatic conception of music', *Journal of the International Folk Music Council*, 13, pp. 64–7, Heffers, Cambridge

Gibbon, Edward (1776 vol. 1; 1781 vols. 2, 3; 1781 vol. 4) *The Decline & Fall of the Roman Empire*, London

Gimm, Martin (1966) *Das* Yüeh-fu tsa-lu *des Tuan An-chieh*, Wiesbaden

Gionbayashi 祇園ばやし (1988) (Preface by Kataoka Yoshimichi 片岡義道) *Gionmatsuri yamaboko rengōkai* 祇園祭山鉾連合會, Tokyo

Glutz von Boltzheim, U. N. and Bauer, K. M. (1980) *Handbuch der Vögel Mitteleuropas* 7. Wiesbaden

(1984) Volume IV, *Voice*: pp. 412, 413

Granet, Marcel (1950) *La Pensée Chinoise*, Editions Albin Michel, 22, rue Huyghens, Paris (XIVᵉ)

Guanzi 管子 (The *Guanzi*-book) (late fourth century BC) See: a Song or Yuan print with preface by Yang Chen 楊忱 (c.1224) and colophon by Zhang Nie 張嶫, reproduced in the *Sibu congkan* 四部叢刊 series

Guevara, Michael R, Glass, Leon and Schrier, Alvin 'Phase Locking, Period-Doubling Bifurcations, and Irregular Dynamics in Periodically Stimulated Cardiac Cells', *Science* 214 (1981), p. 1350

Gujin tushu jicheng 古今圖書集成 (Chen Menglei 陳 and others 1726). See *Qinding gujintushu jicheng* 1884, Shanghai

Gulik, R.H. van (1940) *The Lore of the Chinese Lute*, Tokyo

(1961) *Sexual Life in Ancient China*, Leiden

Gurney, Oliver R. (1968) 'An old treatise on the tuning of the babylonian harp', *IRAQ* 1968, pp. 229–33. See also Wulstan, David, 'The Tuning of the babylonian harp', pp. 215–28, London

(1994) 'Babylonian music again', *IRAQ*, pp. 101–6

Hakuga fue-fu (966); see Marett (1977), pp. 1–3. Only the fourth scroll (of an original set of four) of this flute-score survives. The earliest copies are of the eighteenth century. All include the heading: 'Newly Edited Music Scores, Fourth Scroll, Transverse-Flute' Shinsen gaku-fu maki dai ōteki yotsu 新撰樂譜卷第横笛四. The name 'Hakuga' is the Japanese *on*-reading (Han-Chinese reading) of the Chinese name 'Boya' 伯牙 – a famous Master of the seven-stringed zither: 古琴. An alternative phonetic writing of this name in Chinese characters might be 博雅, with the flattering meaning of 'Transmitting refinement'. Read in Japanese, these latter Chinese characters for 'Hakuga' become 'Hiromasa'. Hence the Japanese form of the name: Minamoto no Hiromasa: 源博雅.

Hanshu 漢書 (begun in AD 54, completed in the second century) Zhonghua shuju, 1964

Harich-Schneider, Eta (1954) *A History of Japanese Music*, Oxford

Harris, David (1989, February 4–5) 'The quest for China's lost city', *The Weekend Australian*, Weekend 2, 4, Sydney

(1991) *Black Horse Odyssey, Search for the lost city of Rome in China*, Wakefield Press, Kent Town, South Australia 5071

Haruyuki, Tōno (1995) *Acta Asiatica* (Bulletin of Institute of Eastern Culture Tōhō Gakkai) 'Japanese embassies to T'ang China and their ships', pp. 39–62, Tokyo

Hawkes, David (1959) *The Songs of the South, an ancient Chinese anthology* (Oxford: Clarendon Press); second revised edition: *The songs of the south: an anthology of ancient Chinese poems by Qu Yuan and other poets*, Harmondsworth: Penguin Books Limited. See also *Ch'u tzu*, David Hawkes, in: Michael Loewe, *Early Chinese Texts...* (1993)

Hayashi, Kenzō 林 謙 三 (1969) *Gagaku – Kogaku-fu kaidoku, Tōyō ongaku sensho* 雅 樂 – 古 樂 譜 解 讀, 東 洋 音 樂 選 書); see *Biwa-fu shinkō* 琵 琶 譜 新 考 (pp. 235–62: p. 258), Tokyo
(1974) *Ongaku kongen shō* 音 樂 根 源 鈔, *Kogaku sho ishu* 古 樂 書 遺 珠, *Zempon sōsho* 全 本 叢 書 16, pp. 103, 119, 123, Tenri; see note (p. 24) and in particular p. 25.

He, Changlin 何 昌 林 (1985) '變 于 闐' – 於 邦 應 時 同 討 論, 1, pp. 94–6, Hua ishu chuban she, Beijing

Helffer, Mireille (1994) *Mchod-rol: les instruments de la musique Tibetaine*, Paris
(1995) 'Recherches récentes concernant l'emploi des notations musicales dans la tradition tibétaine', *Tibet: Civilisation et Société*, Éditions de la Fondation Singer-Polignac, Paris

Henderson, Isobel (1957) 'Ancient Greek Music' in *The New Oxford History of Music* 1, pp. 336–403, London, New York, Toronto

Herbert, P.A.(1979) 'Japanese Embassies and Students in T'ang China', University of Western Australia, Centre for East Asian Studies, Occasional Papers no.4

Higuchi Akira 桶 口 昭 (1980) '*Chūsei o meguru ongaku no shosō* 中 世 を め ぐ る 音 樂 の 諸 相 *Tōkyō ongaku daigaku 'Kenkyūkiyō' dai 5 shū* 東 京 音 樂 大 學 研 究 紀 要 第 5 集, Tokyo
(1968) *Hayashi no samazama* ロ雜 子 の さ ま ざ ま *Gion bayashi* 祇 園 ロ雜 子, ed. Tanaka Tsuneo 田 中 常 雄, pp. 68–85, Kyoto. For a reprinting of music of *Sagimai* ceremony at Tsuwano, see pp. 76–8.

Hirade, Hisao 平 出 久 雄 (1982), entry: *Gagaku*: 雅 樂, *Ongaku daijiten* 音 樂 大 字 典, 2, pp. 527–35, Heibonsha 平 凡 社 Tokyo

Hirano, Kenji 平 野 健 次 (1977) 'The intake and transformation of Chinese music in Japan', *Proceedings of the Second Asian Pacific Music Conference*, Seoul, pp. 26–9 and pp. 26 and 27 in particular

Hirano, Kenji and Mabuchi, Usaburō 馬 淵 卯 三 郎 etc., (1978) 'Rokudan' – koto instrumental music (Discover Japanese Classical Music Series (1)) Toshiba TH-60054, Stereo, 2 discs

Holzman, Donald (1957) *La Vie et la Pensée de Hi Kang*, Leiden

Honchō gunkikō 本 朝 軍 記 考 (*c*.1850), Osaka

Honpō gakusetsu 本 邦 樂 説; see *Gakkaroku* 卷 之 三 十 一, pp. 918–24, *Sada-chō* pp. 924–28 (1936), Tokyo

Hood, M. and Susilo, H. (1967) *Music of the Venerable Dark Cloud*, Los Angeles, California

Huang, Xiang-peng (1980) ' "Chu-shang" elucidated', *Chinese Music*, 20–4, 56–60, Woodridge, Illinois

Hucbald (*c*.900) *De harmonica institutione* (see Gerbert, *Scriptores* I, pp. 104–21

Hulsewe, A.F.P. (1993): see Loewe (1993), '*Han Shu* 漢 書', pp. 129–36

Hymns Ancient and Modern (1st edn 1861; 2nd edn ed. W.H. Monk; Standard edn = 2nd edn with two Supplements 1916, 1940). The tune *Ravenshaw* appears on p. 258 as Hymn 243. The statement that it was abridged from a tune in the collection of M.Weisse appears in the *English Hymnal*.

Ishida, Mikinosuke 石 田 幹 之 助 (1948) *Tō-shi sōshō* 唐 史 叢 鈔, Tokyo

Ishihara, Akira and Levy, Howard S. (1969) *The Tao of Sex, an annotated translation of the twenty-eighth section of The Essence of Medical Prescription* (Ishimpō), Yokohama

Jairazbhoy, Nazir A. (1971) *The rāgas of North Indian music, their structure and evolution*, London

James, Edward (1982) *The Origins of France: from Clovis to the Capetians*, 500–1000, London, Macmillan

Jiaofangji jianding 教 坊 記 箋 訂. The *Jiaofangji* was composed by Cui Lingqin 崔 令 欽 of the Tang dynasty. The *Jiaofang* itself was established in the *Kaiyuan* period (713–41) of the reign of the Xuanzong Emperor, commonly known as Minghuang. See Ren Bantang (1972).

Jiegulu 羯 鼓 錄 (Nan Zhuo 南 卓 *fl*. 847), 中 國 文 學 參 考 瓷 料 小 叢 書, 的 一 輯, pp. 1–16 Gudian wenxue chubanshe, 1957, Shanghai

Jinchi-yōroku 仁 智 要 錄, Manuscript copy (of 12th-century original) made in *Temmei* 天 明 元 年 (1781) (item 593 in the Catalogue of *Kunaichō Shoryōbu* 宮 內 廳 書 陵 部, Library of the Imperial Palace, Tokyo), 音 樂, 雅 樂. *For Ichikotsu-chō* items 1–7 (our numbers) see 卷 第 四, 壹 越 調, 上; for the remaining items in this mode-key (8–23), and for all those in *Sada-chō* (24–31) see 卷 第 五, 壹 越 調 曲, 下, and 沙 陀 調 曲.

Jing Fang 京 房 (*fl*. 45 BC) 後 漢 書, 11

Jinshi cuibian 金 石 萃 編 (Wang Chang 王 昶) (1805)

Jiu Tangshu 舊 唐 書 (Liu Yun 劉 昫 and others, completed 945) Zhonghua shuju 1975, Beijing

Jones, Stephen and Picken, Laurence (1987) 'Tunes of T'ang date for the "Get treasure song" ?', *T'ang Studies*, *Number Five*, pp. 33–44, Boulder CO

Jones, Stephen and Xue Yibing (1991) 'The Music Associations of Hebei Province, China', *Ethnomusicology* 35/1: 1–29

Jones, Stephen (1990) 'A note on Xi'an Ancient Music and its *Yousheng* ', *Music from the Tang Court* 5, pp. 127–8

(1995) *Folk Music of China: Living Instrumental Traditions*, Oxford, Clarendon Press

Joseph, H.K. (1976) 'The Chanda', *T'oung Pao*, 62, pp. 167–98, Leiden

Kabu hinmoku 歌 舞 品 目 (1930, 1978) *Nihon koten zenshū* edn, Kyoto

Karlgren, Bernard (1931) 'The early history of the Chou Li and Tso Chuan texts', *The Museum of Far Eastern Antiquities, Bulletin* 3, pp. 1–59, Stockholm

(1957) *Grammata Serica Recensa, The Museum of Far Eastern Antiquities Bulletin* 29, Stockholm

Kárpáti, János (1990) Japán sínto szertartások zenéje/*Kagura*: Japanese *Shinto* Ritual Music, Hungaroton SLPX 18193 Stereo, 90–3361-Révai Nyomda, Budapest – Felelös vezetö: Horváth Józsefné dr.

Keizū sanyō 系 圖 纂 要 (1973) Heibonsha, Tokyo

Kikkawa, Eishi 吉 川 英 史 (1979) *Nihon ongaku no shikaku* 日 本 音 樂 の 思 格, Tokyo; see p. 73.

(1984) *Vom Charakter der japanischen Musik*, aus dem Japanischen übertragen von Petra Rudolph, durch Quellenhinweise ergänzt, mit Anmerkungen versehen und redigiert unter Mitwirkung von Heinz-Dieter Reese von Robert Günther, Kassel; see p. 64.

Kinnier-Wilson, James V. (with the assistance of Vanstiphout, Herman) (1979) *The Rebel Lands: An investigation into the origins of early mesopotamian mythology*, University of Cambridge Oriental Publications 29

Kishibe, Shigeo 岸 邊 成 雄 (1966, 1981) The Traditional Music of Japan, Ongaku no tomo sha, Tokyo. See pp. 51–3.

(1985) *Tempyō no hibiki* 天 平の 響, Tokyo

Kofu Hōshō-fu ryokan/ritsukan 古 譜 鳳 笙 譜 呂 卷 律 卷, *MS.* in the Collection of Ueno Gakuen University, Tokyo: 上 野 樂 園 日 本 音 樂 瓷 料 室, directed by Professor Fukushima Kazuo 福 島 和 夫. The two sewn volumes are stamped: 日 本 音 樂 瓷 料 室 藏 書 No.6009. For further details see our Fascicle 1 (1981), pp. 33, i4.

Koizumi, Fumio 小 泉 文 太 (1957) *Nihon dentō ongaku no kenkyū* 日 本 傳 統 音 樂 g 研 究, 1, Tokyo

Kokonchomonshū: see Tachibana Narisue and Eckardt, Hans.

Ko sō-fu 古 箏 譜 (10th century?), *Kogakusho ishu* 古 樂 書 遺 珠, 聲 (Volume 16 of *Zenpon sōsho* 全 本 叢 書, Tokyo 1974, pp. 4–55, with commentary by Hayashi Kenzō 林 謙 三)

Kroeber, A.L. (1940) 'Stimulus Diffusion' *American Anthropologist* 42, pp. 1–20; see, for example, pp. 2, 4, 7, 10, 13.

Kuttner, F.A. (1975) 'Prince Chu Tsai-yü's life and work – a re-examination of his contribution to equal temperament theory', *Ethnomusicology* XIX, pp. 163–206, Bloomington

Kyōkunshō 教訓抄, *Kodai chūsei eishūron* 古代中世藝術論, *Nihon shisō taikei* 日本思想大系 23, 1984, pp. 10–215, ed. Ueki Yukinori 植木行宜, Tokyo

Lai, Chun-Yue (1979) *'Lao Liuban'*, *Chinese Music* 2, pp. 47–51, Woodbridge, Illinois

Lawson, Wendy & Graeme (1986) 'Sounds of the Roman World', *Music from Archaeology No.2*, cassette (Dolby, stereo), Archaeologia Musica, Cambridge

Lee Young-hee 李寧熙 (1989) *Mōhitsu ni manyōshū*; もう一つに万葉集, Tokyo

Li, Linfu 李林甫 and others (738) [*Da*] *Tang liu dian* [大] 唐六典, Wenhai chubanshe, Taipei, 1974

Li, Shigen 李石根 (1982) 西安古樂曲集 *Xi'an guyue quji* Shaanxi sheng qunzhong yishuguan 陝西省群眾藝術館; also n. 1, p. 127, Fascicle 5

Li, Youbai 李尤白 (1995) *Liyuan kaolun* 黎園考論, Shaanxi renmin chubanshi, Xi'an

Liang, Mingyue (1969) *The Chinese Ch'in: Its History and its Music*, Chinese National Music Association, the San Francisco Conservatory of Music (1985) *Music of the Billion* 中國音樂通論 Heinrichshofen Edition, New York

Lidai yudi yan'ge xian yaotu 歷代輿地沿革險要圖 (1879), compiled by Yang Shoujing 楊守敬, 觀海堂

Liu, Feng-Shüeh 劉鳳學 (1986) *A Documented Historical and Analytical Study of Chinese Ritual and Ceremonial Dance from the second millennium BC to the thirteenth century.* Ph.D. Dissertation, Laban Centre, University of London, Goldsmiths' College

Loewe, Michael, ed.(1993) *Early Chinese Texts: A Bibliographical Guide*, The Society for the Study of Ancient China and The Institute of East Asian Studies, University of California, Berkeley

Lü, Buwei 呂不韋 (and others) (239 BC) *Lü-shi chun qiu* 呂氏春秋 (1978) ed. Ji Liankang 吉聯抗, 呂氏春秋中的音樂料, Shanghai wenyi chuban she
(1986) eds. Zhang Shuangdi and others 呂氏春秋譯註上，下, Ji Linwen shi chubanshe chuban

Lunyu 論語 (*c*.465–50 BC) Guyi congshu 3 1882

Ma, Chengyuan 馬 承 源 (1981) *Shang Zhou qingtong shuangyin zhong* 商 周 清 銅 雙 音 鍾 *Kaogu xuebao* 考 古 學 報 (1), pp. 131–46. See also English translation by Shen Sin-yan (1980): 'Ancient Chinese two-pitched bronze bells', *Chinese Music* 3 (1980) (4) 81–6; 4 (1981) (1) 18–20, and (2) 31–6

Mabuchi, Usaburō 馬 淵 卯 三 郎 (1989) *Jūshichiseiki-kōhan ni okeru reigaku-shisō to ongaku no yōshiku* 17 世 紀 後 半 に お け る, 禮 樂 思 想 と 音 樂 の 樣 式, 大 阪 教 育 大 學 紀 要 第 1 部 門, 第 一 號, pp. 189–204, Osaka
(1990) 'Zum Begriff *gagaku*', *Florilegio musicale* Festschrift KATAOKA Gidō zum 70. Geburtstag, pp. 25–35, Tokyo

Maceda, J. (1990, i) 'In search of a source of pentatonic, hemitonic and anhemitonic scalings in Southeast Asia', *Acta Musicologica* Heft 2–3, pp. 193–223, Kassel
(1990, ii) 'Review Essay: Bipolarity, Ki Mantle Hood's trilogy, four counts and the fifth interval', *Asian Music, New York*, 21, pp. 135–45, New York
(1994) 'A Logic in Court music of the Tang Dynasty' (18 pp. of text; 21 pp. of figures), Lecture delivered to the Asian-Pacific Society for Ethnomusicology, Seoul, Korea. See *Acta Musicologica* (1995), 67, pp. 109–41, Stuttgart
(1995) 'Bipolarity and the fifth interval in gamelan music and medieval European music' in *The Medieval West Meets the Rest of the World*, ed. Nancy van Deuren, The Institute of Medieval Music, Ottawa, Canada, pp. 91–107

Mallory, J.P. (1989, 1991) *In Search of the Indo-Europeans: Language, Archaeology and Myth*, Thames and Hudson Ltd, London

Mandell, Arnold (1985) 'From Molecular Biological Simplification to More Realistic Central Nervous System Dynamics: An Opinion' in *Psychiatry: Psychobiological Foundations of Clinical Psychiatry* 3:2, J.O.Cavenar *et al.*, eds. (New York: Lippincott, 1985)

Marcel-Dubois, Claudie (1941) *Les instruments de musique de l'Inde ancienne* (Forme et Style), Paris

Marco, Guy A. and Palisca, Claude V.(1968) translation of Third Part of Giuseppe Zarlino's *Le istitutioni harmoniche* from the edition of 1575

Marett, Allan J. (1976) 'Hakuga's flute-score: a tenth-century Japanese source of "Tang-Music" in tablature', Ph.D. Dissertation, University Library, Cambridge, No.9823
(1977) 'Tunes notated in flute-tablature from a Japanese source of the tenth century', *Musica Asiatica* 1, pp. 1–59, Oxford

(1979) 'Hakuga no fuefu no sho kifuhō ni tsuite' 博 雅 の 笛 譜 の 諸 記 譜 法 仁 つ い て, *Gagakkai* 雅 樂 會 54, pp. 171–88, Tokyo

(1985) '*Tōgaku*: where have the Tang melodies gone, and where have the new melodies come from?', *Ethnomusicology* 29, pp. 409–31

(1986) 'In search of the lost melodies of Tang China: an account of recent research and its implications for the history and analysis of *Tōgaku*', *Musicology Australia* vol.9, pp. 29–38

(1988) 'An investigation of sources for *Chū Ōga ryūteki yōroku-fu*, a Japanese flute-score of the 14th-century' *Musica Asiatica* 4, pp. 210–67, Oxford

Markham, E.J. (1983) *Saibara – Japanese Court Songs of the Heian Period* (2 vols.), Cambridge

Markham, Elizabeth J., Picken, L.E.R., Wolpert, R.F. (1987) 'Pieces for *biwa* in calendrically correct tunings from a manuscript in the Heian Museum, Kyoto', *Musica Asiatica* 5, pp. 191–209, Cambridge

Martianus Capella ed. Adolfus Dick, addenda adiecit Jean Préaux (1969), Stuttgardt. See also Stahl *et al.*

Mathews, R.H. (1931, 1943) *A Chinese-English Dictionary* compiled for the China Inland Mission, Shanghai, China Inland Mission and Presbyterian Mission Press, 1931; photolithographed by the Murray Printing Company, Cambridge, Mass.

Matsushima Yorimasa 松 島 順 正 (1952, 1953) *Shōsōin ko retsu meimon shūsei*' 正 倉 院 古 裂 銘 文 集 成, *Shoryōbu kiyō* 書 陵 部 記 要, Archives and Mausoleum Division, Imperial Household Agency: No.2, March 1952, No.3, March 1953

(1978) *Shōsōin hōmotsu meimon shūsei* 正 倉 院 寶 物 銘 文 集 成, Tokyɔ

Meeùs, Nicolas (1987) 'A = 415' Communication 830, Letter to Jeremy Montagu of 14 September, Brussels, *FOMRHI Quarterly* Bulletin No. 49 October, pp. 27, 28, Oxford

Mengqi bitan 夢 溪 筆 談 (Shen Gua 沈 括 1086–93) Congshu jicheng 1937

Micrologus Guidonis Aretini (*c.*1040) ed. Jos. Smits van Waesberghe, *Corpus Scriptorum de Musica*, 4, 1955, American Institute of Musicology

Minamoto no Hiromasa (919–80) (see *Hakuga fue-fu*: HFF)

Minamoto no Tsunenobu 源 經 信 筆 (11th century?) *Biwa-fu* 琵 琶 譜 (facsimile 1990), Tokyo

Mission Paul Pelliot (1960–71) documents conservés à la Bibliothèque Nationale, Vols. 1–3, Paris; 2, *Airs de Touen-houang (Touen-houang k'iu)* Textes à chanter des viiie-xe siècles
Introduction en chinois par Jao Tsong-yi

Centre Nationale de la Recherche Scientifique
Adaptée en français avec la traduction de quelques Textes d'Airs par Paul
Demiéville, Éditions du Centre Nationale, Paris, 1971 [Planches 54–7
(P.3808), Planche 58 (P.3539)]

Miyata Teru 宮 田 輝 (1978) '*Tsuwano no sagimai*' 津 和 野 の 鷺 舞 in
Matsuri to geinō no ryo 5 (see Takahashi & Yamaji)

Mocquéreau, Dom André (1889-) *Paléographie musicale: les principaux
manuscrits de chant grégorien, ambrosien, mozarabe, gallican, publiées en
fac-similés phototypiques par les Bénédictins de Solesmes (– sous la
direction de Dom A. Mocquéreau, J. Gajard.* [Sér. 1.] Vol. 1- Solesmes,
Berne, 1889-

Mommsen, Theodor (1854–6; 1976) *Römische Geschichte*, Leipzig; Munich

Morris, Ivan (Ira) (1964) *The World of the Shining Prince*, London

Moule, A.C. (1909) 'On the musical and other sound-producing instruments of
the Chinese', *Journal of the North-China Branch of the Royal Asiatic
Society*, London, etc.

Moule, A. C. and Yetts, W. Percival (1957) *The Rulers of China* 221 BC –
AD 1949, London

Murasaki Shikibu 紫 式 部 (10th century) *Genji monogatari* 源 氏 物 語 1,
Nihon koten bungaku taikei 日 本 古 典 文 學 大 系 (1958) 14, Iwanami
shoten kankō 岩 波 書 店 刊 行, Tokyo. For the Flower Banquet (*Hana no
en* 花 の 宴) see p. 304, column 12.

Nanchikufu 南 竹 譜 = *Nangūfu* 南 宮 譜 = the lost score of Prince Sadayasu
貞 保 親 王 (921), perhaps incorporated in that of Minamoto no Hiromasa
(Hakuga).

Needham, Joseph (with the research assistance of Wang Ling) (1954) *Science
and Civilisation in China: Volume 1 Introductory Orientations*, Cambridge
at the University Press
(1962) (with the research assistance of Wang Ling and with special
collaboration of Kenneth Girdwood Robinson), *Volume 4 Physics and
Physical Technology, Part I: Physics* (*h*) Sound (Acoustics), pp. 126–228
(1965) (with the research assistance of Wang Ling) *Volume 4 Physics and
Physical Technology, Part II: Mechanical Engineering*, see p 6
(1971) (with the collaboration of Wang Ling and Lu Gwei-Djen) *Volume 4
Physics and Physical Technology, Part III: Civil Engineering and Nautics*,
28 Civil Engineering (7) (*v*) The Grand Canal (Sui and Yuan), pp. 306ff
(1986) (with the collaboration of Lu Gwei-Djen and a special contribution
from Huang Hsing-Tsung) *Volume 6 Biology and Biological Technology,
Part I: Botany* 2 (*i*) *Oecology and phyto-geography in the* Kuan Tzu *book*,
pp. 48–56

Nelson, Andrew Nathaniel (1975) *The Modern Reader's Japanese English Character Dictionary*, 蕞 新 漢 英 辭 典, Second Revised Edition, Charles E. Tuttle Company: Publishers, Rutland/Vermont, Tokyo/Japan

Nguyen-Xuàn-Khoát (1960) 'Le Dàn Bâu', *Journal of the International Folk Music Council*, Volume 12, pp. 31–3, Heffer, Cambridge

Nickson, Noël (1988) 'Structural design of "Chinese" melodies known in Japan before 841', *Conspectus Carminis* – Essays for David Galliver, *Miscellanea Musicologica, Adelaide Studies in Musicology*, volume 15, pp. 58–73, Adelaide

Nihon daihyakka zensho (*shōgakkan*) *dai* 10 *maki*, 54 *peiji*: *sagimai* 日 本 大 百 全 書 (小 學 館) 第 10 卷 54 頁 さ ぎ ま い, Watanabe Nobuo 渡 邊 伸 夫, Shōwa 61 年, 1986, Tokyo

Nihon Gagakkai Kaihō 日 本 雅 樂 會 會 報, 第 9 卷 *Nara Gagaku Kenkyūkai* 奈 良 雅 樂 研 究 會, Heisei 4 (1992) 陵 王 の 墓 前 口 舞 り p. 3, Tokyo

Nihon-koku genzaisho mokuroku 日 本 國 現 在 書 目 錄. See the edn of Yashima Kurosuke 矢 島 玄 亮 (1984), subtitled *Shūshō to kenkyū* 集 証 と 研 究, Kyūko sho-in 汲 古 書 院. The book-list is believed to date from 891.

Nihon minzoku ongaku 日 本 民 俗 音 樂, compiled by Dr Honda Yasuji 本 田 安, 38 LP discs (2166–2204), recorded by NHK in 1955

Nihon Ongaku Daijiten 日 本 音 樂 大 字 典 (1989) eds Hirano Kenji 平 野 健 次, Kamisango Sukeyasu 上 參 鄉 祐 康, *Gamō Satoaki* 蒲 生 鄉 昭, Heibonsha, Tokyo

O'Neill, Patrick Geoffrey (1958) *Early Nō drama, its background, character and development, 1300–1450*, London

Ongaku daijiten 音 樂 大 辭 典, vol.2, Heibonsha, Tokyo, 1982

Paléographie musicale see Mocquéreau, André

Parry, C. H. Hubert 'CODA' in *Grove's Dictionary of Music and Musicians* (1879), London; 1, p. 376

Pelliot, Paul (1934) 'Tokharien et Koutchéen', *Journal Asiatique* 224, pp. 23–106. In regard to *samaca, see p. 104.

Picard, François (1986) 'Sur l'accord de quelques jeux de cloches de la Chine ancienne', *Groupe d'Acoustique Musicale* Laboratoire d'acoustique musicale, Tour 66 – 5ème étage, 4 Place Jussieu, 75005 Paris

Picken, L.E.R. (1954) 'Instrumental polyphonic folk music in Asia Minor', *Proceedings of the Royal Musical Association*, 80th Session, London (1955) 'The Origin of the Short Lute', *The Galpin Society Journal* 8, pp. 32–42, London

(1956, 1957, i) 'Twelve Ritual melodies of the T'ang dynasty', *Studia Memoriae Belae Bartók Sacra*, pp. 147–73, Budapest

(1957, ii) 'Chiang K'uei's "Nine Songs for Yüeh" ', *The Musical Quarterly* 63, pp. 201–18

(1957, iii) *New Oxford History of Music*, I, Ancient and oriental music (ed. Egon Wellesz), p. 94; p. 147

(1962) 'Musical terms in a Chinese dictionary of the first century', *The Journal of the International Folk Music Council*, 14, pp. 40–3

(1965) 'Early Chinese friction-chordophones', *The Galpin Society Journal* 18, pp. 84–9

(1966) 'Secular Chinese songs of the twelfth century', *Studia Musicologica Academiae Scientiarum Hungaricae*, vol.8, pp. 125–72, Budapest

(1969, i) 'T'ang music and musical instruments', *T'oung Pao* 55, pp. 74–122, Leiden

(1969, ii) 'Music and musical sources of the Song dynasty', *Journal of the American Oriental Society*, 89, pp. 600–21, NewYork

(1969, iii) 'The musical implications of line-sharing in the *Book of Songs* (*Shih Ching*)', *Journal of the American Oriental Society* 89, pp. 408–10, New York

(1969, iv) 'Tunes apt for T'ang lyrics from the *shō* part-books of *Tōgaku*', *Essays in Ethnomusicology – a birthday-offering for Lee Hye-ku*, Seoul

(1971, i) 'Some Chinese terms for musical repeats, sections, and forms, common to T'ang, Yüan, and *Tōgaku* 唐 樂 scores', *Bulletin of the School of Oriental and African Studies, University of London*, 34/1, pp. 113–18, London

(1971, ii) 'A twelfth-century secular Chinese song in zither-tablature', *Asia Major* 16, pp. 102–20, London

(1974) *'Tenri toshokan shozō no jūyōna Tōgaku-fu ni kansuru oboegaki'* 天 理 讀 書 館 所 藏 の 重 要 な 唐 樂 譜 に 關 す る 覺 書 *Biblia* 57, pp. 2–12, Tenri

(1975) *Folk Musical Instruments of Turkey*, Oxford

(1977) 'The shapes of the *Shi Jing* song-texts and their musical implications', *Musica Asiatica* 1, pp. 85–109, Oxford

Picken, L.E.R. and Mitani, Yōko (1979) 'Finger-techniques for the zithers *sō-no-koto* and *kin* in Heian times', *Musica Asiatica* 2, pp. 89–114, Oxford

Picken, Laurence E.R. and Nickson, Noël J. (1999) 'The Han "Large Piece" (*Daqu* 大 曲), its surviving vestiges and descendants', *Acta Iranica*

Picken, L.E.R. and Wolpert, R.F. (1981) 'Mouth-organ and lute parts of *Tōgaku* and their interrelationship', *Musica Asiatica* 3, pp. 79–95, Oxford

Pliny the Elder (Gaius Plinius Secundus) *Historia Naturalis, Liber* VI; see Pliny Natural History II, *Libri* III-VII, The Loeb Classical Library (1942, 1947; 1961), Harvard University Press, Cambridge, Massachusetts; Heinemann, Ltd, London

Powers, Harold S. (1980) 'Mode', *The New Grove Dictionary of Music and Musicians*, ed. Stanley Sadie, 12 Meares–Mutis, pp. 376–450, London

Pulleyblank, E.G. (1949–50) 'The *Tzyjyh tong jiann kaoyih* and the sources for the history of the period 730–63', *Bulletin of the School of Oriental and African Studies, University of London*, vol. 13, pp. 448–73, London
(1984) *Middle Chinese: a Study in historical Phonology*, University of British Columbia Press, Vancouver
'Neo-Confucianism and Neo-Legalism in T'ang intellectual life, 755–805', in *The Confucian Persuasion*, ed. A.F. Wright, Stanford, California

Qian Lezhi 錢 樂 之 (Astronomer Royal of the (Liu) Song (劉) 宋 dynasty, *c*.435); see Needham, 3, pp. 346, 384, etc.

Qinding da Qing huidian (1818) 欽 定 大 清 會 典

Quan Tangshi 全 唐 詩 (1986, 1990) 上 海 古 籍 出 版 社 Shanghai guji chubanshe (two volumes)

[*Quxian*] *shenqi mipu* (1425) [膠 仙] 神 奇 秘 譜 (Facsimile printing, with introduction by Zha Fushi 查 皀 西) Yinyue chuban she, 3 volumes, 1956

Rajeczky, Benjamin ed.(1988) *Magyarorszag zenetörténete, I Középkor* (A History of Hungarian Music, I Middle Ages), Budapest

Rameau, Jean Philippe (1722) *Traité de l'harmonie réduite à ses principes naturels*, Paris
(1726) *Nouveau système de musique théorique*, Paris

Rawson, Jessica ed. (1993) *British Museum Book of Chinese Art*, London. See Sheilagh Vainker, 'Ceramics for use', p. 230

Reese, Heinz-Dieter (1986) 'Picken, Lawrence [*sic*] (ed.) *Music from the Tang Court*. Fascicle 2. Cambridge, London, New York: Cambridge University Press, 1985. 108 pp. music, charts, illustrations.' *The World of Music*, 28, 2, pp. 80–2, Florian Noetzel Verlag, Wilhelmshaven

Reese, Gustave (1940) *Music in the Middle Ages*, New York

Reid, James Lany (1946) *The Komagaku Repertory of Japanese Gagaku (Court Music): a study of contemporary performance practice*, U.C.L.A., Ph.D. Music

Reischauer, Edwin Oldfather (1955, i) *Ennin's travels in T'ang China*, New York
(1955, ii) *ENNIN. Diary: The record of a pilgrimage to China in search of the law*; translated from the Chinese by E.O.R., NewYork

Ren Bantang 任半塘 (1972) *Jiaofangji jianding* 教訪記箋訂, Taipei, Hongye shuju; an edition of the Tang *Jiaofangji* (Cui Lingqin 崔令欽 758) with commentary

(1984) *Tang xinong* 唐戲弄, Shanghai guji chubanshe, Shanghai

Renfrew, Colin (1987, 1989) *Archaeology and Language: The puzzle of Indo-European origins*, Jonathan Cape 1987, Penguin Books 1989

Richter, Lukas (1998) 'Antike Überlieferungen in der byzantinischen Musiktheorie', *Acta Musicologica* Vol. LXX/70, pp. 133–208

Rickett, W. Allyn (1993) *Kuan Tzu* 管子, see *Early Chinese Texts: A Bibliographical Guide*, ed. Michael Loewe, The Society for the Study of Early China and The Institute of East Asian Studies, University of California, Berkeley

Riegel, Jeffrey K. (1993) *Li chi* 禮記, *Early Chinese Texts*, ed. Michael Loewe, pp. 293–7

Riemann, Hugo (1893) *Vereinfachte Harmonielehre, oder die Lehre von den tonalen Funktionen der Akkorde*, London (German printed)

Rikkokushi 六國史, 9, *Nihon rekishi sōsho* 日本歷史總書 7, ed. Sakamoto Tarō 土反本太郎 (1970), Tokyo

Robinson, Kenneth (see Joseph Needham, Wang Ling, Kenneth Girdwood Robinson (1962), *Science and Civilisation in China*, volume IV: 1 Physics and Physical Technology, Part 1: Physics (*h*) Sound (Acoustics) [with Kenneth Robinson], pp. 126–228, Cambridge at the University Press

Rosen, S. and Howell, A. (1991) *Signals and Systems for Speech and Hearing*, Academic Press, London

Ruijū sō-fu 類聚箏譜 *Classified Zither-Scores* (Editorship attributed uncertainly to Fujiwara no Tadazane 藤原忠實 (1078–1162) (see Nihon Ongaku Daijiten 日本音樂大事典，平凡社，1989; p. 734b) However, as stated in Fascicle 1, p. 36, upper marginal glosses in both *JCYR* and *SGYR* affirm that Ruijū sō-fu was 'edited by Nochi no Ujidono', and this is the usual name of Fujiwara no Morozane 藤原師實(1042–1101). As such this zither-collectaneum has disappeared, but it is believed that much of its contents survive in the next.

Ruisō-chiyō 類箏治要 *Essential Information for the Zither-Kind*. The University Library, Cambridge has a microfiche of a copy in the library of *Tōkyō Geijutsu Daigaku* 152.

Ryō 令: see *Ritsuryō* 律令, *Nihon shisō taikei* 日本思想大系 3, 1976, 1977, Iwanami Shotenkankō, Tokyo

Ryūmeishō 龍鳴抄: Ōga no Motomasa 大家基政 *Gunsho Ruijū* 群書類從 342, *Kangenbu* Pipes & Strings Class 管絃部，Tokyo

Sachs, C. (1943) *The Rise of Music in the Ancient World, East and West*, New York

Sandai jitsuroku 三 代 實 錄, 卷 14, p. 357 (see *Rikkokushi*)

Sango-yōroku 三 五 要 錄 (Fujiwara no Moronaga compiler) Manuscript of *Karyaku* 嘉 曆 3 (1328) in *Kunaichō Shoryōbu* 宮 內 廳 書 陵 部, Library of the Imperial Palace, Tokyo. For *Ichikotsu-chō* items 1–7 (our numbers) see 卷 第 五，壹 越 調 曲; for the remaining items in this mode-key (8–23), and for all those in *Sada-chō* (24–31) see 卷 第 六，壹 越 調 曲，下 and 沙 陀 調 曲.

Śārṅgadeva (13th century) *Saṅgītaratnākara*; for details see Widdess, 1995.

Schafer, E.H. (1963) *The Golden Peaches of Samarkand*, Berkeley and Los Angeles
(1967) *The Vermilion Bird*, Berkeley and Los Angeles

Seidel, Elmer (1967) *Dominante*, in *Riemanns Musik Lexikon*, Sachteil, p. 237, Mainz, London, New York, Paris

Seidensticker, E.G. (1976) *The Tale of Genji*, London

Shiba, Sukehiro 芝 祐 泰 (1955) 'The Tones of Ancient Oriental Music and those of Western Music', *KBS Bulletin* (*Kokusai Bunka Shinkokai* 國 際 文 化 新 古 會) No. 13, July 25, pp. 6–8, Tokyo
(1972) *Gosen-fu ni yoru Gagaku-sōfu* 五 線 譜 に よ る 雅 樂 總 譜 (4 vols.), Tokyo

Shiji 史 記 (Sima Qian 司 馬 遷, 145 – *c.*86 BC) Zhonghua shuju 1964, Shanghai

Shilin guangji 事 林 廣 記 (1100–1250, a popular encyclopaedia, first printed in 1325), compiled by Chen Yuanjing 陳 元 靚

Shinsen shōtekifu 新 選 笙 笛 譜 *MS. Yōmei Bunko* 陽 明 文 庫 Library: item 94487, Kyoto; see Fascicle 1, p. 30

Shōchū-yōroku-hikyoku 掌 中 要 錄 秘 曲 (1263) *Zoku gunsho ruijū* 續 群 書 類 從 530, *Kangenbu* 4, pp. 226–42, 1912, Tokyo

Shoku Nihongi 續 日 本 紀, *Shin Nihon Koten Bungaku Taikei* 新 日 本 古 典 文 學 大 系 13, 1989, 1990, 1992, Tokyo

Shominzoku no oto 諸 民 族 の 音 (1986), Memorial Volume for Professor Koizumi Fumio 小 泉 文 夫 先 生 追 彝 論 文 集, ed. 柴 田 南 雄, Tokyo

Shujing 書 經 (*c.*450–221 BC) *Shinshaku kambun taikei* 25, 26; ed. Katō Jōken 加 撰 常 賢 (1983) Tokyo

Shuowen jiezi 説 文 解 子 (AD 121), compiled by Xu Shen 許 慎. For editions, etc., see Boltz, 1993.

Signell, Karl (1977) *Makam, modal practice in Turkish art music*, Asian Music Publications, School of Music, University of Washington

Sipos, János (1994) *Török Népzene* I., MTA Zenetudományi Intézet, Budapest

Soothill, W.E. and Hodous, L. (1937) *A Dictionary of Chinese Buddhist Terms*, London

Stahl, William Harris, and Johnson, Richard, with E.L. Burge (1977) *Martianus Capella and the Seven Liberal Arts*, 2 vols. See vol. 2, *The marriage of philology and mercury*, and pp. 359–71 ([930–63])

Steuart, Ethel Mary (1925) *The Annals of Quintus Ennius*, Cambridge

Strunk, Oliver (1950) *Source readings in music history from classical antiquity through the Romantic era, selected and translated by O. Strunk*, New York

Suishu 隋 書, Wei Zheng 魏 徵 and others, 14, pp. 345–6, Beijing, Zhonghua shuju, 1973

Sui Tang jia hua 隋 唐 嘉 話 (Liu Su 劉 餗, *c.* 750) *Zhongguo wenxue cankao ziliao xiao congshu* 中 國 文 學 參 考 資 料 參 小 叢 書 (1958) I, 2, Shanghai; (1986) Hangzhou Zhejiang Guji 杭 州 折 江 古 籍

Tachibana no Narisue 橘 成 季 (1254) *Kokonchomonshū* 古 今 著 文 集; some read: *Kokonchomonjū* (See Eckardt, Hans.)

Takahashi Hideo 高 橋 秀 雄 and Yamaji Kōzō 山 路 興 造 (1978) eds. *Matsuri to geinō no ryo* 祭 と 藝 能 の 旅, 5, Kyoto

Takakusu Junjirō (1929) 'Le Voyage de Kanshin en Orient (742–54), par Aomi-no Mabito Genkai (779)', *Bulletin de l'Ecole française d'extrême orient*, vol. 28, 1928, pp. 1–41
ibid., vol. 29, 1929, pp. 47–62

Tanabe, Hisao 田 邊 尚 雄 (1926) *Nihon ongaku kōwa* 日 本 音 樂 講 話, Tokyo
(1930) *Nihon ongaku shi* 日 本 音 樂 史, Tokyo
'Zhongguo yinyue zai Riben' 中 國 音 樂 在 日 本, *Guangming ribao* 光 明 日 報, October 12, Beijing

Tangdai wudao 唐 代 舞 蹈 (1980), Ouyang Yuqian 歐 陽 予 倩 ed., Shanghai wenyi chuban she, Shanghai. See pp. 122–4

Tang huiyao 唐 會 要 (As *Huiyao* presented to the Throne in the recension of Su Mian 蘇 冕 in 801; today known only in the recension of Wang Pu 王 溥, presented to the Throne in 961) (1955) *Guoxue jiben congshu*, 國 學 集 本 叢 書, Zhonghua shuju, Beijing

Tang Li Shou *mu fa jue tong bao* 唐 李 壽 墓 發 掘 简 報 (陝 西 省 博 物 館, 文 管 會) *Wenwu* 文 物 1974, 9, pp. 71–88. For plates see pp. 84–6. See also: 壁 畫 試 探, pp. 89–94

Tatarskie narodnyie pesni (1964), ed. M. Muzaforov, Y. Vinogradov and others, Kazanskaya Gosudarstvennaya Konservatoriya, Moscow

The Music of Japan (1962) Record 2, *Gagaku*, Bärenreiter Musicaphon

Thrasher, Alan R. (1985) 'The melodic structure of *Jiangnan sizhu*', *Ethnomusicology* 29, pp. 237–63, Bloomington

(1988) 'Hakka-Chaozhou instrumental repertoire: an analytic perspective on traditional creativity', *Asian Music*, New York, 19–2, pp. 1–30

Tinctoris, Johannis (1455–1511) *Opera theoretica, Liber de arte contrapuncti* (Augustus Seay edn 1975), volumes I & II. See p. 22. *Liber tonorum* (1476)

Tōdaiji yōroku 東 大 寺 要 錄 (Heian to Kamakura) ed.Tsutsui Eishun 筒 井 英 俊 (1971), Kyoto

Tongdian 通 典(Du You 杜 佑 – 801 or 803), Siku shanben congshu shibu 1965, Taipei

Tōno, Haruyuki 東 野 治 之 (1995) 'Japanese Embassies to T'ang China and Their Ships', *Acta Asiatica* (Bulletin of the Institute of Eastern Culture Tōhō Gakkai 東 方 學 會), pp. 39–62, Tokyo

Traynor, L. and Kishibe, S. (1951) 'The four unknown pipes of the Shō (mouth organ) used in ancient Japanese Court Music', *Tōyō Ongaku Kenkyū* IX, pp. 26–53, Tokyo

Twitchett, Denis Crispin (1992) *The Writing of Official History under the T'ang* 劍 橋 中 華 文 史 叢 刊, Cambridge. For *The Monograph on Music*, 音 樂 志, see pp. 212–19.

Twitchett, Denis Crispin, and Anthony Christie (1959) 'A medieval Burmese orchestra', *Asia Major*, 7, pp. 176–95, London

Vaurie, Charles (1959, 1965) *The Birds of the Palaearctic Fauna* (1) Order Passeriformes, (2) Non-Passeriformes, London. *Anser fabalis serrirostris*: see (2) pp. 98–101.

Vikár, László (1969) 'Votiak trichord melodies', *Studia Musicologica Academiae Scientiarum Hungaricae* 11, pp. 461–71, Akadémiai Kiadó, Budapest (1989) 'Mordvinian laments', *Studia Musicologica Academiae Scientiarum Hungaricae* 31, pp. 405–20, Budapest

Vikár, László and Bereczki, Gábor (1971) *Cheremis Folksongs*, Budapest, Akadémiai Kiadó

Waley, Arthur (1928, 1945, 1949) *The Analects of Confucius*, London (1935) *The Tale of Genji*, London (first one-volume edn) (1937) *The Book of Songs*, London (1949) *The Life and Times of Po Chü-i*, London

Walther von Wartburg (1928) 6.Bd / I.Teil 1969 *Französisches etymologisches Wörterbuch*, Bonn

Wamyō ruijū shō 倭 名 類 聚 鈔 (10th century, by order, Minamoto no Jun/Shitagau 源 順 between 923 and 930.) Facsimile of printing of 1617, published by 風 間 書 房 刊, Tokyo, 1954. For *Tōgaku* repertory see Chapter 4. This chapter is much later than the tenth century, as pointed out by Demiéville (1925). See Fascicle 3, p. 31, and reference p. 98

Watanabe, Shinta 渡 邊 神 太 *Nihon daihyakka zensho* (*shōgakkan*) *dai* 10 *maki*, 54 *peiji*: *sagimai* 日 本 大 百 科 全 書 (小 學 館) 第 10 卷 54頁 鷺 舞

Waterhouse, David (1991) 'Where did *Toragaku* come from?', *Musica Asiatica* 6, pp. 73–91, Cambridge

Weakland, Rembert, O.S.B. (1956) 'Hucbald as musician and theorist', *Musical Quarterly* 42, pp. 66–84, New York

Wechsler, Howard J. (1979) 'The founding of the T'ang dynasty: Kao-tsu (reign 618–26)' in *The Cambridge History of China*, eds. Denis Twitchett and John K. Fairbank, Chapter 3, Volume 3: Sui and T'ang China, 589–906, Part 1, Cambridge
(1979) 'T'ai-tsung (reign 626–49) the consolidator', Chapter 4, Volume 3

Weisse, M. (Michael) (1531) ed. *Ein neu Gesengbuchlen*, Zum jungen Buntzel (Facsimile, K. Ameln, Kassel, 1937)

Wells, Marnix StJohn (1991-2) 'Rhythm and phrasing in Chinese tune title lyrics (qupai)', *Asian Music*, XXIII-1, Cornell University, New York
(1993) 'Great music of few notes *West River Moon*', *CHIME* – Journal of the European Foundation for Chinese Music Research, 7, 58–89, Leiden

Wenwu 文 物 1974, pp. 71–94. See *Tang* Li Shou.

Wenxian tongkao 文 獻 通 考 by 馬 端 臨 Ma Duanlin (late 13th century or *c.*1308) ed. Wang Yunwu 王 雲 五 (1936), Shanghai

West, M. L. (1992) *Ancient Greek Music*, Clarendon Press, Oxford
(1994) 'The Babylonian musical notation and the Hurrian melodic texts', *Music & Letters*, 75, pp. 161–79, Oxford

Whewell, William (1840, 1847) *The Philosophy of the Inductive Sciences founded upon their History*, 2 volumes, London

Widdess, D.R. (1979) 'The Kudumiyāmālai inscription: a source of early Indian music in notation', *Musica Asiatica* 2, pp. 115–50, Oxford
(1980/1981) *Early Indian Musical Forms*, Ph.D. Dissertation (2 vols.), University Library, Cambridge, No.11727
(1987) 'Laurence Picken with Rembrandt Wolpert, Allan Marett, Jonathan Condit, Elizabeth Markham and Yōko Mitani: *Music from the Tang Court*, Fascicle 1. 82 pp. Oxford: Oxford University Press, 1981. Idem. and Noël J. Nickson: *Music from the Tang Court*. Fascicles 2, 3, 108 pp., 98 pp. Cambridge University Press, 1985', *Bulletin of the School of Oriental and African Studies, University of London*, 50, pp. 176–8. See p. 178
(1993, i) 'The geography of *rāga* in Ancient India', *The World of Music* Journal of the International Institute for Traditional Music, 35/3, 35–50, Wilhelmshaven

(1993, ii) 'Sléndro and Pélog in India?', in B. Arps (ed.) *Performance in Java and Bali*, London, SOAS

(1995) *The Rāgas of Early India, Modes, melodies and musical notations from the Gupta period to c.1250*, Clarendon Press, Oxford

Widia, I Gusti Made (1984) *Kekawin Ramayana*, Volume 1, Indra Jaya Press, Singaraja, Bali

Wilhelm, Helmut and Knechtges, David R. (1987) 'T'ang T'ai-tsung's Poetry', *T'ang Studies* 5, 1–23, Boulder CO

Winnington-Ingram, R.P. 'Greece' *I, *The New Grove Dictionary of Music and Musicians*, ed. Stanley Sadie (1980), pp. 659–72, London

Wolpert, R.F. (1975) *Lute Music and Tablatures of the Tang Period*, Ph.D. Dissertation, University Library, Cambridge, No.9447

(1977) 'A ninth-century lute-tutor', *Musica Asiatica* 1, pp. 111–65, Oxford

(1979) 'The evolution of notated ornamentation in Tōgaku manuscripts for lute', *Sino-Mongolica, Festschrift für Herbert Franke, Münchener Ostasiatische Studien* 25, ed. W. Bauer, Wiesbaden

(1981) 'A ninth-century score for five-stringed lute', *Musica Asiatica* 3, pp. 107–35, Oxford

(1985) 'Colour and the notation of rhythmic variation and modal rhythm in 12th- to 14th-century sources for the *Tōgaku* 唐 樂 "Tang Music" repertory of Japanese Court Music', *Zinbun* 人 文, *Memoirs of the Research Institute for Humanistic Studies*, 20, pp. 51–80, Kyoto

(1988) 'Frogs more frogs', 24 *Deutscher Orientalistentag: Ausgewählte Vorträge* (Stuttgart, 1990)

(1995) 'Towards a grammar of Tōgaku', *Oideion* 2, Leiden

Wolpert, Rembrandt; Marett, Allan; Condit, Jonathan; Picken, Laurence (1973) ' "The Waves of Kokonor": a dance-tune of the T'ang dynasty', *Asian Music, New York*, 1973, pp. 3–9

Wright, Arthur F. (1960) *The Confucian Persuasion*, Stanford, Cal.

(1978) *The Sui Dynasty*, New York

Xin Tangshu 新 唐 書 (1061, Song 宋: Ouyang Xiu 歐 陽 修 and Song Qi 宋 祁) Zhonghua shuju 1975, Beijing

Yamada Yoshio 山 田 孝 雄 (1934, 1969) *Genjimonogatari no ongaku* 源 氏 物 語 の 音 樂, Hōbungan zōban shuppan, Tokyo

Yang, Hong 楊 泓 (1980) *Zhongguo gu bingqi luncong* 中 國 古 兵 器 論 叢, Wenwu chuban she, Beijing

Yang, Yinliu (1980) *Zhongguo gudai yinyue shigao* 中 國 古 代 音 樂 史 稿 (A draft history of ancient Chinese music), Renmin yinyue chuban she, Beijing

Yili Jingzhuan Tongjie 儀 禮 經 傳 通 節 (Zhu Xi 朱 熹 *c.*1220) Lü shi Baogaotang edn, *c.*1700. (A unique copy in the Rylands Library, Manchester)

The work was first published posthumously during the Southern Song (南 宋) between 1217 and 1232 (Jiading 10 to Shaoding 4) [嘉 定 丁 丑 (十 年) 至 紹 定 辛 卯 (四 年)].

A copy of this first printing exists in the Taipei Municipal Library. Even this copy, however, is incomplete and lacks the fifteenth *juan* of the entire work. A printed note in the original text asserts this. Following the heading for the 15th *juan* is the statement: 'This one Section is wanting.' (此 一 篇 闕); presumably it was never available to the printer.

The music for the 12 *Shijing* songs occurs in the 14th chapter (*juan*) of the entire work. This is entitled 'Song Music' and numbered 24th (詩 樂 第 二 十 四), it is also the 7th part of 'Ritual Studies' (學 禮). The original page-numbers for the *Xiao Ya* items (小 雅) run from 1 to 6; those of the *Zhou Nan Guo Feng* (周 南 國 風) from 7 to 11.

Yokoyama Shigeru 橫 山 重 (1964, 1967, 1968) *Sekkyo ōshōhon shū* 説 經 正 本 集, Tokyo

Yoshino Yoshimizu-in Gakusho 吉 野 吉 水 院 樂 書 (17th-18th century), *Zoku gunsho ruijū* 續 群 書 類 從, 532, first published in 大 正 1 (1912), last reprinted in 昭 和 6 (1931), p. 477, Tokyo

Yuefu shiji 樂 府 詩 集 (Guo Maoqian 郭 茂 倩, *c.*1150–1200) Zhonghua shuju 1979, Beijing

Yuefu zalu 樂 府 雜 錄 (*c.*890, Duan Anjie 段 安 節), in 中 國 古 典 戲 曲 論 著 集 成, Beijing 1959, volume 1, pp. 31–89

Yueji 樂 記 (a component of the *Liji* 禮 記). The *Liji* itself, and in its entirety, cannot be earlier than about AD 100. Parts of the *Yueji* may once have belonged to the *Xunzi* 荀 子 (see Riegel, 1993). Xunzi himself may have died in 238 BC; but there are considerable doubts as to the authenticity of the text as a whole, as it now exists in 32 *pian* 篇.

Zarlino, Giuseppe (Rev. Messere Gioseffo Zarlino da Chioggia) (1573) *Le istitutioni harmoniche…*, Venetia. Facsimile, Farnborough, German printed, 1966. (*Le i. pt 3*) *The art of counterpoint by G. Zarlino*; translated by G.A. Marco and C.V. Palisca (Music Theory Series, 2, New Haven, 1968

Zdeněk, Nejedlý (1955) *Dějiny husitského zpěvu* III (Prague, 1955: pp. 222–3)

Zhang, Juzhong and others (1999), *Nature*, vol. 401, September 23, pp. 366–8)

Zhongguo minge 中 國 民 歌 (1959) *Zhongguo yinyue yanjiu bian* 中 國 音 樂 研 究 遍, Yinyue chuban she, Beijing

Zhonghua dazidian 中 華 大 字 典, p. 80, Zhonghua shuju yinhang Shanghai (1952)

Zhongwen ciyuan 中 文 辭 源 (1980) ed. Ding Daichen 丁 戴 臣, Taipei, Taizhong

Zhu Xi 朱 熹, see *Yili Jingzhuan Tongjie* (1217–72)

Zhu Xie 朱 偰 (1962) 中 國 運 河 史 料 選 輯. See pp. 16, 20

Zizhi tongjian 資 治 通 鑑 (1067–84) ed.1956, Beijing

Zoku Kyōkunshō 續 教 訓 抄 (13th century), Tokyo